MUTTON AND OYSTERS

MUTTON AND OYSTERS

The Victorians and their Food

SARAH FREEMAN

LONDON
VICTOR GOLLANCZ LTD
1989

BY THE SAME AUTHOR

Isabella and Sam:
The Story of Mrs Beeton

First published in Great Britain 1989
by Victor Gollancz Ltd,
14 Henrietta Street, London WC2E 8QJ

© 1989 by Sarah Freeman

British Library Cataloguing in Publication Data
Freeman, Sarah
 Mutton and oysters : food, cooking and eating in
 Victorian times.
 1. Britons. Food habits, history
 I. Title
 394.1'0892

ISBN 0-575-03151-4

Typeset by Centracet Cambridge
and printed and bound in Great Britain by
Butler & Tanner Ltd, Frome, Somerset

Contents

List of Illustrations

Preface

This book was started in solemn academic spirit as a straight comprehensive survey of Victorian food and eating habits. It soon became evident, however (as one should have foreseen), that without producing an encyclopaedia comprehensiveness was out of the question; by degrees, it also became clear that the subject one was studying was the Victorians perhaps rather more than food – and not only the Victorians but ourselves. One would have liked to write much, much more – about topics which have only been touched on or omitted altogether, and in greater detail about those which have been included: in their final form, the contents represent the mere tip of a huge iceberg (or rather, the top of a bottomless cooking pot). That they should seem relevant to today is no doubt partly because the temptation to draw parallels with the present is always strong: in this instance, however, the similarities are so close and many that I have come to feel that an alternative title might have been *The First Food Revolution* – the second being in progress now. Here and there I have drawn attention to them in the text, but even since the book was finished more have materialized – e.g. the founding of an exhibition of food at the Science Museum, the current concern about the safety and quality of produce in particular, and proposals to privatize water – in which, on the very day this Preface is being written, it is reported that worms (perfectly harmless, we are assured) have been found (a week or so ago, it was shrimps).

I would like to add that although, like Mrs Beeton, 'if I had known, beforehand, that this book would have cost me the labour which it has, I should never have been courageous enough to commence it' I have enjoyed every moment (or almost every moment) of it.

Acknowledgements

A large number of people and organizations have helped in one way or another in the research for this book and I am extremely grateful to them all. In particular, I wish to thank Christopher Driver for advice; Clare Sheppard for research assistance; Jeremy Bruce-Watt, Pat Edmunds, Glenys Holloway, Audrey Stamforth, and Nina Virtue Lees for the loan of unpublished cookery manuscripts; and for other material or information, Monica Burroughes, David Burnett, Mrs Fernandez-Armesto, the Hon. Jacob Rothschild, Peter and Mary-Ann Sheppard, and the Bedford Estate; Mr Fernandez-Armesto of Charterhouse School, Patrick Strong of Eton, James Sabben-Clare of Winchester, and staff at Marlborough; many libraries in different parts of the country; the Swedenborgian Institute; John Calvert of the Ministry of Agriculture, Fisheries, and Food and Mrs Bull of its nutrition unit; Robert Thorne of the former G.L.C.; the Brewers' Society, the Chocolate and Confectionery Alliance, the Flour Advisory Board, the National Dairy Centre, the Thames Water Authority, and the Wine Development Board; Victor Crosse of Crosse & Blackwell; Alfred Boxer of Lipton's; Mr McGee of the A.B.C.; Fortnum & Mason, Gilbey's, and J. Sainsbury P.L.C.; Percy Smith of the Café Royal; Savoy Hotels, the Trafalgar Tavern, the Magic Moment (formerly Verrey's), Rules, Simpson's, Stone's, and Sweeting's restaurants. I also want to express my appreciation of the unfailing efficiency and good humour of the staffs at the British and London Libraries, the sympathetic secretarial assistance of my daughter Polly, and her and my son's help in testing recipes (of which a great many more were tried than there was eventually space to include). Above all, I owe thanks to my husband for his patience and endurance and to Elfreda Powell not only for her judgement and editorial help but sense of humour and encouragement: without her, this book would never have been finished.

S. F.

1. Shops and Shopping Customs: Normal and Sharp Practices

At the time of the Great Exhibition of 1851, when Harrods was only two years old and shops selling food were comparatively small and specialized, the most famous grocers in London were Fortnum & Mason and Crosse & Blackwell – the latter not yet being known primarily as a manufacturer. Both shops had already been established for a century and a half and traditionally served the upper classes, although Fortnum's origin was hardly pretentious, its founder having been a footman at the court of Queen Anne who started by selling the royal candle-ends, which he received as perquisites. In the Victorian period it was in the same position in Piccadilly as today but occupied a pair of tall Georgian houses, to which a third was added sometime before 1900 (these premises were burnt down shortly after the First World War). It sold wine, every sort of grocery and provision from tea to *pâté de foie gras*, and 'real West Indian turtle', and picnic items such as truffled pheasant, cold roast duck garnished with peas, and Savory Lozenges (presumably a kind of biscuit) to slip into one's pocket when going hunting or shooting. Queen Victoria sent 250 lb. of concentrated beef tea to Florence Nightingale in the Crimea; throughout the war, orders for rather choicer goods were also dispatched to officers, but so often suffered from 'undue leakage of luxuries during the voyage'[1]* that the firm was requested not to put its name on packing cases. A special department was set up to cater for the West End clubs: among regular customers were the Athenaeum, the Garrick, White's, the Carlton, and Brooks's and Crockford's, the last two being particularly noted for good food. Perhaps most celebrated of all, however, were the luncheon hampers prepared for Derby Day, which were given one of the best advertisements a product can ever have had by Dickens in his description of the races for his magazine *Household Words*: 'Never, to be sure, were there so many carriages, so many fours, so many twos, so many ones, so many horsemen, so many people who have come down by "rail," so many fine ladies in so many broughams, so many of Fortnum & Mason's hampers, so much ice and champagne! If I were on the turf, and had a horse to enter for the

---

* References begin on p.295.

Derby, I would call that horse Fortnum & Mason, convinced that with that name he would beat the field. Public opinion would bring him in somehow. Look where I will – in some connexion with the carriages – made fast upon the top, or occupying the box, or peeping out of a window – I see Fortnum & Mason. And now, Heavens! All the hampers fly wide open and the green Downs burst into a blossom of lobster salad!'[2] In order to have the hampers ready in time, the staff had to begin work at 4 a.m. – normal hours being 7.45 a.m. probably to 8 p.m., which would have been considered short by contemporary standards, since many shops stayed open until 10 or 11 p.m. on weekdays and midnight on Saturdays.

Crosse & Blackwell had started as a partnership called West & Wyatt dealing in olive oil, pickles, and sauces – which until cheap sauces could be produced by industrial methods were bought only by the wealthy (most people, if they had them at all, made pickles and ketchup at home). Edmund Crosse and Thomas Blackwell joined as apprentices in 1819; soon after they had served their time, their employers decided to retire, and put the business up for sale for the then respectable but not large sum of £600. This put it just within the reach of the two young men, who bought it and were so successful that fifteen years later they had increased their capital to £25,000, were employing a staff which by 1854 numbered 200, and had moved from a small house in Shaftesbury Avenue into handsome premises in Soho Square. The most conspicuous features of their new shop were a coat of arms over the central doorway which signified that they had been granted the Royal Warrant, and the restrained but picturesque window display. Until after mid century, the possibilities of the latter were limited by the traditional small panes of blown glass (despite the Crystal Palace, sheet glass was a rarity before the 1860s) but a striking, chequered pattern was created by placing a single pot or jar of goods in each one – an arrangement which depended for its impact on the custom of selling expensive products in appropriately costly, often fantastical but sometimes surprisingly beautiful containers. Less eye-catching but very unusual was the fact that everywhere, including the workshops and kitchens where they made most of their stock, was kept scrupulously clean (this was also a distinguishing characteristic and one of the main reasons for the success of Sainsbury's and the A.B.C. Bakeries; neither, however, was founded until the 1860s).

Although they continued to specialize in pickles and sauces, of which they were offering twenty-five and nearly forty kinds respectively around 1840, they extended their range over the next twenty years to cover jams, syrups, essences, invalid foods, pasta, soups, preserved meats and fish, *pâtés*, truffles and truffled products, chocolates, crystallized fruits, and many other delicacies; they did not, however, compete in the picnic field nor sell wine or ordinary groceries such as tea. One of their best known customers was the chef Alexis Soyer, who became a close friend, particularly of Blackwell; almost certainly, having conducted an inquiry into a scandal concerning tinned meats supplied to the navy, he discussed with them and may even have originally suggested the idea of going into tinned foods, which, although used as military provisions and by travellers, had not yet been produced for the general public. Among other notable customers was Charles Elmé Francatelli, Soyer's chief rival, who had worked for both Crockford's and Queen Victoria, and was said by some to be the more distinguished chef.

In the most complete possible contrast to Crosse & Blackwell's and Fortnum's (though no doubt some of its wares originated from them) was a shop on the edge of a notorious slum in Westminster, only a few minutes walk from the Houses of Parliament. It was discovered by a journalist called James Greenwood who, like Mayhew, specialized in studying and writing about the poor, and, although not so talented as a reporter, was quite as sympathetic and realistic about their predicament. He was on his way to the market at Strutton Ground, on which he was planning to write an article when his attention was caught by the copious but rather puzzling spread of food in the window. 'It was as though the fragments of a hundred feasts were here gathered – pecks and bushels of bread-crumbs, and meat-crumbs, and the crumbs of game, and poultry, and jellified soups, and all manner of rich puddings. . . . There were mounds of mutton-bones with a not insignificant amount of meat adhering to them; hillocks of beef-bones, ribs, aitchbones, and sirloins; heaps of lamb and pork bones equally promising of satisfactory picking. These mounds were on the window-board, and were flanked on one side by a vast pyramid of scraps of every conceivable shape, size, and colour and ticketed "odd bits, fourpence a pound," and on the other side by an enormous brown pan filled with broken bread and ticketed a penny a pound.

'Where did it all come from? Clearly the meat was of the best, and it was wonderfully cheap – facts which were not lost on the inhabitants, as it seemed, for, it being just about dinner time, the customers were flocking in, and it was as much as the old man and woman behind the counter could do to serve and take money. Several individuals were crowded about the window, and just to see what was going on, I was rude enough to join the throng and look in too. . . . "What's that there shoulder o' mutton 'un?" inquired a youth in the hare and rabbit skin interest and with his stock in trade slung round his neck. "That'll be three pence," answered the shopkeeper, fishing up the shoulder o' mutton 'un with his fork and holding it up so spitted. . . . I saw a great beef-bone richly ragged of meat, and exactly the thing to make a pot of soup, sold for sixpence, and the trunk of a turkey, by no means bare, for fourpence. I saw twopence put down on the counter, the customer pointing at the same time to the great pile of pudding bits, and I saw as much pudding (of a mixed sort certainly, and consisting of baked and boiled plum and plain) weighed out and delivered for the twopence as any boy possessed of an appetite but slightly inferior to that of Mr Dickens's fat boy could possibly have devoured.'

The shopkeeper was also a pig-keeper, and in his second guise collected the kitchen rubbish from the clubs and local lunatic asylums. The idea of food from the clubs greatly appealed to the customers, but there was some uneasiness about the asylums: ' "How do you know how a luney might serve his wittles? He might put pison on it for all you know." ' Initially, Greenwood was revolted, but after some thought was able to rationalize: 'No doubt, although between the under-cook and his chef the refuse food is regarded as fit only for the hog-tub, the former and the broken-victuals dealer understand each other quite well, so that the latter is spared the trouble of fishing his shop-stock from the pig-food proper. This being the case, nothing objectionable remains. Good bread at a penny a pound, and a meal of prime cold beef and mutton for twopence, is a boon one would like to see extended amongst certain poverty-stricken districts . . .'³ What he did not point out was that, cheap as the food may have seemed, the proprietor could still have made a profit if he had charged only half the prices quoted.

The broken victuals were nevertheless much better value than some of the 'bargains' in the market, where the potatoes looked magnificent but were sold scrubbed, which Greenwood took to be because prolonged soaking increased their weight, though a more valid reason was that it plumped out old, wrinkled ones. The meat was 'skinny and yellow, and bloodless and moist-looking' and altogether so repellent that he felt sure that it had come from animals which had died of disease rather than being slaughtered. (The operative word here was 'skinny', since lack of fat was accepted as the most obvious sign of ill health.)

Far more than today, however, easily the commonest type of shop was the general store, which could be a village shop or in a town back street. This catered for all the everyday needs of the poorer classes and, for reasons of distance or debt, was in many cases the only one they used. Its goods varied according to locality and the shopkeeper's enterprise, but the range of groceries was often limited to little more than tea, sugar, flour and/or oatmeal, cheese, bacon or red herrings, and sometimes bread. An example of a typical shopping list was given in an anecdote about a man on a shooting expedition, which also serves to show that other merchandise

A provision shop, 1866 (Mansell Collection)

might include several now somewhat unexpected items. The man ran out of gunpowder and went into the first shop he could find to buy more, clearly in the complete certainty that it would be kept – as it evidently was. While he was there, a little girl came in and ended an order for 'tea, sugar, soap, currants, red herrings, and flour, with the remarkable demand – "and two ounces of arsenic." '[4] The arsenic was handed over as casually as everything else and carried away by the girl jumbled up with the food and soap in her apron.

Normally, it was used in the home as rat poison,* but its popularity as a means of committing murder, plus the number of accidents which occurred, led to an Act placing some restriction on sales in 1851; for another seven years, however, other poisons could still be bought freely and any shopkeeper was permitted to stock them.†

Another little girl went into a shop in Birmingham and asked for ' "Farden tate, farden teed, farden lang tannen, farden aden" ' – a farthing cake, a farthing's worth of thread, a long farthing candle, and a farthing of change (' "again" '). In 1854, Birmingham had nearly 800 general stores,

* It was also employed commercially in soap preparations to whiten the skin.
† The Act laid down that arsenic could be sold only to adult males or in the presence of a witness known to the shopkeeper; also, all sales had to be recorded. In 1858, licencing was introduced and legislation extended to cover all recognized poisons.

as compared to 500 grocers and only forty-five fishmongers. 'Whichever way one turns in the streets, one sees a shop in which the housewife may buy bread and thread, bacon and shoes, cheese and knitting needles, or whatsoever it may be that she wants.'[5] The tiny quantities bought by the child were typical: working-class people usually shopped by the day, if not from meal to meal – a habit much criticized by those concerned for their welfare but not as uneconomic as one might think because in families where food was short shopping in advance would simply have meant eating in advance.

In Ireland, unlike England, grocers and general storekeepers were allowed to sell spirits without a licence, theoretically for off-the-premises consumption; in practice, however, a make-shift bar was part of their furniture. 'The grocers pile up empty tea-chests, or full tea-chests, as the case may be, round which the women go and get a glass to drink. They get it either for nothing, as being customers to the house on behalf of their employers, or they pay for it and drink it surreptitiously.'[6] It was claimed that much of the drunkenness among Irish servants could be attributed to this custom. At one time the sale of spirits had been forbidden, but evasion of the law by, for instance, offering whiskey from the next house or dividing shops into two and employing someone else to sell it had been so universal that the authorities had capitulated.

Another issue on which legislation had had no effect, insofar as it had been attempted, was truck. This was the payment of workers in kind rather than money and prevailed in a number of occupations, notably mining, ship- and railway-building, and various trades involving piece-work such as lace-, glove- and chair-making; in addition, farm workers sometimes received privileges instead of wages besides board and lodging which strictly speaking, was a form of it, though neither were generally counted as such. In piece-work, however, it seems likely to have developed from the custom of giving board and lodging; in mining and railway building it had originated in the need to provide goods and services in isolated areas. In its recognized forms it was exercised mainly through shops and pubs either owned by employers or where agreements with independent proprietors had been made. The pubs were frequently used as offices, where work and materials were distributed – after a deliberate delay during which the workers were expected to drink. In the shops, which in terms of goods were general stores but in some cases comparatively large, two systems of payment were current: those attached to the mining companies sold on credit (like other shops) while many piece-work firms paid directly in kind.

With minimal risk of bad debts and very often substantial capital behind them, company-owned shops could have been managed to the advantage of all concerned – as, according to evidence given to a Royal Commission later in the century, was in fact sometimes the case: one outstanding example was a store belonging to a north of England ironworks which was not only warmly praised by employees but did excellent business with the local townspeople. The majority, however, were shown to be used by employers merely as an indirect means of exploitation: prices were inflated and quality, though uneven, sometimes as low as in the cheap markets – with the aggravation that customers were not in a position to pick and choose or refuse to buy. A grocer called MacCulloch, commenting on truck in Scotland, said that the shops were 'invariably dearer – much dearer' than ordinary ones, and that in industrial districts even the latter were 'dearer than they ought to be, though nothing to compare with the [truck] stores'[7] (the proximity of a big, high-priced company store tended to distort values in all the shops within reach). In bearing this out, he said that it was reckoned that tea in the Scottish truck shops was at least 1s. per lb. (about 30%) more expensive than elsewhere; he also checked a selection of purchases from two stores (also run by ironworks) and reported: 'Sugar, short weight and bad value; cheese, American,* short weight and very dear; butter, fairish value. . . . Sugar, bad value, short weight, half an ounce in one half pound; cheese, 3 ounces instead of 4 ounces for 2½d. worth 9d. per pound; butter 3½ ounces instead of 4 ounces for 4d., worth 1s. a pound retail.'[8] The second shop defended itself by publishing a table of its profit margins, which looked very modest, but this of course did not include gains from short weight (in many instances, short weight almost certainly represented the shopkeeper's personal rake-off and was practised independently, if not without the knowledge of the employer).

In the South Wales coal-miners' shops, fair weight was usual and the standard of goods exceptionally high, but it was found impossible to justify the prices even allowing for outstanding quality. At some of the piece-workers' shops in the Midlands and elsewhere, similar prices were charged for such items as mouldy flour, rancid butter, and bacon which 'smelt as strong as brandy'[9] – this being forced on a chair-maker who had not actually asked for bacon but wanted a pair of shoes. In his case, payment was in goods only, without the option of any money at all, which was not unusual: when such people needed cash, they were obliged to obtain it by reselling shop purchases. Even when value was reasonable, this could only be done at a loss; in addition, it sometimes entailed considerable cost in terms of potential working time, as was illustrated by

---

* Unlike British, American cheese at this date could have been factory-produced; evidently the example in question was either badly made or overripe (or both), since one woman described it as 'enough to scunner a toad'.

the employees of a Hampshire glove-making firm, who described having
to make rounds of everyone they knew to collect orders. Their shop sold
grossly overpriced food and rather better value clothing material, which
was presumably bought on favourable terms via the business: obviously,
it was in their interest to sell the latter, but they can seldom have succeeded
in doing so because most of those who lived in the area were labourers'
families and too poor to be able to afford new clothes.

Workers were prepared to put up with these and other hardships
because, even by present standards, the unemployment level was appallingly high and the only form of public benefit the workhouse, which was
widely regarded as almost worse than prison; further factors were poverty
and the lack of education. Many pieceworkers were so badly paid that
they were apathetic from overwork and undernourishment: an unusually
prosperous and articulate nailer said that his fellows had 'neither life nor
soul left in them. They are worked down and down until they become
wretched, starving, miserable, and destitute.'[10] Nearly all the nailers'
children had to support themselves by working for their parents rather
than going to school; nor had most of the parents had any education: thus
they were unlikely to question the way they were paid, let alone organize
protests or consider taking other sorts of job. The miners were coerced
into using the shops by blackmail: in many companies, it was generally
understood that men who did not spend a certain amount would be
sacked, or at least the first to be laid off in times of depression;
alternatively, more mildly, the most desirable work would be given to the
best customers or credit refused to those who did not shop regularly.
These sanctions lent disproportionate power to the shopkeepers: hence
Disraeli's caricature in *Sybil* of the villainous Mr Diggs and his son Joseph,
who took sadistic delight in insulting, swearing at, and threatening their
victims not only with the sack but (accurately) rusty bacon.[11]

The fact that the shops offered credit was also some inducement to use
them, though hardly a sufficient one, as the need for compulsion shows.
This was not because people could manage without it – on the contrary,
the miners and their families frequently lived on it entirely, and consequently handled cash as seldom as those who were paid only in goods.
They were not, however, alone in their reliance on it: it was a way of life
throughout society, in all occupations and at all income levels, the only
people who avoided it as a group being artisans and other members of the
lower and lower middle classes with some degree of education – the same
public as the users of the wholesale vegetable markets and future Co-
operative Society shops. Rather than providing a unique service, the truck
shops thus offered no more than others, the majority of which would grant
it to almost any regular or potentially regular customer. The little stores in

A grocer's shop at Christmas, 1850 (*Illustrated London News*)

Birmingham gave it: 'The one thing that the workers of Birmingham (so clever in so many ways) seem wholly unable to do, is to keep their affairs well in hand. Whatever they may be earning, they are always anticipating. If they can get their wages in advance, they do; and whether they can or not, they ask and obtain credit at these hucksters' shops – a week's credit at all events, and, too often, very much more.'[12] In Manchester it was much the same: from a survey of four working-class shopping streets made during an exceptionally severe depression in the 1840s, it was found that over two thirds of the shops offered it – at an average cost to customers of 2s. 6d. in the £.

The need for it, though it often stemmed merely from ignorance and improvidence, was also due to infrequent payment, lack of alternative lending facilities, subsistence wages, and the threat of the workhouse. Some companies paid as seldom as six-weekly or quarterly, which could force even the most careful individual into debt at the beginning of a period of employment: the only constructive suggestion which emerged from the Commission on truck was that weekly payment should be made the rule. Outside the system, shops in effect provided a social security service, supporting people during times of illness or unemployment. The Manchester shopkeepers, faced with a situation in which many of their customers were starving, fed them for as long as their resources permitted, no doubt partly on the premise that in the long run it was more profitable to keep them than leave them to die but also apparently from feelings of genuine sympathy: they knew that those out of work could not help their circumstances, and said that seven out of ten of them would pay their debts if they could. On this occasion, as in other emergencies, the normal system of giving poor relief was totally inadequate to deal with the numbers involved – as would have been the case with any method practicable at that time; in general, however, the law in operation after 1834 probably increased the shops' humanitarian role because, whereas previously people had been granted food or money and allowed to stay in their own homes, thereafter they were supposed to receive aid only as inmates of the 'Bastilles', as the workhouses were popularly called.

Among the upper and middle classes, credit was almost certainly even more widespread than among the lower, mainly for social reasons. In aristocratic or very wealthy households, large staffs headed by stewards or housekeepers were kept, so that household management did not need to concern mistresses at all; nor were many of them at this social level able to undertake it in more than an overall sense because of the size of establishments and the amount of visiting and entertaining expected of them. As, virtually by definition, the middle classes also had servants, or at least a servant, they too often did not need to do actual housework: the example of the upper classes, however, led to the idea that any kind of domestic chore, including cooking and shopping, was socially improper for a lady (as also was any kind of remunerative work, only good works, i.e. for charity, being permissible). Ladies might possibly pay a visit to Fortnum's or some other very exclusive grocer – grocers being considered the least unacceptable type of shop – but otherwise her contact with tradesmen was limited to the occasional, formal interview. If necessary, odd errands were run by servants, but in general, instead of active shopping, goods were bought via order and delivery – which, as they were received below stairs by the staff, meant that immediate payment was inconvenient.

Convenience, in households where birth control was not practised and quantities had to include provisions for servants and possibly living-in employees, was no doubt another reason for the delivery system; nor, as perhaps one might expect, do fashionable prejudices seem to have been as binding in the north as south, at any rate over shopping: the ladies of Liverpool, for instance, regularly attended the central general market – albeit not at the same time as other customers, and perhaps partly because it had prestige as one of the first covered markets to be built, and furthermore was exceptionally clean and well administered. They may also have done so, however, for sound economic reasons, since, as was made

A Christmas display at a butcher's shop in Alton,
c. 1890 (Hampshire Museum)

clear in an article about butchers, style and convenience (as ever, and not only in relation to food) had their price: 'Our grandmothers went to market, and knew the current price of everything; they chaffered and bargained as ladies of considerable fortune do still in the provincial towns of France and Germany. Our ladies of London cannot now go to market. . . . . The rule is a red book, in which the weights sent by the butcher are accepted by cook or housekeeper, or by any grander person who rules the roast. . . .

'This book, very careful housewives – quite the exception – inspect once a week; others, once a month; many glance at it once a quarter, and a great many once a year, when the totals only are examined, grumbled at, and paid. The greater the consumption, the less the attention paid to details. Weights and prices are left to cook or housekeeper, who in mild cases expects a handsome Christmas-box from the butcher, but in the majority of establishments takes a regular "poundage". That is the term familiar to the trade. The kitchen-maid also expects something, and the butler, if he pays the bills, a handsome consideration.

'How few there are who dare to change the butcher, the poulterer, and the fishmonger, without the permission of a favourite cook!

'This system destroys the butcher's conscience, if he had any to start with.'[13]

Until the last quarter of the century, nearly all foods needing preparation were processed by hand, which made large-scale operations impossible: they were therefore wholesaled in a crude state and prepared for retailing by the shopkeeper. Some items, particularly those demanding special equipment or skills, such as vinegar and pickles, sweets, and soft drinks, were made and wholesaled at local level, but usually wholesalers were simply the leading shopkeepers in the area or, even if they styled themselves wholesalers, carried on a proportion of retailing as well. Crosse & Blackwell did both indiscriminately; Lea & Perrins, the makers of Worcestershire Sauce (who were principally chemists) were exceptional in both manufacturing in comparatively large quantities and running as many as five shops by 1850 – most shops being singly owned, or at any rate with only one or two branches. So far as can be discovered, three bread or biscuit factories were functioning by this date; otherwise, the only commodities processed by industrial methods were white sugar, cocoa and drinking chocolate, military provisions, and beer and spirits. Fish and greengrocery were still sold largely in the markets or on the streets, partly because premises for preparation were not required; as they could not be

Interior of a grocer's shop, 1846 (Mansell Collection)

kept for any length of time, sellers also had less need for storage space than grocers. With meat, the case was different, since besides the need for skinning and cutting up, butchers generally bought live animals and whenever possible did their own slaughtering.

Grocers' and general storekeepers' most universal task was blending tea, which was wholesaled unmixed in chests. Brown sugar, substantially cheaper than white and before mid-century more widely used, was similarly distributed unmixed, and as different consignments varied considerably, often 'handled' to give consistent quality. Although coffee could usually be obtained ready roasted, it had to be ground and (as it almost invariably was) mixed with chicory by the shopkeeper. Apart from Worcestershire Sauce, four other sauces and similar products, including Keiller's Marmalade, Colman's Mustard, Cock's Reading Sauce, and Harvey's Sauce (which featured in several of Mrs Beeton's recipes) were marketed nationally, but in tiny amounts compared to present-day standards. Keiller's used a machine for cutting orange peel into strips, and Colman's introduced steam for milling in 1846; it seems to have been rare, however, for the makers of this type of goods to employ machinery. Lea & Perrins' output was 1,000 bottles a day in 1854, but their only mechanical aid was hand-operated grinders: the sauce was mixed and every bottle filled, stoppered, and labelled manually. Twelve years later, Crosse & Blackwell were producing nearly 300 different articles,* all of which, with the probable exception of tinned items, were also apparently made and packed by hand.

In towns, it was customary for bakers and confectioners to work in their shop basements, which in other circumstances would have been used as ordinary domestic kitchens. The exhausting nature of kneading dough and notoriety of conditions in basement bakehouses led to the invention of several mechanical dough-mixers, which, however, were remarkably slow to be adopted, chiefly because of an over-abundance of cheap labour. Carr's of Carlisle were using machinery for mixing, cutting, and stamping biscuits by around 1838; Huntley & Palmer followed suit a few years later, and somewhere about this time a Birmingham miller and baker called Lucy evolved a system which comprised sifter, mixer, and the automatic conveyance of the flour and dough. This was run on four engines, the larger pair of which were of forty and twenty-five horsepower; capacity was approximately 2,000 loaves per day. There is no evidence of similar innovations in confectionery, although some London shops had developed into quite large concerns: *Punch* published a description of a

---

* Their price list attributed a number of goods to other manufacturers; this figure is based on the assumption that everything not so credited was their own.

sweet 'factory' in which a different department or room was referred to for each kind of sweet, e.g. the Bonaparte's Ribs and Brandy-Ball Departments, Hardbake Warehouse, and 'Toffey' and Rock Rooms (Bonaparte's Ribs were lollipops and hardbake a cheap form of toffee). As well as sweets and cakes, confectioners made jam, *petits-fours*, and puddings such as creams and blancmanges for fashionable dinner parties; according to Thackeray, some took this a stage further and provided complete dinner-party catering services which included French or pseudo-French chefs who could be hired to cook in people's homes, plus butlers, waiters, and suitably tasteful crockery and flowers.

As there was no refrigeration, the length of time meat would keep depended on the weather: one sultry summer's night could ruin a whole shopful. For this reason, butchers preferred to time killing to the exact day, which meant that they needed room not only for slaughtering but for keeping livestock. Public abattoirs were provided at the cattle markets, but were unpopular because they could be used only on market days; also, the theft of fat was frequent and the work tended to be done less carefully, and thus less advantageously, than if carried out privately. The wholesaling of carcases, or 'dead' meat, as it was usually called, had traditionally been limited to the cheaper class of butcher, but, as a result of the availability of railway transport and the growing demand for meat, particularly in large towns, was becoming increasingly important: this was acknowledged in London in 1850, when plans were made for building a new dead-meat market on the site of the cattle market at Smithfield. (The main London markets for ready-killed meat at this time were Newgate, which was conveniently near Smithfield, and Leadenhall, where game and poultry were sold.)

Both credit and the preparation of goods on the premises contributed to a characteristic not only of shops but selling of all kinds – the prevalence of cheating, which at the lower end of the market, where it was commonest, had come to be accepted as a normal and even necessary business practice. Basically, it was due to inefficient consumer protection, the gullibility of customers, and the incidence of poverty, which increased the shopkeepers' overheads and the need for cheap goods. Individual production offered almost unlimited opportunities for adulteration, which at mid century was its most publicized form; credit tied people of all classes to particular shops, while in the country the same effect was produced by lack of choice of facilities irrespective of debt. Market and street-sellers, who seldom gave credit and generally sold goods of the kind which could not be adulterated in the usual sense, nevertheless found ways of tampering with them and probably relied more heavily than shopkeepers on short weight.

There were a variety of methods of giving short weight: the most straightforward was to use false weights and measures, which was especially favoured by the London costermongers, at least until they were exposed by Mayhew, but was also a long-standing custom in the markets. Weights and measures inspectors were employed, but not necessarily to much effect, chiefly because of the scale of the problem and wiliness of offenders, the fact that penalties were merely minor fines, and the lack of odium attached to being caught. Probably many of the costermongers escaped detection by their habit of carrying two weights, one fair and one false, which Mayhew was told was so that, instead of being obliged to give short weight to everyone, they could restrict it only to bargain hunters (known accordingly to their slang as 'scaly customers', with whom they felt it a matter of honour to get 'even'[14]). If, however, they were convicted, all that happened was that they paid up and continued as before 'without being a pin the worse thought of'[15]. Two weights were also common in Ireland among traders in corn and other produce, who, far from refinements such as distinctions between customers, simply used one for buying and the other for selling. At Kendal market, in the Lake District, where two 'lookers' supposedly officiated, weights became such a scandal that the police were called in twice and on the second occasion (in 1860) found that virtually all the fair ones in the district had been pawned in order to raise money for drink. The false weights used by the costermongers were hollow and gave 8 oz. to the lb.; the measures consisted of a standard-sized mug with a removable inner container holding half or three quarters of the apparent quantity. Today, it is difficult to believe that people could have been taken in by such reductions: many customers, however, were too poor to be able to buy their own scales and thus could not check weights at home, and even those who realized that they had been cheated had very little chance of redress, since experienced sellers were always ready with a defence and few victims were sufficiently sophisticated, let alone well off, to prosecute. Among other ways of giving short weight were weighing goods with superfluous matter, interfering with scales, and sleight of hand (the latter having the advantage, for what it was worth, of involving no equipment or other concrete evidence). The London street-sellers laid fish on a waterlogged cloth, soaked if necessary in the nearest puddle; at Billingsgate it was the custom to sell eels in sand, usually in a proportion per lb. of about 3 to 20, on the excuse that it helped to keep them alive, or made them easier to handle.

Scales could be set at a couple of ounces and the goods placed at the extreme end of the pan, which yielded a couple more; or the arms could be made of uneven length, or a spring or lead or iron bar attached to them (these devices, again, were reported in Ireland). The superintendent of the

Manchester markets, John Page, who had had more than a decade's experience of sellers of all kinds and possessed considerable talent for writing about them (apparently rather more than for the practical demands of his job) described several methods of sleight of hand which gave the customer quite as little as false weights. One, which was suitable for nuts, was for the vendor to push his measure into the pile with one hand and make a play of filling it with the other: 'the measure, however, remains empty, or nearly so, and all the buyer gets are those only which he has seen heaped on the top of it.' If the seller did not provide bags, he could get away with even smaller quantities than usual, since the nuts would then be dropped straight into people's pockets, which, being at the side, meant that they could not see how many there were; if, after examining them, they went back to complain, the retort was likely to be that they had seen them measured for themselves, and could inspect the measures – '"are they not proper ones?"'[16] Another technique was to drop goods from some distance above; this was particularly well adapted for peas: 'the measure is set level, and the peas lifted with both hands, from which they are let slip through the fingers, so that they fall lightly and perpendicularly into the measure, which is soon – not full – but heaped, and so cleverly can this be done by a perfect hand, that, in some cases, the purchaser – although he has seen the measure, apparently, filled – gets little more than half a peck for a peck.'[17] In this instance, if the knowing customer was near enough, he could give the measure a sharp tap, whereupon its contents would subside to the correct height.

Page also described how old, milkless coconuts (which could easily be distinguished by their lightness) were pierced, filled with water, sealed with blackened cork, and sold to factory workers on Saturday nights. Coconuts, however, were a comparatively unusual commodity; a much commoner trick was boiled oranges: '"I've boiled lots of oranges," chuckled one man, "and sold them to Irish hawkers, as wasn't awake, for stunning big 'uns. The boiling swells the oranges and so makes 'em look finer ones, but it spoils them, for it takes out the juice. People can't find that out though until it's too late."'[18] Other sellers discreetly pricked them and squeezed out the juice for sale to the makers of orange wine. Prunes were also made to look larger by boiling, and it was alleged that cod were plumped out by means of air pipes inserted into their bellies (though whether this was really possible seems doubtful). Since the freshness of fish was normally judged by redness about the gills, the north-of-England street-sellers touched up their wares with a little blood or red paint: a distinctly comic picture is suggested by a chemist's declaration that he had sold paint to any number of them, and watched them applying it while still in his shop – where they presumably stayed because it was less public than the open street. In London, costermongers seem to have relied for the same effect on lighting, or rather the lack of it – stale fish being another commodity customarily sold (in this case after dark) on Saturday nights.

Diseased meat was disguised by a process known as 'polishing', which involved barding the offending carcase with a layer of healthy fat and rubbing it smooth with hot cloths; this, however, was only practicable if the flesh was of normal texture. Sometimes illness had caused parts of it to soften and become flabby; the soft parts were used for sausages, brawn, and probably pies. It is impossible to say how much diseased meat was sold, but the quantity was clearly considerable; an officer of the Board of Health of Newton Heath, near Manchester, said that in his district a dozen diseased cows and two dozen calves were slaughtered per week, and a few years later a Professor Gamjee estimated that it accounted for about a fifth of all the meat consumed. Sausages frequently also contained horse, which, being tough, helped to keep them firm; it was popularly supposed that pies were made of cat, but, if they ever had been on any scale, the custom had ceased by mid-century: ' "People . . . often begin crying 'Mee-yow' or 'Bow-wow-wow' . . . but there's nothing of that kind now. Meat, you see, is so cheap." '[19] Possibly, one discouragement to the use of cat had been the publication of *The Pickwick Papers*:

'Wery good thing is weal pie, when you know the lady as made it, and is quite sure it an't kittens; and arter all though, where's the odds, when they're so like weal that the wery piemen themselves don't know the difference?'

'Don't they, Sam?' said Mr Pickwick.

'Not they, sir,' replied Mr Weller, touching his hat. 'I lodged in the same house with a pieman once, sir, and a wery nice man he was – reg'lar clever chap, too – make pies out o' anything, he could. "What a number o' cats you keep, Mr Brooks" says I, when I'd got intimate with him. "Ah," says he, "I do – a good many," says he. "You must be wery fond o' cats," says I. "Other people is," says he, a winkin' at me; "they an't in season til the winter though," says he. "Not in season!" says I. "No," says he, "fruits is in, cats is out." "Why, what do you mean?" says I. "Mean?" says he. "That I'll never be a party to the combination o' the butchers, to keep up the prices o' meat," says he. "Mr Weller," says he, a squeezing my hand wery hard, and vispering in my ear – "don't mention this here agin – but it's the seasonin' as does it. They're all made o' them noble animals," says he, a pointin' to a wery nice little tabby kitten, "and I seasons 'em for beef-steak, weal, or kidney, 'cordin to the demand." '[20]

A somewhat similar idea to polishing meat was applied to cheeses: usually, the subjects were the hard, skim-milk types made in Yorkshire,

Suffolk, and elsewhere and seldom marketed outside their places of origin, but sometimes it extended to Dutch Edams and Goudas, which, although commoner than other imported varieties, were still unlikely to be recognized in many areas. The upper and middle classes frequently invested in whole cheeses to last them (or rather their servants) through the winter; the lower could seldom afford the outlay, but apparently bargain prices sometimes tempted thrifty housewives to invest in halves. The cheeses were cut and the exposed surfaces covered with a veneer of good quality Cheshire, a piece of which was offered to the customer to taste. As prices ran into pounds whereas fish or even a few servings of meat cost only pence, this was one of the most substantial of all the frauds practised (at least at retail level).

One of the most serious, albeit not much money was at stake, was watering milk, which could be disastrous for children already short of protein. This was not only extremely common but could be carried to considerable lengths: 'Milk will bear an enormous amount of water without being much deteriorated in appearance; you may introduce three-fourths of water . . . and it will still appear to be milk; it has only a bluer tinge.'[21] Eleven out of a series of twenty-six samples obtained in London were diluted by up to 45%: two more lacked cream. Dilution, however, was a relatively minor disadvantage of milk (or would have been if water had not been another potential danger): far more serious was the absence of pasteurization – nobody at this date suspecting its connection with TB although, ironically, one of the alleged risks of eating meat from diseased animals was scrofula.*

More innocuously, beer and gin were also watered, and if necessary recoloured and flavoured with sugar, treacle, salt, and, in the case of gin, Cayenne pepper. Whiskey† was blended with crude spirit (which could be far from innocuous); wine was a veritable fruit cup. Sugar and ground spices were eked out with flour, and honey with sugar and flour; jam was said to be made from the skins and pips left over from jellies; when oranges were dear, marmalade was liable to contain chunks of turnip. Similarly, various substitute vegetables (including turnip) were used in pickles: ' "girkins [sic]," on close examination, often turn out to be but shrivelled or sliced cucumbers . . . "red cabbage" to be nothing more than white cabbage turned red by colouring matter, as a dyer would change the colour of a dress; further . . . amongst the vegetables not unfrequently employed for the purpose of pickle-making are some which do not enter into the calculation of the epicure, as vegetable marrows, – which, when

* Tuberculosis of glands in the neck.
† This refers to both Scotch and Irish; at this date, the spelling of whisk(e)y was indiscriminate.

cut into pieces, form a very respectable imitation of cucumbers, – and sliced turnips, the identification of which would be apt to puzzle even a botanist . . .'.[22]

In London at any rate, wheat flour was not adulterated with other sorts of flour, probably because the composition of bread was already subject to regulations; oatmeal, however, was often cheapened with barley meal (which was roughly half as dear). Cocoa was mixed with starch, but in this instance the reason was gastronomic as well as economic, manufacturers being unable to extract the cacao butter, which meant that unless something was added to take it up, the resulting drink was excessively oily. Chicory in coffee was a comparable issue, since, as today, many people preferred it to the cheaper sorts of pure coffee; this nevertheless hardly justified the fact that some so-called coffee was almost entirely chicory, nor that the latter might contain ingredients such as bean or potato flour, ground acorns, or even dog-biscuit crumbs. Although factories existed for making fake tea out of used tea- and other leaves, the relative size of their output and tests on over 100 teas sold in London indicate that most of those on the market were genuine; black tea, however, was sometimes glossed with blacklead (a poison, which was also used for polishing fireplaces) while green was almost invariably 'glazed' or 'lacquered' with Prussian blue (a mild poison). In these cases, the Chinese were responsible for the dyes, but virtually every British product which could have been coloured to any advantage was: bread was whitened with alum (potassium aluminium sulphate), cheese darkened with arnatto, meat and fish products reddened with earthen dyes, pickles brightened with copper, and sweets, desserts, and cake icing coloured with pigments containing copper, lead, arsenic, and mercury. Harmful as many of them were, colourings were no more to be classed as adulterants than now, but in the confusion which prevailed at mid century, before the question of food standards had been considered, all types of impurity tended to be condemned under the same heading – which made grocers and others seem more dishonest than they actually were.

2. Markets, Fairs and Street-Sellers: Oysters Three a Penny

Liverpool's covered central market, St John's, was opened in 1822, by which time both Liverpool and Manchester's industrial importance was well established. A mid-century guidebook was uncomplimentary about its architecture: 'It was run up in the short space of eighteen months. . . . It is constructed of brick and stone. It has no pretensions to architectural beauty.'[1] It was planned along strictly functional lines and looked rather like a gigantic warehouse from the outside, unlike later, more fashionable edifices such as Birmingham's impressive, severely classical main market hall or Blackburn's mock Venetian palazzo. Workaday as it looked, for its time (which preceded the building of any of the railway termini) it represented a remarkable feat of engineering, since it was nearly 200 yards long and 50 wide, covering an area of almost two acres. Four rows of cast-iron supports created five shopping avenues: the central one was chiefly taken up by fishmongers, greengrocers, and florists, the intermediate ones by the sellers of poultry and dairy produce, and those next to the walls by butchers, bakers, and grocers, for whom, as became customary, small, self-contained shops were provided. The American novelist Nathaniel Hawthorne, who spent several years in Liverpool as consul, probably had the butchers at St John's in mind when he commented on the unattractive scraps displayed in the shops in the poorer parts of the town: 'There were butchers' shops . . . of a class adapted to the neighbourhood, presenting no such generously fattened carcases as Englishmen love to gaze at in the market, no stupendous halves of mighty beeves, no dead hogs or muttons ornamented with carved bas-reliefs of fat on their ribs and shoulders, in a peculiarly British style of art – not these, but bits and gobbets of lean meat, selvages snipt off from steaks . . .'[2]

Alongside the shops were offices for the market staff, who included constables, meat and fish inspectors, and weighers, who checked purchases for a fee of ½d.; porters could also be engaged who would deliver to any address in the town. Five pumps, one for hot (or rather, warm) water provided the means whereby the entire floor was scrubbed after every market day (Wednesday and Saturday). The cross-class nature of the customers is shown by the following: 'On Saturdays . . . [at] about eleven o'clock in the morning the avenues are thronged with elegantly dressed ladies, and persons of the highest respectability; towards the afternoon the market is less thronged until night, when multitudes pour into it, either for the purpose of gazing about or making purchases.'[3] After dark, it was lit by 144 gas lights; closing time was 11 p.m.

Liverpool had three other covered general markets, several uncovered ones, pork and cattle markets, a large covered fish market, and a hay and potato market which by 1866 had been officially designated as its wholesale fruit and vegetable market. Rather as shops fulfilled both wholesale and retail functions, the latter was used not only by the trade but artisans' wives and other private customers to whom the fact that it operated from 4 to 10 a.m. was no inconvenience, since the first factory shift was 6 to 9 – 9 being the breakfast break, when the workers went home; women could therefore leave home at the same time as their husbands and be back in time to prepare the meal. 'The frugal and thrifty working-man's wife is an instructive picture as, with a couple of children "to carry things,"' she moves about buying whatever vegetables and fruit may be in season. Of course she must buy wholesale. She has to take a dozen of cabbages or bundles of rhubarb, &c.; but with her large family all is necessary. . . . She, too, must have her flower-pot or bunch of flowers; and her children are ever ready to remind her if she attempts to go away without her posy. But it is an invariable rule amongst this class of women that all purchases of necessaries are made first, and then the flower-baskets are visited. Frequently we have seen the children fix upon a bright Tom Thumb geranium, a calceolaria, or some other comparatively costly flower, and then all their hopes would be blighted by the mother saying, as soon as she learned the price, "Oh, that's too much. I've spent nearly all my money now; you'll have to make do with a bunch this week."'[4] By the time this passage was written, in the early '70s, there were a larger number of careful wives than in earlier years, and more people able to afford the luxury of flowers – though to the residents of grimy Victorian towns flowers perhaps scarcely counted as a luxury.

This market was run by a staff of eight, plus three police officers, and, again, was extremely efficiently managed. 'Six hours of harder work in selling and buying can nowhere else be seen daily in Liverpool. It is stated that more than four thousand carts – that is carts engaged by the buyers to remove their purchases to the railway or their places of business – will enter this market between the hours of four and ten; and when it is borne in mind what class of drivers acompany these carts, some notion may be formed of the firmness and decision required upon the part of the market officers. . . .'[5] Goods were sold directly from carts, many of which could be converted into stalls by means of let-down sides: one of the tasks of the officials was to arrange them in neat rows and place the inevitable overspill in the surrounding streets, where, as the market was not in the centre of the town, trading could be carried on without hindrance to anyone. As soon as the carts were parked, the horses, which had come distances of up to thirty miles, were unharnessed and led away to stables.

As at all the major markets after mid century, goods came by railway from all over England and Europe and even as far away as Egypt; predictably given Liverpool's position, a large contribution was also sent from Ireland. Much of the particular character of the market, however, derived from the way in which traders from the surrounding northern districts exhibited and sold their produce. 'The carts and wagons heaped, nay piled up with cabbages, the stalks of which are all trimmed, present a very neat and clean appearance. In strong contrast to these stand the carts, crates, and hampers of Irish cabbage, which are thrown and stacked in delightful disorder with the roots on. The sellers of produce are very generally in keeping with the style or taste that their stands, stalls, or carts display. Halsall, Southport, and Ainsdale people present distinct features when compared with the Wirral and Cheshire folk, and their baskets or hampers can be as readily distinguished as their produce after a little close observation. Carts of produce are weekly, if not daily, to be seen here from every township bounded by the Mersey, including Warrington, and a line drawn from there up to Preston, Southport, and the North Meole district; and each district maintains its own way, to some extent, of "bringing the stuff to market." The stolid indifference which appears to be manifested by the majority of salesmen and saleswomen as to whether or not their goods are taken forces itself upon a stranger who has any experience of the markets of southern England. With rare exceptions, there is no attempt to push trade, no effort to attract attention or effect a sale. Most owners or sellers of produce seem to say, "Theer's moy stuff, yo can tek it or leave it, as yo loike." This does not apply to the poor cottagers, who, with their little baskets of fruit, flowers . . . and bundles of herbs, and their clothing wonderfully quaint and scrupulously clean, stand along and by the entrances to the avenues, clinging, as it were, to the skirts of their wealthier neighbours . . .'.[6]

At Manchester's fruit and vegetable market it was the sheer number rather than the idiosyncrasies of sellers which attracted comment and by the same date had given rise to a now all-too-familiar problem. This market, which, confusingly, was called Smithfield, was housed from the late 1850s in an elegant glass and iron structure reminiscent of and, to judge from the detailing, strongly influenced by the Crystal Palace.* As

* The Manchester building continued to stand until 1978.

the building consisted simply of a roof, the walls being left open, it not only gave a pleasingly airy effect but was practical since (although draughty) the unenclosed space discouraged overcrowding; also, a sizeable area for unloading and extra stalls was provided in front. Despite this, because it was situated in the centre of the town, it soon became notoriously overcrowded and caused congestion in all the streets around (a parallel situation having caused the removal of the London Smithfield from a central site two decades before). On market mornings, traffic blocks often lasted from early in the morning until after midday; traders thus had to carry produce considerable distances on foot, deliveries to shops in the area were impeded, pedestrians could not cross the roads because of continuous lines of horses and carts, and residents were not only woken at dawn by carters quarrelling for spaces but were unable to go out because their doors were barricaded by bundles of vegetables. In the '70s, the affected shopkeepers launched a campaign for stricter regulations, including parking restrictions (at Covent Garden, parking was permitted on one side of the street only); inevitably, Page was criticized, but most of their wrath was directed at the Corporation, which (in something like the same spirit as was shown by the City) was unwilling to act because it feared that its short-term interest, i.e. the market's immediate profitability, would suffer.

The London Smithfield – which at that time was a livestock rather than dead-meat market – was moved, after 800 years on its City site, to a more rural position off the Caledonian Road, just north of King's Cross, in 1855. By the time it had been uprooted, in the face of strenuous opposition, it had become even more overwhelming than when Dickens described it in *Oliver Twist*: 'The ground was covered, nearly ankle-deep, with filth and mire; and a thick steam, rising from the bodies of the cattle, and mingling with the fog, which seemed to rest upon the chimney pots, hung heavily above. All the pens in the centre of the large area, and as many temporary pens as could be crowded into the vacant space, were filled with sheep; tied up to posts by the gutter side were long lines of beasts [bullocks] and oxen, three or four deep. Countrymen, butchers, drivers, hawkers, boys, thieves, idlers and vagabonds of every low grade, were mingled together in a mass; the whistling of drovers, the barking of dogs, the bellowing and plunging of oxen, the bleating of sheep, the grunting and squeaking of pigs; the cries of hawkers, the shouts, oaths, and quarrelling on all sides; the ringing of bells and roars of voices, that issued from every public-house; the crowding, pushing, driving, beating, whooping, and yelling; the hideous and discordant din that resounded from every corner of the market; and the unwashed, unshaven, squalid and dirty figures constantly

A SUBSTITUTE FOR THE SEA-SIDE;

Or, SMITHFIELD FOR A CHANGE.

An alternative view of Smithfield Market as seen in *Punch*

running to and fro, and bursting in and out of the throng; rendered it a stunning and bewildering scene, which quite confounded the senses.'[7]

Few private customers were likely to witness it, but the general public was made aware of it by the fact that every Monday and Friday (the two market days) the streets were invaded by droves of animals. Sheep and cattle started gathering in the roads approaching it before midnight on Sundays; in its last few years, more than half had walked only from the railway stations, but some still came on foot all the way from their places of origin. Market hours were 3 a.m. to 3 p.m.; in the middle of the day there was a break, and in the afternoon a fresh concourse appeared and fanned out all over London en route to the butchers' shops. The more prosperous butchers transported the smaller animals in carts, but this was impossible in the case of cattle, who, thirsty, confused, and perhaps enraged by their experiences in the market, every now and again broke away from their drovers and caused chaos, sometimes in the most unexpected places. A bullock made his way into a coffee house in High Holborn and sauntered across the room to a large mirror, in which he 'took a deliberate survey of himself, and not liking the appearance of one or two customers'[8], broke some seats, the windows, and the door; on another occasion, a cow went up the stairs of the London Coffee-House on Tower Hill. A third cow or bullock (which was not specified, but, on the basis that most of the animals sold for meat are male, probably the latter) trotted through a small general store kept by an old woman, started down the stairs to the kitchen, and stuck half way; his drover found him and succeeded in manoeuvring him to the bottom, where he spent the night, and, after vain efforts to hoist him through a grating hole, was slaughtered. No one (except the latter) was hurt in any of these incidents, but in a fourth, a bullock bought by a butcher called William Giblett, whose shop was in Bond Street, ran amok in St James's Place and attacked a broker and two women: the broker spent several weeks in hospital as a result. The bullock was not caught until he had reached Tottenham Court Road, where, after an exciting chase, he was lassoed by Giblett's foreman. Giblett, who was well known in the trade and clearly an exceptionally humane and imaginative man, had subsequently given much thought to the question of a new cattle market, probably partly as a result of this episode; some of his more idealistic notions were obviously impractical, but his views certainly influenced the final plan, and it was at his suggestion that the north London site was chosen.

By 1848, overcrowding had reached the point where the animals were packed so tightly at the tethering rails that they could scarcely move and prospective buyers were unable to gain a separate view of them. The area available, which was six acres, was calculated to accommodate a maximum of 2,750 cattle, 30,000 sheep, and 1,000 pigs; instead, the number of cattle had risen to 3,500. As, despite crowding, not all of them could be placed at the rails, some were formed into circles known as 'droving rings' which were so small that their heads knocked together. The struggle to force them into their places and general difficulty of steering them through the mêlée was exhausting and exasperating, and almost inevitably gave rise to cruelty: regulations and the fact that blows on the body would have been detrimental to the meat helped to protect them from major injuries, but they were beaten about the head and 'goaded', i.e. pricked, on the nose, sometimes to the extent that their horns were broken and the ground underneath them covered with blood; also, no food or water was provided, which meant that they had to go without sometimes for as long as fourteen or sixteen hours. The R.S.P.C.A. was founded as a protest against the hardships to which they were subjected in connection with the market.

An argument which weighed heavily in favour of the move, as might be expected by this date, was that such a gathering and its accompaniment of slaughterhouses, some of which were disgracefully squalid, were unhealthy in a densely populated area. Several medical practitioners claimed that smallpox and typhoid were unusually prevalent in the district; also, the local inhabitants complained of disgusting smells caused by the boiling of offal, drains allegedly clogged with dried blood, and the collection and storage of blood for sale to the manufacturers of Prussian blue. Against this, however, it was pointed out that the market place was occupied only twice a week and for the rest of the time was of benefit to the neighbourhood as a salutary open space. The desirability of keeping the space open was widely acknowledged and formed one of the recommendations made by the Committee which succeeded in bringing in the Bill for removal.

The most powerful factions against removal were the trade itself, few members of which shared Giblett's enlightened views, and the City of London Corporation. The butchers were no doubt swayed largely by conservatism, but their expressed fears were that a market in the suburbs would increase their transport costs and hence the price of meat, and also that banking facilities might not be near at hand (this was a matter of especial concern because payments for livestock were customarily made by cheque and instant cashing required for immediate expenses – Smithfield being only a few minutes' walk from the Bank of England). The City, which made a sizeable income from the market, was so anxious to retain it within its boundaries that it produced an extremely expensive alternative plan which involved clearing an area to the west of the traditional ground and included not only slaughterhouses but also a new dead-meat market:

the proposal, however, was rejected partly on the grounds that it did not allow sufficient room for expansion.

Giblett's vision was of a market-cum-sanctuary of about 200 acres, preferably on a hill, where animals could be rested, fed, and watered and if necessary be left for extended periods;[9] efficient slaughterhouses which would put an end to the hazard of cattle in the streets were also an important feature of his concept. As it was built, the new market covered only thirty acres, but considerably more land was bought and held in reserve; water, sheds, and grazing for the animals, bankers' offices, slaughterhouses, and several hotels with shops, five pubs, and covered parking space for butchers' carts, were provided. The banks and market offices were grouped around a decorative clock tower (which is still there); four avenues radiated outwards dividing the sales area into separate zones, two for grown cattle and two for calves, sheep, and pigs; the hotels and other buildings were placed at suitable points on the perimeter. The City's objections were eventually overcome by the fact that it retained ownership; the design was by the first holder of the post of City architect, J. B. Bunning (who was also responsible for the Bethnal Green workhouse and the original Holloway Prison building).

After the market had gone, a wrangle commenced as to the use to which the Smithfield ground should be put; a number of suggestions were made for turning it into a park, as was consistent with the idea of an open space, but the City had not abandoned part of its earlier proposal and was quietly planning to build a dead-meat market on it. After some years' delay, partly due to excavations for the new Metropolitan Line underground, this materialized in its present form, the architect being Bunning's successor Sir Horace Jones.

The years of the Removal Act and the opening of the new cattle market also saw the abolition of the two main traditional Londoners' fairs, Greenwich and St Bartholomew's. St Bartholomew's had been held on the Smithfield site for almost as long as the old market, and, if the two happened to coincide, had clashed with it 'in a wild uproar'.[10] Unlike Greenwich and the cattle, however, its disappearance was hardly noticed, since although it had once been a rousing event which had continued for fourteen days, it had dwindled to 'only a dozen gingerbread stalls'.[11] (in earlier times, refreshments had included slices of hot plum pudding, oysters, and sausages). The last celebration of Greenwich was attended by Hawthorne, who was struck not only by the size of the crowd but its unattractiveness. 'I remember little more than a confusion of unwashed and shabbily dressed people. . . . It taught me to understand why Shakespeare in speaking of a crowd, so often alludes to its attribute of evil odour. The common people of England, I am afraid, have no daily familiarity with even so necessary a thing as a wash-bowl, not to mention a bathing-tub; and furthermore, it is one mighty difference between them and us, that every man and woman, on our side of the water, has a working-day suit and a holiday suit, and is occasionally as fresh as a rose, whereas, in the good old country, the grimness of his labour or squalid habits clings forever to the individual, and gets to be a part of his personal substance. . . . There are really, if you stop to think about it, few sadder spectacles in the world than a ragged coat or a soiled and shabby gown at a festival.

'This unfragrant crowd was exceedingly dense, being welded together, as it were, in the street through which we strove to make our way. On either side were oyster-stands, stalls of oranges . . . and booths covered with old sail-cloth in which the commodity that most attracted the eye was gilt gingerbread. It was so completely enveloped in Dutch gilding, that I did not at first recognize an old acquaintance, but wondered what those golden crowns and images could be.'[12] Besides snacks and drinking and dancing booths, amusements included plays, wrestling, juggling, an ancient (and singularly harmless) fertility game called 'Kissing in the Ring' (Greenwich took place in spring) and the popular novelty of weighing machines: 'It seemed very singular to see a great many portable weighing machines, the owners of which cried continually and again – "Come, know your weight!" – and a multitude of people, mostly large in girth, were moved by this vociferation to sit down in the machines. I know not whether they valued themselves on their beef, and estimated their standing, as members of society, at so much a pound; but I shall set it down as a national peculiarity, and a symbol of the earthly over the spiritual element, that Englishmen are wonderfully bent on knowing how solid and physically ponderous they are.'[13]

Greenwich was unusual in that it always seems to have been primarily for amusement, but most fairs had, or rather had had, a commercial *raison d'être*: St Bartholomew's had been famous for centuries as the biggest cloth fair in England, and another of national standing, Stourbridge, which was terminated at about the same time, had been known mainly for hops and wool. The railways, by taking constant supplies of goods all over the country, deprived the fairs of their trading importance, in many cases almost immediately; retail marketing was also affected, but less directly. In 1877 a Fairs Act was passed making the procedure of abolishing them simpler; those which survived took on their modern role of gatherings for pleasure, and, although often condemned in large towns, were valued as much as ever in country districts where little outside entertainment was available.

One which continued to be of major commercial importance throughout the 1850s, although a decline in business was noted as soon as the local railway station opened (in 1839), was the Nottingham Goose Fair, which, having formerly lasted two or three weeks, was still deemed to justify a duration of nine days. Its name derived from the geese which before the existence of fattening farms had been fed on the stubble after the harvest and in Nottinghamshire and Lincolnshire were traditionally served at Michaelmas feasts. By this time, horses, cattle, and cheese had overtaken geese as the main items of trade, though the latter, plus onions and other store produce which was customarily sold at autumn fairs, such as apples and potatoes, remained significant; the amusement element, however, was already not only the most popular and newsworthy aspect of the fair but a considerable part of its *raison d'être*. Some idea of the atmosphere it created and the range of entertainments on offer is given by the following extracts from a description of the celebrations of 1860:

'Early in the morning of the long looked-for day, hundreds, we might say thousands, of the youthful portion of the surrounding populations, may be seen pouring into the town from every direction, but all hastening to one point, the Market Place, where a concentration of "wonders" from all parts of the world, and of every conceivable quality, has been sedulously provided for their gratification; it is not altogether clear, by the way, whether some of the monstrosities provided for exhibition at the fair may not be excelled in point of extravagance by the outrageous proportions of some of the young lasses, whose crinolines, swollen to the amplitude of rick coverings when leaving home, are doomed to frightful collapse in the effort to squeeze them through the compact masses of unpitying, or envious, rivals in the race after fashion and pleasure. As the hours advance towards noon, the excitement . . . becomes more intense; the desires of months are upon the eve of fruition, and at the risk of crushed finery, and perhaps spoilt tempers, the country lads and lasses from sheer impatience thread their way from stall to stall – from booth to booth – crushing, squeezing, laughing, and talking, as if the troubles of life were left outside the town boundaries. . . .

'Exactly at noon . . . the Mayor, Edwin Patchitt, Esq., preceded by the mace-bearer, and attended by the usual escort, marched to the centre of the Market Place, and after the prescribed ceremonies had been observed declared the Goose Fair opened. . . . Comparative silence had been obtained in the immediate vicinity of the municipal *cortège*, while the declaration, &c., was made, but the last words had scarcely left the lips of the worthy chief magistrate before the assembled crowd broke through the barrier of self-imposed restraint, and made the spacious area echo with the din of human voices, the clang and clamour of a thousand instruments, from the sonorous gong to the shrill whistle, the roar of caged animals, and the scarcely more musical tones of the showmen who, on every side, were persuasively inviting the crowds before, below, and around them to "Walk up, walk up – just agoing to begin!" . . .

'While some hundreds – a drop in the vast ocean of expectant curiosity – are settling themselves down to see the "Murder of the Innocents," or some other fearful tragedy rendered as comic as possible, within the canvas walls of the theatrical booths, or are looking with intense astonishment and gratification at the wonders of Nature collected for their instruction and amusement in the travelling menageries – of which, by the way, there were several of considerable merit – we will take a squeeze through the well-wedged alleys of the Fair, and if possible have a share in the universal enjoyment around us. . . . We were not surprised . . . to meet with imposters of every grade of vagrant life; pretenders who would make one believe the Pope has three heads, as well as three crowns to cover them with, and speculators who have at their fingers' ends all the gold and diamonds of Golconda, and are burning with desire to distribute the glittering store among the admiring crowds around them. . . .

'[There are] spirometers to test the state of the lungs – weighing machines to indicate your exact weight. Other machines very like railway buffers, for trying a man's strength, and the power of his blow, are also here. . . . The well furnished toy and gingerbread stalls, with their regiment of pretty lasses, now busily engaged in weighing out the best "Grantham," are well worthy of a tread upon one's corns. . . . Here the usual fun of the fair is carried on amidst furious joking and merriment on all sides – everybody taking and giving in jest and repartee with a perfect understanding that "all's fair at fair time." '[14]

Street-selling or hawking, far from being the exception, was as normal as selling in the markets or from shops. Page wrote: 'Napoleon called us "a nation of shopkeepers." ' The remark would have been infinitely more degrading if he had called us a nation of hawkers, but certainly quite as true, for there is not one portion or spot of this island but is overrun with them . . .'.[15] There are no national figures from which the total number of sellers of food can be calculated: hawkers of other goods were supposed to be licensed, though only a small proportion were, but those dealing in edible wares were exempt; Mayhew, however, reckoned that, counting children, there were about 35,000 in London (one in sixty-five of the population).

The chief reason for the commonness of hawking was lack of shops, particularly fishmongers and greengrocers (in London at any rate, the fact that ready-to-eat food was a popular street item was more because of cost and limited menus than shortage of eating-places, where coffee and bread

An early photograph of a pedlar, St Neots, Huntingdonshire, c. 1860
(County Record Office, Cambridge)

and butter was often the only option at a comparable price). Other factors, however, also contributed, notably long working hours, class loyalty, and unemployment. As shops stayed open late, work did not prohibit people from shopping: it did, however, mean that they were likely to be physically tired – wives' exhaustion after a day in a factory probably having much to do with the prevalence of door-to-door hawking in the north as opposed to street-selling on the southern pattern: this in turn, since it obviated the need to attract attention, was why street 'crying' of a seller's wares was virtually never heard in industrial areas. Class was relevant because it was generally assumed that sellers were as poor as or poorer than their customers, whereas shopkeepers, who could afford premises and credit, were popularly assumed to be rich. The significance of unemployment was that people took to hawking, as they might today, when they could not find work in other occupations. Among the London sellers in 1851 were around 1,000 craftsmen of one sort or another, including a patten-maker and a copper-plate printer whose jobs had become obsolescent; there were also ex-labourers, policemen, cab-drivers, journeymen (i.e. assistant) butchers and bakers, and servants. Mayhew told of one former manservant who had been consistently rejected by employers, despite an unexception-able reference, because he was married and had children; his wife, who had also been in service, had suffered similarly (the reason for this being that servants of both sexes were expected to live in). Another example was of a coal-heaver who had been disabled by a fall at work and who (compensation being unheard of) managed to support a wife and four children by running a hot-eel and pea-soup stall – though only just: the children went in rags and had no shoes (the girls borrowed their mother's when they went out) and he depended on an elder daughter to help him. ' "Aye, I can't go without my crutch. My daughter goes to Billingsgate for me. I've got nobody else; and she cuts up the eels. If it wasn't for her, I must give it up altogether, and go into the workhouse outright. . . . My wife can't do much; she's troubled with the rheumatics in her head and limbs." '[16] Many children were sent out by needy parents to sell low-priced commodities such as watercress, oranges, or nuts, as soon as they were old enough to carry their wares and count change – one little girl who sold nuts reporting that her mother (an orange-seller) beat her if she did not make 3d. a day – though in general the latter was 'kind enough'[17] to her and never beat her for any other reason.

Some vendors (though according to Mayhew not as many as one might expect: possibly the question of working hours slipped his consideration) used selling (again as might be the case today) not as their only means of earning a living but as a moonlight occupation, either regularly or as opportunity offered. Of four men who dealt in hot green peas in London, three spent the main part of their day as shoemakers, selling peas at the wholesale markets in the early morning and street markets in the evening. The peas were particularly convenient for part-time purposes because dried ones were used, so that they did not have to be freshly bought but involved only soaking and boiling (even with fresh ones, shelling would have been unnecessary, since at Covent Garden this was done by teams of women employed by the market salesmen – though no doubt at extra cost to the customer). A few low-paid workers sold cakes (which they did not make themselves, but bought from cheap bakeries) on Sundays; until it was ended, hot cross buns were vended chiefly by boys anxious to earn money to spend at Greenwich Fair. Another boy, George Sanger, whose family toured the fairs with a freak show in the summer and in winter made a meagre living by transporting vegetables from London to Newbury, where they sold in the market, was staying in London during an icy spell and hapened to notice that nobody was catering for the skaters on Hackney Marshes. Having been taught to make toffee and rock by the sweet-sellers at the fairs, he went straight out to buy sugar and peppermint flavouring, borrowed some cooking pans, and made peppermint rock. This proved so popular that he had sold out in an hour; he then persuaded his brothers to contribute their few shillings of savings, purchased a much larger quantity of sugar, and on a second expedition made a profit of over £2.

Besides those who adopted it from need or expediency were others who either chose to sell for the sake of an outdoor life and the independence of being self-employed or had been brought up to it and never considered any alternative. The best known example and probably only sizeable group of this type were the 'thoroughbred' London costermongers studied by Mayhew, who were not only distinctive in habits and dress but fulfilled a basic traditional need in retailing only fish and vegetables – London unlike provincial towns and cities, lacking central general market facilities. As a class, the thoroughbred costermongers were contemptuous of the sellers of any other wares, referring to them scornfully as 'illegitimates',[18] although on one occasion a party of the former abandoned their pride so far as to hawk fried fish at the Derby – accompanied not by chips (which were a later innovation) but bread left on the grass by picnickers. These sellers, being relatively prosperous and professional, often had pony or donkey carts and were thus able to drive considerable distances to races and fairs; some of them also made rounds into the suburbs and country, Watford and Croydon (where there was a large Saturday street-market) and even Maidstone and Farnham being popular destinations. Like everyone else, however, they were already taking advantage of the railways: a frequent practice, which was cheaper than travelling with carts on long journeys,

Cleaning fish on the beach at St Ives, Cornwall, 1890
(Royal Institution, Truro)

was to send goods and a hand-barrow in advance, walk to meet them (to save on fares) and sell on the way home. Hand-barrows could be hired for a few pence a day or, along with carts, ponies, donkeys, harness, and everything else needed for the trade, bought at a hawkers' market known as Smithfield Races, which had been held on part of the old market ground on Friday afternoons. Compared to the cattle sales the Races were a light-hearted affair and attracted many of the despised refreshment sellers, who offered hot eels and pea soup, fried fish, pickled whelks, nuts, apples, cakes, rock, and generously watered (and skimmed) milk.

A rather different type of seller were producers such as fishermen, smallholders, and gatherers of wild produce. A. H. Slee, in *Victorian Days in a Devon Village*[19], recalled 'The Fishman' who walked from Barnstaple with a hand-barrow two or three times a week; during the herring season in November, fishermen also came from Ilfracombe, usually in the evening when they had returned from the day's trip, with the very real bargain of sixty for a shilling, the practice being to buy them in bulk to salt at home for the winter. In summer an old blind farmer called Dick Yeo from nearby

Swimbridge, where Mazzard cherries were grown, hawked them with wortleberries from Exmoor, a few miles to the east. All through the year except in summer, women brought round baskets of laver, which was collected from the rocks at low tide, boiled in vinegar, and customarily eaten fried with bacon for breakfast. Laver was also sold round parts of the Welsh and Scottish coasts, where it was sometimes served with butter or shaped into cakes and rolled in oatmeal.

Except in London, where the only general markets were the street markets, hawkers and market sellers were often the same, tradesmen using one or more markets when they were held and the streets for the rest of the time. Somewhat later in the century, a greengrocer from St Albans explained that he paid a rent, or 'toll', of 9d for a place in the market and stood by the roadside on every other day but Monday. A Hitchin grocer was understandably aggrieved because, when stalls were built into the market, he was obliged to take one for 6d, whereas formerly he had been able to sell from his barrow, which he said was larger, for 2d.; on non-market days he visited the neighbouring villages, like the Fishman. In many towns, the building of covered premises and subsequent improvements often acted as a disincentive to their use because higher tolls meant that those with smaller businesses found it more worthwhile to sell in the streets just outside than pay them; if the authorities reacted by charging similar rates for street space, they either retreated still further and sold outside the town boundaries or resisted, as at Bedford, where the collector was pelted with potatoes.

Sometimes selling was undertaken not for its own sake but as a blind for other activities such as prostitution or gambling; prostitutes might carry baskets of fruit, probably oranges, to serve as an introduction in pubs; gamblers kept stalls of cakes, nuts, or any cheap item with general appeal, and, if customers were willing, whipped out baize and dice (there was no possibility of the latter winning unless they happened to be familiar with the methods of cheating used). Burglars too might call from door to door in order to assess premises, but a stock of durable goods suited them better than food, since it was less trouble and more likely to provoke conversation and a longer, more informative visit.

Just as one can only guess at their overall numbers, so the total amount of food distributed by the various types of seller cannot be given; Mayhew, however, published tables of their purchases at the different London wholesale markets, 1850–51, from which their importance in the distribution of fish especially is clear. As he himself observed, the railways, by opening up new sources of supply, had in effect brought a glut of fish to London which had lowered prices and turned it into the staple food of the working classes. The more because it was quick (and thus cheap) to cook

– or in the case of shellfish did not need cooking at all – it was eaten at
every meal and on all occasions: people had red herrings, i.e. kippers, for
breakfast, shellfish for supper and snacks, and plaice, mackerel, sprats,
fresh herrings, and even sole (which was sometimes used by the fried-fish
sellers) for dinner. The more expensive fish, which included salmon and
lobster,* were seldom seen in the streets, but according to the tables, the
sellers bought nearly all the plaice, three quarters of the herrings and
sprats, two thirds of the mackerel, half the shrimps and red herrings, all
the whelks, and three quarters of the cockles and winkles sold at
Billingsgate, which added up to an average of well over half the fish of all
kinds. The stink of stale herrings was characteristic of poverty: 'The rooms
of the very neediest of our needy population always smell of fish; most
frequently herrings. So much so that, to people who, like myself, have
been in the habit of visiting their dwellings, the smell of herrings even in
comfortable homes, savours from association so strongly of squalor and
wretchedness, as to be often most oppressive.'[20] As wages were paid on
Saturdays and tended to have run out by Tuesdays, the usual days for red
herrings were Sundays and Monday: on Sundays, sellers disturbed sleepers-
in by crying their wares under their windows, and on Monday mornings
clustered round workshop and factory gates to catch the workers as they
went home for breakfast. During the Great Exhibition, stalls offering tea
and shrimps lined the streets leading to Hyde Park (where it was held); a
winkle-seller said that he thought his wares were used chiefly as an excuse
for ' "daddling" ' (presumably dawdling): ' "When a young woman's young
man takes tea with her mother and her, then they've winks; and then
there's joking, and helping to pick winks, between Thomas and Betsy,
while the mother's busy with her tea, or is wiping her specs . . ." '†[21] In
inland areas outside London, where before the railways sea fish had
seldom been obtainable, very little was eaten, but it seems likely that the
amounts disposed of in the streets, though small in absolute terms, were
proportionately even higher (Birmingham, it may be remembered, had
only two fish shops).

The quantities bought at Covent Garden and the other London fruit and
vegetable markets (Borough, Farringdon, Spitalfields, and Portman),
though still considerable, were relatively less, largely because fruit was
counted as an extra and the street sale of the cheaper kinds of vegetable,
such as carrots and potatoes, was discouraged by their bulk; also, people
lacked time and often the means and knowledge needed for preparation,
particularly in the case of fruit for cooking, which called for further

---

* According to Mrs Beeton, salmon averaged 1s. 3d. per lb., as compared to 3d. each for plaice.
† The tea referred to would have been after rather than before the evening meal.

ingredients: ' "O, a plum pie's too fine for us, and what's more, it takes too much sugar" ' (in addition, it demanded the ability to make pastry and an oven, both of which were comparatively unusual). In apparent contradiction to this was the fact that three quarters of the gooseberries bought came from costermongers, which, however, was because, as well as being cheap, most of those on sale at this date were of the sweet variety and could be eaten raw; similarly among other fruits favoured by the sellers were red currants, which were used for jelly by the higher classes but eaten raw by the lower.

As acknowedged luxuries, poultry and game were hawked in perhaps surprising amounts, a fifth of the hares and pheasants, a third of the chickens, and a significant number of ducks, geese, and partridges being sold in this way. The main explanation for the presence of game on the streets was that, since quantities depended on sport rather than demand, supplies were erratic and sometimes soared dramatically (poached goods, which were at a premium because they were usually trapped and thus undamaged, virtually never reached the street traders, though out-of-season items sometimes did). The chickens included old hens (presumably those past laying) which, as their legs harden with increasing age, were disguised by softening the latter in water; skinniness was counteracted by means of implants of pork fat under the breast (game old in the other sense required no treatment because, as Page pointed out, it seldom smelt perceptibly from the outside). Buyers were mainly middle-class bargain-hunters or people living in the suburbs where poultry and game dealers were often not yet established. (It should be said in fairness that Mayhew interviewed several sellers who had regular customers and sound as if they gave very fair value.)

In London, the number of different refreshments on sale totalled over thirty, excluding shellfish, fruit and nuts, and variations of the kinds of biscuit, cake, and pie, but including every sort of drink, which comprised tea, coffee, cocoa, hot elder wine, peppermint 'water' (which was also a kind of wine), ginger beer, lemonade, 'nectar' (supposedly mixed fruit juice), 'rice milk' (a very liquid version of rice pudding), and ordinary water or milk. Peppermint water was a rarity, but a number of carriers of ordinary water were still in trade, though they relied more on washer-women and tavern-keepers for business than passers-by. Milk was sold in the markets, as at the Smithfield Races, and in places where people went for walks on Sundays, such as Hampstead Heath; also, cows were kept in St James's Park, where they were milked to order for every customer as a guarantee of cleanliness and purity. Coffee, and occasionally tea and cocoa, plus bread and butter, cake, hard-boiled eggs, ham sandwiches, and watercress (which was a popular breakfast item and also often eaten with shrimps) were available from stalls which functioned from midnight or early in the morning for the benefit of prostitutes and others out late, wholesale market traders, and those who had to be at work by 6 a.m. Working people frequently did not have a hot drink before leaving home because, unless they had invested in a 'Bachelor's Kettle' or some other kind of instant stove (see page 111) the water could not be boiled until the kitchen fire had been lit, which meant getting up considerably earlier than was otherwise necessary – and, if the rest of the family was still in bed, was an extravagance in terms of both ingredients and fuel. Economy, and the fact that it was hot, or should have been (it was kept in an urn with a charcoal fire underneath) were the only things to recommend the coffee made by the stall-keeper to whom Mayhew spoke, which was so weak that even with chicory it cannot have tasted of anything; often, burnt sugar was added to give it colour. The bread was 'second bread'[22], i.e. of second-quality flour, which yielded a coarse (but not brown) loaf; the butter, however, although the cheapest, had to be real because there was no margarine. Neither butter nor eggs featured in the 'cake', which was really a kind of scone containing a little dripping and very few currants and would have been greatly improved by the addition of butter and jam. Excluding any allowance for labour costs, the profits, as of most other refreshments, were around 100%; nevertheless, at 1d. per cup or ½d. per half cup, the coffee was probably cheaper than a pot made for one at home (instant coffee did not exist).

The other hot items, besides rice milk and the elder wine, were muffins, pies, meat and currant puddings, baked potatoes, roast chestnuts, and the hot peas, eels, and pea soup. The last two, which were almost always sold by the same people, were extremely popular, especially the eels, some devotees consuming half a dozen cupsful (each holding about as many small pieces of eel) at a time; the recipe given was perhaps too vinegary for modern tastes, but the soup, which was flavoured with mint and celery, might still (if it were not so unfashionable) be popular today. The eels were served throughout the year, but in summer the soup was replaced by whelks; similarly, the hot rice milk was exchanged for curds and whey, which were the contemporary equivalent of yoghurt: they were prescribed for children (the young Tom Brown, of *Tom Brown's Schooldays*, was made to take them) and, instead of being mixed with fruit, were served with it, the women who dispensed them also carrying cherries or oranges. Like other liquid refreshments, they were served in cups or glasses which required washing up after every customer: Mayhew commented on the neat appearance of the glasses and cleanliness of the curd pan on a stall in Holborn, but in general the difficulty, or at least inconvenience, of obtaining water (which can only have been cold) must have meant that washing up was often done in water so dirty as to be virtually useless; presumably it was for this reason that middle-class children sent to drink the milk in St James's Park took their own mugs (rather than mere snobbery, as the milk-woman seems to have assumed: ' "Some bring their own china mugs to drink it out of; nothing less [is] good enough for them." ')[23]

More convenient for street consumption were baked potatoes, which people could put into their pockets or use as hand-warmers. These were a comparatively new line which had been made possible by the invention of cans with fires at the bottom and double sides to contain hot water; some were very picturesque, with bright paint, brass finishes, and (in one case) coloured lamps. Newer still were ice creams, which were introduced into the streets in 1850 and to begin with were a disastrous failure, despite efficient equipment, because of their effect on people's teeth – those who had never tried them, instead of eating them slowly, cramming them into their mouths in large spoonsful, like pudding.

Pies were a declining trade, not so much because of doubts about their contents but competition from shops, which also affected eel and ginger beer sales. Patent medicines in the shops – plus possibly a greater degree of public scepticism – had similarly caused the virtual disappearance of sellers of remedies from London, the few who were left being vendors of either corn salves (which consisted of resin and tallow plus green colouring) or herbal cough sweets and related products. The most prominent cough-sweet seller, who had once run a sizeable street wholesale business, said: 'The cough and herb trade is nothing now to what it was long ago. Thirty and forty years ago, it was as good as £3 or £4 a week to a person, and was carried on by respectable men. I know nothing of any humbugs in the respectable part of the trade. . . . I am the "original" maker of my goods. I will cure any child of the hooping-cough, and very speedily. I defy any medical man to dispute it, and I'll do it – "no cure, no pay." I never profess to cure asthma. Nobody but a gravedigger can put an end to that there. It's the same with consumption; it may be relieved, but the gravedigger is the only man as can put a stop to it. I sell to very respectable people, and educated people, too; and, what's more, a good deal (of cough drops) to medical men. In course, they can analyse it, if they please.' As was typical of such sellers, he was very secretive about his recipes, but his ingredients included horehound and coltsfoot for coughs, Irish moss for consumption, and hyssop, which was usually used for flatulence, for 'wind in the chest'; he was also prepared to supply the plain herbs and a few other items to order. 'I'm never asked for anything improper. They won't ask *me* for . . . or . . . [probably rue and savin for abortions]. And I'm never asked for washes or cosmetics; but a few nettles are ordered of me for complexions.'[24]

True herbalists were to be found in many parts of the country – Lancashire, according to Page, being especially well known for them; outside London, however, a far commoner group was quacks, who knew next to nothing about herbs or medicine but depended solely on the art of salesmanship. As the nature and worth of their goods could not be taken for granted in the same way as food or medicines prescribed by doctors (or herbal remedies from known specialists) many of them adopted a more elaborate selling technique than merely knocking on doors or shouting their wares and offered entertainment in the form of 'patter' or a speech, necessarily of a more or less amusing kind. In earlier times, they had carried entertainment to the length of employing clowns to accompany them, but by this time clowns had given way to class and they customarily travelled in smart carts attended by liveried footmen (for less obvious reasons but perhaps in order to foster a suitably pale and studious look, they were also in the habit of wearing green-tinted spectacles). Occasionally, they sold patent products such as were in the shops, but usually, to hugely greater profit, made their own: some offered a variety of potions and others only one, which, however, might be claimed could cure a remarkable range of complaints, such as liver pills, which one extremely persuasive seller sold as a cure for everything on the grounds that the liver was the cause of all illness; he also induced people with no symptoms to buy them by pointing out that prevention was better than cure.

A rather different example of single-product sellers, who, to judge from results, must have included some with knowledge of the herbs in question (of which there were several) were worm-expellers, whose stalls looked unusually interesting because the displaced worms were displayed in bottles: sometimes the exhibits were merely sheep's or chicken's entrails, or in one quoted instance a bootlace, but it was claimed that in general fakes were not needed because customers were only too willing to hand over genuine specimens: '. . . lor bless yer, there is no occasion to show anything else but genuine ones when you have been any time in one place'.[25]

A case-book kept by a seller who did not practise patter but went from door to door and offered a range of preparations distinguished by colour but probably little or nothing else shows how easy and lucrative, given the right public, this kind of selling could be.

No. 75. – T. Mackfereson, a publicin, —Street. Sicknes, a scurvy red face, told him it was the scrufle an venrel mixt, age 43. Fisik [physic], 6 bottles of my yello wash, and bid him drink his likers [liquors] mixt and not nate; ped [paid] me, altogether, 2 ginys.

No. 76. – Sakery Moses, one of our tribe. Sickness, bad ies, age 57. Fisik, a bottle of my red drops; ped me 1 shillin, for he wouldn't pay any more; for wich reson I med it strong enough to blind im.

No. 77. – Jem Tomson, a yuth, 2, —coart, —street; narvus weeknes an was ni kild [nigh killed] by D—, age 18. Fisik, 3 bottles of my narvus cordial.

No. 78. – Jane Sikes, a sarvant, out of place, — Row. Siknes, swellin in the lines [limbs?] an vamiten, age 19; 2 bottles of the blue mixtur; ped me 3 shillins.

No. 79. – November 7: Tom Parker, a musishaner, —street. Siknes, grumblin in the guts, age 25. Fisik, a large plaster of cobblers' wax to the pit of the stummik and 2 bottles of the blue drench; ped me 6 shillins and 2 shillins a week till well. Will be a good incum if it lasts.

No. 80. – Marget Darren, Cross-street. Siknes, the hard gripes on gall dropsi, age 47. Fisik, a box of pumpin pills to bring down the water an 3 bottles of red drops.

No. 81. Ellorner Skinner, milkwoman, — lane. Siknes, bellake an water weakness, age 28. Fisik, 22 broun powders an to drink her own milk; ped me, by 2 scores, 8 shillin.

No. 82. – Simon Crab, hater [hatter]. Siknes, kernals in the gullet, age 29. Fisik, cut open the swellins an rubd blue vitrol on it, 3 bottles of blu wash; mind an cal every week.[26]

Smithfield Club Cattle Show, 1851 (*Illustrated London News*)

3. Produce: The Best in the World

The Victorians were immensely proud of their beef and mutton, which by then had benefited from a century of selective breeding and turnip feeding – long enough to have doubled the size of cattle but not for the farmers' achievement to be taken for granted. A journalist enthusing over the exhibits at the 1854 Smithfield Christmas cattle show complacently compared the beef they represented to the 'old cow' with which people had formerly had to content themselves and stressed the up-to-date version's status as a product: 'The Christmas show of fat cattle in Baker Street is the result of an entirely new order of things. The only fair way of regarding beef is to consider it – as it is really – a manufactured article. . . . And, as in manufactured goods – so also in beef – it is produced in various forms, differing in quality.'[1]

The highest quality was, as ever, Scotch; next came Devon and Hereford, and finally shorthorn, which had only recently been bred and, though principally a dairy cow today, was at that time valued not only for milk but its propensity to fatten quickly and provide medium quality beef at popular prices. Until a short time before, excessive fat had been admired, and grotesquely obese specimens were still sometimes seen, but in general a more moderate ideal had come to prevail – albeit not the degree of leanness favoured today (which would not only have conflicted with the belief in fat as a sign of health but caused problems in the kitchen, where the only alternative to animal fats was olive oil). Fattening had by then been studied with scientific care: the part played by warmth and inactivity was appreciated, and a varied, carefully balanced diet recommended, the foods favoured including not only turnips (which alone tended to have a laxative effect) but hay and chaff (which offset it) plus carrots, cabbages, oats and barley, pea and bean meal, malt, and, most effective of all for ensuring gain in weight, linseed and oilcake. For the rest, slaughter was at two to four years old (as compared to our twelve to eighteen months) and hanging time, weather permitting, three or four days: at Smithfield, the custom was to buy, but not necessarily kill, for the following weekend.

The resulting beef was generally accepted as the best in the world – as perhaps it remains: one says this not only because of its greater maturity but the circumstances of the richness of its pasturage before fattening,

A prize Border Leicester ram with the agent and shepherd
of the Rock Estate, 1869 (Rock Farms)

which contained a far wider variety of herbs and flowers than survive in
the present environment – the only type which is comparable being that
from cattle reared in the Highlands, where conditions have changed
relatively little.

Except with regard to age, much the same applied to mutton as beef:
the superiority of Welsh and Southdown was firmly established, and
fattening carried out with a similar range of foods, though less consistently.
In earlier decades, the custom had been to slaughter at five years: the
necessity to send one-year-olds to market, however, was already admitted
by the leading agriculturalist and MP Philip Pusey, who said to James
Caird, author of the classic survey of contemporary farming, *English
Agriculture 1850–51*: 'Your readers ... may not like this rapid production, but it is required by the increase of our population.[2]

Pigs, because they did not require large areas of pasture, were often reared on smallholdings and in cottages rather than on farms, the annual pig paying the rent and in the meanwhile being treated as the family pet. An old couple in Essex kept their pig under the stairs and the wife knitted a little jacket for him; the feminist Frances Power Cobbe, who was brought up in Ireland, told a somewhat disillusioning story (from the mistress's point of view) about a beautiful Irish girl thought to have been trained as the perfect housemaid but who, when she married and was set up in a 'particularly neat'[3], newly furnished cottage, let the pig sleep under the marital bed for six months without clearing up the manure. In Ireland, pigs were often allowed to run free wearing hats with the crowns cut out of them to prevent their rooting up the potatoes. They were also frequently kept as adjuncts to breweries and distilleries, or at dairies, where they were fed on whey and buttermilk (cattle were similarly sometimes fattened on the malt at breweries). As the broken-victuals dealer's activities suggest, they were commonplace in London: according to Mayhew, there were 200 street-sellers of pigwash, which must have accounted for some thousands not attached to supporting businesses; about 3,000 were kept in a slum known, inappropriately, as 'The Potteries' (rather than Piggeries) in

Typical cottage pigs: Gloucester Old Spots (by an unknown artist) (Iona Antiques)

Notting Hill, where a great many slept under the beds. Those raised on miscellaneous scraps were turned into bacon; pigs intended for pork, which were killed at three to six months, were carefully fed, often on dairy by-products, or sometimes maize. At this stage, pork was eaten in nothing like the quantities of beef and mutton, and was therefore much dearer (10d.–1s. for a prime cut as compared to 5–7d. and 6–8d. respectively); demand, however, was increasing rapidly, largely because of the need for variety at dinner parties. Sucking pig, which was sufficiently popular for Mrs Beeton to include it among her menus, cost 5–6s. (slightly less than a turkey).

Game had not been legally saleable until 1831, which had meant that before that date its consumption had theoretically been limited to the holders of shooting rights and their connections, while shooting rights had in turn been restricted to people with property qualifications, i.e. in effect the landed classes. This had given it social cachet the effect of which has not worn off even yet and which ensured that thereafter no dinner party between August and February could be given without it: when it was out of season, poultry was served instead. It also established the tradition of poaching, which by then, despite ferocious penalties, was carried on to an extent which made it a plausible reason for changing the law, though in fact a proportion of the illegal trade was contributed by the rights-holders themselves (who, as a sop to legality, often did not sell for money but in direct exchange for poultry or fish: hence the number of game-dealers who were also fishmongers).

After 1831, the right to kill and sell game was controlled by licence and the penalty for poaching by daylight modified (night poaching, because of the likelihood of violence, continued to be classified as a misdemeanour and as such was punishable by prison with hard labour or, in aggravated cases, transportation). Fifteen years later, despite a far larger volume of legal trade, there was still 'quite as much . . . as ever there was'[4] of the poached – which was surprising only in that one might have expected the amount to have been considerably greater. The reduced penalty (fine, except in default of payment) meant that poaching became a relatively sensible as well as probably the only way for country people to supplement incomes which might be as low as 6s. a week or support themselves during periods of unemployment; also, reform came at a particularly timely moment, since the new poor law, with its promise of the Bastilles, was introduced the very next year. That the legal sector did not destroy the poachers' market was largely due to the condition of their goods; other factors were price, poachers usually being offered less than other suppliers, and demand for out-of-season game.

The situation in the countryside was described by a master poacher called Frederick Gowing who managed to put himself across virtually as a welfare officer. Gowing, who was based at Snape, in Suffolk claimed that he could draw on the services of some forty or fifty local accomplices at any time; in the autumn and winter, however (the game season), he reckoned to be able to count on 100 from some ten or fifteen parishes around. The reason for the increase was that after the harvest there was less agricultural work to be done, and farmers, many of whom were themselves badly off, were often obliged to reduce their labour force. '. . . When the poor men are out of employment, of course they must have something to support them; they will call upon the parish, and the parish refuse to allow them anything, but they may go to the bastile. . . . They come to me sometimes, and then I pity them, and I ask them questions. Supposing they get an order to go into the house, they say, "Well, Frederick, I have got an order to go into the house; I do not like to go there; what should I do?" I say, "Do not go thieving, you do not want to do that." "What should I do? . . . I do not know how to set a wire; I do not know how to get a head of game." "Then," says I, "I will tell you: knock up two or three dozen of wires, and prick them down at a certain height, and you will earn as much, if you are fortunate, in one night, as you would get probably in a week by working for a farmer." Hares are very frequent in our country.' Disposal was relatively easy: professionals like Gowing took out shooting licences to enable them to carry game without interference, and, as the restrictions on killing it were universally resented, virtually everyone was sympathetic: '. . . there are plenty of people to take game; perhaps I take some of it. But there are pig dealers. . . . probably going to market on Tuesday or Wednesday, or Saturday; they will take three or four hares from one man, and two or three from another, and say, "We are going to Woodbridge market; there is a man from Ipswich that will meet us, and we can sell them to him." '⁵

As one would expect, noise and the difficulty of concealment were among the reasons for poachers' avoidance of the use of guns, although James Hawker, author of his *Journal*, kept a sawn-off rifle in his boot, and according to Gowing airguns were popular for night-poaching (which continued, despite penalties, but almost certainly to a lesser extent than before); wires or nets, however, were more efficient than shooting as well as avoiding the disadvantage of wounds. Nor was it only wounds to which people might object: poached items were the rule at City dinners because the participants, who could expect to be tight before the game course arrived, were afraid of swallowing mouthsful of shot. Out-of-season demand was apparently continuous but (again as one might expect) soared on the first morning of the season, when legitimate items could by no possibility have reached the shops – let alone been hung. It was said that

one City poulterer with several scrupulous but stupid customers would go
to Leadenhall market at dawn on the opening day of the partridge season,
take his purchases home, hang them up in his hall, and solemnly shoot
them with a brace of pistols.

The legitimately killed supply was nurtured as carefully and, often,
very much more emotively than regular farm stock – proprietors' anxiety
being reflected in the size and wages of gamekeeping staff. Earl Fitz-
Hardinge, of Berkeley Castle, Gloucestershire, who was a noted sports-
man, kept eight head keepers, twenty under keepers, and thirty full-time
watchmen over 30,000 acres; Lord Salisbury employed seven keepers
plus rat- and mole-catchers over 4,000 acres (tenants on his estate were
not allowed to kill rats and moles for themselves, presumably for fear of
their endangering the game by using poison). The keeper's job included
not only guarding against poachers but combating vermin, which was
much more plentiful than today, one of his most important skills being
to make and set traps for foxes, stoats, weasels, and other predators,
including any dogs and cats which might stray into the preserve: as can
be imagined, this threat to their pets was one of the most active of many
sources of resentment felt by people living in the neighbourhood against
the game-preserving establishment. The greatest problem preservers had,
however, which also involved poaching, was the introduction of new
stock, since, although pheasants were fed (on buckwheat, barley, maize,
lentils, and other foods), breeding, i.e. hatching under hens, was not yet
carried out on a significant scale: relatively small numbers were occasionally reared in this way, and it was used as a means of saving eggs which
had been stolen from nests, but otherwise it had been adopted only by
dealers in live game, some of whose stock was bred and most of the rest
poached – of necessity. The more conscientious (if, again, stupid)
sportsmen resorted to such dealers, but others went straight to the
poachers themselves: thus Gowing, while spending the shooting season
concentrating on edible goods, was chiefly occupied during the spring
and summer in transferring livestock from one estate to another. His
clients included the Marquis of Hertford, who came to know him as a
result of a chase after he had been detected stealing 'store birds'[6] from
his land; subsequently, he was invited into his lordship's drawing room,
where he also met the Duke of Wellington.

A generation later, when Richard Jefferies was writing, breeding had
become general, and later still incubators may have been used: with the
aid of such methods, densely stocked estates and enormous bags were
possible, but at this stage the numbers killed were moderate, except with
regard to hares, which were evidently very abundant in some areas (e.g.
Suffolk where Gowing operated). As one might suppose, however, not all

The Game Keeper at Lacock Abbey, Wiltshire: a photograph taken in
the 1840s by William Henry Fox Talbot (Science Museum, London)

types of land suited them: Earl Fitz-Hardinge took about 1,000 pheasants a year but (which he seemed to consider embarrassingly modest) only 700–800 hares – and, for the same reason, no partridges at all (wild duck, on the other hand, were plentiful on his estate; he also kept deer and had extensive fisheries).

Lord Salisbury averaged, in round numbers, 550 pheasants, 600 partridges, and 475 hares 1842–5; the totals taken on Lord Berners' estate of 4,000 acres at Didlington, Norfolk, 1844–5, were 826 pheasants, 502 partridges, 1,319 hares, twenty-one woodcock, and fifty-three wild duck. Hares and partridges sometimes retailed for as little as 6d. each; pheasants cost 2s.6d.–4s. (as compared to chickens at 2.6d.), wild duck 2s.–2s.6d., and venison from 1s.6d. per lb.

Besides game, a distressingly large number of other wild birds were eaten, including plovers, curlews, ruffs and reeves, dotterels, larks, wheatears, starlings, redwings, and blackbirds (all of which are now protected by law).* Most of them were served during the same season and in the same way as conventional game, with accompaniments of fried breadcrumbs or toast, or, à la *haute cuisine*, a variety of sauces, stuffings, and forcemeats. Another bird occasionally seen on upper-class tables was the ortolan, a European species which had to be imported (live, as in the case of all meat except salted); it was so tiny that Soyer's ultimate extravagance was not stuffing it with truffles but vice-versa. Small birds were usually caught with nets: ortolans, corncrakes, redwings, and ruffs and reeves were fattened thereafter, as no doubt others would have been if it had been practicable; ruffs and reeves were given wheat, bread and milk, and hemp seeds, and redwings mashed figs and juniper berries. Pigeons, which were popular at all levels of society and cooked in many different ways, were bred domestically, being kept either in dovecotes or, like pigs, indoors, where they were encouraged to make their nests on the floor to prevent the young from falling and injuring themselves. According to Cobbett, they were not very profitable, but they were generally agreed to be remarkably pleasant companions and the easiest of all birds to rear. (In Buckinghamshire, Aylesbury ducks similarly were often raised in parlours and sitting rooms.)

The fattening of the larger sorts of poultry for the London market was carried on as a separate business and had become a highly organized, chiefly because of the biannual demand for geese, which were not only

---

* Woodlarks, two kinds of plover, corncrakes, ruffs and reeves, and dotterels are listed under Schedule I, i.e. may not be interfered with in any way.

eaten at Michaelmas but by far the most popular Christmas bird; the fashion for turkeys, however, was growing, presumably for the same reason as chickens suddenly coming into vogue – because of the increasing influence of French cookery, in which both were much more frequently and imaginatively used than was traditional in this country. Except as the means of producing *foie gras*, the French do not seem to have shared the English preference for goose, but their system of land-holding, which led to divided estates and small farms, favoured the rearing of poultry of all kinds rather than cattle: the ascendancy of the former in their diet was also evident from the state of the egg trade, French eggs being cheaper than British and imported in large quantities (100 million in 1852). In England, hen rearing received comparatively little attention until after 1846, by which time the first and most outstanding two of a spate of French or French-inspired cookery books had appeared (Eliza Acton's *Modern Cookery* and Soyer's *Gastronomic Regenerator*); also, a pair of Cochin China fowls, which had never been seen here before, were presented to Queen Victoria and exhibited in Dublin that year. An account of the excitement to which they gave rise was given (or rather quoted) by Mrs Beeton: 'As soon as it was discovered, despite the most strenuous endeavours to keep the tremendous secret, that a certain dealer was possessed of a pair of these birds, straightway the avenues to that dealer's shop were blocked by broughams, and chariots, and hack cabs, until the shy poulterer had been tempted by a sufficiently high sum to part with his treasure. Bank notes were exchanged for Cochin chicks, and Cochin eggs were in as great demand as though they had been laid by the fabled golden goose. The reign of the Cochin China, however, was of inconsiderable duration.' By the time she was writing, in the late '50s, several other exotic varieties had similarly risen and fallen from favour, but the general enthusiasm, or 'poultry mania', as it was dubbed by *Punch*, had by no means died down; one useful result which came of it at a fairly early stage was the foundation of the British Poultry Club in 1852.

An invention which was independent of the 'mania' insofar as that it was not a new idea, but which might have been of some consequence not only to the poultry trade but contemporary game preservers, was an apparently efficient, commercially viable incubator. A number of attempts at artificial hatching had been made earlier in the century, several by the French, another by a breeder called Mowbray, to whom Mrs Beeton referred as an authority on poultry rearing, and yet another by a scientifically minded character named Bucknell, who designed a heated box or chest in which a constant, exact temperature could be maintained (precise heat regulation being impossible with the ordinary ovens of the time). Bucknell displayed his appliance in a showroom in Pall Mall in

1839, together with a promotional booklet in which he claimed to have reared 2,000 chicks with its aid; technical details were not given, but the heat was almost certainly supplied by water, as with potato-cans (or thermos flasks) and by his successor in the field. Enough interest was aroused for the 'Eccaleobion', as the incubator was called, to be remembered some years later, but as a curiosity rather than practical possibility.

The next person to try was William Cantelo, whose 'Hydro-Incubator' was similarly exhibited in a showroom in Leicester Square, also accompanied by a promotional book.[7] By this time (1849) the 'mania' was at its height, which was no doubt partly why the latter attracted a considerable amount of attention – among those who read it, or at least had heard of it, being the Queen and Prince Albert, who invited him to give an exposition of his invention at Windsor. Also, however, the book was clear, readable, and informed. It presented his product as an investment not only for professionals but people such as the old anxious to keep out of the workhouse; nor did he fail to recommend it to game preservers. Further, he gave it additional credibility by stating (which, if it was true, meant that the Eccaleobion cannot have been very efficient) that he was the first to utilize the discovery that the body temperature of birds is 106°F (41°C), rather than the same as that of human beings, as had apparently always previously been assumed.

The incubator consisted of a tank of water kept at 42°C (the extra degree presumably being to allow for cooling) and an egg container or series of containers with perforated bottoms and coverings of rubber or gutta percha (which, since neither material proved durable, were replaced on later models with plate glass). A continuous flow of water was passed over the covers, supplying 'top-contact' rather than all-round heat, which he considered important because it was how warmth was transmitted by the hen, whose treatment of her eggs he imitated as closely as possible in all respects: thus he also advocated that they should be left to cool for twenty to thirty minutes three times a day, as they would have been while she went in search of food, and turned at the end of each interval, as when she disturbed them on her return. He had rational justifications for all these precautions: top-contact heat, he said, caused less evaporation than radiated; when the hen left her nest, the temporary loss of heat reduced the volume of air in the egg so that more was drawn in to fill the vacuum, thus furnishing the embryo with a new supply; moving the eggs ensured that no part of the fluid stuck to the shell and promoted the chick's circulation. It is noteworthy that all three precepts continued to be followed until about thirty years ago.

The incubator was accompanied by a further piece of apparatus for raising the chicks, which he called the 'Hydro-Mother': this consisted of a

set of warm pipes fixed above an adjustable floor which could be lowered
as the chicks grew so that the piping was always at a height just to brush
their backs, the intention being to give them the same sensation as when
huddling under the hen.

Both appliances were offered in various sizes, for the smallest of which
he gave a calculation showing that a profit of about £75 per year exclusive
of the initial cost of equipment could have been made; for a large size,
which hatched 200 chicks a day, profit was £2,500. His figures were
optimistic in that he quoted London prices for chickens, which could not
have been guaranteed elsewhere.

One of his problems was price, since the smallest sizes, plus installation
charge, cost £50, which was more than twice the average farm worker's
whole annual wage and beyond consideration for anyone ever likely to
end up in the workhouse – even £2 (the price, incredible as it may now
seem, of a cheap cooking range) being more than a large proportion of the
working classes, living as they did almost entirely on credit, could manage.
Almost certainly, however, as was indicated by a cartoon in *Punch*
suggesting that food produced unnaturally must be unhealthy, he also
faced prejudice which, though hardly the equivalent of humanitarian
feelings about battery rearing today, bore some relation to them and
discouraged professional and higher-class buyers. Thus salesmanship and
even royal patronage could not bring him more than very limited business:
his showroom closed in 1856.

Although milk and eggs were available all the year round, both were scarce
in winter, for which reason eggs were preserved by one of three methods:
painting with oil or resin, immersion in lime water, or brief boiling –
according to Mrs Beeton, for twenty seconds, to *The Servant's Magazine*,
one minute (their aim in all cases to seal the surface). Grading was not
carried out, though very small ones were sold for ½d. rather than the
standard price of 1d., but their usual size seems to have been much smaller
than today: George Dodd, author of a book called *The Food of London*,
took their average weight as 1 oz., whereas the present size 5 is almost 2,
roughly the same is indicated by the proportions given in recipes. Bought
eggs were bad sufficiently often for Soyer to give the classic advice about
breaking them into a bowl before adding them to the mixture; staleness
was supposed to be detectable by holding them up to the light to see if
they looked dull and opaque rather than clear and slightly translucent.
Prejudice over colour, as with bread and sugar (and women's complexions), went in favour of white rather than brown or (worse: the same
applied to freckles) mottled. In areas where they were available, eggs other
than hens' were often used: Miss Acton, who came from Suffolk, where

turkeys and guinea-fowl were raised, said that guinea-fowls' eggs were 'very rich and excellent'[8] and turkeys' considered locally to be preferable to hens' for all culinary purposes; bantams' were also popular, and ducks', despite their strong flavour, frequently (and with justification) recommended for cakes and puddings. Wild birds', like the birds themselves, could be taken freely, among the most esteemed and commonly eaten being swans', which were sometimes served as delicacies instead of plovers'.

Much less importance was attached to the production of milk than beef at this stage: traditionally, dairy work was done by women, which it is tempting to see, especially during the Victorian period, when the subordination of women was particularly marked, as symbolic of its secondary status. Practical difficulties were no doubt paramount, but at least to the extent that female labour was even cheaper and more plentiful than male, its feminine stamp was perhaps connected with the almost complete lack of innovation which characterized it not only at mid century but for some decades to come. Milking machines had been designed by 1865 but were not put into general use for many years; mechanical cream separators were introduced in the '90s; steam power was occasionally employed for churning butter, but only on the most advanced farms. In the meanwhile, dairy maids had to combine the womanly virtues of good temper and patience with an unfashionable degree of physical strength. It was not uncommon for cows to withhold their milk if they sensed that the maid was irritable: '. . . do what you will, you can't do your duty to the cows if you're cross. There is not a cunninger thing in the world than a cow for finding out what sort of people they are that have the meddling with her. . . . The cow hates snuff-taking, dirty women.'[9] Girls needed strong arms to carry the milk pails and sometimes both persistence and stamina for churning, which could take hours (the hard manual work involved in their job was the basis of their reputation for being buxom and healthy).

The railways were used to transport milk, notably to London, but not to a significant extent until after 1865, when outbreaks of rinderpest and subsequent government action greatly reduced the city's cow population. A main beneficiary of the epidemic was George Barham, founder of the Express Dairies, who had set up a company a short time before to bring milk from the country to London because of growing public concern about the unhealthiness of town-produced supplies. Earlier, when towns had been smaller and space available, keeping cows in an urban environment had not been impractical: Barham's father, who had also been a milk seller, had tended his herd in fields just off the Strand (town production, as a form of shop-keeping, was the exception to the rule of female domination). In 1854, however, a chemist called Normandy who was foolish enough to look inside a dairy in Clerkenwell declared that the sight of the cattle had prevented him from being able to touch milk for six months: 'I saw about 30 or 40 cows in the most disgusting condition one can possibly conceive, full of ulcers; their teats ... most horribly ... ulcerated ... and their legs full of tumours and abscesses ... and the fellow was milking these poor cows in the middle of all this purulent abomination. I have been told since, that it is by no means the exception, but that the animals of a great many cow-keepers are in the same condition; so that what is introduced into the milk besides water, which is comparatively nothing, is actually the product of disease.'[10] In several dairies in Westminster, the cows were kept tethered in double stalls seven feet wide; two buildings had no windows, the only ventilation being through tiled roofs, and gratings in the wall of a third were carefully covered with sacking, probably because of complaints about the smell. Understandably, few cow-keepers cared (or dared) to call in vets, but allowed ailing animals to deteriorate until they dropped dead or their milk dried up, whereupon they were dispatched to the butcher.

Scalding – as opposed to boiling, which was avoided because of the skin and taste – was sometimes used as a way of preventing milk from turning sour; dried and tinned milk were manufactured but, like other similarly prepared food (dried meat and vegetables were also available) were not regarded as articles for general consumption and made only in relatively small quantities. The value of any of these processes as a means of sterilization could not be appreciated because of ignorance of the existence of germs (which was suspected in the early 1850s and first formally propounded by Pasteur in 1856 but did not become common knowledge for many years). In butter-making areas, skim milk was drunk by the poor, who otherwise probably could not afford milk at all; skimming was also often carried out in the home for cream, the milk being left to stand in wide, shallow pans and the cream removed with perforated spatulas.

Methods of making butter varied from place to place according to tradition, the type desired, and whether cheese was also made. For cheap butter, sour rather than fresh cream was frequently used, partly because it could be skimmed more efficiently; in cheese districts, whey cream, either alone or mixed with fresh, was churned, and could yield an almost first-class result, despite the axiom that good cheese and butter were incompatible; sometimes, high-quality fresh butter was made directly from milk, but, because of the amount of labour required, only on farms where steam- or horsepower could be employed. Hand-churning took anything from half an hour to four or five, chiefly depending on the weather – hot weather making for quick churning but inferior quality. The significance of temperature in butter-making was not generally understood: stoves

Cheese market 1850–60 (Salisbury and South Wiltshire Museum)

were used in store-rooms for maturing cheeses, but Caird, who toured the country in the course of his researching his book, said that he did not come across a single dairy with heating facilities. Another unrecognized factor was possible infection with bacteria, which meant that the butter might be tainted for no obvious reason.

Its apparent temperamentality had caused its manufacture to be more surrounded with superstition than any other agricultural activity. The Irish, who exported in large quantities, had a particularly wide repertoire of rites: in County Cork, for instance (where production was carried on for only six months of the year), the beginning of the season was celebrated by sprinkling the cows with holy water, garlanding them with rowan berries, passing live coals around them, gathering up the earth on which they trod when they first emerged from their sheds or paddocks in the morning, and killing any hares found in their fields, on the supposition that they were witches in disguise; elsewhere, a common custom was to put the key of the church door into the churn. Irish butter, which was subjected to a system of inspection, was reckoned to be of consistently fair quality; Cambridge and Epping butter was considered the best sold in London. Accusations of adulteration with lard and horse fat were made, but tests revealed only excess moisture, which was probably unintentional.

The following is part of a journalist's account of Cheshire cheese-making on a farm on the banks of the Dee owned by a widow, Mrs S.: 'I had obtained leave to come at seven in the morning to see the whole process of cheese-making. The maidens, of whom there are always three, and sometimes four, rise at five o'clock. There is the milking and the breakfast; and by seven they are ready to begin upon the cheese.

'The meal of milk of the evening before was put into tubs, except what is wanted for butter, and for domestic use. The tubs which receive the milk for the cheese are two; and there are two more to contain the whey of the preceding batch. When the evening's and morning's meal were poured (mixed) into the two tubs, there were about fifty gallons in each, the yield of sixty cows, ten of the seventy cows on the farm being dry, or calving at the time.

'There are two things to be put into this deluge of milk, one for show and the other for use. For show, a tablespoonful of arnotta is mixed in. The arnotta is a thick, viscid, dark red substance . . . used merely to colour the cheese . . . The other . . . is the rennet. Irish rennet is found to be the best. Some of the farmers in the cheese districts bargain with the butchers, in selling their calves, to have the stomachs back again; but . . . the regular cheese dairies are provided with the stomachs of Irish calves, brought by travelling agents. Mrs S. buys enough in the spring to last the whole year. . . .

'The maids are not idle while the curd is setting. One stout wench draws several pailsful of buttermilk from a copper in one corner, for the pigs; and next, she sets about skimming the whey of yesterday. A thick cream has risen and makes that great tub look exceedingly rich. She skims it, and deposits the cream in an earthen jar, ready for the churn; and then she empties the whey by pailsful into what seems a great copper in another corner; but, as the whey vanishes, it is clear that the copper is a funnel. The whey runs off through a pipe to the piggery. She is a clever girl who does this. She wears a blue bib like a child's, up to her collar-bones, and her gown is short, to a most sensible degree, as is that of the other dairy-maids. They do not go slopping and draggling about, as ladies do in London streets; but have their dress no lower than the ankle, and shoes thick enough to keep them out of the damp of the moist brick floor.

'I stand between fifty gallons of thick custard (to all appearance) on the one hand and fifty gallons on the other. A very long, blunt knife is handed to the widow, who this morning does the honours with her own hands. She scores the curd in all directions. . . . The breaker is next handed. The breaker is like a round grid-iron, delicately made of thick wire, and fastened to the end of a slender broomstick. With a graceful and slow motion, Mrs S. plunges in the breaker, and works it gently up and down, and hither and thither, searching every part of the great tub, that no lump of curd may remain unbroken. When she turns – in ten minutes or so – to the second tub, the curd of the first all sinks to the bottom. Then comes the dairymaid, and fishes and rakes among the whey with a bowl till she brings up the greater part of the curd to her side of the tub. Then she throws aside the bowl; and, while she retains the mass with one arm, she sweeps the whey with the other for all the curd that is yet abroad. There seems to be such a quantity that one can hardly believe that it all goes to make one cheese. Some of the cheeses, however, weigh one hundred weight, or even more, while those made in winter dwindle to sixty pounds or less.'[11]

The curd was heaped into two baskets lined with linen cloths, which were set in oak tubs to drain, and in several hours was dry enough for salting. The next morning the cheeses, as they had then become, were pierced with large skewers to draw the whey from the inside, and the morning after that placed under stone presses. On the fifth day they were transferred to a vast store-room, which was furnished with both stove and thermometer, where they were regularly turned and wiped, and eventually sold, the widow's reputation being such that they seldom reached the markets but were bought by visiting factors, mainly from London and Manchester.

This description was representative in that all British cheese was farmhouse made (the first cheese factory was established in 1870) and Cheshire estimated to be the best-selling kind: Cheddar at this date was marketed only in Somerset and frequently replaced by Cheshire for cooking purposes. Other leading varieties included Shropshire, Derbyshire, Cambridge, Stilton, and double and single Gloucester – single Gloucester being made partly with skim milk; like hard skim-milk types (now seldom produced, for good reason) and Cheddar, however, much of the cheese eaten was made and sold locally. Several tales were current illustrating the extreme hardness of all-skim-milk cheese: it was said of the Suffolk version that 'pigs grunt at it, dogs bark at it, but neither of them dare bite it',[12] while the parings of Cumberland were alleged to be used for mending clogs. The only imported cheeses were Dutch and American at the one end of the market and Parmesan and Gruyère at the other. Soft foreign varieties such as Brie and Camembert were unknown because they could not be transported satisfactorily, although, since mild-tasting fresh cream cheese, which was made in many districts, was widely considered the only socially acceptable sort, Brie would almost certainly have been popular.

An idealized view of a milkmaid
(*London Labour and the London Poor*, Vol. 2)

In general, however, cheese was out of favour in polite society, for a combination of two reasons: it was customarily associated with the working classes, among whom it was a far commoner (because cheaper) accompaniment to bread than butter, and all except cream cheese (which, perhaps significantly, they could not afford) was condemned as indigestible. Mrs Beeton said, '. . . cheese, in its commonest shape, is only fit for sedentary people, as an after-dinner stimulant, and in very small quantity. Bread and cheese, as a meal, is only fit for soldiers on march or labourers in the open air, who like it because it "holds the stomach a long time." '13 Mrs Gaskell, herself a cheese-lover, very effectively attacked this view in *Wives and Daughters*, where Mrs Kirkpatrick, just before she remarried

(it was a second marriage on both sides), protested at her fiancé's liking
for it to his daughter Molly – he being far more genuinely well bred than
his future wife and also (which covered it from the health point of view) a
doctor. ' "Bread and cheese! Does Mr Gibson eat cheese?"

' "Yes, he's very fond of it," said Molly, innocently. "I've known him
eat toasted cheese when he has been too tired to fancy anything else."

' "Oh! but my dear, we must change all that. I shouldn't like to think of
your father's eating cheese; it's such a strong-smelling, coarse kind of
thing. We must get him a cook who can toss him up an omelette, or
something elegant." '[14]* In the lady's defence, it should be said that the
description of it as strong-smelling was probably a good deal truer than
today, partly because of the lack of cold storage and also because of the
relatively full flavour and obviously variable quality of farmhouse produce.
It seems highly likely that the custom of eating it after dinners which had
almost certainly already been extremely heavy was a main cause of its
supposed indigestibility – though, as people were greatly preoccupied with
the subject of digestion, a considerable number of other foods to which
this did not apply were similarly stigmatized. A further discouragement
from eating blue cheese was the consciousness that it contained mould,
which was associated with decay and therefore unwholesomeness – this
objection having arisen as a result of the increasing popularity of the
microscope (by the '50s, looking down a microscope had become a
favourite form of street entertainment and a piece of cheese a common
subject for observation).

Snobbery and digestibility were also responsible for the fact that
vegetables were under a cloud at this time. Peas and potatoes were among
the very few kinds sufficiently cheap and appreciated to cut across the
class barrier; in a more limited way, the same was true of dried peas,
which were traditionally used for soup and pudding; otherwise, pulses
were eaten only in the most gastronomically sophisticated circles, most
people looking on them as merely animal food. Onions, leeks, and above
all garlic were treated with great caution by everyone with any social
pretensions because of the danger of smelly breath: a magazine primarily
dedicated to teaching girls how to behave like ladies warned: 'The smell of
onions . . . is quite intolerable. . . . The loveliest mouth in the world would
have no charm if, instead of a pure – not "*fragrant*" – breath (no breath
ought to be fragrant) it emitted a pungent odour of onions, garlic, chalot,
or any such horror.'[15] Onions and leeks were used sparingly in soups and
stews and, particularly when people were entertaining, very seldom as

---

* This part of the story was set in the '30s, but, as Mrs Beeton's remarks show, the prejudice
against cheese remained.

straight vegetables; garlic, although sometimes discreetly introduced into elaborate dishes created by chefs, was never found in middle-class kitchens. The only vegetables guaranteed perfectly digestible were old potatoes, cauliflowers, broccoli, French beans, and asparagus (which cost 2s.6d. per 100 heads, or approximately 6d. per lb.). Salads were regarded as especially risky because raw items were believed to be the most likely to ferment in the stomach (as was probably the opposite of the truth, it now being thought that they contain enzymes which inhibit bacterial action). Since vitamins were not discovered until this century, nor (except by the vegetarians and other minority groups) was the importance of fibre recognized, whereas the low protein and energy-giving content of most kinds was known, the latter were dismissed by the majority of doctors as useless except as a means of providing variety in the diet: hospital patients were given greens only as a very occasional change from potatoes, and children and nursing mothers similarly permitted no more than small, infrequent helpings of the safe sorts. As a result of the work of the German chemist Justus von Liebig, however, who is chiefly remembered in connection with agricultural chemistry but whose research on animal nutrition was quite as far-reaching, the prevailing view was already being challenged, notably by a doctor called Edwin Lankester, who in particular recommended eating more salads.

Liebig's best known contribution and the one which originally made his name was his advocacy of artificial fertilizers, the use of which dated from the appearance of his celebrated *Organic Chemistry in its Application to Agriculture* in 1840 and was the outstanding innovation of the period in arable farming and market gardening. Four English editions of the book had appeared within a few years, and by 1855 at least a score of firms were manufacturing a variety of products, including superphosphates (which, however, remarkably rapid as the adoption of the new fertilizers was, still accounted for only a very small sector of the market).

Another major advance was the development of mechanized implements, which similarly gained momentum from about 1840, the chief focus of interest at mid century being the early steam ploughs. Forcing under glass (for cauliflowers, which, as they were both dear and classified as digestible, were relatively fashionable) was already used in the market gardens around London in the mid 1840s, but did not become general until later; magnificent hothouse fruit, however, was raised by the higher classes, among whom few status symbols were equal to the display of freshly picked, home-nurtured grapes and pineapples. Great efforts were also being made in breeding, with particularly conspicuous success in the case of apples and tomatoes: Cox's Orange Pippin was produced around

Truffle hunter with dogs, Wiltshire, c. 1870
(Salisbury and South Wiltshire Museum)

1850, though not yet marketed, and tomatoes (or 'love-apples', as was their old-fashioned name), which had previously been ribbed and evidently not very palatable, were sufficiently improved to be popular for cooking; possibly because they were still not suitable for eating raw, however, they were never used in salads at this stage.

Both watercress and mushrooms were extensively cultivated: mushrooms, like pigs and pigeons, were often raised by cottagers and smallholders, who grew them in their cellars, despite the smell of the beds of horse manure on which they were customarily sown. In addition, attempts had already been made to cultivate truffles: in England, a white variety known as 'summer' truffles were found in the woods, notably beech woods on chalky soils (as they still may be occasionally). They were not hunted with pigs, as in France, but dogs, often by gamekeepers: Richard Jefferies, in *The Gamekeeper At Home*, noted that the keeper's wife had some to spare. 'Here also are half a dozen truffles if I will accept them: most that are found go up to the great house; but of late years they have not been sought for so carefully because coming in quantities from abroad.'[16] (This was written in 1878.) As this suggests, English truffles were not usually bought and sold, but black French ones cost 8–15s. per lb., which, though nothing like so expensive in relative terms as today,* was still extremely dear – their popularity being accountable to the wealth of the upper classes rather than price.

On a more ordinary level, not only cauliflowers but broccoli and marrows (or courgettes, according to size) were also dear, a cauliflower being 6d. in comparison to 2d. for a cabbage – the high price of marrows being due to the fact that they had only recently been introduced into this country and were still unusual: hence it was felt necessary to refer to them as 'vegetable' marrows to distinguish them from bone marrow, which was much more popular than today, not only by itself or on toast, but as dumplings or sweet puddings, often flavoured with currants. Pumpkins were not often served as vegetables, but made into jam or 'pies', which, unlike the American version, meant that they were simply hollowed out and stuffed with apples and spices; spinach too was sometimes used for puddings – sweet meat and vegetable dishes being a legacy of an earlier culinary style and still not inconsistent with the pattern of formal dinners, when game and shellfish, vegetables, and puddings were all served at the same course.

An enormous number of varieties of apple were grown, nearly all of which have been superseded; apart from Cox's, the few which are still cultivated include Claygate Pearmain and Sturmer Pippin (the name

---

* According to Harrods, a black truffle the size of a hen's egg would now cost about £100.

'Pippin' originated from the fact that the trees were grown from pips). Much attention had been given to strawberry breeding, but none of the large sorts which were popular at that time have endured, partly because very little was known about disease resistance: as this was not a factor to be taken into consideration, higher priority was given to flavour, which leads one to suspect that strawberries then were rather more worth eating than now. The least changed are probably the small Alpine type, which were favoured because their season could be extended until almost Christmas. Of the three sorts of currant, the most fashionable was white, which was the mildest and considered the most suitable for serving at dessert: the leaves of the black were noted for black-currant-leaf tea, but many people disliked the taste of the fruit, which did not gain ascendancy until its high vitamin content became known. Nearly 200 varieties of gooseberry were cultivated, most of which had been developed in Lancashire and the north midlands, where growing them was a popular working-class hobby, as is indicated by some of their names, e.g. 'Jolly Miller', 'Jolly Painter', 'Lancashire Lad', and 'Pastime'; annual gooseberry shows were held at which a favourite among a selection of similar prizes was a copper tea kettle. Besides eating, gooseberries were used for wine, which was generally acknowledged the best of the numerous sorts of non-grape wine made and produced on a considerable scale commercially, partly (allegedly) for purposes of adulteration. Mulberries were also extensively used for wine; quinces were not often marketed, but when available employed for flavouring apples and marmalade. Pomegranates were planted for their scarlet blossom but did not ripen; outdoor peaches were unflatteringly described by Hawthorne as like the weather – watery.

It perhaps seems surprising that very few of the imported fruits and nuts on sale today were not available by midcentury, although some, notably avocado pears and bananas, were relatively unusual, and many suffered from transport conditions. The future popularity of the avocado was foreseeable, since it was already acclaimed as 'the most delicious [fruit] in the world'[17] instead of being served at the beginning of the meal, however, when the rule was soup and fish, it was dressed with salt, pepper, sugar, and fresh lime juice and eaten for dessert. Imported grapes, which came mainly from Portugal, were packed in jars of sawdust and arrived 'flat and vapid';[18] the scarcity of bananas was presumably due to the fact that they were almost impossible to transport without overripening in ships without temperature control. West Indian pineapples were plentiful, costing 6–9d. each, or 1d. or ½d. per slice – many of those disposed of in this way, however, being 'salt-water touched',[19] and all foreign-grown pineapples, because of their staleness, considered inferior to hot-house produce. Passion-fruit and tamarinds were raised in hot-houses; earlier in the century, Earl Powys in Shropshire had successfully ripened mangoes, but normally they were obtainable only as pickle, and guavas, similarly, as jelly. Mammees were occasionally eaten, and mangosteens, lychees, custard apples, and shaddocks known – the latter being the ancestors of grapefruit, which, although discovered, were not yet cultivated and still unheard-of in this country. Oranges, in contrast, were imported at an estimated annual rate of 300 million, or ten per head of the population, and were four a penny, which meant that they were cheaper than apples; without the Israeli and American trades, the most popular kinds were St Michael's, from the Azores, Maltese blood oranges, and Seville marmalade oranges. Coconuts had long been stowed on sugar ships; small quantities of Brazil nuts were sold; there do not seem to have been any peanuts, but cashews and pistachios were used for cooking, though not eaten *per se*, partly for lack of occasion, since as yet pre-prandial drinks and snacks were never served.

4. Products: The Worst in the World

Despite notable recent improvements at the top end of the market, the general view of bread has not changed much over the years. Bought bread was condemned as worse than in any other country: specific criticisms were that it was unhygienic, unwholesome, bitter, liable to go stale quickly, unsatisfying, and, like so many other things, indigestible – the last three being attributed to the addition of alum (a double sulphate of aluminium and potassium), which was used as a bleach. Its use had become almost universal because of the assumption that the whiter the bread, the higher its quality, and even the poor were not prepared to sacrifice their pride by buying an obviously inferior kind. Bakers were believed to take advantage of it to conceal adulteration with brown or non-wheat flour; concern was also felt about the fact that it slightly increased the absorbability of the dough, thus reducing the amount of flour needed to yield a given weight of loaf. Its effect on the stomach was thought to be astringent or irritating, according to quantity: among other complaints supposed to be caused by it were headaches, heartburn, nausea, constipation, and diarrhoea (though in fact it was probably fairly harmless).

A realistic comment on home-made bread, at least as fabricated in middle-class households, was contained in the following:

> Who hath not met with home-made bread,
> A heavy compound of putty and lead – [1]

Brown bread had been recommended as healthy since ancient times, but the arguments in its favour carried new conviction because it could be supported by chemical analysis – which at this stage, however, led to the erroneous conclusion that the part of the grain containing the most protein was the bran: in a widely quoted work, *The Chemistry of Common Life* by Professor James Johnston, the first Reader in Chemistry at Durham University, bran (which alone has none) was assigned a 14–15% protein content and fine white flour 10%. In fact, as all flour was stone-ground, and thus contained the whole wheat germ, the amount in brown and white differed very little, the balance being slightly in favour of white because the proteinous parts were more concentrated (which is as today except that because roller-milling sifts out the germ, it is returned to the flour thereafter). Fibre and of course vitamins were not mentioned, but the laxative property of brown bread was acknowledged and valued by its devotees.

The complaint that bread was unhygienic arose as a result of the filthiness of bakeries, which itself was the corollary of an extreme (but not untypical) degree of overwork. The state of many London bakeries was first reported by Dr William Guy of King's College Hospital, who, in an attempt to initiate improvement, subsequently became a founding director of the Aerated Bread Company. In the course of conversation, one of his patients told him that he was a journeyman (i.e. qualified assistant) baker and worked a twenty-hour day, beginning at eleven p.m. and continuing until about seven the following evening. Guy, in his 'utter astonishment'[2] (which might not have been so great had he known of conditions in, for instance, the dressmaking trade) felt impelled to question other bakers, and found that he was not exaggerating: a normal working pattern was for bread and rolls to be baked overnight so that they would be fresh for breakfast, mornings to be spent on deliveries and sales over the counter, and afternoons and evenings in making and selling fancy items such as buns, biscuits, and muffins. On most days of the week, the work was over between five and seven p.m., but on Fridays and Saturdays, when demand was heaviest, it sometimes went on without a break until midnight on Saturday.

The thing which most struck him about the bakeries themselves was the smell of drains: this resulted from the combination of lack of upkeep and the fact that bakehouses were generally situated in the basements under the shops, where the domestic kitchens of the houses would have been, and thus (as also were domestic kitchens) were directly next to or over them: in 'a decent-looking shop, in a respectable neighbourhood, I found the soil-pipe within a foot of the trough in which the bread is made; the pipe in a very unsound state, and the floor in some danger of being moistened by its contents. Indeed, I was assured by a baker who accompanied me, that he had himself seen the sewage flowing into the trough.'[3] In a later investigation, inspectors commented on spectacular cobwebs hanging from the ceilings, which were made the more conspicuous by coatings of flour dust, and the quantity of animal life the bakehouses supported. Abbreviated descriptions of individual bakeries included the following: 'Hundreds of cockroaches, ants, and other creeping things running about upon the walls and on the boards on which the bread is made. Rafters black with sulphur and flour-dust, and hanging thick with cobwebs in all directions. ... One of the troughs was open and full of flour, ready for the next batch. Hundreds of animals were running about over the lid and by the side, and upon the wall close by. The other trough was imperfectly shut and many of these animals were crawling in and out. . . . Flakes of cobwebs, heavy with dust, hanging down. Stone floor, very uneven and dirty, and piles of dark brown and black dust and dirt swept up in corners and under the troughs. A number of very dirty utensils and a wash-place close to the trough. Animals numerous. A large business done at this shop.'[4]*

The heat of the ovens meant that the temperature in which the men had to work might be as high as 80° or 90°F, the only ventilation frequently being through the door, which master bakers were in the habit of locking while the bread was being made at night: this, plus the energy required for kneading the dough, caused it to be said that much of the water which went into it was sweat. The heat – if nothing else – also caused the men to drink very heavily, which could have been a reason for the bread being badly made: a more certain one was sheer exhaustion, which meant that they tended to fall asleep while the dough was rising or during baking, so that it was overproved or burnt.

These conditions applied in about half the London bakeries – generally speaking, despite the 'decent-looking' one visited by Guy, the cheaper half; the same was true in Manchester and Birmingham. The root of the problem lay in over-competition springing mainly from the fact that, as materials and equipment were relatively cheap and the value of unpaid credit lower, less capital was needed to set up in baking than, for instance, as a butcher or grocer; staffing costs were kept down by using apprentice labour, which aggravated the problem by forcing qualified men to start up on their own. No action was taken until 1863 (more than fifteen years after Guy's original report), when minimum standards of hygiene and cleanliness were laid down and working hours of apprentices (but not qualified or adult workers) regulated.

The reason for bitterness in bread was that, instead of pure baker's yeast, brewers' yeast was used, which was impregnated with hops: sometimes, this was used direct, or sometimes for a barm, i.e. secondary culture, which helped to modify the taste. Another source of bitterness, or rather sourness, was that yeast, like butter, was liable to bacterial infection, which not only produced undesirable 'off' flavours but could interfere

---

* This may be compared with a report in *The Standard* (19 May 1983) 'Yesterday, Brooks's, the St James's club was fined £700 after Bow Street magistrates heard that "hundreds to thousands" of mice droppings and cockroach remains had been found in the kitchen. In the next few months, the Café Royal will be joined in court by other well-known names all accused of allegedly keeping dirty kitchens. . . .

A few years ago, Bob Crozier [a Principal Environmental Health Officer] saw a photo in a morning paper of a mouse dining off a table in the window of a West End restaurant. At 11 a.m. he visited the kitchen. . . . What he found, he says, was more mice than he had ever seen. "Baby mice were falling into pots and pans and mice droppings were everywhere."'

with its action. As they were age-old, these problems alone probably would not have worried the bakers unduly, although competition increased their significance: by midcentury, however, a further factor had arisen. The way in which yeast worked had long been a subject of curiosity to scientists, but until the spread of Pasteur's ideas was not correctly understood: at this time, the prevailing theory was Liebig's, according to which carbon dioxide was given off not by the living organism but in the course of its decomposition. This had the same off-putting effect on people as the thought of mould in cheese (logically, beer and wine should have been looked on similarly, but beer, which had always been considered healthy, continued to be generally regarded as especially wholesome). Some of the more ingenious bakers reacted by inventing chemical raising methods to replace yeast. The most popular seems to have been sodium carbonate or bicarbonate combined with hydrochloric acid: one recipe was 50 drops hydrochloric acid, 1 drachm sodium bicarbonate, ½ teaspoonful sugar, and ½ pint water per lb. flour; a second (which was published in a woman's magazine), 4 drachms each hydrochloric acid and salt, and ½ oz. each sodium carbonate and smelling salts per 5 lb. flour (plus water).

A more practical but apparently less often adopted alternative was tartaric acid (cream of tartar is, or was, a normal ingredient of baking powder). Yet another was that adopted by the Aerated Bread Company, which was founded to make bread raised directly by carbon dioxide. The process used, which was patented by a doctor called Dauglish who claimed to have been motivated by the indigestibility of the bread in Edinburgh, was to enclose the dry flour in a drum, pump the air out and carbon dioxide in, add aerated water, and mix the dough under air-tight conditions. The attraction of (in effect) no raising agent at all, plus the fact that as it was mixed by machinery, the bread could be guaranteed free from sewage and sweat, was such that within two years twenty-eight shops had been opened and the company had bought its own mill, and thus could also guarantee the quality of its flour.

In earlier times, it had been the custom to both bake and brew at home, which had meant that households were self-sufficient in yeast: also the increase in the number of pubs and abandonment of home brewing, by making women dependent on commercial yeast was one of the reasons for a parallel decline in home baking. By the 1850s, however, the domestic yeast problem had been solved to a limited extent by the introduction of a special baking yeast known as 'German yeast', so named because it was prepared by a method first developed in Vienna: this consisted of cleansing by thorough washing followed by compression to a dough-like consistency much the same as that of fresh baking yeast today. It was welcomed by cookery writers as ideal for domestic purposes, its only drawback being that since it was not made in this country but had to be imported, it was almost stale by the time it arrived, and would not keep. Also, possibly for this reason, it was only distributed in certain areas. Perhaps because of irregular supplies, or the cost, which was naturally higher than that of the brewery product, it does not seem to have been favoured by bakers, although they sold it and may have made barms from it: lack of their custom and the small size of the private market was presumably why it was not manufactured here until around 1900.

A number of factors besides brewing contributed to the decline of home baking: among the poorer classes, a significant one was the expense of fuel after the enclosure of common land, which proceeded throughout the first half of the century and meant, among much else, that people could no longer gather free firewood; another was the need for suitable ovens. In old houses, capacious brick ovens had been built in, but this custom ceased when free-standing iron stoves and ranges became available; thereafter, as today, inhabitants were frequently expected to provide their own: hence the fact that large numbers of the poor did not have one. Even when they did, they were usually obliged to make do with a size totally inadequate for the necessary quantity of bread, which, in families where little else was eaten, was 2–3 lb. per head a day; nor could people afford the time (or fuel) to bake oftener than once a week. When a baker was near, dough was sometimes taken to his oven, but this meant that it was probably spoiled by draughts or cold – besides which the presence of a baker was in any case a disincentive to bake. A further difficulty was the lack of adequate written instruction at this time, knowledge of how to make bread – as of other cooking – was dependent on a chain of personal instruction: when women went to the baker, thus breaking the chain, they were condemning the next generation to the 'compound of putty and lead'.

In some areas, where there were old buildings, or farms where labourers and dairy-maids lived in (large numbers to be fed made the economic saving more worthwhile), or truck in the form of grain or gleaning permitted, baking nevertheless survived. It was reported, for instance, that in York, Leeds, and Bradford there were very few bakers because home baking was the custom – though here one has to allow for a lower bread consumption than in the south because oatcakes and porridge were also eaten. As late as the 1870s, an Essex farmer observed that 'nearly all the cottagers baked their own bread, doing this once a fortnight; thus one week baking, next week washing'.[5] In Sussex, the farmers' wives not only baked but brewed. 'I dare say you remember the very long table in the farmhouse kitchen at Huggett's Furnace. We all sat down together at it, Master, Missus, maids, and men. We each had a large lump of fat boiled pork as big as my fist to eat with our bread, and washed it down with small beer which was made at home. Every farmer brewed, and made home-made cheese in those days, as well as baking bread, cakes, and pies. Oh! I have seen the whole of the oven floor covered with big loaves and then, when they were taken out, there were twenty cakes and pies ready to go in.'[6] This was a brick oven, which even in cottages was six foot square; they were operated by lighting a fire inside and rapidly clearing it out before beginning cooking, bread being put in first (because it requires a high temperature), then pies and cakes, and finally, if such luxuries could be afforded, custards. In this neighbourhood, gleaning was also customary: the grain was ground by the local miller in return for the bran, which was used as animal food (in such cases, families had no choice but to eat white bread). In one instance, a widower with children to feed got up at 3 a.m. once a week to bake before going to work because he was paid part of his wages in flour.

Bread thus made may have been excellent − when fresh: once-weekly baking, however, meant that it was usually stale; also many housewives, to prevent more than was strictly necessary from being eaten, made it a rule to keep it for several days before allowing anyone to touch it − an economy conveniently justified by the notion (once more) that new bread was indigestible. Mrs Beeton said severely, 'Hot rolls swimming in melted butter, and new bread, ought to be carefully shunned by everybody who has the slightest respect for that much-injured individual − the stomach,'[7] and (very credibly) gave as the reason that new bread formed into 'leathery poreless masses' which the gastric juices could not penetrate. As is shown by the bakers' custom of baking overnight to ensure fresh bread for breakfast, however, few people heeded: indeed, one has no doubt that, once the bakers were there, the attraction of fresh bread daily overrode all other considerations.

The kind of country cottage where baking was likely to be carried on would almost certainly have had no running water: instead, people relied on water butts, wells, springs, and rivers − as was still not uncommon until well into this century. Even in towns, the poor were often supplied only externally by stand-pipes or were similarly dependent on natural sources. In London in 1850 about 6% of the houses were entirely without water and a large number more provided only by stand-pipes which probably had to serve whole streets or courts. In Manchester, although by this time improvement was in hand, the situation was far worse, since less than a quarter of the houses had an indoor supply and scarcely more than another quarter stand-pipes. Also, in both towns the method of supply was not continuous but intermittent, i.e. turned on for a limited time, so that people with running water had to store it in cisterns which rapidly became dirty and insanitary, and others could only fetch it at those times; this affected everyone in Manchester, whether they were supplied or not, since the same hours were observed at the wells, which were kept locked during the intervening periods. Many Mancunians were so short of water that (like the street-sellers) they used it over and over again, and made a habit of not washing themselves at home but waiting until they were at work and could take advantage of their employers' facilities.

When it was clean, water was probably pleasanter to drink and made better flavoured tea and coffee than the chlorinated supplies available today. A number of northern towns, notably Bolton and parts of Glasgow, where it was also delivered continuously, were known for their pure water; London and Manchester, on the other hand, besides being inadequately served in terms of distribution, were notorious for its filth. A surgeon described the latter's as 'evidently and perceptibly polluted'[8] and cited an instance of a man whose eyes became sore as a result of washing with it (but of course this may have been water which had already been used). London was supplied by nine separate private companies, five of which drew it from the central stretch of the Thames, where the sewers also terminated, and two more from nearby points on tributaries which were no cleaner; six of them claimed to filter it, but only in one case efficiently enough to have a significant effect. *Punch* described their wares as 'a full-bodied liquid, in which are included not only an ordinary drinkable but a variety of eatables, possessed of numerous flavours and qualities. . . . We scarcely require soup kitchens when we can get a thick, substantial *potage à la Thames*, supplied to us at comparatively trifling expense'.[9]

The relation between cholera and dirty water had already been established beyond reasonable doubt: numerous instances were cited of people catching the disease after drinking from particular sources, which often turned out to have been polluted with cesspool water. Opinion as to its exact cause was divided between 'vibriones' (a term used to denote minute animal organisms, i.e. germs) and fungi, both of which had been discovered in connection with other disorders (in the case of fungi, skin complaints). The doctor and nutritionist Edwin Lankester came to favour the latter: during an epidemic 1853–4, he and Dr John Snow, the anaesthetist who first administered chloroform to Queen Victoria, analysed the water from a well which had killed 500 people in less than a week and found nothing remarkable in it except a thread-like type of fungus. They carried this out at considerable personal risk: meanwhile, another doctor, Arthur Hill Hassall, with even greater selflessness, examined the drinking water, clothes, blood, and excreta of a cholera victim, which he had to do entirely alone because no one had the courage to help him, and isolated the cholera bacillus. As he did not feel justified in drawing a positive conclusion from

A DROP OF LONDON WATER.

The first microscopic analysis of London's water
as caricatured in *Punch*

a single example and in the face of conflicting evidence, he merely commented: 'Without ... at all supposing that there is an essential or primary connection between these vibriones and cholera, their occurrence in such vast numbers in the rice-water discharges of that disease *is not without interest and possibly is of importance*.'[10]

Arthur Hassall's work on water was, and still is, somewhat overlooked in favour of a similar investigation of foods, in the course of which he examined thousands of samples of products, including beer and milk, and exposed the practice of adulteration; as a result, a Committee was called and in due course the first Food and Drugs Act passed. Though he was not the first to make such discoveries, earlier investigators had failed to attract much attention, chiefly because they had had to rely on chemical evidence:

the introduction of the achromatic lens, however, meant that Hassall was also able to use the microscope and popularize his results by means of illustrations. His first series of the latter were of the contents of drops of London water, which were the more effective because (hand)-coloured; subsequently, he published numerous drawings of food, which, although less dismaying in terms of import, included a striking picture of the lice with which he revealed almost all the brown sugar on sale was infested.

Water, however, was his earlier and perhaps remained his first concern: thus he was extremely upset by the abandonment of a plan for supplying London from the Bagshot area in Surrey rather than the Thames: when considered alongside the schemes adopted by Liverpool and Manchester, it was not as idealistic as it may at first sound, but it entailed buying out all the private companies, who, when it came before a Parliamentary Committee, succeeded in quashing it, though they were obliged to accept a number of provisions for improving existing supplies. As one of the most ardent supporters of the project, he virtually lost his temper (which, although he made a few scathing comments, he never did in relation to food): 'The results of all the evidence given before this committee, and of its deliberations, have ended as most other questions, in which on the one hand the rights and interests of the public are opposed by powerful and interested monopolies on the other, do end in this country, in a compromise. . . . The metropolis and its suburbs are still to be supplied with water from the Thames, although this is not to be taken below Kingston; the water is to undergo a process of filtration; and the reservoirs in which it is to be stored are, we believe, to be covered; these provisions come into operation in 1856. These changes, as far as they go, are no doubt in the right direction, but the evil is that they do not go half far enough. . . . The interests of each of the metropolitan water companies were represented by one or more Old Bailey barristers, some of whom thought that they could not properly or sufficiently discharge their duty to their clients, except by bullying and insulting every adverse witness who had the courage to appear on behalf of the public. . . .'[11]

Subsequently, he was commissioned to analyse supplies following the date by which the improvements were supposed to be implemented, and reported unfavourably; his results were confirmed shortly afterwards by the Great Stink of 1858, when the Thames smelt so abominably that Parliament was forced to rise before the end of the session. Another cholera epidemic broke out in east London in 1866, but it was the last. The need for more efficient filtering in particular was driven home, and immediate steps taken by instituting regular examinations of water; also, a Royal Commission was called to reconsider the question of long-distance supply, various sources being suggested on this occasion, including Wales.

Again, the outcome was compromise, but significant advance was made in that it was laid down that continuous supplies should be introduced – though it was several decades before the latter could be fully carried out. Despite the Commission's recommendation and a number of further attempts, the overthrow of the companies and establishment of a single, publicly owned Water Board was not achieved until 1902.

By the time the original plan for bringing non-Thames water to London had been suppressed, Manchester had transformed its supply from one of the worst to one of the best. As early as 1847 (the year after its purchase of market rights) the Corporation had taken control of water and begun work on a project for drawing it from the Longdendale valley in the Pennines; this was in operation by 1852, and made available water of remarkable purity, continuously delivered, to all houses, though some were still served only externally. Liverpool acted similarly, and started using water from Rivington, near Bolton, a few years later – some delay being caused in this instance by difficulties with the two private companies concerned. During the '50s and '60s, supplies were improved in many other towns, and some, including Leeds' and the Welsh mining town Merthyr Tydfil's, likewise municipalized, but private ownership and intermittent delivery continued to be common for some time.

In terms of price, though not preference, tea and coffee were the reverse of today because of heavier import duties on the former; in the eighteenth century, consumption of both had been limited to the higher classes, but during the nineteenth it rose steadily, aided, particularly in the case of tea, by reductions in duty: by 1857, the amount of tea drunk had reached an average of nearly 2½ lb. per head a year, or one or two cups a day each (rather over a third of the present quantity). Prices, and its novelty value to many people, plus the fact that it was sometimes the only hot element in their diet, must have increased the lower classes' appreciation of it, but there was a unique gastronomic feeling for it at all levels of society. The poor were not merely prepared to make sacrifices to have it, but insisted on reasonable quality: a spokesman for a leading tea firm said, ' "No class of the community are so particular in having good tea as the labouring poor" '[12] this was borne out by the fact that a substantial drop in duty in 1834 had wiped out demand for the cheapest sort. Among the higher classes, tea was the only item customarily made in the dining or drawing room by the mistress of the house herself (admittedly, making tea was clean and easy, which was relevant, but scarcely detracts from the compliment). As drawing-room articles, tea urns were expensive and ornate – urns being needed because of the scale on which fashionable hostesses entertained; often, tea was served from specially designed tables called teapoys: the Dickenses had a rosewood one in their dining room at Devonshire Terrace. One of the most capacious tea drinkers in a Dickens novel was the 'young 'ooman' at a temperance meeting in *Pickwick* who had drunk 'nine breakfast cups and a half; and she's a swellin' wisibly before my wery eyes'[13] (the thirst of deprived temperance reformers was a standard joke). Two well known non-fictional addicts were Gladstone, who was reputed to put tea into his hot-water bottle so as to have a supply ready during the night, and Carlyle, who was so fond of black tea that when invited out he made his own pot before going in case his hostess should offer him green instead.

All the tea drunk before midcentury and most of that in the '50s was China. The possibility of growing tea in India had been considered since the 1770s but was not seriously pursued until the East India Company's monopoly expired, which gave the subject urgency because of the practice of paying for tea with opium: as importing opium to China was illegal,

Advertisement for tea – not the recycled variety

this was a predictable source of problems, and some people feared that the outcome might be that the Chinese would cease trading altogether. Two types of plant were cultivated, one a variety indigenous to Assam which had been discovered some years before but not definitely identified, and the other of Chinese origin. The first samples reached London in 1839 and '42 respectively, and caused great excitement: thereafter, despite initial difficulties and the damaging effects of subsequent 'tea mania', the new industry rapidly established itself and production escalated. In the '50s, however, Indian tea was still very much a connoisseur's item: even by the end of the decade, when production reached 1,000,000 lb., it accounted for only a seventh of total consumption, and was correspondingly expensive (Twining's stocked two grades of Assam at this date, one of which was almost the dearest article on its list).

The poor probably had to drink it black or with skim milk, and brown sugar, but the correct way to drink tea was with cream instead of milk and very small lumps of sugar – lump rather than powdered being customary for practical reasons; practical considerations also meant that it was generally served, not with cakes, but bread and butter or muffins. Since all but the upper classes dined early, it was similarly logical that the conventional time for it was in the evening rather than the afternoon: dinner invitations included tea, or guests might be asked to it separately after the meal. The upper classes, who did not dine until later in the day, were the first to adopt afternoon tea, which was introduced by the seventh Duchess of Bedford and had become a fashionable form of entertaining by about 1865.

Ever since tea and coffee had first been drunk in this country, there had been argument over whether caffeine was harmful, but by this time it had been accepted as at least better than alcohol; green tea, however, not only seems to have had an excessive stimulant effect on some people, but was occasionally reported to produce symptoms which sound like those of poisoning – and perhaps were, since it was virtually always 'glazed' or 'lacquered' with colouring containing Prussian blue: this was by no means as harmful as some of the dyes used for sweets, but was nevertheless pronounced 'capable of exerting an injurious action'.[14] The victims suffered from stomach ache but, one is happy to say, soon recovered; certainly, nobody was ever known to have died from drinking tea. Sometimes black varieties were also coloured, but not poisonously – unless with the intention of imitating green (the most expensive tea on the market was green Gunpowder). As was natural in connection with an article on which people set such store, there was great, but, except over the question of dyeing (which was usually merely cosmetic), to some extent unnecessary, concern about adulteration. From time to time, excise officials had seized teas made from other leaves – in a recent instance, horse chestnut and sycamore – or reconstituted used tea leaves: Mayhew was told that nearly 80,000 lb. a year of the latter were collected and processed in London. 'The exhausted leaves of the tea-pot are purchased of servants or of poor women. . . . The *old* tea-leaves, to be converted into *new*, are placed by the manufacturers on hot plates, and are re-dried and *re-dyed*. To give the "green" hue, a preparation of copper is used. For the "black" no dye is necessary in the generality of cases. This tea-manufacture is sold to "cheap" or "slop" keepers, both in town and country, and especially for hawking in the country, and is almost always sold ready mixed. . . . The trade is one peculiar to great cities, and most peculiar, I am assured, to London . . . .'[15] Though it may sound substantial, 80,000 lb. was hardly a large proportion (1/700) of current total consumption, even when considered in relation to London alone: it was not surprising that in rather more than 100 samples taken from dealers and grocers, Hassall, in the course of investigating adulteration, did not find any leaves of this kind. The content of nearly all the black teas he examined was genuine, and four-fifths of the green: one of the latter included alien leaves, but most of the adulterations were with a pre-prepared mixture of tea-dust and other debris supplied (though not necessarily added) by the Chinese. In all probability, adulteration had been commoner when the duty was higher (as also had been the use of substitute drinks such as black-currant-leaf tea); to ameliorate the situation further, Hassall recommended that the existing duty should be lowered, but on black only, on the basis that its consumption would rise sufficiently to maintain the revenue while people would be discouraged from drinking the tinted, less reliable green. In the event, this was partly carried out: though no distinction between the kinds was made, the duty was halved in stages over the next few years.

There was also much agitation over what was termed the adulteration of coffee with chicory, which, before 1852, was almost invariable when sold ready ground. In fact, mixing with chicory was legally authorized and preferred by a large proportion of customers because, although they did not necessarily like the taste, its strength made the coffee more economic – an attitude which expresses the difference between the popular regard for coffee and tea. From 1852, sellers were supposed to label chicory mixtures as such, but many did not bother, or failed to display the wording, so that it still took persistence to buy pure ground coffee.

Chicory was clearly a chief reason for awful station coffee – a tradition as old as stations themselves. Eliza Acton wrote: 'We hear constant and well-founded complaints both from foreigners and English people, of the wretched compounds so commonly served up here under its name, especially in many lodging houses, hotels, and railway refreshment

A London coffee stall (*London Labour and the London Poor*, Vol. 1)

rooms. . . . At some of the principal stations on lines connected with the coast, by which an immense number of strangers pass and repass, the coffee is so bad, that great as the refreshment of it would be to them, particularly in night travelling, in cold weather, they reject it as too nauseous to be swallowed. A little *national pride* ought surely to prevent this, if no higher principle interfered to do so . . . .'[16]

Another reason for bad coffee was boiling. By this time, pots with filters were obtainable (or muslin could be used) but in many households the earlier method of making it was still preferred. This was to simmer it for ten minutes or longer and keep it hot for a further ten minutes or so to allow the grounds to settle; sometimes it was then cleared with isinglass or egg-white, or (horrifyingly) mustard. A recipe given in a guide to gastronomy called *Hints for the Table*, published in 1859, advocated mixing the dry coffee to a paste with two eggs and boiling for an hour, starting with cold water.

Cocoa and chocolate for drinking rather than eating were the usual forms of cacao product consumed because until the 1860s the relatively primitive manufacturing methods used in Britain meant that it was difficult to make chocolate sufficiently well flavoured for eating. Nearly all the eating chocolate sold was imported from France and hence a luxury to be served at dessert rather than merely indulged in at whim or given to children. The pioneer of English eating chocolate, as of other innovations in the British industry, was John Cadbury, who was selling 'French' Eating Chocolate in 1842; a rival product firm Fry followed five years later. Cadbury riposted with milk chocolate, which was advertised as made to the recipe given by Sir Hans Sloane, founder of the British Museum, who had travelled to South America in the previous century and recommended adding milk to cocoa to increase its nutritional value. By 1866 both Cadbury and Fry had added chocolate cream to their repertoire – Cadbury two years later also introducing traditional chocolate-box packaging with boxes decorated with paintings by the then joint managing director Richard Cadbury. Until this time, drinking chocolate continued to be a composite drink containing cocoa fat and varying amounts of starch, which must have made it thick and soup-like and probably very disagreeable by modern standards: also in 1866, however, Cadbury pulled off probably its greatest coup in terms of its future success by being able to offer pure 'Cocoa Essence' produced by a process invented by Coenraad van Houten and already in use in Europe – the only cocoa previously available in pure form having been the roasted but otherwise unprocessed beans, or the shells, which were cheap but inconvenient since hours of boiling was needed to detach the edible remnants stuck to them.

Unlike many of the impurities he found, Hassall's discovery of lice in sugar had not been detected by earlier analysts and understandably came as probably even more of a shock to the grocers than the public: they were still smarting painfully some five years later, when their trade magazine, *The Grocer*, was founded, in which (foolishly) they tried to defend their product by likening the lice to mould in cheese. Hassall suggested that they were the cause of an irritating occupational complaint known as 'grocers' itch', but did not go into the question of whether they were harmful when eaten; nor did he point out that they would have been killed by cooking, though he tested them in water and found that they survived for a considerable time, even when it was 'very warm'[17] – not, however, indicating whether this meant as hot tea or coffee. Much of the brown sugar he examined also contained fungi, as well as bits of cane and grit, and a few examples were adulterated with flour; in conclusion, he advised the public to buy the purer but more expensive white.

Sugar prices and consumption followed a similar pattern to those of tea – consumption of the two being closely related. By midcentury, the figure for sugar had similarly reached between a third and half the present quantity, which meant that people used it for drinks but that the majority still could not afford such items as jam or puddings (in the absence of popular – as opposed to fashionable – concern about slimming, and despite poverty, the only people to whom it seems to have occurred to drink tea or coffee without it were Quakers and Methodists, who abstained as a protest against the slave trade). Prices rose around 1840 as a result of the abolition of the latter, which caused labour shortages on the plantations, but fell within a few years as the situation settled; duties were reduced, though by less than tea, at midcentury. In addition, whereas the differential between brown and white had once caused even the wealthy to be very sparing with the latter, the gap was narrowing as a result of improvement in refining techniques, which made Hassall's recommendation more practicable than it would formerly have been. In 1842, the average cost of brown was 7–8d. per lb. and of white 9–10d.; by 1860, it was 5d. and 6d. Technical improvements also meant that, as with coffee, filtering was replacing the traditional method of clearing the sugar with albumen (impurities were collected by the protein); in this case, blood was used, and, although not evident to the ordinary consumer, a sanguineous residue remained in the finished product.

Another disadvantage of white was that it was not sold in a free-running state, but in solid, conical 'loaves' a yard or more long (the size depended on quality): this was because in the final stage of refining, the molten sugar was set to drain in moulds of this shape, where it solidified; as no means was known of preventing it from recaking, it was not pulverized but left to be pounded as required in the kitchen. This added considerably to the cook's work and was one of the reasons why many items which might now be made at home, such as cakes and creams, were left to professionals. Without pre-prepared icing sugar, even people who made their own cakes seldom attempted decoration; ready-made sugar decorations, often of a very elaborate nature, were therefore sold separately. Lumps, which were cut with special, pincer-like cutters, were obviously labour-saving for drinks and whatever else was practical, e.g. preserves.

It is difficult to assess the amount of harm done by poisonous confectioners' colours: Hassall described a quarter of the sweets and cake decorations he analysed as positively poisonous, but they differed from most of the rest only in degree, since the majority were toxic to some extent. Instances were cited of their causing people to be taken seriously ill, but one does not know to what extent these cases were exceptional. A doctor called Henry Letheby gave the example of two children who were taken to the London Hospital after eating items containing arsenic, copper, lead, iron, and zinc, all but the last being attributed to confectionery bought in Petticoat Lane: later, it was found that thirty or forty other children who had eaten goods from the same seller had been similarly affected. Letheby commented: 'Within the last three years no less than seventy cases of poisoning have been traced to . . . [confectionery]; and how many, may we ask, have escaped discovery?'[18] All the children recovered, but a man who had perhaps been unusually greedy over a green blancmange at a public dinner in Nottingham died. Several dangerous green pigments were popular, but the most injurious, and probably the source of the arsenic consumed by the children, was a new, very bright emerald dye called Scheele's Green, which was also used for fabrics: it was said that dressmakers were afflicted by mere proximity to it. A particularly brilliant yellow and some reds and oranges contained lead; iron was an ingredient in Prussian and another blue, and gold and silver were made with copper and zinc. The kind of goods the children had eaten was not specified, but every other case mentioned concerned cake decorations or puddings rather than sweets, which was as might be expected, since, although about half of Hassall's definitely poisonous samples were the latter, the former were bigger and thus tended to be eaten in larger quantities (now, very fortunately, much less frequently). A year or so after his report appeared, Hassall noted, with due satisfaction, that fewer confectioners were using mineral pigments; nor was the change restricted to the confectionery trade, since up-market grocers (who invariably tinted pickles, preserves and other items) also reacted – Crosse & Blackwell (who gave evidence at the Committee) being among the first to institute reform.

Hassall himself disapproved of artificial food colouring of any sort, with which today it is easy to agree; at the time, however, tastes were influenced by a tradition of fanciful presentation, particularly in confectionery, which obviously offered most scope to the aspiring *artiste*. In earlier times, chefs of the aristocracy had served intricate models sculpted in sugar or huge architectural structures of fruit and flowers as the centrepiece and culmination of the dinner at dessert: Soyer upheld the custom by modelling in cake, one of his creations being a 'Peacock *à la Louis Quatorze*' decorated with pink icing, red and green sugar crystals (coloured harmlessly with cochineal and spinach) and glitter in the form of cubes of jelly made up with 'gold water'[19] (Danziger Goldwasser, a liqueur containing flakes of gold leaf); another was a chocolate-covered ship in full sail complete with rigging, ladders, and guns. He also had a weakness for *trompe l'oeil* jokes, such as a cake boar's head or pheasant, turkey, or '*Selle de Mouton à la Jardinière en Surprise*', which was iced with various shades of chocolate to imitate the fat and lean and accompanied by vanilla-flavoured chocolate sauce for gravy and green sugar-coated currants for peas: these, he declared, 'had often caused the greatest hilarity at table; some parties, unacquainted with them, have ordered their removal, thinking they belonged to the first course, whilst others have actually carved them before discovering their mistake.'[20] This theme was followed up on a more modest scale by confectioners, who, besides making sugar pheasants and almost every other sort of animal, offered in one instance a rasher of bacon, again carefully coloured to imitate the fat and lean, and in another a mutton chop on a blue-bordered plate. They also displayed other sorts of humour: in Ireland, according to *Punch*, juvenile rebels could satisfy their appetites with liquorice cannon-balls, red-hot sugar coals, and so-called chocolate muskets and pikes (which were almost certainly made of brown-dyed sugar rather than real chocolate). Another line was mottoes, which were printed on lozenges, or, in the case of one London street confectioner, hidden inside sticks of rock, to be revealed as eating progressed: one read '"Do you love me?"' and another, rather less romantically, '"Do you love sprats?"'[21]

5. Drink: The Grape v. The Gooseberry

The traditional view of alcohol was that it was as natural and necessary for survival as food. Before the introduction of tea and coffee, the only practical alternative had been water, which people often distrusted because of the taste if for no other reason, besides not liking it as a staple drink any more than today. That beer had been considered as important to public health as bread is suggested by the fact that the composition of both had at various times in the past been regulated by law (nor, apart from alum, did Hassall's tests reveal adulterants in either, or at least in beer as it left the breweries). Board and lodging for employees had automatically included a beer allowance, and sometimes still did, although by this time it was often commuted to extra wages in order to give them the choice of tea instead (the increments for servants recommended by Mrs Beeton were about a seventh of their basic rates). The provisions fixed for the navy in 1833 included a daily ration of as much as a gallon of beer per head; table, i.e. weak, beer was served at public schools; afternoon callers were offered wine (generally homemade or sherry); doctors advocated alcohol as a tonic in illness and convalescence, pregnancy and lactation, stress, depression, and old age.

By mid-century, however, the traditional view had been challenged, first on a practical level by the temperance movement and later by the more radical end of the medical profession. Certainly to begin with, the chief considerations of the temperance reformers were the social and economic aspects of drinking, i.e. drunkenness and the effect of the cost of liquor on a poor family's budget; not until they had provided abundant evidence that teetotalism was consistent with good health, and more modern ideas on nutrition were coming to be accepted, did doctors begin to reassess their values. It was natural, given the almost revolutionary nature of the whole concept, that the earliest societies to be formed were not teetotal but against spirits only, though the complete abstainers were only a few years behind; nor was it surprising that, while the spirits-only campaign gained substantial support in conventional circles, complete abstinence was regarded for years as eccentric almost to the point of insanity (the same being felt about vegetarianism, of which it was an invariable accompaniment). The first known tract advocating the latter (by a vegetarian) appeared in 1819; ten years later the first anti-spirits societies were founded in Ireland and Scotland. The next, and easily most influential single force in establishing the credibility of teetotalism was the personality of the Irish Franciscan temperance reformer Theobald Mathew, who by sheer charm inspired something like a million drinkers to take the pledge, and in so doing noticeably improved the material condition of the Irish – until his efforts were cut short by the potato famine. Just before it struck, when he was at the height of his renown. Thackeray happened to meet him: 'On the day we arrived at Cork, and as the passengers descended from "the drag," a stout, handsome, honest-looking man of some two-and-forty years [actually, he was then fifty-two], was passing by, and received a number of bows from the crowd around. It was Theobald Mathew, with whose face a thousand little print-shop windows had already rendered me familiar. He shook hands with the master of the carriage very cordially, and just as cordially with the master's coachman, a disciple of temperance, as at least half Ireland is at present. . . .

'The world likes to know how a great man appears even to a valet-de-chambre, and I suppose it is one's vanity that is flattered in such rare company to find the great man quite as unassuming as the very smallest personage present. . . . There is nothing remarkable in Mr Mathew's manner, except that it is exceedingly simple, hearty, and manly, and that he does not wear the downcast, demure look which, I know not why, certainly characterizes the chief part of the gentlemen of his profession.'[1]

A few years later a Unitarian doctor and naturalist, William Carpenter, who subsequently became Registrar and a leading figure in promoting the extension of London University, wrote a prize-winning essay called *The Uses and Abuses of Alcoholic Liquors* in which he set out to prove that not only was alcohol unnecessary for survival but actually a poison. Part of his argument was that as it contained no essential nutrients, notably protein, it could not be used to build muscle or any other functional tissue such as nerves and therefore had no real strengthening power; he also (more or less correctly) maintained that the initial stimulation it produced was the result of irritation and always followed by corresponding depression, which, if regularly repeated, impaired both mental and physical health and, far from benefiting the old and sick, shortened life. He cited numerous examples to illustrate its disadvantageous effects, including the case of temperance ships, on which spirits were replaced by coffee or cocoa and the sailors said to be not only demonstrably fitter but more willing and tractable than on others; similar claims were reported from soldiers, miners, furnace-workers, and harvesters, all of whom maintained that their working capacity had increased after varying periods of abstinence; in addition, he quoted figures from an insurance society and pointed out that no company would insure anyone known to drink excessively.

His warning against excessive drinking was quite as unsparing as any anti-smoking propaganda: 'Delirium Tremens ... There is an almost entire want of sleep; and even if repose be obtained, it is very imperfect, being interrupted by frightful dreams. On the other hand, the waking state is frequently so disturbed by illusions ... that it differs but little from that of sleep, save in the partial consciousness of external things. The following is a vivid picture of this condition given by one who has himself experienced it: "For three days I endured more agony than pen could describe, even were it guided by the hand of a Dante. Who can tell the horrors of that horrible malady, aggravated as it is by the almost ever-abiding consciousness that it is self-sought? Hideous faces appeared on the walls, and on the ceiling, and on the floors; foul things crept along the bed-clothes, and glaring eyes peered into mine. I was at one time surrounded by millions of monstrous spiders, who crawled slowly, slowly over every limb. ... Strange lights would dance before my eyes, and then suddenly the very blackness of darkness would appal me by its dense gloom. All at once, whilst gazing at a frightful creation of my distempered mind, I seemed struck with sudden blindness. I knew a candle was burning in the room, but I could not see it. All was so pitchy dark. I lost the sense of feeling too, for I endeavoured to grasp my arm in one hand, but consciousness was gone. I put my hand to my side, my head, but felt nothing, and still I knew my limbs and frame *were* there. And then the scene would change. I was falling ... far down into some terrible abyss; and so like the reality was it, that as I fell I could see the rocky sides of the horrible shaft, where mocking, gibing, mowing, fiend-like forms were perched; and I could feel the air rushing past me, making my hair stream out by the force of the unwholesome blast." '[2]

Meanwhile, physiological evidence of the effect of alcohol had been supplied by a series of experiments carried out on a young Canadian fur trapper, who, as a result of an accident, literally gave doctors insight into the stomach. He was not a regular drunkard, but from time to time he went on the spree, after which the lining of his stomach became inflamed and covered with a rash of raw, bleeding spots: 'Inner membrane of Stomach unusually morbid; the erythematous appearance much more extensive, and spots more livid than usual, from the surface of which exude small spots of grumous blood. ... The gastric fluids extracted this morning were mixed with a large proportion of thick, ropy mucous and considerable muco-purulent matter, slightly tinged with blood, resembling the discharge from the bowels in some cases of chronic dysentery." [3]

Given the implications of temperance reform with the traditional place of alcohol in the diet, plus the amounts consumed by certain occupational groups (not only the navy but many of the London coal porters drank a gallon of beer, or rather ale, per day, and Scottish iron workers half a bottle of whisky), it perhaps seems surprising that average consumption per head was rather less than today. Admittedly, that of spirits was about the same, but the figure for beer was significantly lower, and for wine, which (except British-made varieties) was drunk only by a small minority, far lower.[*4] Drunkenness, however, was almost certainly much more in evidence, and perhaps more frequent, for a number of reasons. In particular, it attracted attention because of poverty, which meant that drunkards' families often ended up in the workhouse (though of course it was also largely poverty which kept the overall average down); since Saturday was pay-day, consumption tended to be concentrated on the weekend – one of the most undesirable practices of the time being the distribution of wages in pubs, which naturally led people to start drinking immediately (some wives were wise – or foolish – enough to meet their husbands there in the hope of rescuing the housekeeping money before it was too late). From 1839, pubs were supposed to close from midnight on Saturday to 1 p.m. on Sunday, but no other closing time was laid down until 1854, nor, unless customers became violent or totally incapable, were publicans likely to interfere; furthermore, drunks on the streets were commoner than today because transport conditions meant that a far larger proportion had to walk home.

Before 1860, when customs began to change, what people drank was strictly limited by circumstance, i.e. class and place. In England, the basic lower-class drinks were beer, ale (which was not hopped), and gin, varied by cider in the cider districts, perry, British wines, rum, and 'British' brandy – the latter allegedly being distilled from refuse items such as spoilt wine and damaged grain. The upper and middle classes confined them-selves chiefly to wine and imported brandy, a surprisingly large proportion of which was in the form of the two combined; i.e. brandied wine; as they had become accustomed to it at school, men quite often favoured beer, but never gin, which had had disreputable associations ever since it was first introduced into this country. In Ireland and Scotland, a similar prejudice existed against whisk(e)y, but was less inflexible: in Ireland,

* U.K. consumption in 1850 was just over 1 gallon of spirits per head, 19.6 gallons of beer, and .2 gallons of imported wine; 1987 figures were the same for spirits, 24 gallons of beer, and about 17 bottles of wine.

although not served at 'the bettermost sort of tables', it was 'always to be had for the asking'[5]; the status of Scotch was greatly enhanced by Queen Victoria, who drank it when she visited Balmoral and stamped it with her approval by granting the 'royal warrant' to the local distillery (Begg's). Neither Scotch nor Irish were consumed in England at this stage, not for social reasons but because, like other goods, they were produced only on a small scale and very seldom exported: Thackeray thought it necessary to warn English readers to be 'very careful of whiskey. . . . Natives say that it is wholesome . . . but . . . two glasses will often be found sufficient to cause headaches, heartburns, and fevers, to a person newly arrived in the country.'[6] The drink with the broadest spectrum of consumers was perhaps British, i.e. non-grape wine, which half a century earlier had been considered a necessity even in households where French wines were drunk: although looked on condescendingly by some, it was still made and/or

consumed at all social levels except the very highest and lowest, partly because it was a useful way of conserving seasonal fruit. The poorer growers of suitable produce were often deterred from making it (as with fruit puddings) by the cost of the other ingredients (which in this case, besides sugar, frequently included brandy) but might occasionally buy a bottle of the commercial versions, as also did the urban middle classes: presumably because the latter tended to be extremely sweet, they were generally referred to as 'sweets' – and recommended by Soyer (in the least patronizing way possible) as suitable for ladies' lunches. Besides the sweets made and sold for what they were, it was alleged, probably justifiably, that large amounts were produced specifically for imitating or adulterating other wines, which somewhat clouded their general reputation.

Of the various sorts of beer, one of the most popular was porter, which is supposed to have been so named because it was originally especially favoured by market porters. It was thick, dark, and bitter, which gave the illusion of strength, though in fact, as usually drunk, it was weaker than the average lager (the latter was not made in Britain until the 1880s). Among the strongest brews on the market were Welsh and Edinburgh ale and Guinness's Double Stout, which had been exported since the '20s and, along with several other Guinness products, was already widely known in England for its flavour. Although the strengths of beer given by several authorities were in general higher than today, according to Hassall's tests this was not the case, even when samples were taken directly from the breweries: in pubs, beer was customarily weakened by about 1% of alcoholic volume, salt being used to make up the flavour (but not, as earlier analysts had alleged, a variety of more recondite items including grains of Paradise, quassia (to increase bitterness), and a poisonous Indian berry, *coccolus Indicus*, which had supposedly been added to produce extra froth). Possibly, a factor in the success of Guinness was that it was distributed in bottles and therefore impossible to dilute: though bottling became commoner as the century progressed, most beer at this time was drawn from the barrel; since carbonation was not yet known, it was always naturally matured (i.e., left with a slight yeast content).

The most notable feature of gin was the part it played in the transformation of pubs into the famous Victorian gin-palaces, the first of which was opened in the early 1830s. The palaces were originally conceived in response to the publicans' need to compete with beer-houses, of which a large number sprang up as a result of an attempt to decrease the consumption of spirits by exempting the sale of beer from licensing. The idea of attracting people by means of glamorous surroundings, obvious as it seems now, was new to the catering trade at the time and the cleverer both because of the squalor of many other drinking-places and the dinginess of the slums in which customers probably lived. Instead of dirt and dark rooms were bright paint and pretty girls, plus drinks with such evocative or exciting names as 'Cream of the Valley', 'The Celebrated Butter Gin', 'The Real Knock-me-down' and 'The Regular Flare-up'[7] – which must have made quite as much of an impression as those of American cocktails among the higher classes a generation later (and perhaps derived their inspiration from the appellations given to gin a century before when for a brief period it had been so heavily taxed that it had been sold illicitly under other names).[8] In general, the notion of glamour or, as one might now refer to it, creating an atmosphere was taken up remarkably slowly, but the employment of attractive girls in the new (and otherwise typically terrible) station refreshment rooms can perhaps be attributed to the palaces.

Whisk(e)y meanwhile was going through a period of lull between the excitement of illicit distilling and controversy towards the end of the century caused by the use of the patent still and increasing popularity of blends. The patent still, unlike the traditional type, was capable of production on an industrial scale, but yielded virtually tasteless spirit: it was realized, however, that if this was mixed with single whiskies of the old sort, a much cheaper but still acceptable compound could be made. It was invented in 1831 and employed in Scotland from around 1840, but did not constitute a serious threat to the producers of single whiskies until the '70s. According to a book commissioned in defence of their products by the four leading distillers of Dublin whiskey, some of the early blends were truly fearsome in their effects, partly because manufacturers were inexperienced in handling the new stills and partly because they cut costs by using immature (and hence cheaper) traditional whiskies for blending, both of which could mean that toxic elements remained in the drink; also, they were suspected of flavouring their products with methylated spirits (which are poisonous). Other supposed adulterants were creosote, which was thought to be added to imitate the smokiness of Scotch, and 'Hamburg sherry' (the name was taken from the port of export) to give the hint of sherry imparted to Irish by the custom of maturing it in old sherry casks. The results were said to give rise not only to hangovers fully worthy of Thackeray's warning, but a peculiarly violent form of drunkenness: one story was told of a boy who, after only a glass and a half of a particularly virulent mixture, was so maddened that he leapt into the air and then tried to commit suicide; more generally, the new liquor was blamed for increasingly disorderly behaviour in towns (for which there may have been any number of explanations).

As they were not drunk in England while he was concerned with adulteration, Hassall did not test whiskies; nor, presumably because of the kind of fraud involved, did he analyze wines. Wine, however, was very much in the news at this time because, after a long period of high duties, a committee had been called to consider the practicality of lowering them – one of the main arguments put forward in favour of change being that it would lessen the incentive for adulteration. The committee was told that an estimated fifth of all wine drunk was fake in one way or another – which may have been alarmist but in this instance strikes one as credible, not so much because of the scale of profits involved (tea was also very highly taxed) but because of the relatively impregnable position of the trade. Since many (though by no means all) the frauds allegedly carried out were qualitative only, i.e. the substitution of one wine for another, they could not necessarily be detected by analytical means; furthermore, because of high duty and prices, the average customer was extremely unlikely to have had sufficient experience of wine to be able to spot them. The intrinsic variability of the product was another factor to the merchants' advantage; so was its social significance, which, then as now (and as with food in general) made criticism impossible in the interest of plain good manners. By the time a commercial treaty had been made with France, according to which the duties were almost halved (wine was dropped from nearly 5s. 10d. to 3s. per gallon, brandy from 15s. to 8s. 2d.) the probability of adulteration had been increased by vine disease,* which between 1852 and 1858 reduced European output by (again) a fifth (and served to stimulate British interest in the then nascent American wine industry).

From reports received, it would seem that standards in the trade were about the same in France and elsewhere as Britain. The centres of the European fake wine industry were Sète and Marseilles, in Provence, where it was said that every known kind of vinous drink, from any country, was imitated. One of their better known creations was Hamburg sherry; others were Spanish claret, which was alleged to be endowed with the appropriate bouquet by means of orris, Champagne, including variations made from non-grape wines (though most of those on sale in Britain were probably of domestic origin), and a version of port so lusciously flavoured that British sellers sometimes passed it off as Masdeu (a much more expensive French wine which had recently become fashionable). Pure port, i.e. composed only of Douro wine and brandy, was almost impossible to obtain irrespective of profiteering by individuals because of Portuguese government regulations, according to which, to comply with supposed British taste, all the wine had to reach a minimum standard of body and strength: this was enforced by a team of almost certainly (as was alleged) corrupt and unqualified tasters, who visited the vineyards soon after pressing and dosed the future wines with a mixture known as 'Jeropiga', which consisted of sweetening matter, spirit 20% above proof, grape juice, and elderberry dye.

This, however, was trivial when compared to the treatment port apparently received after reaching Britain. One of the most respected wine writers of the day, Cyrus Redding, quoted two recipes from a book called *The Victualler's Guide*, which, as he observed, must have had a sizeable circulation since it had run to four impressions: the first called for forty-two gallons of rough cider, eight of rectified spirit, and three of Cognac per twelve gallons (only) of strong port, and the second for forty-five gallons of cider, six of brandy, and two of sloe juice per eight of port; instructions for ageing corks and producing a crusted effect at the tops of

* Oidium, caused by fungus, rather than phylloxera.

bottles were also given. (The decline in the relative popularity of port which took place over this period has often been attributed to the fact that it was so disgusting.)

The most commonly mentioned British imitation champagne was goose-berry wine, which a number of apparently sophisticated people testified could be remarkably like the real thing: whether this says more about their powers of discrimination, the skill of the gooseberry wine-makers, or the usual quality of Champagne is hard to say, but it was perhaps relevant that all the Champagne imported into Britain, genuine or otherwise, was full, and some of it brandied. Other alleged substitutes for the latter were perry and wine from home-grown grapes, though the latter seems improbable because very little attempt appears to have been made to produce British grape wine at this period. Of all types, the easiest wine to counterfeit was (Spanish) sherry, since South African alternatives were available and until 1860 (as colonial products) admitted at half the normal rate (cider, perry, and home-grown wines were not charged at all). As 80% of the total wine drunk was sherry and port, and much of the rest Champagne, most of the suspicion, and probably (except in the case of sherry, which did not need it) the greatest ingenuity were concentrated on these three; Redding, however, had a good story about claret and the Prince of Wales. Apparently, the Prince had a limited stock of exceptionally fine claret – so good that when in due course he ordered it for a dinner, all but two bottles had been drunk by his household. In some perturbation, his chief butler went to a wine merchant in the City, who told him to give him one of the two remaining bottles and see that the replacements he sent were drunk immediately (which seems to have been a standard condition when drugs were used for flavouring). The dinner was duly held and the wine savoured without any of the diners realizing, or at any rate daring to comment on what it was; thereafter, any conscience which members of his household may have had about helping themselves was evidently dispelled, since they had recourse to the same tradesman on several subsequent occasions.

The overwhelmingly high proportion of fortified wine drunk, and possibly also the character of 'sweets', had led to the widely held assumption that the British preference was for strong, sweet wine – all the sherry exported at this date being full, and not only Champagne but many Burgundies fortified; presumably, the nature of the predominant wines was also responsible for the tradition of drinking principally after rather than before or during dinner (though sherry was acknowledged as an accompaniment to all courses, and even port was sometimes served during a meals). Although many people felt that this apparent preference was due to environmental or inherent factors, i.e. climate, the national style of

EFFERVESCING GOOSEBERRY WINE

INGREDIENTS – To every gallon of water allow 6lbs. of green gooseberries, 3lbs. of lump sugar.

Mode. – This wine should be prepared from unripe gooseberries, in order to avoid the flavour which the fruit would give to the wine when in a mature state. Its briskness depends more upon the time of bottling than upon the unripe state of the fruit, for effervescing wine can be made from fruit that is ripe as well as that which is unripe. The fruit should be selected when it has nearly attained its full growth, and consequently before it shows any tendency to ripen. Any bruised or decayed berries, and those that are very small, should be rejected. The blossom and stalk ends should be removed, and the fruit well bruised in a tub or pan, in such quantities as to insure each berry being broken without crushing the seeds. Pour the water (which should be warm) on the fruit, squeeze and stir it with the hand until all the pulp is removed from the skin and seeds, and cover the whole closely for 24 hours; after which, strain it through a coarse bag, and press it with as much force as can be conveniently applied, to extract the whole of the juice and liquor the fruit may contain. To every 40 or 50lbs. of fruit one gallon more of hot water may be passed through the *mare*, or husks, in order to obtain any soluble matter that may remain, and be again pressed. The juice should be put into a tub or pan of sufficient size to contain all of it, and the sugar added to it. Let it be well stirred until the sugar is dissolved, and place the pan in a warm situation; keep it closely covered, and let it ferment for a day or two. It must then be drawn off into clean casks, placed a little on one side for the scum that arises to be thrown out, and the cask kept filled with the remaining "must," that should be reserved for that purpose. When the active fermentation has ceased, the casks should be plugged upright, again filled, if necessary, the bungs be put in loosely, and, after a few days, when the fermentation is a little more languid (which may be known by the hissing noise ceasing), the bungs should be driven in tight, and a spill-hole made, to give vent if necessary. About November or December, on a clear fine day, the wine should be racked from its lees into clean casks, which may be rinsed with brandy. After a month, it should be examined to see if it is sufficiently clear for bottling; if not, it must be fined with isinglass, which may be dissolved in some of the wine: 1oz. will be sufficient for 9 gallons. In March or April, or when the gooseberry bushes begin to blossom, the wine must be bottled, in order to insure its being effervescing.

Seasonable. – Make this the end of May or beginning of June, before the berries ripen.

from *Beeton's Book of Household Management*, Isabella Beeton (Jonathan Cape, facsimile of 1861 ed. pp. 883–4)

cookery, or mere gastronomic barbarity, it was (as usual) mainly attribut-
able to political and economic, and, in the case of the properties of wine,
technical circumstances. Quarrels with France had resulted in 150 years of
discrimination against French wines, which from the beginning of the
eighteenth century until 1831 had been charged a third more than Spanish
or Portuguese; in 1831 the differential had been removed but the rate was
still too high for consumption to increase, partly because the duty
prohibited the importation of the cheaper types of wine. In addition, one
has to remember that port and sherry were more economical in effect than
straight wines, not only because they went further but kept after being
opened. The sweetness of sherry was because the significance of '*flor*'-, or
'flower'-producing yeasts, which are necessary for the production of dry,
was not understood (the driest available was Amontillado); yeast was also
the reason for the fortification of non-grape wines, since not enough grew
naturally on most of the materials used to produce adequate fermentation:
according to the classic authority on the subject, MacCullock's *Remarks
on the Art of Wine Making*, all kinds could be made successfully without
any addition except sugar, but in general people found that the only ones
which turned out strong enough to keep by this method were gooseberry
and rhubarb.

When the question of the duties was discussed, those who ascribed the
taste for strong, sweet wines to non-economic factors naturally argued
that lower prices would not significantly alter drinking habits; some
evidence, however, was given which suggested not only that the port-
and-sherry drinking public would welcome variety but that a taste for
wine might extend to people who had never been able to afford it before.
It was pointed out that holiday-makers in Europe, who were becoming
increasingly numerous as a result of railway travel, came back full of
enthusiasm for the light local wines they had sampled; also, the proprietors of an establishment selling wines by the glass claimed that many
of their customers were bus and cab drivers who had taken to drinking
sherry instead of gin, although it was twice the price (4d. instead of 2d.).
The inquiry was held in 1852, eight years before the treaty with France
was signed: during this time, two other indications of broadening
preferences appeared, one of which was the successful introduction of
dry sherry and the other the founding of the firm of Walter and Alfred
Gilbey, who set out initially to sell cheap, unadulterated South African
wines.

The measures introduced in 1860 included not only lowering the duties
but extending sales outlets by allowing eating-house-keepers (eating-
houses were the equivalent of cafés), grocers, and other retailers of food to
take out wine licences – the only places where it had been permissible for

Banquet for Viscount Palmerston at the Reform Club, 1850
(*Illustrated London News*)

wine and food to be sold together before having been clubs and hotels (which had been logical insofar as they had been the only places used by the traditional wine-drinking public). As a result, imports of French wine immediately doubled; ten years later they had almost quadrupled, and were far ahead of port; by 1880 they had also overtaken sherry. The first to benefit were the Gilbeys, who promptly widened their range and took advantage of licensed grocers to sell their wines in different parts of the country: within seven years they had moved into an enormous building in Oxford Street called the Pantheon, which had once been an opera house, and not long afterwards bought their own château in the Médoc. As is shown by subsequent consumption figures, however, most of those who purchased the new wines were of the European-holiday class, i.e. the former sweet-and-strong port-and-sherry brigade, who were now able to enlarge their repertoire, rather than new converts – consumption of both beer and, after a slight temporary drop, spirits remaining unaffected by the change (the sherry-drinking bus and cab drivers thus being atypical:

possibly, they were members of the anti-spirits movement, some of whom
did not realize that such wines were fortified).

Perhaps partly because of the limited nature of the wine supply, mixed
drinks such as punch, shrub, and cups of various kinds had long been
popular; the use of ice for cooling drinks was also spreading rapidly. Thus
the only unusual feature of an iced drink from America, Mint Julep –
which at this stage was customarily made with brandy – was that the ice
was used, not merely to cool it, but as an integral ingredient, which meant
that it was colder than was usual with English drinks; also, as a
consequence of this (as with ice-cream, because of the effect on the teeth),
it was supposed to be drunk through straws – which was hardly in keeping
with Victorian notions of propriety. It was said to have been first
introduced into this country by Captain Marryat, author of *Children of
the New Forest*; an early recipe, attributed to an unnamed American
(presumably someone else) was also given by Eliza Acton in 1845.

Six years later, in 1851, Soyer opened an American bar as part of a
restaurant complex in South Kensington designed to cater for visitors to
the Great Exhibition. The bar was in a double sense a novelty, since,
besides offering a long list of unfamiliar drinks, plus (one assumes) the
option of straws, the idea of a smart drinking place, as opposed to pubs
and beerhouses, was unknown. Like many other notions ahead of their
time, it caused a certain amount of comment but had no immediate
outcome: despite the fact that the restaurants served 1,000 people a day,
American drinks continued to be regarded as oddities and it was a decade
before another bar was founded. To some extent, its lack of impact was
due to the unprecedented and altogether extraordinary nature of the
overall enterprise: restaurants in the modern sense, as these have to be
counted, were also virtually unknown – far less those serving ethnic food,
as Soyer set out to do, his concept being a 'Gastronomic Symposium of All
Nations' where foreigners coming to London could order their own
national specialities. In addition were his fantastic decorative effects,
beside which glamour in pubs becomes totally unnoticeable: the stairs
were dominated by an enormous mural painted by the journalist George
Augustus Sala and, as was indicated on the prospectus, every room planned
according to a different theme, e.g. The Gallic Pavilion, or L'Avenue des
Amours, The Temple of Phoebus, The Celestial Hall of Golden Lilies; the
effect being compounded by a confusing plethora of plants, vases, foun-
tains, pictures, statues, and other ornaments. The credibility of the project
was further impaired by the fact that it closed unexpectedly, largely
because of a perhaps not surprising but almost certainly unmerited query
as to its respectability. The premises were a mansion situated where the
Albert Hall now stands, Gore House, which (appropriately, since the food

was reported to be on the whole good) had formerly been the residence of a noted gastronome, the Count d'Orsay; the bar was under an ornamental bridge (itself, inappropriately, in the Italian style) in the gardens. Some forty drinks were advertised, including, besides Mint Julep, Sherry Cobbler, Egg-nog, and Brandy Smash.

A few years later, a selection of recipes for 'American Summer Drinks', which included not only Mint Julep and Sherry Cobbler but Gin Sling, appeared in the *Illustrated London News* – this possibly being the first time that a recipe was published in this country for an upper-class type of drink based on gin. It was subsequently quoted by the writer Timbs in his little book, *Hints for the Table*, which also contained a recipe for Gin Punch and a round-up of information about wine (it came out just before the reduction in duties was announced). This was followed by a cookery book for the middle classes by the chef Francatelli, who included a brief but to-the-point chapter on serving wine, another on cups, a third on 'English and Foreign Summer Drinks', which were mostly soft but included a second recipe for Gin Punch, and a fourth on American drinks, where there were three recipes for gin and one for whisk(e)y. He made no comment on the latter, presumably because it was still unusual in England, but, to make it clear that he expected expensive rather than cheap gin to be used, specified that it should be 'old'. The justification he gave for straws was positively puritanical – if, in view of the reason for which the early cocktails were often drunk, ironic: 'I am afraid that very genteel persons will be exceedingly shocked at the words "suck through a straw;" but when I tell them that the very act of imbibation through a straw prevents the gluttonous absorption of large and baneful quantities of drink, they will, I make no doubt, accept the vulgar precept for the sake of its protection against sudden inebriety.'[9]

Somewhere around this time, another bar, evidently of a fairly modest character, since it was referred to as 'a small drinking saloon'[10], was set up just behind the Bank of England in the City: the menu included drinks with such eye-catching names as 'Connecticut Eye-openers', 'Alabama Fog-cutters', 'Lightning Smashes', and 'Thunderbolt Cocktails'. Probably, it lasted no longer than Soyer's; unlike his, however, it had a direct sequel, since it was claimed to have been the inspiration for a book published shortly afterwards in New York entirely devoted to mixed drinks. The book was in two volumes, one being on how to mix them and the second on making the basic ingredients, i.e. distilling, syrups, and so on. The author of the latter, which was not of the same lasting interest as the former, was a Professor Schultz; the part on mixing was by a bartender called Jerry Thomas, whose publisher – or, more probably, he himself – said in the preface, after giving an impressive list of his credentials, that he had had the idea of the book when, on a visit to London, he had noticed a crowd in the street outside the bar staring at the menu: 'It struck us, then, that a list of all the social drinks – the composite beverages, if we may call them so – of America, would really be one of the curiosities of jovial literature ...'.[11] The owner of the bar was described as 'a peripatetic American' – who in fact was again probably Thomas himself.

Whether this was so or not, he had certainly researched drinking in this country thoroughly, since, besides American and other recipes, the book contained a collection of traditional British mixed or made drinks which must have been the most comprehensive ever published. The first part was devoted to punch, of which eighty-six different kinds were given, including gin, milk (which was customarily served after turtle soup), Irish and Scotch whisk(e)y, Glasgow, Yorkshire, Oxford, Duke of Norfolk, Uncle Toby, Philadelphia Fish-house (perhaps the most famous American version), Louisiana Sugar-house, Rockey Mountain, and even a D'Orsay; there were also two cups invented by Soyer during the Crimean war, Crimean Cup and Balaklava nectar. Like the book itself, Thomas's general directions for making it became classic: 'To make punch in any sort of perfection, the ambrosial essence of the lemon must be extracted by rubbing lumps of sugar on the rind, which breaks the delicate little vessels that contain the essence, and at the same time absorbs it. This, and making the mixture sweet and strong [one has to allow for the context in which he said this], using tea instead of water, and thoroughly amalgamating all the compounds, so that the taste of neither the bitter, the sweet, the spirit, nor the element, shall be perceptible the one over the other, is the grand secret, only to be acquired by practice.

'In making hot toddy, or hot punch, you must put in the spirits before the water: in cold punch, grog, &c., the other way.

'The precise proportions of spirit and water, or even of acidity and sweetness, can have no special rule, as scarcely two persons make punch alike.'[12]

The 'American Summer Drink' recipes included cobblers, sangarees, slings, sours, egg-nogs and flips, juleps and smashes, and cocktails and crustas: there were half a dozen juleps, the same of egg-nogs, eight cobblers, and eleven cocktails, two of which were made with gin; altogether, the book gave seventeen preparations based on gin. The cocktails, which were distinguished by containing bitters, were described as 'a modern invention ... generally used on fishing and other sporting parties, although some *patients* insist that it is good in the morning as a tonic'.[13]

As brandy with water or other accompaniments, along with green tea, were the most popular remedies for hangovers, it was natural that at first cocktails should be used in this way, which was perhaps not very helpful to their acceptance (drunkenness had once been fashionable but by now, as was consistent with Francatelli's remark, was considered even more reprehensible among the higher than the lower classes); the chief reason, however, for the fact that they were slow to catch on was simply that drinking aperitifs was not yet the custom. The next stage in their progress was the founding of a successful bar by a partnership of Australians (rather than an American), but it was still half a century before they became established, or Thomas's book was published in this country. The corollary of their rise was a broadened market for spirits rather as duty had widened the taste in wine, the traditional higher-class restriction to brandy giving way to the alternatives of whisk(e)y and gin.

6. Cooking: Management of the Fire

The change in drinking habits came as a complement to the increasing influence of French cooking, which, like French wines, had formerly been restricted to a small minority. As with wine, the lower classes were hardly affected, despite the efforts of well meaning cookery writers to persuade them of the merits of soups and stews, which were so unpopular below a certain social level that, as was observed by the reviewer of another of Francatelli's books, *A Plain Cookery Book for the Working Classes*, husbands would have been more likely to throw them at their wives than eat them (this remark was prompted by a particularly economical recipe for 'Pot-Liquor Soup', the main ingredient of which was oatmeal). Similarly, the use of ice, which had once been the prerogative of the owners of ice-houses, was becoming a necessity to fashionable middle-class hostesses, not only for serving drinks but ice cream and iced puddings; the cost of refrigerators, however, plus the lack of any alternative to solid ice for cooling them, which meant that space was at a premium, prevented their being used for general purposes.

In the field of cooking equipment, the great controversy of the day was gas: its most conspicuous advocate was Soyer, whose influence was probably largely responsible for the fact that more interest was shown in it in the '50s than for some years afterwards. Soyer, whose talents as an inventor were at least equal to his skill as a chef also designed the 'Magic Stove', a portable spirit ring which fulfilled the need for a quick, independent source of heat and, among other cookers, an army stove which is still in use, essentially unchanged, today. Presumably for the same reason as in the dairy, least attention seems to have been paid to the development of labour-saving devices – by far the most significant contribution in this direction being the introduction of gas.

Until refrigeration was widely used for storage and the large-scale production of jams and preserves became possible, a far larger proportion of the work of the kitchen than it is now easy to imagine was concerned, not with the direct preparation, but preservation of food. 'The mistress who wishes to guard against *all waste* and to turn everything to the best account either for her own family, or her poor neighbours, will have the whole contents of the larder spread before her. Raw meat will be examined, and, as the case may require, be directed for the service of the day, or put in salt, or again hung up for use on a future day. In summer time especially, care will be taken to remove kernels which might be likely to taint the meat, and to wipe away fly blows; suet will be skinned and chopped for use, or, if not likely to be wanted while fresh, will be nicely melted down. . . . The salt-pan must be daily attended to, – that meat is properly salted, turned daily, and dressed in due time. . . . Bacon, hams, and tongues should be tied in brown paper and laid on a rack, or hung in a dry place, not too warm. . . . Game will keep much longer if not paunched.'[1]

This came from a cookery book published in 1838, though it might just as well have been '58, or even '78. It appeared a few years before the beginning of major expansion in the ice business, which can be dated from the early '40s, when two firms, the Wenham Lake Ice Company and Thomas Masters', were founded. The former offered refrigerators which at first were lined with zinc but later patent glass enamel, and natural ice

Alexis Soyer demonstrating his Magic Stove on the Parthenon
(*Culinary Campaign*)

for cooling shipped from Wenham Lake, near Boston; Masters patented an ice- and ice-cream-making machine:* this had the advantage that, as substances with lower freezing points than water were used for the ice, lower temperatures could be achieved. By the time of the Great Exhibition at least nine other firms were competing, including two more importing American ice, and George Kent, who manufactured 'Ling's Patent Ice-Safe' and other appliances and later co-operated with Masters. Refrigerators, however, were relatively expensive (Masters' prices were £6 6s.–£16 16s.) and a considerable proportion of their bulk was occupied by the ice and insulation. As frozen joints were referred to in 1859, meat was evidently sometimes kept in them, but the size of cut which was usual must have meant that often it would not go in (many models were designed, not with open interiors, in which a low temperature was relatively hard to maintain, but as a series of ice-packed drawers): generally, apart from ice-cream, they were used for fish and small, choice items such as stuffings and sauces, high-quality unsalted butter, eggs, and strawberries. And the tops, which were cold, formed convenient surfaces for making and rolling out pastry.

The same cookery book which was written by a woman who lived in the country, also gave instructions for keeping vegetables and herbs: '. . . potatoes may be preserved in a warm, dry store-room, covered with straw, or dig a trench in the earth four feet deep, into which lay the potatoes as they are dug up, then cover them with earth, raised in the middle, and . . . straw or tiles, to carry off the rain; in this way the frost will not injure them. Carrots, parsnips, and beetroot, to be packed in boxes, or hampers, with sand or dry mould. Onions roped, and hung in a dry place, not too warm, or they will be likely to sprout. Shallots roped or hung up in a net. . . . Sweet herbs, including thyme of various sorts, marjoram, and savory, sage, mint, and balm, hyssop and penny royal†, should be gathered when the plants come to full growth, but before they begin to flower. They must be gathered on a dry day, when the dew is off; perfectly clear[ed] from dirt and insects, the roots cut off, and the herbs tied in small bundles. The quicker they can be dried without scorching the better . . . when quite dry, rub them to powder, and sift through a coarse piece of muslin, put them in bottles closely corked and labelled.'2

The number of people to whom this was relevant diminished as urbanization progressed (it had reached just over the half-way mark by

---

* Altogether, he gave 37 freezing mixtures, in some of which natural ice was an ingredient; 3 made without it were: 5 parts each ammonium chloride and potassium nitrate to 16 of water; the same plus 8 parts sodium sulphate; 6 of sodium sulphate to 5 of ammonium nitrate and 4 of dilute nitric acid. These were supposed to give 40°, 46°, and 64°F of cold respectively.
† The last three were used for remedies rather than cooking.

1851) but making jams, pickles, and other preserves at home continued to be general: Mrs Beeton, writing for the suburban housewife, gave nearly ninety recipes of this class and a list of seasonal chores which included the following: 'In June or July, gooseberries, currants, raspberries, strawberries, and other summer fruits should be preserved, and jams and jellies made. In July, too, the making of walnut ketchup should be attended to, as the green walnuts will be approaching perfection for this purpose. Mixed pickles may also now be made, and it will be found a good plan to have ready a jar of pickle-juice. . . . into which to put occasionally some young French beans, cauliflowers, &c.

'In the early autumn, plums of various kinds are to be bottled and preserved. . . . A little later, tomato sauce, a most useful article to have by you, may be prepared; a supply of apples laid in, if you have a place to keep them, as also a few keeping pears and filberts. Endeavour to keep also a large vegetable marrow, – it will be found delicious in the winter.'[3]

An egg-beater consisting of a series of spikes inside a mug, which was shaken to effect beating, was patented by an inventor called Larkin in 1850; a fruit-presser had been designed by 1862 and a fruit- and vegetable-peeler by 1863; several chopping machines were shown at the Exhibition, including a sausage- and herb-cutter which was in effect a mincer: this was hand-operated, but several years later it was reported that a number of London butchers were making sausages by means of steam power. Cheap labour, however, plus perhaps the fact that, like other inventions, they were not necessarily very efficient when first introduced (certainly, one does not have much faith in Larkin's egg-beater) meant that at this stage such aids were not adopted in the ordinary private household. Eggs were beaten with simple (non-rotary) whisks or forks, and mincing, or as near its equivalent as possible, carried out with knives. Eliza Acton was explicit as to how to avoid a mangled, stringy result when attempting the latter: 'Mince . . . quite fine with an exceedingly sharp knife, taking care to *cut* through the meat [the recipe was for potted ham], and not to tear the fibre, as on this much of the excellence of the preparation depends.'[4]

Much more work than today was entailed by groceries, since grit and pieces of stalk were left in rice and dried fruit, which had to be picked and washed before use; raisins needed stoning, candied peel chopping, and mace and nutmeg, and often ginger and cinnamon pounding or grating – the last two being available ready ground but frequently bought whole to avoid the risk of adulteration. Making a cake was thus not a matter of minutes but a prolonged operation: either there were fruit and spices to prepare, or sugar to pound, and sometimes both, although, at least before the discovery of lice, fruit cakes were generally made with brown; as baking powder was the exception (from which it more or less follows that there was no self-raising flour) and many people disliked the taste of bicarbonate of soda, the eggs were frequently the only raising agent, which meant that instead of merely being mixed or beaten, they had to be thoroughly (and laboriously) whisked. The final challenge was that the heat of the oven, which came directly from the fire, could not be accurately regulated nor (as Bucknell's Eccaleobion suggests) a constant, and in particular constant low temperature maintained.

Lack of temperature control was the most serious shortcoming of solid-fuel iron ranges; others were that (as in bakeries) the need for a fire caused kitchens to become very hot, and generated a great deal of smoke and soot; also the heat came from the side rather than the bottom, although by now this had been more or less effectively overcome. They had first been introduced at the end of the previous century, when coal became a popular fuel, and were available in a remarkably wide range of prices and sizes. The basic arrangement was a fire in the middle, which might be open or closed over the top, with an oven on one side and boiler on the other; if the fire was enclosed, the whole upper surface could be used as a hot-plate. The larger ones often had two or more ovens, either beside or above one another to one side of the fire or one on each side, in which case the boiler was generally at the back. Flues were used to equalize heat and convey it to ovens not directly next to the fire; a small one which is on view at the Science Museum also has a revolving grid to ensure even cooking. The latter is two feet high and two and a half wide, with an oven ten inches square (just large enough to take two 2–lb. loaves) and boiler holding three and three-quarter gallons. An enormous one, called the Improved Oxford Range, had a fireplace six feet square, two ovens, two charcoal stoves, a broiling stove, two hot closets for keeping food warm, a heated table for dishing up, and boiler, the capacity of which was not given, but Soyer's roasting fire at the Reform Club, which was roughly the same size, served one of 100 gallons. The table and one of the hot closets were heated by steam; the charcoal stoves, of which only the tops were usable (grills, charcoal or otherwise, were unknown) were included to provide independent hot plates for items requiring slow stewing and simmering. Though the latter were popular in France, they were seldom used in this country outside establishments where French cooking was practised; by the 1850s, several manufacturers had already replaced them with gas.

Soyer's Magic Stove was not necessarily the first of its kind, since several were designed on similar principles at about the same time: it was, however, by far the best known, and innovatory in the social sense, since it was remarkably small and elegant and intended for use not in the kitchen but above stairs and outdoors, i.e. on sporting expeditions and picnics and in the dining and drawing room – and ballroom: according to his biographer, Helen Morris, it became fashionable to invite him to balls to cook individual *bonnes bouches* in front of the guests, one such occasion being a party at Castle Howard at which the Queen was present. One half of the stove, consisting of an upper fuel holder and two wicks, looked rather as one imagines Aladdin's lamp: the first wick heated the fuel, which flowed down a slim, curved tube to the second, where it was ignited; the heat was then transferred via a short pipe to the hob. The recommended fuel was spirits of wine, but any spirit (including brandy) could be used. A frying pan was included with the basic unit, but a stewing pan, saucepans, kettle, and coffee-pot were also available, comprising a complete 'Magic Kitchen'; in addition, the hob had a cover so that cooking could be carried out in the rain. The basic price was £1 15s. which, relatively speaking, was dear: nevertheless, Helen Morris records that when Soyer went on a promotional tour of the country, £5,000's worth were sold in fifteen months.

The poor man's equivalent was the 'Bachelor's Kettle', invented by Thomas Tozer: this was a grate designed to burn specially made wooden wafers, each of which was supposed to last just long enough to boil a shallow kettle; a frying pan (but apparently not saucepans) was also supplied. It was welcomed chiefly as a way for a man living in lodgings to make a cup of coffee before leaving for work in the morning or cook himself supper late at night, when his landlady's fire was out and the servants had gone to bed. The grate, presumably with kettle, cost 3s., and the wafers 1d. each.

In contrast to the Magic Stove, the army stove looked like a dustbin (both can be seen in the Science Museum). Soyer designed it before going to the Crimea for use in both camps and hospitals; it too came in several sizes, the camp size being calculated to be large enough to cater for half a company, i.e. sixty men, but at the same time light enough to be filled with fuel (wood) and carried by one mule per pair – one mule per company thus being needed. A fire was made in the bottom half, while a pan, fitted into the top for boiling and stewing; without it, the stove could be used for roasting. Maximum economy of fuel was ensured not only by the fact that the fire was completely enclosed, but that the pan, instead of being a saucepan, was shaped like a bowl so that as large an area as possible was exposed to the heat (the amount of fuel needed for open fires, which the stoves superseded, had caused a major transport problem).

In his first book, *The Gastronomic Regenerator*, Soyer described his kitchens at the Reform Club, where he had several charcoal and two gas stoves, and said that gas afforded 'the greatest comfort ever introduced into any culinary arrangement'. The gas stoves, which, like charcoal ones,

Alexis Soyer demonstrating his army stove
(*Culinary Campaign*)

consisted of hot plates, only, were 'divided into five compartments . . .
each having a separate pipe and brass cock, with a separate main pipe to
each stove, which supplies sufficient gas to burn the whole five compartments at once, or only one by not turning the gas into any of the other
compartments, or if all burning at once the fire may be regulated to any
height you may think proper. . . . You obtain the same heat as from
charcoal the moment it is lit, it is a fire that never requires making up, is
free from carbonic acid which is so pernicious, especially in small kitchens,
and creates neither dust [n]or smell. . . . The gas stoves also tend to greater
economy, as they are not lit till the moment wanted, then only in the
quantity required, and may be put out the moment it is done with, I think
it a great pity that they can only be fitted in London and other large towns
daily supplied with gas. . . .'[5] He gave them another puff in his next book,
Modern Housewife, and on at least two occasions roasted a whole ox by
gas, the first being for a Royal Agricultural Society dinner at Exeter, where
a special brick structure and 216 gas jets were used; cooking time was five
hours, at a cost of 1s. per hour in fuel. In addition, he demonstrated the
different methods of cookery using gas at a charity ball (to raise money
for a soup kitchen) and designed a gas apparatus capable of cooking for
seventy.

Looking back, it may at first be difficult to understand why everyone
did not share his enthusiasm. The fact that it was forty years or more
before gas became established has often been attributed to conservatism,
which, if taken to include the issue of roasting, certainly contributed;
practical considerations, however, also played their part. Manufacture
began in the late 1830s (the rings at the Reform were installed in 1841)
and, though some of the early models were clearly satisfactory, others
equally evidently were not. Again (no doubt as always in cooker design),
one of the main problems was heat distribution, which in this instance
seems to have been complicated by lack of understanding, on the part of
both the public and manufacturers, of the principle that hot air rises –
assuming that it has room to circulate. The latter's ignorance is apparent
from their descriptions of cookers; the public complained that tall, thin
ovens with burners at the bottom did not cook at the top – which was
almost certainly because the passage of heat had been blocked by baking
sheets or dishes placed over the whole interior. In an attempt to overcome
this, roasting compartments were made with jets from the roof, so that the
food was grilled instead of roasted, and (since people were not used to a
flame from above) burnt. Especially confusing for cooks was that in frying
or broiling over an open fire, where heat was rapidly dissipated, items
requiring slower cooking were held higher up and those needing stronger
heat lower down (as applied in all forms of cooking to people without

stoves). Another fault, which presumably arose from the designers' anxiety to ensure maximum efficiency, was lack of ventilation, as a result of which dishes supposed to have been roasted came out soggy, having in effect been steamed, and smelling unappetizingly of a mixture of staleness and gas. In addition, which was not the fault of the cooker manufacturers, imperfect purification meant that the gas itself sometimes stank, generally partly of hydrogen sulphide, which gives off the stench of rotten eggs. Smells, plus the knowledge that gas was poisonous if inhaled, were largely responsible for a widely held belief that food cooked by it must also be poisonous.

Another, and, as was demonstrated, the main reason for its hesitant start was expense. Although, especially before 1850, when it dropped considerably, its relative price *per se* was very high, Soyer's view of its

James Sharpe gas cooker by W. M. Lankester c. 1850. This was an example of a tall, narrow cooker (Science Museum, London)

economy in use seems to have been generally accepted. A number of other customers made similar comments, and also stressed the amount of work it saved, which several claimed was equal to that of one servant. *The Illustrated London News*, reviewing the cooking equipment at the Exhibition, said: 'We are not quite convinced of the economy of gas for roasting, but ... we feel bound to state that some of our first practical men have the highest opinion of gas ranges. ... For boiling, stewing, and baking, there can be no question of the economy of gas.'*[6] The point was later proved by Magnus Ohrens of the Crystal Palace District Gas Company, who carried out various experiments to test its efficiency including comparing the costs of coal and gas by roasting a series of joints (two pairs of legs of mutton weighing 8–10lb. each and two pairs

Gas cooker of Alfred King's (of Liverpool) design 1859

* Besides a number of gas appliances at the main Exhibition, a supplementary display was put on at the Regent Street Polytechnic. This was because exhibits at the Crystal Palace could not be shown working.

of ribs of beef weighing 11–13lb.): the coal came to 1s 3½d. and the gas 9½d.

The difficulty (as ever) lay in the capital outlay required. The price of solid-fuel ranges 1850–60 varied from a bargain £1 18s. To about £25 for a large model fitted with extras, whereas a small gas cooker was £16 and a medium-sized one £28, to which had to be added a modest installation charge and £2–£6 for meters; the City of London, which installed gas in the crypt of the Guildhall in 1856 for cooking the famous Lord Mayor's Day dinners, paid a total of £447 (a cooker made to measure for the Rothschild's house in Piccadilly cost £20,000 – which, however, was almost certainly a record). The problem was solved via renting: this was first tried, apparently with some success, by the Ipswich Gas Company in conjunction with a leading manufacturer, Ebenezer Godard, as early as 1849 or 1850; twenty years later, Ohrens and his company followed suit, charging 1s. 6d. per quarter. The result was dramatic: thereafter, renting out became an accepted practice and the use of gas rapidly spread.

Even by 1880, however, when production had expanded into a sizeable industry, manufacturers still had to face controversy on the subject of the traditional British roast. Before the introduction of gas, the process then referred to as roasting had always been carried out over the open fire: no approximation to it had been possible with the old brick ovens, which did not retain sufficient heat for long enough, and as the fire was still available when ranges came to be used, there had never been any real justification for change. Cooking inside the oven, either in a jug or jar (the equivalent of a casserole) or in the way which would now be called roasting, was then classified as baking – and, even with modern ovens, no one who has tasted meat roasted in the open will deny the difference. At the time, the distinction had especial significance because, far more than now, roasting was the national gastronomic ideal: less importance was attached to it at the top of society where haute cuisine prevailed, but at the lower level a good meal had only one meaning. The gas industry maintained all the established trappings of roasting: hooks were supplied from which meat could be hung rather than its having to be placed on racks in trays, and special, box-like contraptions were designed for spit-roasting large joints: one such was used by Soyer for cooking his second or third whole ox. All such efforts, however, were in vain, since the issue (leaving aside the question of technical problems) was simply the need to enclose the meat in ovens – many people objecting even to surrounding it with screens because they claimed that it gave it a baked taste.

Those who had no other means of cooking apparently roasted by hanging their meat on pieces of string, or (according to Francatelli's directions) a skein of worsted – though one would have thought that with both there was risk of singeing; presumably, it was turned by being given a push every now and again by members of the family. In better appointed kitchens, normal-sized joints – which meant up to about the weight of Ohrens' examples (Mrs Beeton assumed that sirloins and ribs of beef would be around 10 lb.) – were hung and turned, first in one direction and then the other, by clockwork bottle-jacks; these were suspended on adjustable chains from arms which swung out in front of the fire with a number of ratchets so that their height and distance before it could be varied. Spits were needed for larger items, or when several had to be cooked simultaneously; in addition, 'cradle' spits, which held the object in a framework rather than piercing it, were desirable for anything likely to lose its shape or fall apart, such as boned, stuffed poultry. Spits were made to revolve by means of an ingenious device called a smoke-jack, which had been invented in the eighteenth century (before clockwork) and was powered by the draught from the fire.

Generally, roasting apparatus was fixed to ranges, but spits and bottle-jacks were also attached to curved or three-sided screens, known as 'roasters', which were sometimes used to economize on heat: neither Eliza Acton nor Mrs Beeton, however, recommended them, despite the fact that they must have afforded a considerable saving, because the meat was thus partially surrounded, with the implied threat to flavour. Instead, they advocated using one-sided, i.e. flat ones: these were often quite substantial pieces of furniture, since they were fitted with shelves and could be employed as hot-closets and plate-warmers, which was especially useful in kitchens where the range was small and hot-space limited; they had doors at the back through which items could be lifted and moved on castors.

The need for constant basting was stressed by every cookery writer except Soyer who did not believe in it, but instead often recommended wrapping joints, with a selection of vegetables for flavouring, in buttered foolscap (which served instead of cooking foil). Fat was caught in wide, shallow pans sloped towards a well in the centre in which the gravy collected; mutton fat was unpopular for most purposes because of its rankness, but lard and beef dripping were clarified, i.e. purified by boiling or washing in boiling water, and used for basting subsequent joints, frying, and the everyday type of cake, pudding, and pastry. (A subsidiary complaint about gas for roasting was that the fat was spoilt for further use because it continued to cook in the bottom of the oven, whereas it remained relatively cool in pans in front of the fire.) Since one of Liebig's pronouncements of which especial notice was taken (at least by cookery writers) was that protein was soluble, from which it followed that the meat juices contained significant amounts of nourishment, people were advised to seal the surface of joints by cooking them at as high a temperature as was practicable for the first quarter of an hour, and also to discourage the juices from running by not adding salt until they were almost ready. The dictum on salt was in line with traditional practice, since if too much gravy escaped, the meat became dry; initial rapid cooking, however, was more inconvenient, partly because a brown or burnt appearance prompted cooks to serve items underdone, and also because it was believed that sealing the surface formed a barrier to heat as well as juice. For the rest of the cooking time, roasting was either carried out slowly, which was heavy on fuel but said to make for greater succulence, or, as was commoner, at a slightly higher heat than is the custom in ordinary ovens today.

Broiling, the equivalent of grilling, was always carried out over the open fire, generally on a gridiron with a long handle; as a precaution against falling fat, which caused the fire suddenly to flare up and meant that the grid had to be lifted out of reach until it had settled, some had grooved bars to conduct the fat and small pans at the base of the handle to receive it. As it tended to cling to the bars in any case, broiling was always carried out on a slant so that it either flowed into the pan or fell behind or in front of the fire rather than into it: this made for uneven cooking, which, as in ovens, could be remedied by the use of revolving grids. To minimize the amount of fat involved, none was added until after cooking, when pats of butter were sometimes placed on the serving plate; to considerable detriment to flavour, salt was not used at any stage of cooking either. As the unprotected food was placed straight over it, the fire required more attention than with any other method of cookery: besides having to be brisk (but not too fierce), it was essential that it should not be smokey – roasts, even when swift cooking was required, being sufficiently far in front of it to be out of the smoke line. A more convenient way of broiling, or approximation to it, was to use upright irons, which were similarly set before it and avoided the smoke: they had two disadvantages, however, one of which was that they could not be stood close enough to it to satisfy purists, who, rather as with the distinction between roasting and baking, maintained that they did not broil in the accepted sense but toasted; the other was that because the food was gripped between two grids, they were unsuitable for certain items, notably fish and game, which were respectively too fragile or lumpy to be held in them, or, similarly, anything on skewers or coated with egg and breadcrumbs. Skewers were often used for bacon, and always for kidneys, which, as the bars of gridirons were set wider than on modern grill pans, would have fallen into the fire if cooked independently; egging the breadcrumbing was as popular as for frying, partly because it ensured that neither fat nor juices escaped. One dish which is no longer served but was common then was oxtail (previously stewed) coated with breadcrumbs; another was rib-of-beef bones, the equivalent of pork ribs, which today are not cut separately but sold as part of the joint: when obtainable, however, they are exceptionally crisp, and, the meat being right on the bone, have more flavour than usual. The way beef was cut also affected steaks, which were always rump or chuck because the fillet was left on the sirloin.

Though chops and steaks were as popular as ever among the better-class eaters-out (hence chop-houses), broiling was almost certainly much less often employed in the home than grilling today, partly because of larger numbers to be catered for; it was also impractical for a main-course dish because it demanded constant attention at the same time as other items (which might be numerous) had to be dished up. Similar considerations applied to frying, which was also carried out over the fire, in this case so that heat could be controlled by the height of the pan (fried fish, however, was relatively convenient because, except in families who could afford nothing else, it was served as the first course, when portions were smaller and there were fewer accompanying dishes).

The commonest method of domestic cooking after roasting – indeed, certainly as common among the middle classes – was boiling, which had the advantages of being both light on fuel and, or so it was generally supposed, the easiest. Mrs Beeton, however, felt it necessary to stress that it was not as easy as all that: 'Boiling . . . requires skilful management. Boiled meat should be tender, savoury, and full of its own juices, or natural gravy; but, through the carelessness and ignorance of cooks, it is too often sent to table hard, tasteless, and innutritious. To ensure a successful result in boiling flesh, the fire must be judiciously regulated, the proper quantity of water must be kept up in the pot, and the scum which rises to the surface must be carefully removed.'[7]

The main problem, as indicated by the use of charcoal stoves, was that it was relatively difficult to reduce the fire sufficiently to achieve simmering rather than vigorous boiling, which inevitably makes for toughness; failure to skim merely had unfortunate cosmetic results, since the scum stuck to the meat and made it look grey and dirty. Again, Liebig's protein theory impinged: meat for the table was supposed to be plunged into boiling water, while that for stock, when the aim was the opposite, i.e. to draw out as much protein as possible, was to be put into cold water and brought to the boil very gradually. This meant that meat for stock had to be bought and cooked specially, which might have involved considerable extra trouble and expense: in fact, however (like salt), because of the predominance of roasting and plain boiling (as opposed to *pot-au-feu*-type cookery), it almost certainly merely confirmed the existing tendency.

The accepted proportions for stock were 1 lb. of meat per pint of water for superior and half as much (roughly the amount used for *pot-au-feu*) for ordinary quality: thus the principal ingredients of Mrs Beeton's 'Rich Strong Stock' were 4 lb. shin of beef, 4 lb. knuckle of veal, and ¾ lb. ham per 8 pints of water; 'Medium Stock' demanded 4 lb. of either beef or veal (or 2 lb. of each) plus ½ lb. of ham to 9 pints of water, and 'White Stock' 8 or 4 lb. knuckle of veal and about ¼ lb. of ham per gallon of water. In her recipes, stock of one sort of another was specified for a large number of soups, e.g. cabbage, celery, oyster, mock turtle, and mulligatawny, plus gravies, glaze (for cold ham), several meat dishes, e.g. oxtail, and a variety of sauces, notably béchamel and those based on it, and celery, chestnut, 'Sauce Robert' (for steaks), and brown mushroom sauce. Understandably, however – or so it seems to us, though evidently it did not to French and other tourists – sauces of this type (and probably other stock-based preparations too) were relatively uncommon in this country, a far more typical accompaniment being 'melted butter' – which according to Eliza Acton was notorious abroad as *"the one sauce of England"*.[8] 'Melted butter' was not in fact just that but thickened with egg yolks or cream for a more luxurious result or made to go further with milk or flour and water: hence complaints that it was curdled or lumpy – lumpiness being a constant hazard with any sauce thickened with flour, even when the cook was relatively careful, because the present standard method of making a roux, by which the fat is melted and the flour added before the liquid, had not yet been established: sometimes the flour and fat were rolled or mixed together before heating (which was relatively reliable), sometimes the flour and liquid worked into a batter, and sometimes all three ingredients put into the pan together. Melted-butter sauces included parsley, fennel, one version of caper, anchovy, shrimp, lobster, and oyster: parsley sauce accompanied, among other things, boiled calf's head, which was a popular traditional dish (calves' heads were also in demand for mock turtle soup); fennel accompanied boiled mackerel (both mackerel and sole were often boiled; anchovy was served with haddock, pike, and grey mullet, shrimp and lobster with sole, salmon, and turbot, and oyster with cod, boiled fowl, boiled turkey, boiled veal, and steaks; in addition, plain oysters, which scarcely differed, since the sauce was merely whole ones in the butter, were used to stuff roast veal and mutton (one of Dickens's favourite dishes was roast leg of Welsh mutton stuffed with oysters), with minced veal and in mutton sausages, in omelettes, and even toad-in-the-hole (which was usually made, not with sausages but steak or kidneys), and, in much the same way as garlic or mushrooms now, to add interest to stews, pies, puddings, and re-heated dishes – all this besides being fried, scalloped, stewed, pickled, and made into soup, patties, curries, and sausages in their own right. At prices of ½d. each to three for a penny (this was for the inferior Channel variety, which were generally used, at least by the middle classes, for cooking) no explanation for their popularity is needed; they also had the advantage, however, that they could be kept alive for over a week, which counted for the more in view of the premium on refrigerator space.

Advocates of French cookery and/or those trying to persuade people to buy cheaper cuts of meat, notably Soyer and Eliza Acton, lamented that stewing and oven cookery, i.e. braising and baking, were not more widely used in this country. Soyer said, 'Braising . . . like the sauté, belongs entirely to the French school'[9]: this was true in the strict contemporary sense, according to which it meant applying heat to the top as well as bottom of the pan, not by means of an oven but placing charcoal embers on the lid; in certain parts of Britain, however, it had been the custom to cover cooking pot. with warm peat, which produced a very similar effect – bread and other items having also been baked in this way.[10] Baking had been, and still was, discouraged by the limitations of ovens, which in the case of ranges was the same as with boiling, viz. the difficulty of obtaining very low heat: this had led to the habit of not using them for slow cooking but placing the dish in front of the fire instead, often enclosed by a form of screen known as a Dutch oven, which was similar to a roaster. With many ranges, too, though clearly less inadequate than in the faultier gas ovens, ventilation probably meant that complaints about the 'baked taste' had more justification than today. There were one or two traditional baked dishes, e.g. (besides ham) pike and pork; nevertheless, out of a total of around 300 recipes for meat, Mrs Beeton gave only a dozen for baked items, though, thanks to Miss Acton (from whom she took many of her recipes) she included a much higher proportion for fish.

The very advantage of stewing, i.e. its suitability for cooking inferior meat, was also presumably the reason for its low status – the English tending to evaluate dishes (perhaps still?) according to their ingredients rather than the skill required in their preparation. A sign that stews and similar composite dishes were seldom made in middle-class homes was that in a sample of a score of MSS. notebooks kept by housekeepers and mistresses, meat dishes hardly featured at all, which suggests that their compilers relied on methods for which specific recipes were not needed, e.g. roasting and boiling. Also, stewing was seldom referred to by cooks and maids: Hannah Cullwick, for instance, a maid, part of whose diaries have recently been published, several times mentioned roasting ('Got the dinner & cleaned away after, keeping the fire well up & minding the things what was roasting & basting 'em till I was nearly sick wi' the heat

& smell'[11]) but never stewing. similarly, a cook, in a letter complaining of her mistress's thoughtlessness, cited roasting, boiling, and pastry-making as though they were her entire repertoire: 'She never nose till a Quarter of an Hour too late whether the meat is to be rost or biled, or what Pastawry she will have; consequence is, Master being fond of Puncuation, and always home to a minnit within six o'clock, I am frequently reprooved for keping back the Dinner, or sending it up Hunderdun . . .'.[12] Also, apart from ovens, stews in particular suffered from the inhibition over garlic and onions – Eliza Acton frequently hesitating over onions, saying that they could be added or omitted as desired[13]*: there was, however, the compensation of oysters (another possibility, though hardly in keeping with the prevailing anti-stew feeling, was truffles). The lower classes' alleged aversion to soups and stews seems to have stemmed partly from dislike of sloppy food, which was perhaps connected with the fact that, either from preference or lack of implements, many of them were in the habit of eating with their fingers; in addition, it was claimed that soup was unsatisfying, for which one is tempted to blame the examples dispensed for charity – such soups being the only kind the poor were likely to have tried, and, to judge from recipes, not merely unsatisfying and innutritious, but almost totally tasteless.[14]

The following is a recipe invented by Soyer for feeding the Irish during the potato famine: chiefly because of its tiny meat content, assuming that ½ lb. of barley was used, it was worth about 165 cal. per pint. The cost as shown was 7d. per two gallons. (By way of contrast, one may care to compare it with the recipe on p. 135.)

Two ounces of dripping	0½
Quarter of a pound of solid meat, at 4d. per lb. (cut into dice one inch square)	1
Quarter of a pound of onions, sliced thin	[neg.]
Quarter of a pound of turnips; the peel will do, or one whole one cut into small dice	1
Two ounces of leeks; the green tops will do, sliced thin	[neg.]
Three ounces of celery	1
Three quarters of a pound of common flour	1
Half a pound of pure barley, or one pound of Scotch	1½
Three ounces of salt ⎫	0¼
Quarter of an ounce of brown sugar ⎭	
Fuel	0¾
Two gallons of water	0
	7

* e.g. In her recipes for Beef Roll, Beef Kidney, A Good Family Stew of Mutton, Irish Stew, and Baked Irish Stew.

The English equivalent to soups and stews was pies and puddings, which (except for extremely cheap soups) were probably quite as economic in their way because they made fillings go further – how much further is illustrated by a reminiscence of Alice Catherine Day about an old woman who made a hen (admittedly, in terms of size as well as age, no chicken) serve herself and her husband for dinner for eight days: 'Autumn was coming on, and Mrs Dean said to me, "I'm afeard, Miss, I must kill that hen you admire so much." She was a large, dark Sussex with pheasant-coloured markings round her neck. "Food is dear, she has left off laying, and I can nowise afford to keep her." . . .

It was perhaps a fortnight later when I next called at the cottage. "Please, Miss, I hope you will not be angry, but I had to kill your pet hen."

' "Why should I be angry, Mrs Dean? She was yours, not mine."

' "Well, I had a little flour, so I divided the hen into four lots, and made four little puddings. My Master and I we had one pudding between us the first day. The next day what was left over from that one – and so on; each pudding made two dinners for both of us. So I hope, Miss, you will not think I was very extravagant in killing and eating the old hen." '[15]

Pies (of the sort meant to be eaten cold) were also a convenient way of preserving meat. One 'titanic' pie was still going strong (one hopes not in two senses) well over four weeks after being started, and had probably been made a couple of weeks before that. This was a traditional Yorkshire Christmas, or goose, pie – and as such contained considerably more than just goose. 'What a conglomerate it was! The mere catalogue of the contents of that pie would be a small volume. It was an edible Chinese puzzle. There were, first and foremost, two young twin green geese (removed in the very April time of their sweet youth), one innocent tucked inside the other – folded, as it were, in the arms of his bigger brother – and both embalmed in salt, pepper, mace, allspice, and an ambery agglomeration of jelly. They were boneless; for so the learned embalmers had wisely willed it. Then, in a snug and stately corner, lay a savoury turkey, brooding over a duck, a fowl, and a small covey of partridges, mingling and interchanging flavours. After a whole month's devotion to this pie, breaking into a bin of forcemeat with the flavour of fresh herbs, we dug out (after much labour and research) the rosy tongue of some unknown animal. Somewhat later, a hare rewarded our exertions, hidden in a retired nook where it had secreted itself with the well-known cunning of that timid but delicious creature.'[16]

The top lifted off like a lid, which, as was usual, was decorated with pastry fruit and flowers: the largest and brownest-baked flower served as a handle. The crust was not intended for consumption (and anyway would

CHRISTMAS PIE

First, bone a fowl, a wild duck, a pheasant, and two woodcocks, &c.; having spread them open on the table, season them with aromatic herbs, pepper and salt; garnish each with some forcemeat, sew them up with small twine; place them on a sautapan with a little clarified butter, and set them to bake in a moderate oven, until they are done through; when they must be withdrawn from the heat, and put in the cool. Meanwhile, place the carcasses in a stewpan, with two calf's feet, carrot, celery, onion, a clove of garlic, two bayleaves, thyme, cloves, mace, and a little salt; fill up with four quarts of water; boil, skim, and then set this by the side to continue gently boiling for three hours, when it must be strained, freed from grease, and boiled down to thin glaze, and kept in reserve.

Make four pounds of hot-water paste, and use this to line a raised pie mould; line the inside of the pie with some of the forcemeat; arrange the baked fowl, duck, &c. in the centre, placing at the same time layers of forcemeat and seasoning, until all the preparation is used up; put a cover of paste on the top; weld it all round; cut the edge even; pinch it with pastry-pincers; ornament the top with leaves of paste; egg it over, and bake the pie for about two hours and a half; and when it comes out of the oven, pour in the game-glaze through a funnel; put it in the larder to get cold; and previously to sending it to the table, remove the lid, garnish the top with aspic jelly; place the pie on a napkin, in its dish, and ornament the base with a border of fresh-picked parsley.

Note. – The addition of truffles would be an improvement.

from *The Cook's Guide and Housekeeper's and Butler's Assistant,*
Charles Elmé Francatelli (Bentley, 1861, pages 289–90)

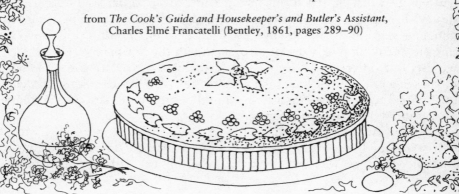

Though not at all the same, a very good pie for about sixteen can be made with twice the quantity of the pastry recommended for mutton pie (see page 161) plus:

1 free-range chicken, boned, skinned, and cut into chunks
2 pheasants, boned and cut into chunks
8–12oz (250–350g) lean ham or bacon, diced
8 hard-boiled eggs, sliced
2 smallish or 1 large onion, finely chopped
3–4 segments of garlic, finely sliced
small bunch parsley, finely chopped
1 tablespoon chopped fresh or 1 teaspoonful dried thyme
finely grated rind of ½ lemon
1 glass port or red wine
salt and freshly ground black pepper

This requires a shallow pie- or other oven-proof dish about 35×25cms and 5cms deep (a shallow dish ensures even cooking and makes serving easier).

Do not cook the poultry first. Line the dish with pastry. Mix the onions, garlic, herbs, and peel, and arrange the ingredients in the dish in layers, seasoning the meat lightly with salt and a little more heavily with pepper. Pour in the port, top with pastry, decorate with pastry leaves if desired, and bake in a pre-heated oven at 180°C, 350°F, gas mark 4, for 1½ hours. Cover the pastry with a sheet of foil if it becomes too brown.

have become increasingly stale) but was purely protective and preservative. Though omitted in several contemporary recipes (and apparently in this example), a distinctive feature of earlier versions of such pies was that they were not merely like Chinese puzzles but Russian dolls, a number of the different ingredients being boned and stuffed into one another: Hannah Glasse, writing in the previous century, directed that a pigeon should be stuffed into a partridge, the partridge into a fowl, the fowl into a goose, and the goose and its contents into a turkey, which, as she said, had to be a large one; additional items were a hare, to be laid down on one side of the turkey, and further game, including woodcocks, to go down the other. Somewhat later, Elizabeth Raffald gave a simpler variation in which the hare was stewed and pounded into forcemeat for the turkey, which was then stuffed into the goose – the reversed order of the latter presumably being because by this time bigger geese were bred. The rest of her ingredients were two ducks to place at each end of the dish and six woodcocks to fill out the sides. In her instructions, it was specified that the pie should not be cut for eight to ten days after baking.

The description quoted came from Dickens's *All the Year Round*, successor to *Household Words*: many years before it appeared, Dickens himself had been sent an example, and completely overwhelmed by its size.

Devonshire Terrace

Twentieth December 1841

My Dear Smithson,

The Pie was no sooner brought into my room yesterday evening, than I fainted away.

Topping put his shoulder out, in carrying it from the waggon to the hall-door; and John is in hospital with a damaged spine – having rashly attempted to lift it.

There never *was* such a Pie! We are mad to know what it's made of, but haven't the courage to cut it. Indeed we haven't a knife large enough for the purpose. We think of hiring Fletcher to eat it. We sit and stare at it in a dull astonishment, and grow dizzy in the contemplation of its enormous magnitude.

It prevents my writing at any length, as my faculties are absorbed in crust.[17]

A less spectacular but perhaps more truly tempting sort of pie was ordinary English game pie, for which Eliza Acton's recipe was neck of venison and boned, stuffed hare, the stuffing being made with lemon peel and herbs for eating hot or sausage-meat, preferably truffled, if for serving cold: this differed from venison pasty in that the latter was supposed to contain venison only, with a barding of mutton fat if the meat was very lean. Other particularly attractive pies were grouse and partridge, in which the game was set on a base of steak in the first instance and veal and ham in the second; similarly, lark was based on veal and ham, and pigeon and goose giblet (another traditional Yorkshire pie) on steak. A traditional Shropshire pie consisted of pork and rabbit with artichoke bottoms, and cockscombs; Leicestershire was pork flavoured with sage; Cheshire, pork and apple, and Devonshire 'squab' pie, mutton, onion, and apple. Both those made with apple were sometimes slightly sweetened, which was partly why the writer on *All the Year Round* found squab pie peculiarly loathsome: 'The odious composition is made of fat, clumsy mutton chops, embedded in layers of sliced apples, shredded onions, and – O tempora! O mores! – brown sugar. The result is nausea, unsociability, and, in course of time, hatred of the whole human race.' Nor did he like the Devon and Cornish fish pies: 'Ling is a sickly, unwholesome-looking fish, like a consumptive cod, and can never thrive – in or out of a pie. Cod is too dry and tasteless for a pie. Pilchard pie, mixed with leeks and filled up with scalded cream, announces its own horrors. Oyster pie, however [here he moved away from the West Country], intermingled with slices of sweetbread, and the faintest and most ethereal seasoning of salt, pepper, and mace, is a dish for the gods, painful to dwell upon when not on hand to refer to. Eel pie needs no eulogium. . . .'[18] (Eel pie was almost as well known as a speciality of Richmond as whitebait of Greenwich.)

Puddings were more a poor man's dish than pies because they did not require ovens, needed less fat than the richer sorts of pastry, and could be made with a smaller proportion of filling, or none at all, as in the case of dumplings or roly-poly puddings: that fillings were sometimes equally luxurious, however, was especially clear from Miss Acton's book, where, among other possibilities, she suggested venison and truffle, woodcock, snipe (snipe pudding, as opposed to pie, was a recognized delicacy), and, again, sweetbread and oyster. Despite the fact that she had lived or at least spent time in France and was in most respects a convert to French methods, she was a great believer in puddings, implying that they were the one culinary area in which the British had something to teach the French: 'The perfect manner in which the nutriment and flavour of an infinite variety of viands may be preserved by enclosing them in paste, is a great recommendation of this purely English class of dishes, the advantages of which foreign cooks are beginning to acknowledge.'[19]

To judge from the number of recipes she gave, her feeling not only for the equivalent varieties of fruit pudding but sweet puddings in general was quite as strong. She included over two dozen for the suet type (one

says suet although other fats were also used), among which were a
blanket recipe for fresh fruit, where she particularly recommended
morello cherries or apples and morello cherries mixed, and no fewer than
thirteen using dried fruit, i.e. forms of plum pudding – which can be
taken as an illustration of how popular it was. Although, despite her
faith, the solider sorts of sweet dish were becoming less fashionable,
plum pudding was not only included on dinner-party menus but second
only to roast (in this case, invariably beef) in the lower classes' order of
gastronomic priority: it was almost always served at feasts such as
harvest suppers, or dinners given for tenants, and at Christmas people
made sure of being able to afford it by joining 'plum-pudding clubs' run
by grocers. She gave several recipes for Christmas pudding, but, although
suitably plum-laden and alcoholic, they were neither her best nor most
extravagant plum-pudding-type dishes: the former was a 'Vegetable Plum
Pudding' made with mashed potato and carrot, and the latter a more
recondite composition which she satirically named 'The Publisher's
Pudding', of which she said, 'This pudding can scarcely be made *too
rich*.'[20] The main ingredients were 5 oz. each of beef marrow and suet,
¼ each of breadcrumbs, crushed macaroons, raisins, and dried cherries,
½ lb. of candied citron, 6 oz. of finely pounded sugar, ¾ pint cream, 7
eggs (yolks only), 6 oz. pounded almonds, which were not included in
the finished dish but used only for flavouring, and a wineglassful of the
best Cognac. Her other suet pudding recipes include a 'Kentish Well
Pudding', the 'well' being a pool of butter boiled in the middle on the
same principle as with Chicken Kiev, a lemon marmalade pudding called
'Snowdon Pudding' which came from a hotel at the bottom of the
mountain, and 'The Welcome Guest's Own Pudding', flavoured with
citron and lemon and orange peel. (She had a delightfully dry sense of
humour and gave nice titles to several other puddings, e.g. 'The Elegant
Economist's Pudding', which was a way of using up left-over plum
pudding, and 'The Poor Author's Pudding', a bread-and-butter pudding
made only with milk and cinnamon, in contrast to 'Rich Bread-and-
Butter Pudding' which contained cream, currants, candied peel, and
brandy.)

Among her recipes for other kinds of pudding were five for batter
pudding, eleven for custards, excluding dishes made with it such as bread-
and-butter pudding and trifle but including fruit custards, in which eggs
were used to thicken fruit juice instead of milk or cream, and a total of
eighteen for rice, which, though by no means so universally popular as
plum pudding, was favoured not only as a dish for children but for its
affinity with fruit. One was a rice cake to accompany cooked fruit; in

VEGETABLE PLUM PUDDING (cheap and good)

Mix well together one pound of smoothly-mashed potatoes, half a pound of carrots boiled quite tender, and beaten to a paste, one pound of flour, one of currants, and one of raisins (full weight after they are stoned), three quarters of a pound of sugar, eight ounces of suet, one nutmeg, and a quarter of a teaspoonful of salt. Put the pudding into a well-floured cloth, tie it up very closely, and boil it for four hours. The correspondent to whom we are indebted for this receipt says, that the cost of the ingredients does not exceed half a crown, and that the pudding is of sufficient size for sixteen persons. We can vouch for its excellence, but as it is rather apt to break when turned out of the cloth, a couple of eggs would perhaps improve it. It is excellent cold. Sweetmeats, brandy, and spices can be added at pleasure.

Mashed potatoes, 1lb; carrots, 8oz; flour, 1lb; suet, ½lb; sugar, ¾lb; currants and raisins, 1lb each; nutmeg, 1; little salt: 4 hours.

*　　　*　　　*　　　*　　　*

This is a boiled version of carrot or passion cake, and delicious – in the author's opinion, much better than conventional Christmas pudding.

Half the quantities given are enough for 6–8.

It is obviously much easier to boil it in a basin than a cloth; cover the top with cooking foil.

from *Modern Cookery*, Eliza Acton (Longman, 1859 ed., page 417)

other cases, the rice was boiled with the fruit (raisins, apples, or goose-berries) or layered with it (cherries or red currants); there were also 'Snow-balls', which were whole apples or oranges coated with it. In addition were rice puddings enriched with butter and eggs and flavoured with orange or lemon peel, spices, or, more unusually, coconut, and a lemon-and-brandy-flavoured ground rice pudding which was served as a tart and is something like a cross between hot cheesecake and syllabub. The other sweet dishes she gave included fritters, fruit salads, ices, an especially good recipe for syllabub, and jellies, which, although prepared gelatine was available, were often still made in the traditional manner with calf's-feet stock, and very fashionable, partly because they could be moulded into decorative shapes and colourful fruits such as strawberries embedded into them (fancy moulds were also used for suet puddings, despite the fact that, because it gave them room to swell, they were said to be lighter if boiled in cloths, in which case they came out round like footballs: hence contemporary illustrations of spherical puddings and the recent fashion for making them in this shape.

The many traditional puddings and sweets featured in the book were one of the reasons for its apparently typically English character – another being her slightly severe, unassailably British middle-class style; even in these chapters, however, French (and a few other foreign) dishes made their appearance. The rice recipes included 'Gâteau de Riz', 'Gabrielle's Pudding', and a Portuguese rice dish called 'Aroce Doce',[21]; 'Gâteau de Semoule', and 'Pudding à la Paysanne', which was similar to summer pudding but baked rather than chilled; she was emphatic about the superiority of the water ices which were favoured in Europe to English ice creams, and instead of stewed fruit gave recipes for compôtes, which were cooked with prepared syrup rather than sugar: 'We would *especially* recommend these delicate and very agreeable preparations to such of our readers who may be unacquainted with them, as well as to those who may have a distaste to the common "*stewed fruit*" of English cookery.'[22]

Elsewhere, her French bias was more apparent. She disapproved of boiling: 'Boiling, in the usual English manner, is the least advantageous of all modes of cooking meat, because a large proportion of the nourishment it contains is withdrawn from it in the process, and it is usually very insipid in flavour.'[23] Similarly, she was unenthusiastic about plain roasts, preferring the French custom of boning and stuffing (her instructions for boning remain classic). Her first soup recipe, bar one for Liebig's 'Extract of Beef', to which she gave precedence for health reasons, was for bouillon; her sauces included l'ail à la Bordelaise, several versions of béchamel, sauce tournée, remoulade, and mayonnaise (which was not yet familiar in this country). In addition, among many other

French preparations, were 'French Beef à la Mode', 'Mutton Kidneys à la Française', 'Norman Harrico', 'Boudin of Pheasant à la Richelieu', 'French Receipt for Boiling a Ham', and 'French and other Receipts for Minced Fowl'. The proportion of French recipes in her book does not give a true idea of how French-oriented it was, since it does not take account of her fundamentally French approach, but for what it was worth it was about a quarter.

At the time it came out (1845) the expansion in publishing which took place in the second half of the century had scarcely begun, and there were relatively few cookery books of any kind on the market: still one of the most popular at this date was *The Cook's Oracle* by an eccentric gentleman of leisure, William Kitchener, which had first been published in 1817; another was the extremely practical book already quoted giving details of how to preserve meat and garden produce. Both were firmly in the English tradition – which perhaps was why the latter attracted much less attention than it deserved. The only successful book to appear on French cooking was *The French Cook* by a chef called Louis Ude, who had made the gaming club Crockford's famous for its cooking much as Soyer subsequently did the Reform (and became the latter's friend and mentor in the early days of his career in this country). Meanwhile, a new public had been created by the growth of the middle classes and proliferation of clubs, the number of which rose between 1800 and 1850 from three or four to around twenty-five – the clubs, which in effect replaced restaurants, being the means by which experience of French cooking spread beyond the minority who could afford personal chefs (though this too was increasing).

The very next year, Soyer and Francatelli published (respectively) the *Gastronomic Regenerator* and *Modern Cook*, both of which consisted chiefly of their authors' professional repertoire, and as such had no direct relevance in the ordinary home: just how elaborate some of the recipes were is illustrated by an example taken more or less at random from the former (the somewhat breathless style, which makes it seem the more formidable, was because at this stage Soyer's mastery of English was imperfect: on the evidence of his later work, however, jounalism has to be counted as another of his talents.

Poularde* à l'Ambassadrice

Procure a nice white poularde [sic], cut it open down the back, and bone it without breaking the skin, make two pounds of forcemeat (No. 120), with which mix six large French truffles cut into slices, spread the

---

* A spayed hen, i.e. the female equivalent to a capon.

forcemeat half an inch in thickness upon the inside of the poularde, then
have ready boiled and nicely trimmed a small ox tongue, cover it with the
forcemeat, fold a slice of fat bacon round, and put it in the middle of the
poularde, which roll up and sew from end to end, fold the poularde in
slices of fat bacon, and tie it up in a cloth, have ready prepared some
vegetables of all kinds cut in slices, put them in a convenient-sized stewpan,
lay the poularde upon them, the breast downwards, but first moisten the
vegetables with a little salad oil, add half a pint of Madeira wine, and
sufficient white broth to cover the poularde, set on a sharp fire to boil,
skim, and let it simmer for three hours, prepare the following garniture:
braise two spring chickens (trussed as for boiling) three quarters of an hour
in the braise with the poularde, have ready prepared a croustade* ... ,
upon which place a larded sweetbread nicely cooked and glazed, place a
fine cockscomb and a large truffle upon a silver attelet, and run it through
the sweetbread, sticking it upright in the croustade, then take the poularde
out of the cloth, take off the bacon, pull out the string it was sewed up
with, dry it in a cloth, and place it upon your dish with the garniture
arranged tastefully around it; have ready the following sauce: chop half a
bottle of fresh mushrooms very fine, put them into a stewpan, with one
ounce of butter and the juice of half a lemon, boil over a sharp fire five
minutes, add two quarts of white sauce (No. 7) with one of the braise, let
boil, keeping it stirred until it adheres to the back of the spoon, rub it
through a tammie into a clean stewpan, adding a few spoonfuls of white
broth if too thick, season with a teaspoonful of sugar and a little salt, cut
a few very black truffles in slices, and chop a couple very fine, place them
on a plate in the hot closet ten minutes; put your sauce again on the fire,
and when boiling add a gill of whipped cream, pour the sauce over the
poularde and chickens, lay the slices of truffles here and there upon them,
and sprinkle the chopped truffles lightly over, the blackness of the truffles
contrasting with the whiteness of the sauce has a pleasing effect; serve
directly you have poured the sauce and sprinkled the truffles over. The
bones being taken out of the poularde it must be carved crosswise, thus
carving through tongue and all.[24]

As well as recipes of this class, however, the *Regenerator* included a
chapter at the back called 'My Kitchen At Home' in which Soyer gave a
number of recipes suitable for middle-class households: possibly partly
because of this, which aroused especial interest and was later reprinted in
The Ladies' Newspaper, and also aided by the fact that he had already
become a public figure, the book (originally published by subscription) ran
to seven editions in four years (Miss Acton's ran to five in its first year;
eight of *Modern Cook* had been issued by 1863). Thereafter, he followed
up 'My Kitchen' with a complete book for the middle classes, *Modern
Housewife*, which was infused with Britishness by means of collaboration
with a typical reader, Mrs B——, and in pitch and content was roughly

---

* Decoratively cut piece of fried bread used as a base for ornaments.

the equivalent of Miss Acton's work, the number of French recipes in this instance being about a third. He then wrote a book for the lower classes which (in contrast to the equivalent by Francatelli) sold nearly 200,000 copies – though, if only because the price was 1s rather than the 2d. or 3d. which was generally reckoned their limit, one can be fairly sure that the purchasers were higher class than his intended public. Soon after this, he went to the Crimea, where his work complemented that of Florence Nightingale, and contracted T.B., of which he died on his return (he wrote several other publications, but his two other major works were not cookery books nor influential in the same way as the latter). Until his death, Francatelli, perhaps in deference to his success, published nothing more: at this point, however, his produced the *Cook's Guide and Butler's Assistant*, a third book aimed at the middle classes – though a more up-market section of them than the other two – and almost at the same time, a specialized book on confectionery and pâtisserie, the *Royal English and Foreign Confectioner*, in which the foreign element considerably outweighed the English. By this time, Isabella Beeton's *Household Management*, which was originally written for the readers of a woman's magazine and was aimed at a young, not particularly smart or well-off public, had appeared. Far from being as quintessentially English as it is now regarded, it was compiled largely from the work of the 'the best modern writers on cookery'[25] – who included Soyer and possibly Francatelli (the *Guide*, however, which would have been the most useful of his books to Isabella, came too late) but, perhaps far more than she herself realized, owed its gastronomic character, as well as a large proportion of its recipes, to Miss Acton.

As early as 1849, Thackeray was complaining: 'Everybody has the same dinner in London, and the same soup, saddle of mutton, boiled fowls and tongue, *entrées*, Champagne, and so forth. . . . If we receive very great men or ladies at our houses, I will lay a wager that they will select mutton and gooseberry tart for their dinners, forsaking the *entrées* which the men in white Berlin [cheap] gloves are handing round. . .'.[26] (Entrées, which were relatively light meat dishes, were regarded as the principal test of the cook's skill and the items which set the tone of the dinner, and were thus the most likely to be French.) A decade later, Francatelli gave a series of dinner-party menus in the *Guide* in which French dishes were served throughout the meal; Mrs Beeton, in a similar series of menus, included between one and half a dozen (often, but not always entrées) out of a total of between twelve and twenty-eight different dishes – which suggests that even at a modest social level at least a token acknowledgement to the French style had to made. In a table of family menus, on the other hand

(admittedly labelled 'plain', which was the accepted term for unfashionable, i.e. English rather than French), she gave only eight in the course of
a list comprising meals for a fortnight for every month of the year. (In that
it was used largely as a status symbol, and also in that it made for a less
solid type of dish, the effect and position of classical French cuisine at that
time somewhat remind one of *nouvelle cuisine* – which was a reaction
against the richness and elaboration of the former.)

7. The Cooks: Aspiring Heroines and Artistes

Dickens, though his tastes were strictly English (Cockney, in fact), was intensely interested in food and not only referred to it constantly in his novels but published a number of articles about it in his magazines, *Household Words* and *All the Year Round*. The first, which appeared in an early issue of the former, began: '"Wanted, a good plain Cook," is hungrily echoed from the columns of the *Times*, by half the husbands and bachelors of Great Britain. According to the true meaning of the words "A good plain Cook" – to judge from the unskilful manner in which domestic cookery is carried on throughout the length and breadth of the land – is a very great rarity.' (A 'plain' cook was generally understood to mean one who did not claim to be able to undertake French cooking.) The writer went on to quote from two other well known publications, the *Examiner* and *Blackwood's Magazine*: '"What is commonly self-called a plain cook . . . is a cook who spoils food for low wages. She is a cook, not because she knows anything about cookery, but because she prefers the kitchen fire to scrubbing floors, polishing grates, or making beds. A cook who can boil a potato or dress a mutton-chop is one in a thousand." . . . "The true difference . . . between English and foreign cookery is just this: in preparing butcher's meat for the table, the aim of foreign cookery is to make it tender, of English to make it hard., And both systems equally effect their object, in spite of difficulties on each side. The butcher's meat, which you buy abroad, is tough, coarse-grained, and stringy; yet foreign cookery sends this meat to table tender. The butcher's meat, which you buy in England, is tender enough when it comes home; but domestic cookery sends it up hard. Don't tell me the hardness is in the meat itself. Nothing of the kind; it's altogether an achievement of the English cuisine."'[1]

No doubt there had always been complaints about cooks, as of other servants: Hannah Glasse had given the culinary ignorance of the average servant as the justification for her book*, and another pre-Victorian writer, Mrs Rundell, who for many years had been a housekeeper, i.e. in charge of all the servants in a large household, said that she had studied cookery more carefully than she might otherwise have done because good

* *The Art of Cooking Made Plain and Easy* (1747).

cooks were so hard to find. The fact that there was a great deal of comment about bad cookery at around midcentury was certainly partly due to the higher expectations aroused by the new cookery books and (in the case of men) eating at the clubs; also, more was said than formerly simply because of the growth of the periodical press. Nevertheless, for a combination of social and economic reasons, namely the background and education of servants and upbringing and education of mistresses, plus the greater demand for cooks brought by increasing prosperity, one is inclined to believe that cooks really were more ignorant and less willing than at an earlier date.

Typically, servants were the daughters of farm labourers, i.e. from the country, where there were often no other employment possibilities: few came from industrial areas because, despite the exploitative nature of piece- and factory-work, virtually any alternative was considered preferable to domestic service, even working in the fields*. A reason for favouring factory – but not piece- or field-work – was that it was better paid; more fundamental however, was that domestic service meant leaving home and family, and sometimes the area, and, above all, loss of independence. Servants were not only obliged to live in, but, as members of their mistresses' households, submit to control over every aspect of their lives, from dress, hair-styles (curls were considered unsuitable), visitors ('followers' were almost universally forbidden) to going out, when, as they rarely had regular time off (except for a brief period in the evenings, which was their only chance of pursuing personal interests or indulging whims) they had to ask special permission – and, as a rule, give details of where and with whom they were going.

The circumstances of farm workers in different parts of the country were noted by Caird in his survey of agriculture: in the north, the proximity of industry ensured full employment and a comfortable wage level, to which benefits in kind, including board or board and lodging, were often added; in southern counties, however, wages were sometimes hardly more than half the northern average and additional benefits much rarer. Although customary in certain localities, board and lodging (which, as board always seems to have been generous, ensured that at least workers had plenty to eat) was less common, partly because large farms meant that it was impracticable; also, labourers suffered from the withdrawal of several bonuses which in the past had helped to maintain a tolerable standard of living, viz. supplementary aid under the unreformed poor law and free fuel and grazing, which had once been provided by the commons

---

* According to the 1851 census, women accounted for an eighth of total agricultural employees, but most of this number were dairy-maids or did other 'indoor', as opposed to outdoor, work.

but disappeared with enclosure. The result was that families sometimes had to subsist on virtually nothing but the cheapest food available, i.e. starch, and frequently could not afford even enough of that (their one advantage was that repeal of the corn laws kept down the price of bread – but at the cost of temporary agricultural recession). In one of the counties where wages were lowest (Wiltshire), a typical diet was flour porridge with a scraping of butter for breakfast, bread for lunch – which only those without children could afford to accompany with cheese – potatoes for dinner (with which again, only those without children could afford a little bacon), and bread for supper (no mention was made of tea). Caird, evidently deeply shocked, commented, 'The appearance of the labourers showed, as might be expected from such a meagre diet, a want of that vigour and activity which mark the well-fed ploughman of the northern and midland counties.'[2] On further inquiry, he was told that in fact the men were so undernourished that they could not do a fair day's work – the farmers' policy being to overstaff and underpay to reduce unemployment. Accommodation and furnishings were often equally deficient: cottages were in advanced stages of disrepair, the inmates stuffing up leaks and cracks with the only material to hand – rags; large families (as in towns) lived in only one room, shared by whatever animals they might keep (which might formerly have included cows and geese, but these were discouraged by lack of the commons); shortage of beds meant multiple occupancy or sleeping on the floor – with or without mattresses; cooking utensils were probably limited to a pot and kettle, plus pail for fetching water, and tub, preferably wooden to reduce risk of breakages, for washing up (scouring was carried out with bunches of hay and ashes from the fire). In these surroundings, a cooking range, however modest, would have seemed out of place – as well as superfluous when there were only potatoes to cook.

By now, however, the advantages of education were recognized, and even very poor parents often made great sacrifices to send their children to school, albeit only for a short time (the cost was generally ½d. per day per child). Boys tended to stay for only a year or so, since the usual age for starting was not until seven or eight and at nine or ten they were old enough to contribute to the family income by scaring birds or doing some other job around the farm; this meant that some were only just able to read by the time they left. Girls, on the other hand, for whom there was very little chance of a job, frequently attended until they were twelve, learning to read fluently, write, if not spell, and do simple arithmetic. If parents could not afford an ordinary school, children were nevertheless not excluded from the possibility of education because they could go to Sunday school, which also enabled many to read fluently. Apart from a series set up under the workhouse system, no schools, either for the lower or – with one, and possibly a very few other brave exceptions – the higher classes taught practical subjects such as domestic science: in the case of those for the lower, this was chiefly simply for lack of means, but in addition the assumption had always been that practical skills would be taught by parents at home. As girls were not accepted for service until fourteen (the same age as boys began apprenticeships), they had two years during which to help their mothers in the house and thus in theory prepare for their careers: in practice, except for looking after younger brothers and sisters, which was (to some extent) useful if they wanted to be nursemaids, there was very little that they could learn in a deprived home which was likely to be relevant in a higher-class establishment. This meant that they had to be trained virtually from scratch by their employers or their staffs – which did not matter if their mistresses were like Tom Brown's mother in *Tom Brown's Schooldays*, who was 'a rare trainer of servants, and spent herself freely in the profession; for profession it was, and gave her more trouble by half than many people take to earn a good income';[3] similarly, in large households, experienced cooks, housekeepers, or, best of all, chefs – who could turn them into more than just 'plain' cooks – were available to give them instruction. If, however, there were no knowledgeable (or willing) senior servants, and their mistresses had been fashionably brought up, their only resort was to trial and error or cookery books and articles – which, although they were by now able to read, were seldom any use in the era before Mrs Beeton except to those who were already experienced cooks.

By far the most constructive aspect of the poor law reform was the establishment of so-called 'industrial schools' for long-term pauper children (mostly orphans) for whom, in the absence of parents or home, the need to be trained in domestic or other skills which would enable them to earn a living (and thus stay out of the workhouses thereafter) was recognized. At these schools, classroom studies were taught in the mornings and agricultural or domestic work in the afternoons: an exceptionally big, ambitious one at Liverpool offered boys the options of tailoring, shoemaking, or carpentry, but this was unusual; none of the schools provided alternatives to general domestic instruction for girls. This comprised sewing, laundry and dairy work, and cooking (the reason for teaching dairy work was not that pupils were expected to work on farms but that country houses customarily had their own dairies). Details of the cookery were not given, except that it often included making bread, but it can only have been of a very plain sort because of financial limitations (which also severely restricted farming projects for the boys). Reports on how the girls turned out were very variable: according to official sources,

Domestic servants of the Curtis family, Hampshire 1865
(*Hampshire Museum*)

a number of employers in the Midlands were so favourably impressed that they reapplied to the workhouses for successive servants; in Bath, on the other hand, where Frances Power Cobbe worked for a time, mistresses complained that they were backward and incompetent; Miss Cobbe also referred to a survey of ex-pupils from a London school which showed that all without exception had ended up on the streets. No doubt standards between the schools varied widely; one also has to consider the predicament of the children, who were undernourished, in some cases severely (probably, though not necessarily, more so than those who came from very low-paid labourers' families) and must also have suffered from lack of affection, to which as soon as they left the schools was added discrimination – feelings against charity children being very strong and likely to be the harder to endure in the closed community of a household; also, servants were reputed to be especially snobbish, as was perhaps a natural reaction to their translation to a higher-class environment. For this reason, most of the girls moved after their first placement (which, as it was arranged by the workhouses, was probably local) to distant employment where their background could be concealed: thus their progress thereafter remained unknown. With such incomplete information, both about the teaching and the pupils' careers, plus the difficulty of evaluating other factors, no judgement on the effectiveness of the schools, at least so far as the girls are concerned, can be made; they were, however, a sensible concept and are of interest not only for their job-training scheme but as the first example of state planning in education (all other schools at this date being independent).

The workhouse girls, however, whatever their qualities and qualifications, accounted for only a few thousand of about a million servants employed in Britain at midcentury – of whom, as housekeepers, cooks, kitchen-maids, and maids of all work, over two thirds had culinary duties of some kind.[*4] The fact that none of the rest were taught domestic subjects at school was widely deplored – and, in the absence of any existing establishment for the purpose, led to at least two proposals for founding colleges of domestic science; it was not, however, the main issue (or, depending on how one looks at it, only one side of it) over which many of the higher classes were concerned in connection with popular education. The convenience of servants who could read or write out shopping lists, check bills, and, on a more modest level, weigh and tell the time accurately (which of course they could not do unless they recognized figures) was acknowledged – but not with anything like the warmth with which the vanity, affectation, fancifulness, pertness, and general restlessness and discontent said to be caused by literacy were condemned. A few years later, these manifestations were classified as 'servantgalism', the main blame being laid on romantic novels, which, since there were as yet no thrillers or detective stories, were the only form of light literature available – and, apart from gossiping, the only form of entertainment open to house-bound servants; some more intelligent girls and women, however, who would now probably have gone on to higher education, had more serious, self-educative tastes (with the general recognition of the value of education went a drive towards self-education, as is instanced by the fact that encyclopedias and other informative books were one of the first areas to be developed in popular publishing.

All this would have been coped with far more easily by mistresses – whose fashionable notions were almost certainly another factor which encouraged vanity and affectation among servants – if their own education and interests had been less restricted. One, with considerable literary flair (she too would have been a candidate for higher education and was evidently of not much more than university age) exclaimed: 'Education (so called) has been tried. It has done much, but has it done much good? . . . For ourselves, we have always been sceptical how far the present system of education would improve the character and principles of those who are

* The 1851 census listed 47,000 housekeepers, 44,000 cooks, and 575,000 maids of all work.

placed in the position of earning their bread by domestic servitude. We have attended the boys' and girls' schools, and marvelled how far the information we heard instilled into their young minds would aid them in their after career. . . . How useful it must be in making a bed or tossing a pancake, to be quite *au courant* "of the latitude and longitude of the Morea!"' This woman's patience had been tried by a succession of five 'servantgal' or otherwise unsatisfactory cooks in a row. The first was middle-aged (probably about twice as old as her mistress) and not only irritatingly well informed, particularly in languages and geography, but so domineering that she soon made the latter feel that 'we had no pretension to call ourselves mistress in our own house; that we were never more to eat a dinner of our own ordering, nor be permitted to have a wish, however modest, gratified . . .'. Having 'gently, and in proper terms' given the reason for her dissatisfaction and dismissed her, the lady engaged 'a *Paragon*; six years' character from her last place, left no doubt that we were decidedly *suited*. Oh! that word: how much it does comprehend. Paragon wore little natural ringlets; we wished so much they had been assisted by art, we could have suggested a little less exuberance in that particular. She used very choice language, would occasionally regret she had received an indifferent *bolletin* of her mother's health; and in lamenting "that the beauteous days of summer were ore," would ask gracefully, and with a lisp, "what vegetation was to be served that day." Whilst Paragon fulfilled her duties which came under our observation, we could not object to the rosewood desk, taken from the drawer of the kitchen dresser, and . . . [ostentatiously] placed for immediate use; nor did we make any observation on accidentally intruding in the regions of this refined cook, and seeing her with an ornamented pen, writing verses – an Ode, possibly, to a patty-pan. Six months we were gracefully and poetically served; one morning, with a more marked lisp, we were begged to "suit ourselves" at our earliest convenience. Cook said, "she found that her talents were completely rusting in our service; in the simple and quiet habits of the family, we gave no opportunity for their display." . . .

'A sickly cook succeeded. She had been crossed in love – tea-caddy, every household necessity purchased, – she had been deserted for another. A tear moistened the hashed mutton, – sudden despair would seize her in the act of whipping a cream. . . . We grieve to see others suffer, and particularly hopelessly. We murmured a kind advice to be cheerful; and at length being unable to cheer this Niobe, who, in the solitude of her room each evening, would indulge her feelings of anguish, and would *not* come out to make the toast, to the housemaid's great disgust, we were necessitated to suggest change of air and scene . . .'.

The fifth cook turned up for her interview suitably plainly dressed and, although 'pleasant-looking', managed to give the impression of being perfectly straightforward; she had, however, 'with some skill concealed the turn of her mind, which was insatiable love of the admiration of others, and a very extensive private admiration for her own attractions. Before a week had elapsed, rumours reached the drawing-room of such elaborate toilettes every evening, that as the only single man in the house was the eldest son of the family, not yet three years old, and not capable consequently of appreciating her [charms], little hope remained that so much labour would be long exercised, where it was in vain.'[5] The mistress's fear was justified: the girl left as soon as she had completed a month's trial period.

The remaining cook, 'Cheerful Susan', who had been a kitchen-maid in an aristocratic establishment, was the only one about whom there was nothing fancy: instead, she drank, for which cooks were notorious, presumably because, like bakers, they suffered from having to work in hot kitchens; also, even if they did not make themselves thirsty by voluntarily picking at food all day, the fact that recipes often did not give quantities meant that the only way to judge amounts of seasoning and flavouring was by tasting (to ensure that they retained discriminating palates, gourmets sometimes recommended that they should be made to fast at regular intervals. In addition was the possibility of cooks being tempted by the wines and liqueurs used in cooking, though, like most of the rest of their class, they usually seem to have got drunk on gin: Cheerful Susan's tipple was not specified, probably because her mistress was too genteel to name it, but (for which at least her mistress should have been grateful), rather than stealing from the household she bought it at the pub with her 'butter' (i.e. tea, sugar, etc.) money.

Not the least notable feature about the lady's recital was that it did not contain any complaints about her cooks' culinary abilities, nor indeed, apart from the reference to 'vegetation' and another equally incidental allusion to a pudding, include mention of food or cooking at all. This suggests that all the cooks were passably competent – to which extent many people would have accounted her lucky; even if this had not been the case, however, she would have been unlikely to dwell on gastronomic details, or make this kind of criticism on her own account – complaints about bad cooking almost always coming, or at least being represented as coming, from husbands. This was no doubt partly because the latter could draw on their experience of eating out; also, however, ladies were again restrained by considerations of propriety. Once, it was nostalgically asserted, food had been one of their first concerns and every higher-class girl taught to cook as a matter of course: now, according to the writer in *Household Words*, cookery was considered a subject unworthy of their attention: 'rather, than apologetically, with a simpering sort of jocularity, or as something which it is "low" to know anything about. When a certain diplomatist was reminded that his mother had been a cook, he did not deny the fact; but assured the company, "upon his honour, that she was a very bad one." People in the best society do not hesitate to bore others with their ailments, and talk about cure and physic; but conversation respecting prevention – which is better than cure – and wholesomely prepared food is tabooed'[6] (the last sentence referred to his contention, put forward earlier in the article, that the reason for the prevalence of indigestion and other stomach complaints in Britain was not, as was often alleged, overeating, but faulty cooking).

That ladies should not display interest in food can be assumed to have been an extension of the ban on work – the idea that they should not have to supply material necessities leading to the physical (as opposed to moral and spiritual) attributes of life: a better known example of this attitude was prudery over sex. Another element in it was puritanism and its more specifically Victorian manifestation evangelicalism – which probably also affected views on drunkenness. On a much more prosaic level, the chef Ude's explanation for ladies' anti-gastronomic tendencies was simply that the food served in the nursery and at boarding-schools was so boring that it deadened the palate for ever; there was also a practical reason for women not eating much at dinner parties (as opposed to failing to show discrimination), since the current fashion for enormous crinolines balanced by tiny waists was accompanied by corsets which were sometimes so tight that they cannot have accommodated more than a few dainty mouthsful (doctors acknowledged that in their case it was tight-lacing which caused various internal disorders).*[7]

Nobody, not even Dickens's journalist or starving husbands advertising for cooks in *The Times*, dared to suggest that higher-class women should actively cook (unless perhaps in the dining room with a Magic Stove). If there was an interregnum in the kitchen, the maids rather than the mistress took over, which was always possible because a family who could afford a cook would also employ at least one maid. If only a maid was kept, she was expected (notwithstanding the lack of labour-saving devices) to cook, shop, deal with tradesmen, wait at table, and wash up, as well doing all

---

* One may compare this with the present attitude, as represented by *The Official Foodie Handbook*, – sub-titled 'Be modern – Worship Food' 'You feel no need to conceal your – excitement (it used to be called greed). . . . Food talk is the *staple* diet of social intercourse now. Foodism crosses all boundaries and is understood in all languages. Food is the frontier to be on.

'You are the New Man – and the New Woman. . . .

'The gourmet was typically a rich male amateur to whom food was a passion. Foodies are typically an aspiring professional couple to whom food is a fashion. A fashion? *The* fashion. Couture has ceded the centre ground to food.'

the other household and family chores, including sewing, possibly the laundry, and perhaps even her mistress's hair: in one skit in a magazine, a particularly unreasonable mistress was depicted as insisting that, so that she should not waste time, she should scrub the doorsteps while the breakfast eggs were boiling (with the inevitable result that they were always hard-boiled). Some mistresses never set foot in the kitchen at all, in which case the cook tended to regard it as entirely her own; more conscientious housewives inspected the larder and examined the pans and pudding-cloths for cleanliness (servants sometimes did not bother to scour the insides of pans because only the outsides showed when they were hung up). Again, the trend in behaviour was supported by fashions in dress: crinolines would have picked up the soot and dirt of the kitchen from yards around, and must have made it virtually impossible to approach near enough to the range to touch a cooking-pot – in addition to being liable to catch fire; women who carried out inspections did so in the morning, before they were formally dressed (servants, fortunately from the point of view of safety, were not only forbidden to wear them but unable to afford them; though they might improvise when they went out and did sometimes indulge in tight-lacing).

As they were not supposed to work (and as well as being inhibited from earning could not theoretically own money after they were married because until 1870 married women had no legal right of ownership) higher-class girls were almost as restricted as servants in their choice of career, the only options in their case being marriage, an existence of vicarious vacuity, or defying convention. The primary aim of most schools therefore was to enhance their chances of marriage: for this reason particular attention was paid to social and artistic accomplishments, i.e. music, dancing, drawing, and deportment, of which music was given top priority because of the opportunity it gave for attracting notice by performing at parties. As it was considered essential for ladies to be able to speak French, stress was also laid on languages; otherwise, too much interest in academic subjects was discouraged, partly because men were presumed not to like 'blues', but also because thinking was believed to be tiring in the same way as physical exercise, and undue exertion of any sort bad for women, who were supposed to reserve their strength for child-bearing; in addition, the study of phrenology had led to the notion that, because their skull measurements were smaller, women were intrinsically less intellectually capable than men. Needless to say, domestic skills were totally disregarded (it was no accident that not only Eliza Acton but Mrs Beeton spent part of her youth abroad).

There was, however, at least one atypical, unfashion-conscious school, which did teach domestic subjects, including cookery: this was the

Freemasons' Girls' School, in London, where Soyer's Mrs B – sent her daughters. Here – very economically – servants were not employed, all the domestic work of the establishment being done in turns by the girls themselves (it was a boarding school). Probably Soyer had this example in mind when, deluded by the success of the *Regenerator* and *Modern Housewife* into thinking that culinary interest had reached the point where such a project would receive support, he drew up a proposal for a College of Domestic Economy (as domestic science was then termed). In the attempt to offset its *raison d'être* – and also perhaps because he himself was deeply imbued with respect for class – he did not adopt the Freemasons' liberal approach but planned it along strictly conservative lines: every possible allowance for class feeling was made, no practical work being suggested for young ladies, who were expected to study theory only – which, though obviously a compromise, was generally accepted as sufficient to enable mistresses to instruct servants; further, which sounds obnoxious now and was not the practice at schools even then (aristocratic girls, however, were not customarily sent to schools, but taught by governesses at home), classes were to be grouped according to social status, so that upper-class girls did not have to mix with the middle classes, the upper-middle with the medium-middle, and so on. Also, to ensure that pupils' more socially acceptable studies should not suffer, music, drawing, and foreign languages were to be included in the curriculum (in all of which, one might add, Soyer's nationality, interests, and connections put him in a position to ensure first-rate instruction).

Each group was to consist of five young ladies and two lower-class students, one of whom was to be a novice, called a 'servitor', and the other a more advanced 'improver', i.e. servant who already had some proficiency in cooking; though the latter could attend classes, part of their training was to consist of serving the former, theory and practice thus being combined. To reassure parents as to their morals and character, it was stated that no working-class girl would be accepted without thorough investigation of her family. The domestic subjects to be studied, as at the industrial schools, included not only cooking but dairy work, laundering, and sewing (in this instance dressmaking); courses for higher-class students were to last three, six, or nine months, divided into three-month terms, at the end of each of which were to be exams – these being an unusual feature in young ladies' education and proof that, notwithstanding his social concessions, Soyer did not intend that the atmosphere should be dilettante: diplomas were to be awarded on the basis of results. The minimum time of attendance for lower-class pupils was only a month because it was envisaged that they would be sent, not by parents but employers, who could not necessarily be expected to spare them for longer.

The College was to be financed, or partly financed, by subscription, the proposed rates being £50 per free place every other month (presumably in perpetuity) for servants and £100 every other term for young ladies. That subscriptions did not forthcome needs no comment in the case of the latter and is even less surprising in the case of the former – £50 being more than even the highest-paid cook's annual wage and about four times that of a maid; also, there was the risk that servants sufficiently favoured to be sent would promptly leave for better-paid jobs on the strength of having attended.

Given that the sum involved would be too great for servants themselves or their parents to manage, this problem was inherent in any scheme within the current social framework – all education except at the industrial schools (which were paid for out of the poor rates) being financed independently; another idea put forward a few years later, however – in fact, exactly ten years before the Education Act – was that a network of colleges for future servants should be financed by means of a national tax or levy; somewhat ingenuously, it was proposed that they should be staffed by superannuated servants (who as things were frequently ended up in the workhouse), the colleges thus serving a subsidiary purpose as old peoples' homes.

Meanwhile, the prevailing situation in the kitchen was succinctly illustrated by the following:

LADY. – Cook! the dinner was very bad yesterday. Your master was very much annoyed.

COOK. – Was he, ma'am? I am very sorry. (We imagine Cook to be civil and well intentioned but ignorant. Perhaps an inexperienced girl at £10 or £12 a year.)

LADY. – The fish looked black and was falling to pieces; and the melted butter was all lumps. You must not put lumps in the butter.

COOK. – (Humbly, but with an inward consciousness that she is innocent of that great offence.) No ma'am, I won't.

LADY. – And the mutton was all dry and burnt outside.

COOK. – I'm sorry, ma'am, it was overdone.

LADY. – But it was not overdone; it was underdone inside.

COOK. – I am sure I can't think how it happened, ma'am.

No more can the lady; and so cook returns to her kitchen, and though willing to improve, serves up [the same] day after day . . . till one fine morning her mistress gives her warning, saying that 'Master does not like her cookery;' and dismisses her, to get in her stead perhaps a worse servant in other respects.[8]

Apart from Ude, Soyer, and Francatelli, little is known, either personally or professionally, about the several thousand chefs working in Britain at this time – even Francatelli's life being traceable only in outline. Very few wrote books because, although some were British, the majority were French or Italian and suffered from the language barrier; in addition, like cooks, they came from working-class backgrounds and were not necessarily sufficiently educated to be literary. Nor, since they were regarded as mere servants, and did not give rise to public outcry against their incompetence, did many people see fit to write about them: Abraham Hayward, author of *The Art of Dining*, and Soyer's first biographers, Warren and Volant, were exceptional in having given some thought to their situation, but even they were not very informative.

It is nevertheless clear that as a group they were at least as discontented as cooks. Hayward said, 'It is a curious fact that almost all the great artists in this line are erratic, restless, and inconstant. They seldom stay long with the same employer, be he as liberal, indulgent, and discriminating as he may. Is it that they sigh, like the Macedonian, for new worlds to conquer, or that – extending the principle of the German *Wanderjahr* to the whole of human life – they fancy that knowledge and intellect are cramped and restricted by becoming stationary? The phenomenon well merits the serious attention of the metaphysician.'[9] Soyer, before being appointed to the Reform, had had four jobs in five years; Francatelli, by the time he was about forty, had run through five top-flight posts, including that of head chef at Buckingham Palace, and almost certainly a long string of less distinguished ones earlier in his career.

One element in many chefs' problems which demands no more than common sense to perceive was their position as Frenchmen in the confines of a British household, which because of a long tradition of Francophobia, was parallel to that of the workhouse girls except that in this instance it was frequently mitigated by the presence of their countrymen; in the sort of establishment where they were employed there would probably also be French ladies' maids, French governesses, and perhaps foreign assistant chefs (the workhouse girls' difficulties were exacerbated, in contrast, by placing them in their first jobs in houses where they were the only servant). One basis for prejudice was religion, about which many people felt very strongly – Catholics, or 'Papists', being hated by Protestants of almost all shades of opinion (many Protestant nonconformists were members of the servant classes): even if the subject was treated with discretion, such differences could not be hidden because religious observance was taken for granted and anyone not attending normal church services was conspicuous by their absence. In addition, as a result of the Revolution, the French were regarded with suspicion as republicans; their tastes in food, of which not only soup but frogs' legs featured prominently in the popular imagination, also caused them to be looked on with distrust; nor were the chefs' pretensions and amusements calculated to help them to mix easily with the rest of the staff.

A further fruitful source of below-stairs tension was their salaries, which were far higher than those of anyone else, even stewards, who took the place of housekeepers as heads of very large establishments. Assistant chefs were more modestly paid, but master chefs could expect a couple or several hundred a year – as compared to about £80 for stewards and a ceiling of £40 for housekeepers and cooks. Salaries at the clubs (partly because lodging was not included) were larger still: Soyer's at the Reform was £1,000, and Ude's at Crockford's a record £1,200.

Generous salaries (the chief reason for their being here) also highlighted the question of their status in Britain, which to the vocal, successful few was a major source of grievance. In France where cooking was rated more highly, they were acknowledged, within the limitations of their background, as professionals and artists: in this country, however, except by Hayward and a small, sophisticated gourmet minority, they were regarded merely as domestics – despite the fact that in financial terms they were often as well off as established middle-class families employing two or three servants. This seems to have troubled Soyer in particular, perhaps partly because he had been made very aware of it when, as a young but already acclaimed chef, he had fallen in love with his future wife and been rejected as a suitor by her stepfather because of his humble occupation. Later, the desire to be accepted, if not quite as a gentleman, at least as of higher than working-class status, appears to have been the underlying driving force of his life: it was almost certainly mainly for this reason that he eventually resigned from the Reform. Francatelli too, to judge from his literary tone and Hayward's description of him as 'a man of cultivation and accomplishments'[10], was extremely sensitive about his social position: he likewise ceased in regular employment for a time, but this may have been due to external circumstances.

Francatelli – rather than Soyer, who looked on it more as a science – was also emphatic about the standing of cookery as an art. On this point, Ude had been uncompromising, maintaining that a really good chef who perfectly suited his master should be valued in the same way as the greatest painters – citing as comparable examples artists such as Raphael, Rubens, and Titian. Francatelli, as a man of culture, was more cautious but no less firm, declaring, 'The palate is as capable, and nearly as worthy of education, as the eye and the ear': he also defined cookery (as professionally carried out) as 'an art by which refined taste is to be *gratified* rather than a coarse appetite *satisfied*.'[11] A nice illustration of the chef as *artiste* was a story about a young Italian confectioner who worked for the Duke of Beaufort (who also employed a first-class French chef named Labalme): 'His Grace was one night in bed, and fast asleep, when he was roused by a knock at his door, which was impatiently repeated. He asked who was there. "It is only me, Signor Duc," said the artist; "I was at the Opera, and I have been dreaming of the music. It was Donizetti's, and I have got an idea. I have this instant invented a sorbet; I have named it after that divine composer, and I hastened to inform your Grace." '[12] Just as cooks read improving books, the chefs were conspicuous for their support of the performing arts, in particular. Ude (among other careers) had tried to go on the stage before committing himself to cooking; Francatelli's cultural preferences are unknown, but Soyer – whose wife was notable for her promise as a painter – was an addicted theatre-goer and balletomane, even going so far as to write the story for a ballet which, though never performed, was subsequently set to music.

Charles Elmé Francatelli
(*The Royal English and Foreign Confectioner*)

It was thus a cause of the more frustration to them that their efforts were not always appreciated, or that appreciation was not as freely expressed, as they might wish. A problem in addition to non-discussion of food was that was that although employers (some of whom were quite as eccentric as the chefs may have seemed) appear to have been not only generous but kind, the demands of entertaining meant that chefs might be kept by hosts who themselves had no interest in food at all (a parallel situation existed in relation to game, which a few landowners preserved for the benefit of guests although they themselves were non-sportsmen). The classic example of such an employer was the Duke of Wellington, who was so indifferent to food that he was said not to notice rancid butter and, on the return march from the Peninsula War, invariably replied, when asked what he wanted for dinner, '"Cold meat"'[13]; nevertheless, he subsequently had a chef (known as 'Bony', after Bonaparte) who was reputed to be one of the best in England at the time (and who stayed with him for over a decade, which would have been a remarkably long period of employment in any circumstances). According to a well known anecdote, however, one of Bony's successors returned to his former master in despair, exclaiming that the Duke was as pleasant and considerate as possible, but: '"I serve him a dinner that would make Ude or Francatelli burst with envy, and he says nothing; I go out and leave him to dine on a dinner badly dressed by the cookmaid, and he says nothing. Dat hurt my feelings, my lord."'[14]

Remarkably, another example of a discouraged chef was given by a woman, in the course of a plea, not for anything so radical as the teaching of cookery in schools, but simply for girls and mistresses to be more observant, by which means, she claimed, they could pick up a useful amount of knowledge without sacrificing anything. 'We were visiting once at a country house where a first-class cook was at the head of his proper department. He was a Frenchmn, and being an enthusiast in his profession, he usually did his best; but many moments of mortification and discouragement did this great artist pass through, knowing that he was wasting his savouriness and his sweetness on the insipid [sic] and the obtuse, that his efforts were overlooked, that his inventions were unappreciated. One morning when he came to his lady's boudoir to submit to her inspection the bill of fare for the day, a visitor of rank and discriminating tastes happened to be present, who paid him some judicious compliments upon his performance of the day before. A glow of pleasure and gratified pride overspread the melancholy countenance of the *artiste méconnu* as he bowed his thanks; and on leaving the room, he was overheard to say ... "*Pour aujourd'hui au moins, il vaut la peine de faire une bonne cuisine. Madame la Comtesse est là qui l'appréciera.*"

'We would, then, exhort our readers, especially the younger part of them, not in the pride and beauty of their accomplishments, too scornfully to look down upon this humble branch of study.'[15]

Not even the chefs' sensibilities, however, could withstand the power of the pound and ambition. Prosperity meant that the job market was expanding rapidly, and it was easier for a young man to make a name working for an aristocratic family, where only one or two chefs were kept and guests potential employers, than in the more competitive, anonymous conditions of a Paris restaurant. The Count d'Orsay, a reluctant exile in France (having been forced to return to his native country by the pressure of creditors), reported: '"I must confess with regret that the culinary art has sadly fallen off in Paris; and I do not very clearly see how it is to recover. . . . It has emigrated to England, and has no wish to return. We do not absolutely die of hunger here, and that is all that can be said."'[16]

8. The Cookery Writers: Frugality and Economy v. Extravagant Farragos

Since both knowledge of cookery and earning money were unacceptable for ladies, cookery writing was doubly so: thus, not surprisingly, women cookery writers tended to keep a low profile – many, like other female authors, writing anonymously, as the number of cookery books listed as 'By a Lady' shows. Partly because of this reticence, very little more is known about most of them than the chefs: it follows, however, that they must have been exceptionally independent-minded and determined. This was certainly true of Mrs Beeton, the only one of whom it has been possible to write biographies and who, if she had lived longer or belonged to the next generation, would have been termed a 'New Woman'; frustratingly little has so far come to light about Miss Acton, but it seems that she too was remarkably purposeful, persisting in her writing career despite much ill health: in her case, one cannot be certain whether she was spurred on by a financial incentive, which was not a major consideration in the case of Mrs Beeton but undoubtedly was for others.

The earliest Victorian woman writer of note was Esther Hewlett, who is chiefly known, not for a cookery book as such, but a book on cottage housekeeping: it is perhaps stretching a point to describe her as Victorian, since her book first appeared in the 1820s, and, as a member of an older generation and having lived, if she did not originally come from the midlands and north, she was impervious to mid-century fashions; subsequently, however, she produced two outstandingly practical cookery books which, though not particularly successful, probably served as models for her successors. Her speciality was writing for the developing lower-class market, which was a new literary area at the beginning of her career and one which she was unusually well qualified to enter, since, unlike Soyer or Francatelli, or even the politician and journalist William Cobbett, who wrote a rival work on cottage management, she clearly knew the poor and how they lived on an intimate, day-to-day basis. By the time her book for cottagers, *Cottage Comforts*, appeared, she was already the author of some thirty titles: since moral and religious instruction were considered the most urgent needs of the new readership, however, they were mostly moral tales and Sunday-school tracts, which, for cheapness, were short and printed as pamphlets, so that she was not quite so prolific as this suggests.

Cobbett's book on cottage living, *Cottage Economy* (which, mainly because it has recently been reprinted, is better known today), appeared several years before hers, and considerably annoyed her, partly because it was a polemic extolling self-sufficiency, which she felt was misleading to an under-educated public, and partly because of his reactionary views on working-class education, which, both as a popular writer and – as seems fairly clear – Sunday-school teacher, she naturally resented. In contrast to him, she aimed simply to give a straightforward, reasonably complete guide: whereas he concentrated chiefly on home brewing and baking and rearing stock, she covered such topics as choosing and equipping a cottage, managing wages, bringing up children, and looking after the sick, and, although she included subjects such as brewing and baking, did not attach especial significance to them – and indeed confessed that until a short time before, she had not seen the advantage of home baking; similarly, as part of her overall plan but not as her main theme, she gave a few other general recipes, mostly for very economical dishes such as pease soup and porridge, plus a fairly inclusive range of preparations for invalids. As with all her work, *Comforts* was distinguished for common sense, her easy, unselfconscious style – unlike others addressing their social inferiors, she was neither condescending nor preached, but used stories to emphasize her points – and the precision and detail of the directions, in which she endeavoured to leave nothing to prior knowledge or imagination.

Many years later – by which time she had also published a comprehensive cookery book for the middle classes – she wrote a series of articles for a popular paper, the *Family Economist*, which were collected into a companion volume, *Cottage Cookery* and especially notable for her realistic – perhaps, notwithstanding her tact, too realistic – remarks about economy and enlightened approach to recipe writing. At the beginning of the book was a discussion of food values (based, but rather shakily, on Liebigian principles, see Ch. 11), in the course of which she condemned the extravagance of toast, which many people ate because they claimed not to be able to afford meat: she pointed out that it added the cost of fuel, time, and butter to the bread, but no nourishment beyond the latter (whereas toast is unpalatable without it, people habitually ate bread without butter). She also suggested that needy families should not spend money on tea, beer, and tobacco: 'In a poorly-furnished cottage, not a hundred miles from where I write, little John and Sally, when they ask for more bread or porridge, often get the answer, "There's no more to give you;" and the poor mother looks thin as a herring. No wonder; for she has a strong child, more than a year old, dragging at her bosom . . . And yet the husband . . . may be seen, at least every evening, with a pipe in his mouth, and fetching, or sending one of the children to fetch, a mug of beer from the public house.

'There is another matter worth consideration. Without wishing to cry out against a cup of tea for those who can afford it, *can* it properly be afforded where people run short of nourishing food?'[1]

Not much more acceptable to southern readers was the idea of oatmeal, which she tried to sell with the following: 'A lady desired her servant, among other errands, to bring in 3 lb. of Scotch oatmeal. "Scotch oatmeal!" exclaimed the girl with astonishment. "Do *you* use *that*? Why it is what they give the poor folks in the union work house." "Yes," replied the lady, "and it is what the Queen gives her children." '[2]

Previous writers had taken a working knowledge of cookery for granted (except Miss Acton, who wrote *Modern Cookery* in the interval between the appearance of Mrs Hewlett's two cookery books): the latter, however, assumed total ignorance, and in both books devoted much of her space to explaining basic principles and processes; she was also unusually conscientious about giving exact quantities, and sometimes (though not always) began her instructions with lists of ingredients. Although the usefulness of this now seems obvious, it was not so then: instead of presenting recipes as formulae, writers had given them as essays consisting only of the method, not introducing ingredients until they occurred, which meant that if cooks did not read them carefully all the way through before starting they might not realize that they lacked a vital component until too late.

The recipes in *Cottage Cookery* (which were limited in number because of her detailed directions and the modest size of the book) were perhaps too basic to be of interest to modern readers: her book for the middle classes, *The Housekeeper's Guide* (already quoted on the subject of preservation of food), on the other hand, is one of the richest sources available of unpretentious traditional country dishes – e.g. fried lampreys, stuffed eels, lambs' rumps and ears (once considered a delicacy), haggis, jugged hare, rice pancakes; there was also an unusually large selection of farmhouse-type cakes and home-made wines. Though she did not stint on her ingredients, economy was again stressed – one of her particular points in this context being that by avoiding waste, mistresses could considerably alleviate lower-class hardship with charitable soup and other items at minimal expense. This tone was set in her opening paragraph: 'Integrity is the first moral virtue, benevolence the second, and prudence the third . . .'[3] Twenty years later, Mrs Beeton began her book: '*As with the Commander of an Army*, or the leader of any enterprise, so it is with the mistress of a house . . . Early Rising is one of the most Essential Qualities which enter into good household management. . . . Cleanliness *is also indispensable to Health*, and must be studied both in regard to the person and the house, and all that it contains. . . . *Frugality and Economy are Home Virtues*, without which no household can prosper.'[4]

The only positive facts which can be gleaned about Mrs Hewlett's life are that in 1823 'domestic afflictions of a most trying nature'[5] had interrupted her work for several years – possibly the death of her husband the Rev. J. P. Hewlett – and that in 1825 she had a 'flourishing'[6] brood of children and was living in Oxford; that at some time she lived further north, however, is indicated by her recommendation of oatmeal and the cake recipes in the *Guide*, which would have been suitable for high tea. Her emphasis on economy did not necessarily reflect her own situation; if, however, she was left with a large family to support, one may reasonably suppose that at least part of her motive for writing was money. Her output was fairly steady until around 1840, after which it became more fitful; her last title was dated 1859.

It has been suggested that Eliza Acton had a daughter (Gabrielle of Gabrielle's Pudding perhaps?) whom she may have maintained or for whom she loved to provide; otherwise, as a spinster disappointed in love, she can be assumed to have written purely from ambition and the desire for fulfilment through a career. She was the daughter of a brewer, John Acton, who moved soon after she was born from Sussex to Suffolk, where she spent her childhood. At some point, she was sent to France, allegedly because she was delicate: the idea has been put forward that in reality it was because she was pregnant, the ensuing daughter being brought up by her sister[7], but her later illness and general concern for health favours the former claim, besides the pregnancy anticipates rather than follows from the next known incident in her life, which was that she became engaged to a French army officer in Paris; the marriage, however, did not take place. In 1826, when she was twenty-seven, she published a volume of poems by subscription in Ipswich, possibly because of adverse criticism, she did not follow it up for nearly a decade, during which her activities are a complete blank, but 1835–6 a few more of her poems appeared in a local annual, *The Sudbury Pocket Book*, and the next year another in a further local publication, *Fulcher's Sudbury Journal*. By this time (she was now nearly forty), she had moved to Tunbridge Wells to look after her mother – her residence there being established by the fact that when Queen Adelaide, widow of William IV, visited the town, she presented her with a suitably complimentary poem. This probably encouraged her to take her work to the publisher Thomas Longman, who rejected it with the suggestion that she should write a cookery book instead – a sop which even now an aspiring poet might well regard as a mere insult but which he certainly meant seriously insofar as that, aware of the potential of the subject of food, Longman's were trying to extend their list in this direction (they were one of the publishers of *The Housekeeper's Guide*, and also brought out Hassall and Hayward's books). Her work took her over seven years to complete – nearly twice as long as Mrs Beeton's: although, as the product of an unknown woman, it was not acclaimed with the almost ridiculous enthusiasm of Soyer's books, it brought her due recognition: within a few years she had become cookery correspondent to the most prestigious woman's magazine of the day, *The Ladies' Companion* (in which, exceptionally, she signed her articles), a contributor to *Household Words* (where, because of Dickens' stricter policy on anonymity, she did not) – and found herself plagiarized, which although so common among cookery writers up to this time that one would expect her to have taken it for granted, greatly agitated her. Fortunately for her peace of mind, *Household Management*, which can almost be regarded as the popular version of her work, was not published, at least in volume form, until after her death. Either because she was already unwell or tended to hypochondria (which, given her situation and evidently far from placid temperament, seems quite likely), or because of her ageing mother's condition, health was clearly a matter of major concern to her even while she was writing her book, in which she referred, not merely often but constantly, to the wholesomeness and digestibility of dishes: in the '50s, she certainly suffered increasingly, probably from cancer, and although one gathers from a number of her remarks that she had a third work in progress, the only book besides *Modern Cookery* which she succeeded in finishing was *The English Bread Book*, which appeared in 1857, two years before she died.

Modern Cookery not only established her in culinary terms but, though she herself probably never realized it, was the ideal outlet for her literary talent. Realizing, like Mrs Hewlett, that inexperienced readers needed exhaustive, precise directions, she described the method for each dish so conscientiously, and with such gastronomic sensitivity, that her book was as much a work of art on food as it was functional: every preparation, even the plainest, sounded special simply because of her care. The effect was enhanced by her periodic sharp comments – on stewed fruit, station coffee, British bread, and also (despite her love of puddings) cakes, which she condemned in almost the same terms as the recent NACNE report: 'We have inserted here but a comparatively limited number of receipts for these "sweet poisons," as they have been emphatically called, and we would willingly have diminished still further even the space which has been allotted to them, that we might have had room in their stead for others of a more really useful character; but . . . we will . . . content ourselves with remarking, that more illness is caused by habitual indulgence in the richer and heavier kinds of cakes than would easily be credited by persons who

A GOOD MUTTON PIE

Lay a half-paste of short or puff crust round a buttered dish; take the whole or part of a loin of mutton, strip off the fat entirely, and raise the flesh clear from the bones without dividing it, then slice it into cutlets of equal thickness, season them well with salt and papper, or cayenne, and strew between the layers some finely-minced herbs mixed with two or three eschalots, when the flavour of these last is liked; or omit them, and roll quite thin some good forcemeat (which can be flavoured with a little minced eschalot at pleasure), and lay it between the cutlets: two or three mutton kidneys intermingled with the meat will greatly enrich the gravy; pour in a little cold water, roll the cover half an inch thick, or more should the crust be short, as it will not rise like puff paste, close the pie very securely, trim the edges even with the dish, ornament the pie according to taste, make a hole in the centre, and bake it from an hour and a half to a couple of hours. The proportions of paste and meat may be ascertained by consulting the last receipt. Gravy made with part of the bones, quite cleared from fat, and left to become cold, may be used to fill the pie instead of water.

*   *   *   *   *

For 4–6:   2lb (900g) lean lamb or mutton
              4 lambs' kidneys
              ¼ pint (125ml) water or a little less is all that is
                  needed to moisten the pie; an alternative is a small
                  glass of red wine.
              garlic and/or mushrooms can be added.

Bake at the bottom of the oven at 180°C. 350°F, gas mark 4 for 1½ hours. Lay a sheet of cooking foil over the pastry if it becomes too brown.

A quickly made, easy-to-handle flaky pastry recipe, based on Eliza Acton's own suggestion, is as follows:
              4oz (100g) plain white flour, plus an extra 2oz (50g)
                  and a little for dusting
              4oz (100g) wholemeal or granary flour
              ½ pint (250ml) double cream
              4oz (100g) chilled butter, chopped into thin slices
                  pinch salt

Mix the flours and salt, keeping the extra 2oz (50g) of white flour aside; add the cream and form quickly into dough. Work in as much of the extra flour as is absorbed (the dough should be as dry as possible). Roll out and proceed as usual for puff pastry.

from *Modern Cookery* Eliza Acton (Longman, 1859 ed., page 355)

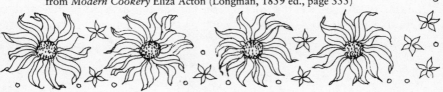

have given no attention to the subject.'[8] (Consistently with this, although in fact she gave quite a number of recipes, most of them were for small, lightish cakes and biscuits, among which were half a dozen for gingerbread, including coconut gingerbread and her well known 'Acton' gingerbread, are notable.)

It is clear from the number of foreign recipes (other than French) which she published that, like most people genuinely interested in food, she loved experimenting. In her book, she devoted half a chapter to curries and a whole one to 'Jewish and Foreign Cookery', in which, among other dishes, were Jewish smoked beef, chorissa with rice, Indian, Syrian, and Turkish pilaffs, Risotto à la Milanaise, and Saltzburger Nockerl; further such items, e.g. the Portuguese 'Aroce Doce', a selection of German puddings and pudding sauces, and West Indian 'Mandram' (cucumber dressed with onion, lemon, and wine) were scattered throughout the main chapters. Curries had long since been popularized among the higher classes by East India Company employees (and later received another boost as a result of the development of the Indian tea trade), but virtually all the rest were novelties in this country. In addition, she seems to have made a point of including as many foreign recipes as she could collect in her magazine articles, where, among those not in the book, were 'Sil Salad', a Swedish dish based on beef and herrings, a vegetarian curry (intended for Lent), 'Reis-content', a cinnamon-flavoured German chocolate pudding, 'The Ohio Way of Baking Apples', and apple strudel; in the same spirit, she printed a series of extracts from an early eighteenth-century cookery manuscript, among which were directions for furmity, almond posset, cheese-curd bread (a cross between bread and cheesecake), and 'Lord Howard's Bouillon de Santé'.

According to both contemporaries and a random survey, the majority of earlier books had been compiled simply by copying existing recipes, authors making no attempt to test them either themselves or via their cooks. Mrs Hewlett's thoroughness and precision can be taken as proof that her recipes were tested very possibly, given her general outlook, by her personally; similarly, the way in which Mrs Beeton presented her recipes, plus the fact that she made slight alterations to many of them (and their reliability) leave no doubt that they were tested and strongly suggest that she tried them out herself (albeit with extensive assistance from her cook). Miss Acton said in her Preface, '. . . our receipts . . . with a few trifling exceptions which are scrupulously specified, are confined to such as may be *perfectly depended on*, from having been proved beneath our own roof and under our own personal inspection'[9] – the truth of which, again, is shown by the quality of her directions. Both this and other remarks in her book, however, such as 'We have not been able to have it

tried'[10] and 'We had it tested with the best end of a fine *neck* of veal'[11]
imply that she herself did not do the cooking. One might argue that she
used this phraseology merely for the sake of appearances, but when one
comes to the *Bread Book* one realizes that, as a sick woman, she would
almost certainly not have been physically capable of handling the quantities sometimes given, e.g. 3 pecks, or roughly 21 lb. or 9 ½ kg. flour
(which was supposed to be enough for bread for one family for a week):
sadly, therefore, one is obliged to conclude that the greatest woman
cookery writer of the century, perhaps ever, did not actually make the
dishes she publicized but wrote merely from observation and reportage.

Isabella Beeton was even less likely as a candidate in the field than an
aspiring poet, and certainly very different from the middle-aged, somewhat
forbidding housekeeper one might imagine, since she was twenty-one
when she started writing her book, had housekept for only a few months,
and certainly then and probably never had any personal ambition beyond
the conventional wish to do her duty as a wife; her own family situation,
however, had been bizarre and her capabilities sharpened by a first-rate
German rather than the usual type of English education. Her mother,
having been left a widow pregnant and with two younger children when
Isabella was four, remarried a widower also with four children, who, as
clerk of the Epsom racecourse, had the use of the racecourse grandstand:
as his house proved too small for eight children, they, plus others as they
arrived (with perhaps not such enviable fecundity, the couple went on to
produce thirteen more) were sent to live there under the supervision of
Isabella's grandmother, with Isabella, as the eldest girl, as second in
command – the grandstand at that time being a four-square classical
structure with a huge, columned entrance hall, curving stone staircase, and
saloon decorated for Queen Victoria with satin wallpaper; the children's
quarters were presumably the committee rooms, which were less imposing
but nevertheless hardly very homely. The stepfather prospered: eventually
he became sufficiently wealthy to set up his family in typical nouveau-riche
style in a country house near Croydon; meanwhile, anxious to ensure that
his daughters were turned into properly brought up young ladies, he sent
Isabella at the age of about thirteen to a boarding school in Islington. For
unspecified reasons but probably partly because her intelligence caused her
to rebel at its inadequacy, she was taken away after a short time and sent
instead to a school with a high academic reputation in Heidelberg, where
she clearly received an excellent intellectual training and, since her
headmistress commented on her culinary interest, was apparently taught
cooking (the instruction, however, was certainly of a limited nature,
possibly to making cakes and puddings only, which in Germany were
often made by the mistress of the house herself).

Her stepfather, who seems to have been especially fond of her, naturally hoped that she would make a good marriage – with the more justification as she was extremely good-looking – and was greatly upset when she fell in love with and, despite his disapproval, married a City tavern-keeper's son, Samuel Beeton – who, however, had not opted for his father's occupation but set himself up as a publisher and already launched two innovatory magazines, the *Englishwoman's Domestic Magazine*, and (just before the marriage took place) the *Boy's Own Magazine*. Beeton, who was quite as remarkable and deserving of memory as she, was a discreet but firm believer in the equality of women and in equality of education and in the *Domestic Magazine* aimed to broaden his readers' minds by such means as avant-garde (rather than romantic) fiction and essay competitions; as its title suggests, however, he also set out to respond to current feeling by remedying their ignorance in the domestic and culinary field, and accordingly included a cookery column. No sooner was Isabella established as his wife than the cookery contributor dropped out: the column remained in abeyance for six months, by the end of which he had persuaded her to write it, no doubt arguing that to do so was not only a wifely service to him but to all the other husbands who would benefit. She began it, having also planned the book, which she intended as a compilation of her articles, just before her first baby was due: probably she would not have thrown herself into writing *Household Management* so completely if her son had lived, but he died a few months later, to which her reaction seems to have been to deaden her grief through work – in which sense the book can be regarded as the baby's memorial.

By the time it was finished she was firmly established as her husband's chief adviser and editress, following up her column with dressmaking and fashion; she became fashion editor on her husband's next publication for women, *The Queen* (the only one which, as *Harpers & Queen*, still survives today) and co-founded a third, *The Young Englishwoman*. Her life, however, overshadowed from the outset by births and deaths, continued to be so: a second son died in infancy, and, although she had two more, both of whom survived, she herself succumbed to puerperal (childbed) fever at the age of twenty-eight.

As is suggested in Miss Acton's case by the fact that she did not cook for herself, neither the latter nor Isabella invented, or claimed to invent, many recipes: Eliza identified a few dozen out of a total of around 1,500 as her own, and Isabella only one – 'Useful Soup for Benevolent Purposes'. Both endeavoured to collect them from friends and acquaintances, Miss Acton considerably the more successfully: Isabella had originally hoped to acquire hers through the readership of the *Domestic Magazine*, but, although invitations to contribute were published over several years and

2,000 sent in, she only used about a third – the rest presumably either not working or being repetitive (to judge from those she did include, most, as with the manuscripts mentioned earlier, were for puddings and sweets). She made up the balance from published sources, principally *Modern Cookery*, from which, not counting a large number probably more freely adapted, she took over 150 – which, presumably because of Eliza's protests against plagiarism, she was careful to appropriate by making insignificant changes to the ingredients. This, however, was by no means the extent of her debt to the latter, who supplied her with so much general information that, leaving aside whatever she may have learnt at school, one can fairly say that she taught her to cook; it was also almost certainly Eliza's work which gave her the idea which effectually made *Management* the first modern cookery book. Miss Acton, unlike Mrs Hewlett, did not list ingredients at the beginning of recipes, but put summaries, which included ingredients, quantities, and cooking times, at the end – not invariably, and never in her articles, presumably because of space, but much more systematically than the former; though not laid out as lists, those in the *Bread Book* were indented, which helped to catch the eye. Isabella introduced the now standardized formula for laying out recipes, with amounts and ingredients at the top, followed by the method and cooking time; she also gave number of servings, costs, and seasonability. The value of this was not immediately recognized, but it transformed cookery writing not only because it enabled cooks to see what was needed at a glance, but forced writers to give precise details.

The other outstanding feature of her work, which, although not of the same significance, is at least as historically interesting today and (if only because it was the mistress who bought the book) unquestionably more influential in terms of immediate sales, was the part of it devoted to the latter. There was nothing unusual in cookery books containing information about housekeeping in general – Isabella, rather like Mrs Hewlett in *Cottage Comforts*, aiming to cover everything a wife might need to know: the sections on etiquette and her general behaviour, however, which added up to a guide on how to be a lady, were unique, not in concept but concision and practicality. A magazine founded a few years after the *Englishwoman's Domestic Magazine* and, although much more conventional, its rival, ran a series of diverting but rambling, often silly, and far from comprehensive articles on the subject, or women could refer to a ponderous volume by a Mrs Sarah Ellis: in *Management*, in contrast, a section of only a few pages gave not only a check-list of the formalities of dinner- and other kinds of party-giving, card-leaving, and call-paying (the accepted way of maintaining a social circle and thus having guests to invite) but advice on the finer points of how to dress, make conversation, and (most difficult of all) leave gracefully: '*After luncheon, morning calls and visits* may be made and received [the word 'morning' was used here in its older sense, which referred to the time before dinner rather than lunch – lunch not yet being a recognized meal]. . . . These visits should be short, a stay of from fifteen to twenty minutes being quite sufficient. A lady paying a visit may remove her boa or neckerchief, but neither shawl nor bonnet.

'When other visitors are announced, it is well to retire as soon as possible, taking care to let it appear that their arrival is not the cause. When they are quietly seated, and the bustle of their entrance is over, rise from your chair, taking a kind leave of your hostess, and bowing politely to the guests. Should you call at an inconvenient time, not having ascertained the luncheon hour, or from any other inadvertence, retire as soon as possible, without, however, showing that you feel yourself an intruder. . . .

'In all these visits, if your acquaintance or friends be not at home, a card should be left. If in a carriage, the servant will answer your inquiry and receive your card; if paying your visits on foot, give your card to the servant in the hall, but leave to go in and rest should on no account be asked. The form of words, "Not at home," may be understood in different senses; but the only courteous way is to receive them as being perfectly true. . . .'[12]

Isabella's opposite number on the *Domestic Magazine's* competitor, *The Ladies' Treasury* – who, since a journalist with the same style and pseudonym wrote for *The Queen*, was apparently afterwards poached by the Beetons – contributed under the name 'Aunt Deborah' and maintained her role by formulating her articles as letters to her newly married (and therefore in culinary terms supposedly completely ignorant) niece: thus she started by taking the latter through the three courses of a simple dinner, dealing with fish in her first piece, mutton (significantly) in her second, and puddings in her third; subsequently, her themes were chosen according to season, e.g. Preserving in June and oyster cookery in August (at that time, the oyster season was taken as beginning on 5 August). Whoever she was (one presumes it was a she) she worked hard to make her articles readable: 'So you wish to set before your husband and a few friends, a *boiled Leg of Mutton*, so cooked as to remove the prejudice he has conceived against that dish, in consequence of his having, while at . . . school, had to sit down day after day for three years, to a plateful of sodden, half-raw, insipid cuttings, "dabs," as he classically terms them, of the joint aforesaid. . . . As to cooking [it], it is thought to be the easiest thing in the whole of gastronomy. Hence a young lady who, like yourself, entered the marriage state without much experience of housekeeping, fixed

MUTTON SAUSAGES

... very choice. Chop a pound of raw or underdone mutton (the middle of the leg is best), chop it fine, and season with pepper, salt, and beaten mace. Chop also half a pound of beef suet, two anchovies, a dozen oysters, a quarter of a pound of grated bread, and a boiled onion. Mix the whole with some oyster liquor, and the whites and yolks of two eggs well beaten. Form into lengths or cakes and fry them.

*   *   *   *   *

This makes 10–12 cakes.

If no oysters are available, a couple of extra anchovies can be used instead. The suet can be partly or completely omitted.

As eggs at that time tended to be small, use sizes 4 or 5, or have a couple of ounces of extra breadcrumbs to hand in case the mixture is too moist to keep its shape. The cakes can be treated exactly like beefburgers, i.e. grilled or baked as well as fried, and served in buns, which makes them ideal for barbecues.

from *Ladies' Treasury*, 'Aunt Deborah' (Volume 2, 1858, page 154)

upon this plain and simple dish as one in preparing which she was not likely to err. But having had three or four legs of mutton in succession, roasted and boiled, and boiled and roasted, her domestic ventured to suggest that it might be as well to introduce some change. "Well, Mary," said the wife, "I have thought so too, and so I think we'll have a *leg of beef next.*" '13

Though she did not give lists or summaries, her instructions were on the whole clear and exact; she was also very conscientious about giving practical details such as how to choose and keep fish and meat, which sort of pans to use for pickling and preserving, and so on. Though Soyer's (rather than Eliza Acton's) influence was perceptible, most of her recipes, as was consistent with her plan, were fairly simple; among the most attractive were those for oysters, which included scalloped, stewed, pickled, patties, and mutton and oyster sausages, there were also pleasantly imaginative suggestions for salad (spoiled by the amount of vinegar she recommended for dressing) and a sensibly scaled-down version of Christmas pie.

Isabella's method of laying out recipes represented one turning-point in the development of cookery writing; another was the introduction of short, specialized books as opposed to one comprehensive one. Not counting one-off works on confectionery, bread, and other topics, or the publication of *Household Management* in parts (which, as each part dealt with a particular subject, was a near equivalent to a number of specific books), the first exploitation of this idea was a series of a total of seventeen books by a young woman called Georgiana Hill. She started by writing a general cookery book, *The Cook's Own Book*, which appeared just before the volume version of *Management*; it was not especially successful, but a couple of years later she followed it up with a book on puddings, *Everybody's Pudding Book*, which did well enough for her to go on to produce, first a book on cooking apples, then *The Breakfast Book*, then, as a series under the title of 'How to Cook . . . in a Hundred Different Ways' (to which *How to Cook Apples* also belonged) books on fish, rabbits, eggs, and potatoes (all 1866) then soups, game, onions (surprisingly) and preserves (all 1867) and finally (1868–70) cakes, vegetables, stews, sweet and savoury puddings, salads, and pickles.

Only the *Pudding* and *Breakfast* books and a couple of the Manuals are now available, but from these it is clear, as the titles and her speed of production suggest, that her chief interest – apart from making money (presumably she had a commission) – was in giving housewives and hostesses ideas. In its way, this was fair enough, indeed, in view of the average mistress's limited scope, much needed; unfortunately, her instructions were so perfunctory that the books were of little further use. It seems unlikely that Ms Hill had ever entered a kitchen, for observation or any other purpose: these, for example, were her directions for making mayonnaise (in their entirety): 'Beat together the yolks of two raw eggs, a little vinegar, salt, and pepper; gradually add a sufficiency of fresh olive oil, and continue beating the whole until a smooth cream is formed. This sauce may be made to look green by adding a small quantity of spinach juice.'[14] (Anyone who doubts the inadequacy of this is challenged to follow it.) After this, she desisted from writing for twenty years; then, in the '90s, she published a history of fashion and a two-volume account of *Women in English Life* which was well researched, sharply written, and altogether in a different class; from its slant and tone, one is inclined to wonder whether she became a suffragette.

Both Ude and Soyer were introduced into the culinary world by members of their families, Ude by his father and Soyer by an elder brother, who was also instrumental in his emigration to England. Ude was the son of an assistant chef in Louis XVI's kitchen, and had been partly trained by his father when he suddenly had second thoughts about his career and ran away; besides acting, he tried working for a jeweller, engraver, printer, haberdasher, as a travelling salesman, stockbroker, and inspector of gambling houses before returning to his original profession. His most distinguished employer in France was Mme Letitia Bonaparte, from whom, however, 'some difference of opinion . . . in matters arithmetical'[15] caused him hastily to depart and embark for England. He then spent the remarkably long period of twenty years with the Earl of Sefton, who seems to have bribed him to stay throughout his lifetime by promising to leave him a pension (which he did); he was also employed by the Duke of York before going to Crockford's, where he remained until he retired around 1840. He was an extremely amusing man, his theatrical talent apparently consisting in a bent for mimicry, and very kind to the youthful Soyer; his hot temper and miserliness, however, were notorious. The story goes that before making a proposal of marriage, he listed all the expenses it would entail, including the amount he planned to grant his wife as an allowance; then, satisfied with the outcome of his calculations, he set about embedding his proposal in an almond cake (pâte d'amande). Unfortunately, he enclosed the wrong piece of paper, so that the lady received, not a romantic request for her hand, but the statement of her allowance – to which she very appropriately replied that it was not enough. (It seems that the marriage took place nevertheless.)

Alexis Soyer's parents were shopkeepers in Meaux near Paris; since as a boy he had a good singing voice and, as it happened, an uncle who was a

priest at Meaux Cathedral, he was sent to the school attached to the
cathedral as chorister (i.e. in effect, scholar) in preparation for going into
the Church. He so hated school life and the thought of becoming a priest,
however, that, when his parents were adamant about not allowing him to
throw away his opportunities by leaving, he determined to get himself
expelled: this turned out to be comparatively difficult, and by the time he
had succeeded, which he did by raising a false fire alarm, he had been at
the school several years, and, albeit in spite of himself, received a very
sound classical education. At least inasmuch as that it meant that he had a
trained mind, this probably helped him to master English, and certainly
explains his ability to write what was in some ways his most interesting
book; he did not take advantage of his academic training when it came to
choosing an alternative career, which, as he was then almost old enough
to take up an apprenticeship, was his next problem. It seems that he settled
on cooking, not because it especially attracted him, but merely because his
brother was a chef – and probably also because it meant going to Paris
rather than staying on at home with his parents, whom one can imagine
were extremely disappointed and displeased with him (so far as is known,
they had nothing more to do with him – but it may be simply that any
correspondence between them is lost).

For the next four years he served an apprenticeship at one of the top
Paris restaurants of the day, Grignon's, after which he was employed at
another, equally prestigious, Douix's, where he made such an impression
that he was promoted to head chef within a matter of months. By then he
was seventeen, and as a young man about Paris had already become
addicted to the theatre; over the next year or so, as one might expect, he
also became interested in girls, with the result that he made one of them
pregnant – which, as his secretaries and subsequently biographers Volant
and Warren put it, was 'rather troublesome to him'[16], and may well have
been one of his considerations in deciding to come to England (which
reminds one of Ude, and makes one wonder how many other chefs came
to this country for reasons of expediency).

It was not the only factor in his decision, however, since at this point his
career was disrupted by his involuntary part in the 1830 July Revolution.
He was temporarily working for the Foreign Minister when the revolution-
aries broke into the Ministry kitchens and shot two of the chefs: possibly
to escape the pressure of the crowd, he jumped on to a table, and then,
perhaps realizing that he had become a prime target, began singing the
national anthem, the *Marseillaise* – which was associated with the original
French Revolution. Evidently taking this as a sign of support, the rebels,
instead of shooting him, seized and carried him through the streets as their
hero. Either as a direct or indirect consequence of this, he was sacked from

the restaurant soon afterwards, which not only left him jobless and (assuming that he had no savings) almost penniless, but afraid that he had no further prospects in Paris. Since his brother was already in London working for the Duke of Cambridge, and could apparently guarantee him employment, joining him no doubt seemed the most practical course to take.

In England, after an initial job at Cambridge's, he went for short periods, presumably as an assistant chef, to the Duke of Sutherland and the Marquis of Waterford, then spent several years with a Mr Lloyd of Aston Hall, Shropshire; he then became chef to the Marquis of Ailsa, soon after which he was appointed to the Reform, where he stayed for the next thirteen years. During this period, his first achievement outside his normal duties as chef was to design and equip the club kitchens, which he had the opportunity to do because the club, which had only recently been formed, had commissioned new premises; otherwise, for the earlier part of his time there, his energies seem to have been absorbed by cooking and marriage and its aftermath. Subsequently, however, he went through an intensely creative phase, designing not only the Magic Stove and at least two conventional cooking ranges (his gas and army stoves came later), but a long list of minor items ranging from a coffee pot to a pair of carving scissors called the 'Tendon Separator'; he also invented a total of five bottled sauces, a beef extract named 'Ozmazone', and 'Soyer's Nectar', drink of raspberry, apple, quince, and lemon juice, laced (primarily for preservative purposes) with wine and brandy: this was one of the most successful of all his products, partly because it became popular as a cure for hangovers. In addition, he wrote his ballet, the *Regenerator*, *Modern Housewife*, and a pamphlet of recipes for feeding the poor, the *Poor Man's Regenerator*, which was a spin-off from his contribution during the Irish famine, when he gave demonstrations of making soup suitable for soup kitchens and himself became involved in running them, opening one in Leicester Square and another, at government request, in Dublin. The famine clearly made a deep impression on him: whereas until that time, if only because of the nature of his job, his interest had been in catering for the very rich (in which part of his success was due to his sense of drama), thereafter he became increasingly concerned with the problems of the sick and undernourished.

By this time, however, he had been afflicted by the misfortune which governed his needs and outlook for the rest of his life, and, in that he would otherwise certainly not have felt free, nor probably have wished, to go to the Crimea, shortened it. Not long after taking up his post at the Reform, which (since it meant that he no longer had to live in) enabled him to set up an independent household, either his conscience was stirred

Alexis Soyer demonstrating the use of a frying-pan (*Culinary Campaign*)

by the thought of the girl with his baby or his mind turned to someone else in Paris: deciding (here again, one is reminded of Ude) that a suitably romantic way of re-establishing contact would be to send his portrait, he visited an artist to commission one – the artist he chose being the stepfather of his future wife, Emma. It seems to have been a case of love at first sight; because of the stepfather's disapproval, Ude gave away the bride. The marriage was in several respects parallel to the Beetons', since besides parental opposition was the fact that Emma too, with every possible encouragement from Soyer, worked in a professional capacity throughout – and that she died, totally unexpectedly, in childbirth; in this instance, the baby, who was premature, also died. Like Isabella, Soyer's reaction seems to have been to take refuge in work: his disorientation was also expressed in his affected style of dress, which, from having been merely rather more colourful than sober English fashion dictated, became distinctly eccentric: '. . . he takes off one of his dress boots and shakes it, and we hear money rattle inside the heel (one of his whims). His hat, too, was built on one side, so that, whichever way worn, it would be slightly coquettish, or, as he used to call it, "*à la* zugzug," meaning zigzag. We could not also but notice the *outré* cut of his clothes; the vest gold-braided, and made to fold half a dozen fashions . . .'.[17]

A desire to attract attention and restlessness following his bereavement were certainly part of the reason for his eventual resignation from the club, which ostensibly was over such a trivial issue that even at the time it was recognized as only an excuse. His first initiative on leaving was to draw up the proposal for his college, the idea of which was perhaps a contributory reason for his departure; then came his brief spell as restaurateur. It was just at this particularly public point in his life that, after twenty-one years' silence, his son, now of age, came to England to visit him: certainly the more because of his situation (one can only speculate on how he would have felt if Emma had lived), he was clearly delighted, notwithstanding the social threat the young man represented: he introduced him as his nephew in this country, which seems to have passed without comment, but later returned his visit and acknowledged his true identity in Paris, whereupon, having already been given his father's Christian name, Alexis junior also took his surname.

After the closure of his restaurant, he spent a considerable amount of time on charity work and published his least and most successful books, *The Pantropheon* and the *Shilling Cookery*. The former was a history of food based on the classics, and, although less readable than his other works, chiefly because he did not distance himself sufficiently from his sources to write with his usual fluency, was notable as the first attempt of its kind and the forerunner of a family of gastonomic dictionaries which appeared later in the century.

The *Shilling Cookery*, his book for the lower classes, preceded by a year and (since he paid his own expenses) presumably financed, his trip to the Crimea. This was undertaken on a sudden but sound, albeit fatal impulse after reading about the conditions prevailing among the troops and in the hospitals there in *The Times*. He described his experiences in his last publication, *Soyer's Culinary Campaign*, from which it is clear that, as in other cases, the extremities of war, by giving him a sharp, immediate *raison d'être*, restored his confidence and sense of identity: had he survived, he might henceforth have been a much happier man. He was seriously ill in the East (as also was Florence Nightingale) and, although he recovered temporarily, died soon after returning to England.

Such a thing was of course unthinkable at the time – perhaps, in relation to chefs, still is – but one feels that he should have been given a knighthood, if not for his services to the army, then for his contribution to cooking generally.

Charles Elmé Francatelli, who succeeded Ude at Crockford's, and also followed Soyer to the Reform (though not immediately), came from a family of Italian immigrants; he was born in London, trained in Paris under Carême, and first made his reputation working for Lord Chesterfield. He left Crockford's to become head chef to the Queen, but was dismissed after two years because he lost his temper and hit a kitchenmaid; thereafter, he went to the Coventry House Club before retiring for a period with 'a handsome competence'[18]. He returned to employment as chef at the St James's Hotel (later the Berkeley) and ended his career at the Freemason's Tavern. According to Hayward, purely as a chef his talent was greater than Soyer's: Hayward seems to have had a grudge against the latter, perhaps for the very reason of his success, but his judgement is borne out by Francatelli's books, in particular *The Housekeeper's Guide*, his work for the middle classes, which, both in terms of recipes and planning meals, is much more modern and sophisticated than *Modern Housewife* – though, to be fair, it was written a decade later and clearly aimed at a more up-market readership. As a writer, he was no more than competent, with none of Soyer's individuality; as if he had taken his cue from Isabella, however (but in fact almost certainly because of the especial importance of precision in cake-making and confectionery), he did give separate lists of ingredients for the cake and biscuit recipes in the *Guide* (though not for others) and consistently in *The Royal English and Foreign Confectioner*.

Soyer, in the course of conversation with a doctor in Istanbul, said: 'Since I have turned my attention to it, I am more and more fortified in the opinion which I have expressed before several medical boards, that a doctor, to be well qualified, should have some knowledge of the art of cookery, and this he ought to acquire in the first stage of his medical education.'[19] It is perhaps not surprising, in view of the obvious importance of food to health and increasing knowledge of and interest in nutrition, that, of upwards of seventy other authors of cookery books in the first two thirds of the century (who, under the pseudonym of 'Lady Maria Clutterbuck', included Dickens's wife), several should have been doctors. One was William Kitchener, whose father was a coal-heaver turned merchant who became sufficiently prosperous to send his son to Eton; after Eton, he qualified as a doctor in Glasgow, but, having no financial need to practise, settled down to a gentlemanly life of enjoying music, experimenting with optics and recipes, entertaining a circle of friends to lunches which became celebrated, and writing a string of books on subjects ranging from telescopes to how to prolong life. His cookery book, *The Cook's Oracle*, was enormously successful, and deservedly so, since it combined the most practical instructions to date with acerbic wit. One of his aphorisms was: ' – Those who say, 'Tis no matter what we eat or drink – may as well say, 'Tis no matter whether we eat or drink.'[20] His comments

Dessert dishes by Francatelli
(from top left: Charlotte – La Parisienne,
Meringue on a Stand, Swan à la Chantilly)
(*The Royal English and Foreign Confectioner*)

on existing cookery books were: '. . . except in the Preface, they are "Like in all else as one Egg to another."

'"*Ab uno disce omnes*;" cutting and pasting have been much oftener employed than the Pen and Ink. . . . The strange, and unaccountable, and uselessly extravagant farragos, and heterogenous compositions, which fill their pages, are combinations no national being would ever think of either dressing or eating.'[21]

This description admirably fitted the cookery section of another success-ful book by a doctor, or rather surgeon, John Henry Walsh, alias 'Stonehenge', who practised medicine for twenty years before abandoning it in favour of writing and indulging in his overriding love of sport, which encompassed hunting, shooting, coursing and breeding greyhounds, and tennis: he was a co-founder of the National Coursing Club and the All-England Tennis Club (he lived near Wimbledon), and an expert on guns. His books included *The Greyhound: on the Art of Breeding, Rearing, and Training Greyhounds*, the *Manual of British Rural Sports*, *The Horse in the Stable and in the Field*, and *Dogs of the British Islands*; he also became editor of *The Field* and founded the *Coursing Calendar*. Initially, he too was unfortunate in his wives, since not one but two died, presumably as a result of pregnancy, within nine months of marriage; a third, however, survived motherhood and almost certainly assembled the 'Committee of Ladies' who supplied the recipes for his *Manual of Domestic Economy*. This was a lengthy guide to all aspects of estate and household manage-ment, in which he included cookery for the sake of completeness but did not write about it himself because, except with regard to Liebig's principles about nutrient values, he did not claim any knowledge of it (probably, he had studied Liebig either in the course of his medical career, or, as was perhaps more likely, in connection with sporting and agricultural pursuits). Since the work as a whole was an immediate success, an enlarged edition was brought out in parts, the second of which was devoted to cooking: this in turn was developed into a separate book, *The English Cookery Book* – which, happily for the interests of cookery, did not share the *Manual*'s popularity but is notable as an illustration of the average mistress's (and cook's) ignorance. Ingenuously, Walsh said: '[It has] been compiled with the assistance of several ladies who kindly took an interest in the subject and who, being at the head of well-conducted establishments . . . may be expected to be good authorities on the value of the receipts they have furnished. A great many of these are from their own family scrap-books, and almost all have had an actual trial; so that they may be safely recommended for use in our English kitchens.'[22] He can at least be given credit for acknowledging the need for trial; he also took the extra precaution of having the book checked by an allegedly experienced cook.

The result was a collection of 'strange ... and uselessly extravagant farragos' indeed: one example was a recipe for Bath buns which called for 1 lb. of butter to ½ lb. of flour, a glass of wine, and six eggs, which could have only ended up as a liquid mess on the bottom of the oven. The *Manual* ran to six editions, but the cookery book on its own only two, the second of which did not appear until the '80s, and then in heavily revised form.

9. Meals and Entertaining: From Porridge to Poularde à la Nelson

The time of dinner, the main meal of the day, had originally been determined by daylight hours – the undesirability of cooking and washing-up by candle-light being obvious. In Jane Austen's day, it had been at about 4 p.m.; by Mrs Beeton's, gas lighting and/or working customs had pushed it back to between 5 and 6 among the lower and middle classes (the Beetons dined at 5.30, the Dickenses at 6); in upper-class circles, however, where lateness had long been fashionable, it was between 8 and 9 (Queen Victoria was served at 8.45). As today, some sections of the population, who included children, domestic servants, many living-in agricultural labourers, and the inmates of workhouses, dined in the middle of the day – in which case, the next meal was high tea or supper; otherwise, lunch was a minor event, and tea, which would have been at almost the same time as most people's dinner, was served an hour or so after rather than before it: to be invited to tea meant that one was expected to stay for the evening. Lunch as an occasion for entertaining was introduced in the late 1850s, and afternoon tea a few years later, but it was several decades before either became common.

This pattern left breakfast as the second most important meal of the day. Then, as now, its possibilities were usually limited by time, but for those not bound by the clock and economy it might be almost as varied and elaborate as dinner. The only items considered unsuitable were soup, large, hot roasts (because of the time they took to cook), green vegetables, and hot puddings; potatoes and truffles, however, were perfectly permissible, and cold roasts, dessert dishes such as jellies, compôtes, and *petits fours*, and also alcoholic drinks (which had once, it must be remembered, been the norm) were invariably offered at smart functions.

Of all breakfasts, the most spectacular were those served at country-house parties, with which the 'Upper Ten Thousand', i.e. Society, having spent the Season in London and thereafter gone abroad or to the north for the beginning of grouse shooting, entertained each other during the autumn (the fact that many of them were MPs did not interfere with the country social round because at this date Parliament did not sit before Christmas – much political discussion and manoeuvring, however, taking place at such gatherings). The particular feature of these breakfasts was the hungrily described 'mighty side-table . . . garnished and groaning with every sort of *pièce de résistance*, game and fowl, that the season or the spit can set upon it . . .',[1] everything displayed on the sideboard was cold: as well as game and fowl, which were presented not merely as such but under a snow of béchamel or as pies, galantines, or mayonnaises, would be larger items such as a lamb, sucking-pig, rolled goose, or turkey, possibly stuffed with a tongue, plus smoked, pickled, and potted game, meat, and fish, perhaps a platter of olives, and sometimes caviare, though this was still a novelty – every dish being decoratively moulded or arranged, and garnished, often out of all recognition, with truffles, lobster coral, herbs, eggs (plovers' or otherwise), aspic, which was favoured because of its shininess, and vegetables, which, though not served *per se*, were used in this context as a means of adding colour.

The choice of hot items might include patties or vols-au-vent, salmis (the fashionable term for ragouts or casseroles), devils, curries, savoury puddings, sausages – perhaps oyster – broils ranging from trout to venison chops, omelettes or other egg dishes, and truffles, which might be fried or baked and served with lemon juice, or stewed in Champagne. Besides dessert items such as jellies and compôtes would be fresh fruit from the gardens and hot-houses, perhaps cream cheese or cheese canapés, and candied fruit and bon-bons such as burnt almonds or coffee drops – all this in addition to rusks, hot rolls, toast, buns (known as 'breakfast cakes'), and brioches (croissants do not yet seem to have become popular), with, of course, marmalade, and tea, coffee, and wines, plus brandy and soda or nectar for those who needed it.

In contrast to dinner, breakfast was informal, and for this reason often considered much the more enjoyable meal. Guests seated themselves rather than being placed by the hostess, which was favourable to relaxed conversation, and could eat as much (or little) as they liked without attracting notice; also, although in some establishments all the dishes were scheduled for a particular time and people expected to be punctual, a more popular arrangement was for hot items to be prepared to order, as in a hotel, which had the advantages both that there was a chance of eating them hot and that nobody, with the exception of sportsmen, who sometimes had to make an early start, was obliged to get up before they wished. Freedom as to time applied as much as the host and hostess, for whom it would have been bad form for anybody to wait, as the guests – not that all hosts, even those with no interest in sport, were tardy in the mornings. One who was always the first downstairs, not from love of sport or even (apparently) greed, but early-morning insomnia, was the collector of erotica and gourmand Lord Houghton, formerly Richard

Monckton Milnes, who was famous not only for his house-parties at Fryston, in Yorkshire, but his breakfasts in London – and his matutinal wit; another, who appeared both early and late, was Lord Lytton, father of Bulwer, who would dash into the dining-room in an old dressing-gown, grab a cup of tea, and disappear without speaking to anyone; some time later he would make a second entrance, brushed, dressed, and smiling, and wish his guests good morning as if he had not seen any of them before – the explanation for this being that he thought that they had not seen him, since he genuinely believed that he could make himself invisible.

It was also fashionable to give breakfast parties as such, but, like business lunches today, more as an occasion for discussion than straight-forward social purposes – the topics favoured, however, being politics, literature, or other subjects of an intellectual nature rather than business (in which people of this class were seldom actively engaged). Literary breakfasts are supposed to have been introduced by the poet and banker's son Samuel Rogers, who began giving them at the end of the previous century and lived to become a friend of Dickens – and enemy of Disraeli. Neither of the latter, because of the demands of work, normally accepted breakfast invitations: Thackeray and Gladstone, however, were enthusi-astic breakfasters, especially Gladstone, who, with his brother-in-law Lord Lyttleton, father of the diarist Lady Frederick Cavendish, plus Rogers, Houghton, and the MP and naturalist Sir Mountstuart Elphinstone Grant Duff, was among the leading breakfast-party hosts – Houghton and Duff not merely giving parties but co-founding breakfast clubs (Gladstone became a member of Grant Duff's). Often, because of women's lack of professional status and educational limitations, these gatherings were exclusively male: although they do not seem to have issued invitations, nor were members of the clubs (or certainly not Duff's), women neverthe-less sometimes attended, either in their own right or as company for the hostess. Lord Lyttleton's guests included the literary hostess Caroline Norton, the Duchess of Sutherland, who was noted for charity work, and a Miss Williams Wynne, who was presumably asked for the benefit of Lady Frederick (then still Lucy Lyttleton). Houghton entertained Florence Nightingale (before she went to the Crimea) and her mother and sister Parthenope, Elizabeth Barrett as well as Robert Browning, and Thomas and Jane Carlyle. A description of one of his parties, and also of Elizabeth Barrett Browning, was given by Nathaniel Hawthorne (who, being Ameri-can and not knowing what to expect, had had breakfast before he went): 'Mr Milnes introduced me to Mrs Browning, and assigned her to me to conduct to the breakfast-room. She is a small, delicate woman, with ringlets of dark hair, a pleasant, intelligent face, and a low, agreeable voice. She looks youthful and comely, and is very gentle and ladylike. And so we proceeded to the breakfast-room, which is hung round with pictures, and in the middle of it stood a large round table, worthy to have been King Arthur's, and here we seated ourselves without any question of precedence or ceremony. On one side of me was an elderly lady with a very fine countenance, and in the course of breakfast I discovered her to be the mother of Florence Nightingale. One of her daughters (not Florence) was present. Mrs Milnes, Mrs Browning, Mrs Nightingale, and her daughter were the only ladies at table; and I think there were as many as eight or ten gentlemen, whose names – as I came so late – I was left to find out for myself, or leave unknown.

'It was a pleasant and sociable meal, and thanks to my cold beef and coffee at home, I had no occasion to trouble myself much about the fare; I just ate some delicate chicken, and a very small cutlet, and some dry toast, and thereupon surceased from my labours. Mrs Browning and I talked a good deal. . . .'[2]

Houghton founded his breakfast club, the Philobiblon Society, in 1853 with the Minister for Belgian Affairs in London, a M. van de Weyer, who was an energetic socialite and equally familiar with Grant Duff – as was to be expected, since members of Society all knew each other, and when in London, as James Pope-Hennessy has pointed out, were almost immediately accessible to each other, since they all had houses within the small area of Mayfair (the exception as it happened, being Duff, who earlier in his career lived in the newly developed Queen's Gate, South Kensington, which at that time backed on to an orchard). The latter and four friends formed a club, called simply the Breakfast Club, in 1866: membership was limited to twelve, plus honorary members absent on a long-term basis, and each member expected to act as host in turn. As the Club's chief *raison d'être* was political (Liberal), meetings were scheduled to take place during the parliamentary session – which anyway was when members were likely to be in town; in particular, it was biased towards foreign affairs, most of those who were honorary being in office abroad: Duff, who himself became Under-Secretary, first for India and then for the Colonies, and finally Governor of Madras (he was also the chief instigator of the Clarendon Report on the Public Schools), recorded: 'The Breakfast Club has prospered exceedingly. . . . In the year 1885–6, it was ruling India, the Dominion of Canada, Madras, and Bombay – a curious record for so small a society.'[3] Characteristically, although he often gave other details of meetings, such as who was host and what was said, he mentioned the food only once, in 1880, when Lord Lansdowne attended bringing a contribution of fresh mangoes, the first ripe ones he had ever seen. Georgiana Hill, however, although aiming at a rather less socially elevated readership, gave some idea of the kind of menu served, which, because numbers were smaller, consisted of fewer dishes than at large house parties (where there were sometimes as many as twenty or thirty guests). The following was for twelve or more in spring, when game was out of season but during the session:

Middle of the Table.
Target of Lamb.

6 By-dishes, Cold.

Pickled Gherkins.	Preserved Tunny Fish.
Fillets of Anchovies.	Bayonne Goose.
Potted Hare.	Pickled Ox Palates.

6 By-dishes, Hot.
Small Patties of Shrimps.
Haunches of Rabbit, *en Papillotes.*
Smoked Salmon, tossed.
Lambs' Tongues, with Parmesan.
Trout Cutlets, broiled.
White Puddings, tossed.*

4 Entrées.

Veal Cutlets, tossed.	Curried Chicken.
Smelts, in cases.	Duck Pie.

2 Entremets.

Omelette of Veal Kidney.	Young potatoes, *au naturelle.*

Cream Cheese, Candied Fruit, etc., according to fancy.[4]

Everyday menus in middle-class homes were more on the scale of the generally accepted version of the traditional British breakfast. The journalist and painter of the mural at Soyer's Symposium, George Augustus Sala, named some of the commonest dishes in an alleged consultation with a doctor about his liver: 'I used to eat a mutton-chop, or a rump-steak, or a good plateful from a cold joint, or a couple of eggs broiled on bacon,† or a haddock, or a mackerel, or some pickled salmon, or some cold veal-and-ham pie, or half a wild duck, or some devilled partridge, with plenty of bread-and-butter, or toast, or muffins, and perhaps some anchovy sauce, or potted char [a kind of trout], or preserved beef; the whole washed down by a couple of cups of tea or coffee. . . .'[5] The main omissions from this list were hot rolls straight from the bakery, kidneys, which, with mutton chops, were said to be the most popular of all cooked breakfast items, and boiled eggs, which, however, were a constant source of irritation

---

* These were not suet puddings but spiced sausages made with egg and beef marrow.
† Presumably he meant broiled bacon with eggs baked on top afterwards, either in the oven or, as was a common way of cooking them, simply set in front of the fire.

because of the difficulty (aggravated by lack of grading) of timing them correctly. Often, muffins were replaced by crumpets (which were cheaper); bacon was sliced at home and therefore tended to be thicker-cut than is customary today; the equivalent of scrambled eggs was 'buttered' eggs, so called because of the large amounts of butter used (Soyer recommended two ounces per three eggs).

Except for health reasons (hence its popularity for children), nobody who could afford fish or meat chose porridge instead – though they might have been tempted by modern breakfast cereals: the need for porridge, however, was obvious among the lower classes, who, failing herrings, either simply had bread, accompanied whenever possible (in descending order of cost) by butter, local cheese, treacle, or dripping, and, because of the desire for a drink and something hot (which porridge fulfilled), tea or coffee, or a variety of porridge-type preparations, e.g. the Wiltshire labourers' flour porridge; in Ireland, cornflour, which was promoted after the famine, was sometimes similarly used, and, although unpopular, was more convenient because it readily thickens smoothly without fat; unexpectedly but intelligently, one Irish workhouse (Kilrush) tried to make it more acceptable by mixing it with rice. In northern England, conventional porridge or a quicker alternative called 'stirabout' were favoured – the latter being oatmeal dribbled through the fingers into boiling water until the desired consistency was reached; in Scotland, where real porridge was considered a luxury because of the length of time it took to cook, an even quicker alternative was 'brose', which was simply oatmeal softened in hot water. However it was prepared, the oatmeal was eaten (again in descending order of cost) with cream, whole milk, or skim milk, and sugar, treacle, or salt (sometimes, but probably not for breakfast, it was made with stock, or rather, the water in which meat or vegetables had been boiled, which made it a poor relation of stews – which in turn were often thickened with it).

Unless they had midday dinner, labourers and factory workers took a ploughman's lunch to work, if not of bread and cheese, of plain bread, bread and (boiled) bacon or pickled onion, a pasty or piece of pie, or oatcake; since by general consent the lion's share of the food went to the chief wage-earner, wives and children were more likely to have only plain bread. Middle-class wives dutifully ate up cold meat – their husbands meanwhile patronizing the chop-houses. The Upper Ten Thousand, for whom lunch was more important because of the later time of dinner, took their choice from a spread of a similar nature to breakfast. The first lunch party recorded by Lady Frederick was during the Season of 1859; Grant Duff, however, did not report lunching out for another decade, when he went to a party given by Dean Stanley – again apparently predominantly male: 'Lunched with the Stanleys, at the Deanery, to meet Prince Christian, the Duke of Augustenburg, Browning, Layard, Reeve, Grote, the Duke of Argyll, Sir Henry Holland, Kinglake and Richmond the painter.'[6] (His most interesting lunch, at least in retrospect, was with Karl Marx ten years later still, when Marx, discussing war, predicted with astonishing accuracy the establishment and escalating cost of the arms race.)

Lady Frederick's first mention of tea was early in 1866: 'May Lascelles came to see me about 4, after which I smiled for a few minutes at a little tea-business at Auntie P.'s [Mrs Gladstone's] . . .'.[7] Duff's was late in 1869 (not long after the lunch party): 'Presented by the Duke of Argyll to the King of the Belgians, who came to a sort of afternoon tea at the India Office'[8] (one notes that neither of them yet felt able to refer to it simply as tea).

Neither lunch parties, with their implication of greater emphasis on lunch, nor afternoon tea (which, one has to remember, consisted only of tea and thin bread and butter) were sufficiently established at this stage to affect dinner: this too, however, was in a state of transition. The change did not stem from any intentional alteration in menu or style of cooking, nor from the spread of French ideas — indeed, in name at least, it was a rejection of them — but from the introduction of a new style of serving, which, far more quickly than competition from other meals, reduced the number of dishes served on fashionable occasions, and also modified garnishings. When Soyer and Francatelli published their first books, the traditional method, known as *service à la Française*, was universal; by the time Francatelli's second book and Isabella's *Household Management* had appeared, Society had adopted the more convenient but (from the point of view of staff) much more demanding *service à la Russe*.

A dinner served *à la Française* was divided into three courses plus dessert, which was in effect a fourth course, followed by a drinking interval for the men (a custom already vigorously resented by women) and coffee. The first course was soup and/or fish — always both for parties of six or more, and never anything else, such as pâté, or even dishes of cold shell- or smoked fish (though oysters were sometimes served as an appetizer before the soup); often, the fish rather than the main course was accompanied by potatoes. In less sophisticated circles, the English custom of serving green vegetables with the meat was retained, but otherwise, except for acknowledged partnerships such as duck with green peas, the second course consisted solely of meat dishes: these were divided into 'removes', or '*relevés*', so named because they were placed at the ends of the table, where they 'removed' the soup and fish, and entrées, which were side-dishes (rather, as yet, than intermediate dishes designed to precede the main meat course – although, in 1861, Isabella was already listing them before the 'Second Course' removes, instead of after, as had been the earlier custom). The removes were the larger, plainer items such as roasts, and the entrées the smaller, fussier dishes such as fricassées, rissoles, the vols-au-vent: whereas, at least among the middle classes, the guests' principal interest (and the host's main challenge) lay in the removes, the hostess's particular worry was whether the cook had been successful in making the entrées. The third course was made up of items classed as delicacies, which included game, poultry, or shellfish (often lobster), perhaps a savoury dish such as fondue or *pâté de foie gras*, and, if the French custom was followed, vegetables; in addition were the puddings and sweets, excluding ices, the lighter type of cake, and fresh and cooked fruit, which, with *petits fours*, nuts, imported chocolates, and other confectionery, formed the dessert. All the items were taken into the dining room whole, to be carved or portioned by the host or hostess, and, except for the soup and fish, and sometimes game and savouries, the entire course laid out on the table at the same time.

This would have been all very well if the number of diners and dishes had been the same as today; even among the middle classes, however, parties tended to be larger – ten or twelve being unexceptional – and, rather than simply preparing more of the same item, it was the custom, as at breakfasts, to offer guests a choice. Again (but slightly more precisely) variety was scaled roughly according to numbers: the minimum for six (the least which was counted as a party) was two or three dishes for the first course (one soup and one or two fish) and four or five for both the second and third; for twelve, it was usual to provide three to four for the first course, six to eight for the second, and eight to ten for the third, usually with a further eight to a dozen for dessert. A menu *à la Française* for twelve compiled by Isabella read as follows:

DINNER FOR TWELVE PERSONS (December).

First Course.
Game Soup.   Clear Vermicelli Soup.
Codfish au Gratin.   Fillets of Whitings à la Maître d'Hôtel.

Entrées.
Filet de Boeuf and Sauce Piquante.   Fricasseed Chicken.
Oyster Patties.   Curried Rabbit.

Second Course.
Roast Turkey and Sausages.   Boiled Leg of Pork and Vegetables.
Roast Goose.   Stewed Beef à la Jardinière.

Third Course.

Widgeon.   Partridges.

Charlotte aux Pommes.   Mince Pies.   Orange Jelly.

Lemon Cream.   Apple Tart.   Cabinet Pudding.

Dessert and Ices.[9]

At large upper-class dinners, the puddings were divided in a similar way to the meat dishes into removes and *entremets*, the removes tending to be the choicest or most picturesque items; also, hot or cold hors-d'oeuvres, or 'flying dishes', were handed round to occupy diners (and help to prevent them from drinking too much) during the interval between the first and second courses. The menu opposite, devised by Soyer in 1849, was for a dinner for twenty served *à la Française* at Grendon Hall, Warwickshire, to celebrate the christening of the owner's grandson; it gives an incomplete idea, however, of the splendour and luxuriousness of the meal, and in particular its visual impact: the *Poulardes à la Nelson*, for instance, were stuffed with cockscombs and truffles and garnished to resemble a ship; the *Hure de Sanglier* en Surprise Glacé* was one of his *trompe l'oeil* cakes.

* Boar's head.

Deux Potages.
One of Clear Turtle.
Ditto à la Nivernaise.

Deux Poissons.
Crimped Severn Salmon à la Regence.   Turbot à la Cardinale.

Deux Relevés.
La Hanche de Venaison.   Deux Poulardes à la Nelson.

Six Entrées.
Les Ortolans à la Vicomtesse.
Epigramme d'Agneau à la purée de concombres.
Grenadine de Veau aux petits pois.
Filets de Caneton au jus d'orange.
Côtelettes de Mouton à la Provençale.
Turban de Volaille à la Perigord.

Deux Rôtis.
Cailles bardés aux feuilles de vignes.
Gelinottes des Ardennes.

Huit Entremets.
Turban de Meringues aux Pistaches.   Pain de Fruit aux Pêches.
Galantine à la Volière.   Croustades d'Artichaux à l'Indienne.
Vegetable Marrow à la Béchamel.   Miroton de Homard à la Gelée.
Bavaroise Mousseuse à l'annanas.   Blanche Crème au Marasquin.

Deux Relevés.
Hure de Sanglier en Surprise Glacé à la Vanille.
Petits Biscuits soufflés à la Crème.

Ices Pine Apple and Strawberry

St James's Cake, the first ever made.[10]

Rissolettes de Foie Gras à la Pompadour.

Rissolettes de Foie Gras à la Pompadour.

The visual potential of this method of serving largely accounted for its popularity: even Isabella's comparatively plain dinner would have looked like a feast with the simultaneous display of turkey, goose, pork, and beef, of pudding, mince pies, tart, cream, and jelly (which would have been made in an elaborately patterned mould and might have had slices of orange embedded in it); it also had the practical advantage of enabling diners to see the dishes on offer before deciding which to choose. Its disadvantage was of course that the food was cold by the time it came to be eaten: this was true for both obvious reasons and others which no longer apply. As can be imagined, garnishing multiple items caused delay in the kitchen, which, however, was often less significant than it might have been because of the heat of kitchens and provision of hot-plate space; much more relevant was the journey to the dining room, which, instead of being near or adjacent, was customarily placed as far away from the cooking area as possible to prevent the penetration of smells. The transport factor counted least in town houses with basement kitchens and service lifts; in country houses, on the other hand, the food might have to be carried enormous distances (if not as far as at the Rothschild château Ferrières, near Paris, where it travelled from underground kitchens situated some 150 yards from the main building). Dishes were covered with huge silver dish covers, such as are still sometimes seen in restaurants, but at the risk of spoiling the crispness of roasts and fried items because of condensation; also, women complained that when the covers were lifted and, as was inevitable, withdrawn over their heads, their bare shoulders were sprayed with drops (evening dress was invariably worn at dinner parties). Even if a course was still hot at this stage, carving and the strangulating effect of etiquette ensured that it seldom remained so until serving was finished. The importance of skill at carving, which, as one might expect, was always left to men, was stressed by Eliza Acton, Soyer, and Isabella – Soyer, perhaps partly as a male, but also as result of his observation of Club members, being particularly sympathetic towards the inept performer: 'you are all aware ... of the continual tribulation in carving at table, for appetites more or less colossal, and when all eyes are fixed upon you with anxious avidity. Very few persons are perfect in this useful art ... it certainly often happens that the greatest gourmet is the worst carver, and complains sadly during that very long process, saying to himself, "I am last to be served; my dinner will be cold."' All he could suggest for hopeless cases was aplomb: 'We remember to have seen a man of high fashion deposit a turkey in this way in the lap of a lady, but with admirable composure, and without offering the slightest apology, he finished a story which he was telling at the same time, and then, quietly turning to her, merely said, "Madam, I'll thank you for that turkey."'[11]

Service à la Russe increased the chances of the meal staying hot by two means: carving and portioning were carried out, in theory at least more swiftly and dexterously, by the servants, and the dishes, instead of being grouped into three composite courses, were served in pairs or sets of alternatives, each of which was presented as a course in itself. Since at first almost, if not quite, as many dishes as before were considered necessary, the result could be somewhat ridiculous, not to mention taxing to the diners, as another sample from Isabella shows (the number for which it catered was not specified, but it was presumably meant for parties of over two dozen):

MENU.
SERVICE À LA RUSSE (NOVEMBER).

Ox-tail Soup. Soup à la Jardinière

Turbot and Lobster Sauce.   Crimped Cod and Oyster Sauce.

Stewed Eels.   Soles à la Normandie.

Pike and Cream Sauce.   Fried Filleted Soles.
Filets de Boeuf à la Jardinière.   Croquettes of Game aux Champignons.

Chicken Cutlets.   Mutton Cutlets and Tomata Sauce.

Lobster Rissoles.   Oyster Patties.

Partridges aux Fines Herbes.   Larded Sweetbreads.

Roast Beef.   Poulets aux Cressons.
Haunch of Mutton.   Roast Turkey.
Boiled Turkey and Celery Sauce.   Ham.

Grouse.   Pheasants.   Hare.

Salad.   Artichokes.   Stewed Celery.

Italian Cream.   Charlotte aux Pommes.   Compôte of Pears.

Croûtes Madrées aux Fruits.   Pastry.   Punch Jelly.

Iced Pudding.

Dessert and Ices.[12]

Far more tempting was a series of menus for dinners given by Disraeli at his London house in Grosvenor Gate, at which, although the choice of

dishes was still wide, the length of the meal was limited to seven courses
(plus dessert) – which makes the written menus look very similar to those
for *service à la Française*, although the impression given by the actual
dinner would have been very different. The following was served at a party
for Prince Napoleon:

MENU DU 20 JUILLET 1862

Potages.
Consommé de Volaille.   Purée de Pois Verts.

Poissons.
Whitebait.   Turbot.
Tranches de Saumon à la Perigord.

Entrées.
Timbales au Salpicon.
Poulets à la Zingara.
Côtelettes d'Agneau aux Petits Pois.

Grosses Pièces.
Poulardes et Langue à la Toulouse.
Epaule d'Agneau.
Hanche de Venaison.

SECOND SERVICE.

Rôtis.
Levraux.   Canetons.

Entremets.
Salade d'Homard.
Gelée au Fruit.
Gâteau aux Cerises.
Vol-au-vent de Framboises et Groseilles.
Boudin de Vénus.

Talmouses au Parmesan.[13]

As the dishes were handed round directly and never laid on the table,
which otherwise would have been bare, flowers and fruit were used to
decorate it throughout the meal; in addition, so that diners knew what
was to come, menus were provided. An incidental advantage of the new
system was that without a display of food and the consequent need for
table space, hostesses were free to seat their guests at a number of smaller
tables rather than one large one, which enabled them to give bigger parties
– and probably favoured conversation. Naturally, lack of display also
meant that there was no longer occasion for works of culinary art such as
Poulardes à la Nelson; on the other hand, the fact that attention was

focused on every dish in turn called for a more sophisticated overall standard of cooking. Until a long succession of courses ceased to be fashionable, a further demand made by *à la Russe* was that, in addition to the need for more crockery and cutlery, a larger number of staff were required to serve and ferry the dishes to and fro.

Even without the added pressure of *à la Russe*, more was expected of waiters than is usual except in the most select or expensive establishments today because etiquette dictated that, whatever their ratio to the diners, none of the company should pass, ask for, or help each other or themselves to anything: not only the principal dishes but minor accompaniments such as pepper and mustard were supposed to be handed by the servants – this rule being sufficiently widely observed and inflexible for an eccentric police magistrate turned essayist called Thomas Walker, who wrote a remarkably enlightened series of articles on dining (his eccentricity lay in his ideas on health)*[14] to put forward as a genuine innovation the suggestion that, to avoid each item being 'provokingly lagging, one thing after another, so that contentment is out of the question',[15] diners should pass each other such things as pepper and bread and butter or potatoes with fish. Among the upper class, where the custom of helplessness originated, waiting at table was performed by footmen, whether there was company or not: professionalism was ensured by daily practice and the supervision of the butler, who was in charge of dining-room organization, and it was taken for granted that when large parties were given, numbers should be increased: in London, people often borrowed staff from one another (this applied not only to waiters but kitchen staff, including chefs) and on country visits, guests customarily took their own lady's maids and valets, the latter of whom were expected to look after them at meals. Waitresses, then as now, were considered *déclassé*, and never employed at this social level (one pragmatic reason given for their disqualification was that they were not strong enough to carry the heavier dishes). Families without butlers or footmen, however, were served on non-entertaining occasions by house- or parlourmaids. Hostesses who wished to conform to upper-class style therefore had to import waiters, which, unless they applied to the confectioner (and even then, experience could only be presumed) meant exchanging practised service for that of amateurs and making do with such numbers as they could raise. Those who kept them brought in coachmen, stable-boys, and gardeners, who cleaned themselves up as best

---

* Two of his propositions seemed odder then than they do now, viz. That good health is largely a matter of will-power, and that abstemiousness produces sense of elation; a third, however, which was made much of by Hayward in *The Art of Dining* (part of which was based on a review of Walker's articles) was that when people were in perfect health, 'active exhalation' via the skin carried off impurities and made washing unnecessary.

they could for the occasion – apparently not always successfully enough for the more fastidious, such as Mrs Gaskell (one has to remember that among ordinary people, having a bath was considerably more complicated than just turning on the tap). Failing this, the greengrocer was sent for: why it should have been the greengrocer is not clear, except that of the various tradesmen who called at the house, he was less pretentious than the grocer (who might aspire to hiring waiters himself), less prosperous than the butcher, and less overworked than the baker's man; whatever the reason, his monopoly in this field was referred to by Mayhew and acknowledged by a full-page article in *Punch* – from which it is difficult to decide who benefited most from his visit: 'About five o'clock there is a quiet ring at the door labelled "Servants".' The next minute a pair of heavy feet is heard tramping along the hall. You look out, and see a huge mass of great coat. In one second, it has dived down the kitchen staircase. It is the Greengrocer.

'Soon afterwards the sound of feet is heard over-head. The elegant figure of a man, with his hair curled, is on the top of a pair of steps, arranging the chandelier. His costume would be of too stern a blackness, if it were not delicately softened by the purity of a white neckcloth. . . . The extreme neatness of the pump, if nothing else, would tell you that it is the Waiter. . . .

'Call on him to-morrow. Catch him behind his apron, and you will not recognize in the soiled hands that are playing at marbles with the potatoes, the BEAU BRUMMEL of the Berlins [cheap gloves] who helped you so gracefully to blanc-mange the evening before. Or observe him when he is on the front bar of a covered van, whipping a jaded white horse. . . .

'The waiter that is only laid on for the night is always better tempered than the waiter who is a regular fixture. The tender way in which the Greengrocer behaves to children would be a cheap lesson to many a big-calved Johnny.* He never kicks them or calls them "brats." He lets them pilfer the "sweets" as much as they please, and if they get between his legs when he is carrying some mighty dome of a silver dish-cover, he manages somehow to bear up against it, where any other servant would be violently upset. He compliments the lady's maids, and jokes with the cook, helping her to unspit joints and untie pudding bags. There must be something in the atmosphere of spring onions and summer cabbages. . . .

'After the fatigues of the evening, his temper is as little ruffled as his fine linen shirt. He helps on great coats, and fastens galoshes, with the most nimble readiness. . . . Then comes the washing-up, and then – painful

* Footmen's liveries included stockings, which meant that well shaped legs were a crucial element in their appearance (as was shown by a cartoon elsewhere in *Punch*, the possibility that padding was used was a standing joke).

duty! implying distrust, but which he cheerfully goes through – the counting "the plate."

'He sits down to supper – and all the good things you had at dinner are brought out for his meal. . . . There is a large tankard foaming with fresh beer. There are innumerable glasses of wine, which he criticizes, as he takes a sip of each. His opinion is greatly respected, for who tastes more wine in the course of his life than the greengrocer who waits at parties? . . . He is a great personage, for . . . in addition to his other duties, he is a large purveyor of situations. . . . He knows the wages of the best houses, the most becoming liveries, and the perquisites, and the strength of the beer, attached to each. He is a portable Servant's Bazaar – a living column of "Want Places,". . . .'[16]

When the middle classes were not entertaining, their dinners were fairly similar to today's, the chief differences being the service of the maid, that they were more likely to consist of two meat dishes and one vegetable than one meat and two veg., and, as by now hardly needs stressing, tended to be much more monotonous, with roast, boiled, and cold meat in almost unbroken succession. If there was a choice of meats, one was probably yesterday's remains, either cold or made into a hash – hashes often being not much more than the sliced meat warmed in gravy, and cold, instead of being given interest by a salad, accompanied only by boiled or mashed potatoes (hence widespread use of bottled sauces, which not only enlivened plain cold meat but could be added to the gravy in hashes). Nor was there much variety in the type of meat, since, despite the obligation to serve poultry and game at dinner parties, they were too expensive to be favoured on other occasions. Allegedly for reasons of both health and economy, by far the most popular meat was mutton – which, taken in conjunction with chops and kidneys at breakfast and chop-house lunches, meant that mutton was the middle-class staple, just as, albeit in a much stricter sense, bread, potatoes, or oatmeal were of the poor. On purely logical grounds, it is difficult to understand why it should have been preferred to beef: lb. for lb., it was slightly more expensive, the fat and stock were less useful (which, however, given the unlikelihood of advantage being taken of them, was perhaps irrelevant), and, although traditionally considered more wholesome, it had been proved to doctors' satisfaction to be less digestible; possibly the amount of fat carried by stall-fed bullocks, its greater tenderness raw, which meant that it could be trimmed or cut into chops more easily at home, or the fact that it could be boiled directly whereas beef for boiling was generally salted, had something to do with it. The equivalents of mutton at the pudding course (for which one needs no explanation) were apples, gooseberries, and dried fruit (Georgiana Hill claimed to have written her *Pudding Book* as a result of staying with an

LEG OF MUTTON WITH OYSTERS

Parboil some fine well-fed oysters, take off the beards and horny parts, put to them some parsley, minced onions, and sweet herbs boiled and chopped fine, and the yolks of two or three hard-boiled eggs; mix all together, and make five or six holes in the fleshy part of a leg of mutton, and put in the mixture, and dress it in either of the following ways: tie it up in a cloth and let it boil gently two and a half to three hours according to size, or braise it, and serve it with a pungent brown sauce.

*   *   *   *   *

For 4–6:   3–3½lb (1.4–1. 6kg) leg of lamb or mutton
12 small (e.g. Normandy) oysters or 6 large ones
3 hard-boiled egg yolks
1 raw egg (which may not be needed)
2 tablespoons finely chopped parsley
2 small or 1 large clove garlic
a little freshly ground sea-salt; rather more black
    pepper

Instead of slitting the meat as directed, bone the leg, which can then be stuffed and roasted in the usual way.

Open the oysters over a small saucepan to catch the liquor. Beard, and set the oysters aside. Add as near as can be judged enough water to the liquor in the saucepan to cover them, bring the contents of the saucepan to boil, add the oysters, and boil for one minute. Remove the oysters, strain the liquor, and allow to cool.

Finely chop the oysters, onion, garlic, and parsley; mix thoroughly with the hard-boiled egg yolks, add the oyster liquor, and, if the mixture remains dry, the egg. Season slightly with sea-salt and a little more heavily with freshly ground black pepper. Stuff and bind the leg.

from *What Shall We Have for Dinner?*, 'Lady Maria Clutterbuck'
(Bradbury & Evans, 1852 ed., p. 48).

old lady who had apple puddings continuously for one half of the year and gooseberry ones for the other).

One suspects that dinners among the better off, better educated lower classes, where wives took advantage of the wholesale markets and did the cooking themselves, were more varied and interesting than those of the middle- and healthier too, since they probably included more vegetables and less meat. Markets and street sellers, if not second-hand shops, also gave some degree of choice to the urban poor, who for the price of a couple of pounds of potatoes could have bought (allowing for season) two pounds of sprats, a pair of herrings, four pounds of peas, two pints of haricot beans (which, however, no one would have chosen), one pound of ox-cheek, or a substantial quantity of 'bits and ears'. These were the scraps of meat left on the hides after the carcases had been skinned by the butchers, and came, not from the food, but the skin markets, where they were collected by gangs of boys: 'There were the heaps of ox-hides, and busy about them half a dozen privileged boys with their ragged trousers rolled up above their knees, and their feet red as high as the ankle. . . . They hunted carefully upwards, beginning from the tail, and when they had gleaned all the bits and arrived at the ears, they sliced them off with a dexterity that showed how used they were to the business.'[17] The bigger 'bits' were fried; the smaller ones and ears (complete with hair) made what was declared to be a 'jolly good'[18] stew.

For many of the rural poor, however, only poaching, or perhaps the occasional charitable gift, relieved the monotony of a diet consisting of almost nothing but starch. A breakfast of bread or some kind of porridge and lunch principally of bread or oatcake might be followed by dumplings, potatoes, more porridge, or (despite Esther Hewlett) tea and toast. A common dish in Scotland was kale brose, the brose (made with kale water) forming the first course and the kale itself the second. The simplest sort of dumplings were Suffolk and Sussex ones, which consisted only of flour and water; in Norfolk, they were made of bread dough, so that they were in effect boiled rolls – and eaten as such, with a knob of butter; in Essex, fat was added and the greasy liquor in which they had been boiled used for mixing another type of flour-based dish, 'floaters', which were a kind of thick pancake. Potatoes were almost always boiled because other methods of cooking demanded fat, or, in the case of baking, took longer – baking anyway being impractical when they formed the entire meal because of the quantity needed (nearly three pounds for a dinner of 1,000 calories). As with dumplings, however, details varied: in Lancashire, they were peeled before cooking and dried by the side of the fire so that they were light and floury; in Yorkshire, they were cooked and served in their skins and the insides scooped out with a fork; in Ireland, they were cooked as they came, unpeeled and unscrubbed, and the skin stripped off as they were eaten – in the fingers, thus dispensing with utensils (not that the Irish were alone in eating without knives and forks, since many families could not afford enough to go round; similarly, lack of plates sometimes meant that meals were eaten in turns). The Irish method had the advantages of being not only the most economical in terms of labour and waste, but the soundest nutritionally, since the skin and outermost layer of flesh contain most protein; when possible, animal protein was added by using the sour skim milk left over from butter-making as a dip like yoghurt or sour cream.

Although against the original intention of the law, or rather it would have been if more of the pauper population had been able-bodied, the food served in the workhouse was considerably better balanced and apparently more luxurious than that of those who lived on bread and potatoes outside. The reform of 1834 had been introduced in response to the rise in the poor rates caused by the spread of poverty, and, the true nature of the problem not being recognized, aimed (like the recent changes) to deter all but the genuinely needy from applying: thus conditions in the houses were designed to be, not actively uncomfortable but sufficiently austere to be less attractive than in people's own homes. Food obviously played an important part in this: to remind paupers of their debt to charity and promote a suitably pious atmosphere, it was dictated that a rule of silence was to be observed at all meals; the composition of the latter was laid down in a series of six alternative diets which (ironically on both counts) were intended to be adequate but as plain as acceptability permitted. Fortunately (and predictably) the rule of silence seems to have proved unenforceable; the diets, of which a selection was given to allow for regional differences, included a high proportion of bread, but also hot meat-and-vegetable dinners on an average of twice a week, with fairly generous portions of meat, and meat soup on average three times a fortnight. Sometimes, meat pudding replaced plain meat; otherwise, the mode of preparing meat was not given because it was taken for granted that it would be boiling, which was the easiest way of catering for large numbers (in nearly all cases, roasting was made impossible by the fact that very few houses were built with suitable fireplaces); nor, except in one instance, was the type of meat stated, presumably because it was similarly assumed that it would be the cheapest available, i.e. bacon, pickled pork, or beef. Much the same applied to the kind of vegetable: potatoes were specified twice, but otherwise the choice was left open. Once- or twice-weekly meals of dumplings or rice or suet puddings (without meat) brought the ratio of hot dinners to just over two thirds; the rest of the dinners, and nearly all suppers, were bread and cheese. Two sets of breakfasts were

Soup and bread in the workhouse

also bread and cheese, but hot porridge was substituted for the cheese in the others. The only feature of the diets which prospective applicants would have recognized as undesirable (but it was a major one) was that no tea or beer was granted to the able-bodied. From the outset, however, a sharp distinction was made between the latter, who, since they were capable of work, were condemned according to the prevailing doctrine of *laissez-faire* as the sole authors of their own misfortune, and the old, infirm, and children, who were acknowledged to be more deserving of public sympathy. Thus all those aged sixty or over were to be given allowances of tea and sugar, usually instead of porridge for breakfast, and the infirm and children under nine fed at medical discretion – which, though far from a guarantee of generosity, ensured that the children had milk and many of the former prescriptions of beer or other alcoholic drinks (notoriously port).

In the event, hatred of the 'Bastilles' plus the fact that outside relief for the able-bodied was often continued notwithstanding, meant that residents consisted almost entirely of those in the second category, i.e. the helpless. For a few years, a number of houses adhered to the original diets; probably partly because of their nursing home/nursery function, however, a large proportion had modified them in the direction of further luxury by the 1860s, when a survey of workhouse food was carried out by a doctor who specialized in the nutrition of the poor, Edward Smith. According to Smith, who gathered information from sixty-five houses (a tenth of the total), mutton was served as well as beef and bacon, meat pudding had been replaced by pies and hashes, and in a few houses such able-bodied paupers as were present were regaled with tea, coffee, or cocoa. Nearly all the dinners were hot: sixty per cent of the sample offered meat and vegetables three times a week and pudding once, all but six houses soup or broth (made from the meat-liquor) two or three times, and only nine bread and cheese, of which only one served it more than once a week. Hot suppers with porridge or broth instead of cheese were common, and porridge was always provided for breakfast.

Smith had several reasons for disapproving of this. In the conclusion to his report, he upheld the deterrent principle and criticized the increased proportion of hot food on moral grounds; this, however, was almost certainly merely a formal declaration, and in any case of very limited relevance, since it applied only to the able-bodied minority. He was much more concerned to halt the trend from the practical and humanitarian point of view, one of his discoveries being that the effect was counter-productive because the meals were often so unpalatable that no one, let alone the old and sick, could have been expected to eat them – with the result that large amounts of food were wasted despite the fact that some of the paupers were almost starving. One of the difficulties was that, as one might expect but far more necessarily than elsewhere, hot dishes were cold by the time they reached the diners – or rather, in this instance, the diners reached them. This of course was particularly true of meat because of the problem of carving for large numbers – which, as there was usually only one carver (the master of the workhouse) was at its very worst; the method adopted for serving soup and broth, however, was almost as unfavourable, since, instead of being brought to table in a tureen, they were dispensed in the kitchen and carried into the dining-room in individual mugs (possibly, the reason for this was that the quantity needed made a single vessel impracticably heavy). In addition, delays were sometimes caused by the fact that allowances for each person were rationed, which meant that in theory every portion had to be weighed or measured; this, however, was not always carried out (though distribution was reported to be fairly even). Much more decisively, apparently for reasons of order – which seems especially silly when one considers the feeble condition of most of the company – nobody was allowed to enter the dining-room until serving was finished and the plates of food set round the table. Two further points, which one would have thought hardly counted after the rest but which Smith nevertheless felt worth emphasizing, were that dining-rooms were cold – which must have been independently unpleasant for the diners – and, to save on breakages, tin ware was used rather than pottery, which (because thicker) would have held the heat better.

Other problems were the usual culinary ignorance, economic pressures – which, as Smith hinted, were no doubt aggravated by additional servings of meat – and lack not only of staff but probably also supplementary help. In some cases, faulty ingredients were used as a result of attempts to cut costs by ordering from the cheapest sources; sometimes, recipes were so pared down that dishes were not only unappetizing but hardly worth eating in the nutritional sense: this certainly applied to porridge, and probably soup. Sometimes, on the other hand – as also applied to porridge – the proportions used were indeed so uselessly extravagant (though hardly farragos) that the results were gastronomically even more unfortunate. Cooks, for whatever they might have been worth, were not employed, the cooking being done by the matrons with the help of some of the paupers – which was the more necessary because the former had other duties: if the types of resident had been more evenly balanced, help would have been automatically forthcoming, since, as the term 'workhouse' implies, employable inmates were expected to work for their keep, men being given the less desirable sort of manual job such as pounding bones (for use as fertilizer) and women sharing the domestic chores; matrons, however, bribed their assistants – usually with beer, or, significantly, extra food – perhaps sometimes merely to secure good will but presumably basically because scarcity of the able-bodied meant that they had to induce the old (who were exempted from the obligation to work) to volunteer.

The porridge in the different houses ranged from a murky, dirty-looking fluid made with a scarcely credible three quarters of an ounce of oatmeal per pint to a gritty, probably burnt-tasting mass with four, which was too thick for the starch to expand properly and would almost inevitably have stuck to the pan – the normal version, however, being a thickish gruel* of one and a half. The so-called meat soup varied from a peas-and-oatmeal broth with no meat at all to a heartening, stew-like dish containing four ounces per pint. Suet pudding similarly contained from a quarter of an ounce of suet per pound of pudding, in which case it was in fact dumpling,

* It was in fact customarily called gruel, not, however, because of its consistency but because, according to the workhouse definition, gruel was made with water and porridge with milk.

to four ounces – which was alleged to be excessive to the point of yielding a 'sticky and repulsive'[19] mess, but in reality would have given a perfectly acceptable result if the right amount of liquid had been used and the boiling carried out with due care. Rice ones ranged from solid rice, rather like plain risotto (they were usually unsweetened) to rice 'milk' made with half an ounce of rice per pint of liquid and water thickened with a little flour instead of milk; when it was used, milk might be 100 per cent pure or seventy-five per cent diluted. The only composite article with a consistent content was bread, which was wholemeal and frequently made on the premises; surprisingly, it was declared to be in general excellent, which was probably sometimes because their labour problems had forced some of the houses to invest in dough-making machines.

The portions allowed were also wildly inconsistent: amounts of bread ranged from four to eight ounces, of meat from three to a comfortable six, of cheese from one or two and a half, of soup from one to two pints, and so on. In many cases, attempts were made to equalize differences via the rest of the diet, e.g. whereas larger helpings of pudding were served as entire dinners, smaller ones were usually accompanied by meat or vegetables; these, however, were haphazard and often, as the substitution of vegetables (certainly if green) for pudding shows, unsatisfactory. Accurate balancing in an overall sense was impossible because there was as yet no means of measuring energy, i.e. calorie, values, but (apart from vitamins) all the major constituents of food had been identified and every common foodstuff analysed, which meant that at least starch could have been exchanged for starch and protein foods for protein (butter and cheese were sometimes interchanged): that a more informed, systematic approach was not adopted was presumably due to the ignorance (or negligence) of the local doctors who attended the houses and were apparently responsible for adapting the diets.

On the other hand, since not only the calorie content of foods but people's requirements could not be calculated, doctors were at fault only in terms of common sense in misjudging total needs. With such diversity, there were probably quite a number of diets which erred on the side of plenty: Smith, however, made the overall comment (which, one has to remember, referred mainly to old people) that although the general condition of the paupers seemed fair, they did not get any fatter; his actual, cautiously worded statement was: 'The aspect of the inmates is not commonly that of robust health, neither is there usually any marked accumulation of flesh; but the aspect is not generally unhealthy, and the appetite, spirits, and general strength are fair.'[20] He also noted that the children were not well grown for their age. Allowances have to be made for a life-style which included no central heating on the one hand and the

How the poor ate: a scene in the kitchen of a cheap lodging-house
(*London Labour and the London Poor*, Vol. 1)

habit of abstemiousness on the other, but on the basis of modern
assessments his remarks are accurately borne out by a calorie count of the
original diets (which were non-specific for children) and those in use at
about that time in two houses, chosen simply because details of portions
are available. Unfortunately, none of these examples included recipes, but
taking the norm of one and a half ounces of oatmeal per pint of porridge,
the maximum four ounces of meat per pint in soup and suet per pound of
pudding, and assuming that all vegetables were potatoes and milk full-
cream and undiluted unless otherwise stated,* the original diets provided
from under 1,800 to upwards of 2,400 for able-bodied men and just over
1,600 to nearly 2,200 for women; at Newport Pagnall, Buckinghamshire,
and Mere, Wiltshire, the average daily totals were respectively 2,172 and
2,532 for able-bodied men, 1,848 and 2,269 for able-bodied women and
children of both sexes aged nine to sixteen,† 1,552 and 1,186 for children

* It has also been assumed that soup contained one ounce of starch per pint, suet and rice
pudding eight ounces of flour and three ounces of rice plus one pint of full-cream milk per pound,
and milk and water (which was given to children) fifty per cent of full-cream milk. Broth has been
counted at 130 calories per pint, meat at seventy per ounce, and cheese at 100. Where rice and
suet pudding were given as alternatives, suet has been taken, which is significant because, with
contents as assumed, it had nearly two and a half times the calorie value of rice and considerably
raises the averages.
† This was stated at Newport Pagnall, but not Mere, presumably because it was standard and
taken for granted.

aged five to eight, and 1,321 and 1,302 for two- to four-year-olds. The elderly at Newport were given sugar and butter instead of porridge to about its value, and at Mere unspecified amounts of milk and sugar plus an extra four ounces of cheese and butter per week 'if *deemed expedient*'.[21] According to these calculations (which, besides being based on more favourable data than probably applied, necessarily exclude the question of whether the food was actually eaten – and, conversely, ignore the possibility that the old were given alcohol) the only group of residents who probably had enough to eat were elderly women, who at Mere were given slightly more than their likely requirements, particularly with extra butter and cheese (which, however, may have been intended as compensation for those who habitually did not eat other items), and at Newport just – but only just – enough. Elderly men at Mere also received just enough, but were several hundred calories short at Newport; similarly, younger women and older girls had sufficient at the former but several hundred too little at the latter. The rest of the children and able-bodied men were underfed by progressive amounts at both houses. The two- to four-year-olds received 200 too little – which, because of their lesser needs, was more proportionately – the five- to eight-year-olds 200 and 400, and older boys 400 and 800. In other words, Oliver Twist's plight was very real, and far commoner than perhaps Dickens realized. Besides the retardation of the children's growth noted by Smith, this would certainly have affected their health in other ways, and gone very far towards nullifying the efforts made with their education. Others who commented on them (on the principle that poverty equalled inherent inferiority) ascribed their apparent lack of promise to heredity. Men, on the assumption that they were doing moderately heavy work, received something like 500 and 1,000 calories too little: that they sometimes suffered from extremities of hunger was shown by a scandal concerning Andover workhouse, Hampshire, in 1846. It has been explained by Ian Anstruther[22] that this house was atypical in that its board of overseers was motivated by the desire for revenge on the local population for losses incurred during agricultural riots; almost certainly more significant to the food situation, however, was that because of poverty in the area it was also unusual in sheltering an appreciable number of able-bodied men. The latter were employed at pounding bones until it was discovered that they regularly picked them over and gnawed them, despite the fact that they might be uncooked and stinking, and sucked out the marrows – the latter at least having the advantage of being clean. Usually, the bones came from butchers' and kitchens, or sometimes stables (though most of the men were careful to avoid those which looked like horse), but it so happened that at the time of the publicity some had been disinterred from a neighbouring graveyard and were therefore human. This affair put an end to the pounding of bones in workhouses – but not, except for a very temporary improvement, to the insufficiency of the allowances at Andover.

The doctors' ignorance of advances in nutritional knowledge was exposed with embarrassing clarity over a subject of concern at the other end of the economic spectrum – slimming; nor does Smith, who was one of several who tried to defend the profession, emerge especially creditably although the practical advice he offered was sound. One might imagine, after studying fashionable menus, that overfeeding prevailed almost as necessarily among the affluent as undernourishment in the workhouses – and indeed some remarkable feats of gourmandizing were recorded; in general, however, there was probably less cause for overweight even at this social level than today. Besides the factor of living conditions, i.e. heating and transport, people had fewer meals – in most cases, not much lunch, and no tea, for which supper seldom compensated; corsets and notions of femininity inhibited women at least from being seen to eat large amounts; above all, opportunities and hence the temptation to eat between meals were greatly reduced by the convention of not hanging about in the kitchen or going shopping, and also by the fact that the sort of instant snack which now supplies many of our calories, e.g. crisps,*[23] cheap chocolate, and soft drinks, was not available. Since fashion favoured curves rather than thinness, girls and women (except in the matter of waists) had a relatively undemanding ideal – boniness (as Smith stressed) in fact being considered almost as much of a disadvantage as excessive plumpness. Nevertheless, neurosis about being fat, possibly even including anorexia or something very like it (though illness from too-tight lacing, partly because easier to diagnose, was more often reported) seem to have been as potent, and not only among women, as ever.

In France, interest in gastronomy was accompanied by study of its effects from a comparatively early date. In 1825 the French writer Jean-Anthelme Brillat-Savarin said, with a characteristically human touch: 'If I had been a qualified doctor [he was in fact a qualified lawyer], I would in the first place have written a monograph on obesity; then I would have established my empire in that sphere of the profession. I would thus have enjoyed the dual advantage of having the healthiest of people as my patients and being daily besieged by the prettier half of the human race ...'.[24] He went on to give considerably sounder advice, both from the physical and psychological point of view, than was usual in this country

---

* The *London Standard* wrote recently: 'The Ministry of Agriculture, Fisheries, and Food reported today that during the last three months of 1984 an astonishing 1,244,242,000 small (up to 35 grams) packets of crisps were consumed in England and Wales.'[23]

forty years later. The majority of British doctors, since they could not give informed advice on diet, had to rely on the alternative of exercise – the effectiveness of which, because the basic metabolic needs of the body were underestimated, was correspondingly overrated: Brillat-Savarin nevertheless rejected it as a practical form of treatment because he felt that women in particular would be even less likely to keep it up than dieting; for the same reason, he also dismissed the parallel notion of cutting down on supposedly very low-energy-consuming sleep. Even at this stage, nearly twenty years before the publication of Liebig's books, it was known that starch was fattening, both through chemistry and empirically: citing the example of animals fattened for market on grain, he therefore recommended a low-starch diet. It is not clear whether he also appreciated that fats and sugar were significant, though he was aware that they were inflammable, which implies a high energy yield; he did condemn sugar, however, as making flour products more attractive and encouraging people to go on eating after the genuine needs of hunger were satisfied.

Accepting the difficulty of entirely giving up bread, he started by suggesting that rye should be substituted for wheat, partly because he thought (wrongly) that rye was lower in starch, but also on the assumption that less of it would be eaten: '. . . it is less nutritious, and less agreeable too; but that only makes our precept easier to obey. For to be sure of yourselves, you must always avoid temptation. Remember that: it is a sound piece of moral advice.' He then guided his readers through the courses at dinner: 'You like soup: let it be clear, à la julienne, with green vegetables, cabbage, or roots; but croutons, noodles, and thick soups are forbidden.

'For the first course you are free to eat anything, with a few exceptions, such as chicken and rice, and the pastry of hot pâtés. Eat well, but prudently. . . .

'The second course is due to appear, and here you will need all your philosophy. Avoid all things floury, in whatever guise they come; for you are still left with the roast and the salad and the green vegetables. And if you must have something sweet afterwards, choose a chocolate custard, or a jelly made with orange or punch.

'Here comes dessert. . . . Mistrust the savouries (they are always brioches more or less adorned); avert your eyes from the biscuits and macaroons; there still remain all kinds of fruit, jams [purées], and many other things which you will learn to choose for yourself if you adopt my principles.'[25] He struck a remarkably modern note by advising white meat and light white wines rather than red; more dated was his suggestion that slimmers should wear an 'anti-obesical belt' to prevent sagging (a similar idea to the tight binders women customarily wore after childbirth). He also told the story of Louise, a girl whom he had known and admired in his youth (he stressed that his relationship with her had not progressed beyond admiration) who apparently died of drinking vinegar – which at that time was popular as a means of losing weight. 'Louise was very pretty, and above all possessed, in a just proportion, that classic fulness of figure which . . . is the glory of the imitative arts. . . .' Noticing that she was thinner, he questioned her and at first received a defensive reply; after watching her for several weeks and becoming increasingly worried, he finally cornered her at a ball and persuaded her to admit that, as a result of teasing from some of her friends, she had determined to slim, and had drunk a glass of vinegar every morning for a month. 'I shuddered when I heard this confession, for I knew the full extent of the danger; and the very next morning I told [her] mother, who was no less alarmed than I. . . . No time was lost; doctors arrived, examined, and prescribed. All in vain!. . . . She died gazing sadly towards a future which, for her, would never exist.'[26]

It was a little ironic that, having given such a moving warning against vinegar, he advocated quinine (which had long been used as a cure for fevers) instead; fortunately, he recommended only a very moderate dose (one teaspoonful every other morning for a month).

His (and other, probably also foreign) dietary ideas were not unknown in this country among the cosmopolitan upper class: Queen Victoria wrote to her eldest daughter soon after the latter's marriage to Frederick William of Prussia: 'I really hope you are not getting fat again? Do avoid eating soft, pappy things, and drinking too much – you know how that fattens.'[27] (By drinking, she probably did not mean alcohol, but anything, since there was a widely held belief, which did not originate with Brillat-Savarin but was presumably connected with fluid retention and/or the weight of fluids, that liquid was fattening *per se*.) Such theories, however, had been heard of only by the very few: in general, people knew nothing about eating in order to slim until the appearance of a pamphlet by an elderly middle-class business man called William Banting, who related how, after over twenty years of worry and unhappiness about his increasing weight and near-torture at the hands of doctors, he had succeeded in losing thirty-five pounds by cutting down on starch, sugar, and fats. Not only because of what he said, but his simple, unpretentious style (which contrasted sharply with that of the first doctor from whom he provoked a response), the pamphlet had such an impact that dieting (rather like exercise today) became the fashion.

Banting himself had no fashionable aspirations, but was as plain-living and apparently modest as his writing suggests: he had dinner at midday and presumably, until he went on his diet, high tea (which Thackeray panned as the most 'odious custom'[28] he could think of), and claimed to

have written his pamphlet, which he published himself and, initially at
least, gave away free, for no other reason than to help his fellow sufferers,
declaring that he had that form of publication because he felt that he was
too ordinary for a newspaper or magazine to be likely to accept his work
(he might have added that the most suitable magazine, *The Lancet*, could
hardly have been expected to welcome what he had to say). He was,
however, remarkable for his determination, endurance, and excellent
health, which, especially in view of his age – he was sixty-six at the time
the pamphlet appeared – might well have broken down considerably
sooner and rather more seriously than was in fact the case. He had not
been fat as a young man, he said, nor did he come from an overweight
family; nevertheless, becoming fat had always been his particular dread
(possibly, it stemmed from self-consciousness about his height, which was
only five feet five). When, therefore, he found himself beginning to put on
weight at the age of about forty, he immediately saw a doctor, who,
predictably, prescribed exercise; accordingly, he tried rowing for two
hours every morning before work – presumably, as it seems that he lived
in London, on the Thames. This developed his muscles and no doubt
increased his general fitness – but also gave him such an appetite that he
gained weight faster than ever. No sooner had he reported this adverse
result to the doctor than the latter, an 'eminent surgeon' unfortunately
died; he then embarked on an increasingly dispiriting round of consulta-
tions with others – always, as he stressed, selecting those of the highest
reputation: *'never any inferior adviser'*. Their treatments, all of which he
declared that he had followed for long enough to have given a fair trial,
comprised 'sea air and bathing in various localities, with much walking
exercise', swallowing 'gallons of physic and liquor potassae' – the latter
presumably as a diuretic – riding, taking the waters, and living 'on
sixpence a day, so to speak, and earn[ing] it, if bodily labour may be so
construed'; finally, he tried Turkish baths, which became popular around
1860. All that any of the doctors said about diet was that it should be
light and moderate, which, as he pointed out, was too vague to be helpful;
it is also possible that, as was common at this date, he took it literally, i.e.
judged 'lightness' by weight, which would have indicated such items as
bread and butter rather than relatively heavy, unsatisfying fruit and
vegetables (or liquids). It was perhaps as a result of restricting himself in
this way – which was the more probable because of his confessed liking
for bread and pastry – that he eventually came out in boils, and also two
'rather formidable carbuncles, for which I was ably operated upon and fed
into increased obesity.'[29] Almost as discouraging was the doctors' attitude,
which was that putting on weight was a natural concomitant of getting
old, and that, as such, it was wrong to interfere with it, both on

physiological and (because of the idea that people should accept themselves as God made them) moral grounds – which excluded the possibility that it might be detrimental to health.

His next consultation was not directly about his weight, which at this point had reached its apogee of 202 lb., but about his hearing. Somewhat surprisingly, it turned out that the specialist to whom he went (a Mr Harvey) regarded obesity as a major cause of deafness, and had therefore studied it as part of his professional expertise. He told Banting that diet was crucial in losing weight, but that, rather than eating 'lightly', or little but indiscriminately, he should cut down on foods high in carbohydrate. The diet he suggested (which was fairly extreme) completely excluded milk, butter, potatoes, pastry, beer, certain wines, notably port and Champagne,* and sugar as such; a little starch in the form of bread or biscuit, a small quantity of sweetened cooked fruit, and relatively generous amounts of light wine or sherry, however, were allowed – neither he nor any other doctor, either for reasons of practicability or (despite temperance) health, advocating giving up alcohol altogether. Nor were portions of permitted foods strictly limited, the wisdom of which was appreciated by Banting, who found that, because he never had to go hungry, he had no temptation to break the diet. The regime he followed was: breakfast: four or five ounces of meat or fish, an ounce (a thin slice) of dry toast or a small biscuit, and a large cup of tea without milk or sugar; dinner: five or six ounces each of fish, meat, and vegetables, an ounce of dry toast, a serving of poultry or game, the fruit but not crust of a pudding, and two or three glasses of claret, sherry, or Madeira; tea: two or three ounces of fruit, one or two rusks, and a cup of milkless and sugarless tea; supper: three or four ounces of meat or fish and one or two glasses of claret; and before bed, a tumbler of unsweetened grog or one or two glasses of claret or Madeira. Assuming that he added no accompaniments such as sauces, nor ate the fat on meat, this would have given him under 1,500 calories a day excluding alcohol: he lost about a pound a week on it and declared that he felt marvellous.

Three doctors, one of whom was Smith, reacted by similarly writing pamphlets: the other two were a Dr Watson Bradshaw, author of a book called *The Anatomy of Dyspepsia*, and a Dr John Harvey (not the same Harvey as the ear specialist). The chief concern of the latter two was to counter the implication that overweight was not a threat to health: thus they concentrated exclusively on its medical aspect and made no mention of its aesthetic disadvantages. Bradshaw's summary of its significance was

---

* One has to remember that the content of drinks was not always the same as today, e.g. Champagne was sweeter: this accounts for some, but not all, the apparently odd distinctions made between them.

as follows: '. . . without a scintilla of doubt, the presence of fat to an immoderate extent on the surface of the body, either locally or generally, is a disease. . . . Of course, while fat continued to deposit itself externally, it would not matter much how great the quantity was, even if it succeeded layer after layer, so long as the individual bearing it, could move about and perform the part of a living animal; but the great danger to be apprehended is, lest fat should show itself in internal organs or external parts, and materially interfere with nature's duties. . . . If this condition of matters goes on within . . . the system becomes so encumbered with fat, that the diaphragm cannot act with natural ease – and the heart may lose its power. . . . no wonder that fat persons should so often, when their friends have considered them in perfect health, fall down dead suddenly, or be found corpses in their beds.'[30] His concept of disease was founded on the idea that since fat people did not necessarily eat more than thin ones,*[31] the cause of fatness was not what was eaten, but the body's use, or rather misuse, of it. On this basis, he argued that different cases of overweight called for different treatment: thus proper medical examination was essential, and Banting's pamphlet, because it encouraged people to act independently, pernicious (which was of course in principle perfectly right). In places, his meaning was obscured by cumbrous language and apparent inconsistencies, but his main point as far as diet was concerned was that the sort of food was less relevant than quantity – which led him to give the usual advice to eat 'moderately',[32] and would have been liable to the bread-and-butter interpretation had he not added, rather as an afterthought, that nevertheless animal food was probably the most suitable for slimmers; he also forbade sugar and beer, and made the general recommendation of taking a fair but not excessive amount of exercise, cutting down on sleep (and especially not having a nap after meals), and wearing plenty of warm clothes to promote sweating.

Harvey's list of the evils of obesity comprised tumours, asthma, obstruction of the heart and liver, compression and displacement of the womb, and – which one would have thought might have been regarded as symptoms of distress about the look of fat – hysteria and nervousness:†[33] Smith (who entered the discussion last) endorsed this list, and also, presumably having studied the same authors, shared Harvey's ideas on diet. Both of them divided foods according to Liebig's classification into those which did and did not contain protein, or, in their terms, nitrogen,

---

* In fact, recent research has proved that they do: see, e.g., *The Observer* 'New research destroys the old idea that you can eat little and still stay fat if you have a "slow metabolism".'[31]

† A modern list runs as follows: 'While plumpness is a matter of aesthetics, real obesity . . . increases your risk of developing heart and gall-bladder disease, diabetes, back trouble, arthritis, varicose veins and high blood pressure.' According to *Living Magazine*, the idea that cutting down on sleep is a useful aid to slimming still persists.

and identified the fattening ones as non-nitrogenous (or low in nitrogen) and composed (or chiefly composed) of carbohydrate. In addition, however, it seems that both had read a recent paper by a French dietitian called Dancel, according to whom all kinds of fish except shellfish, hot tea and coffee, and vegetable acids and 'gum' (in effect, fibre) were also fattening: among the vegetables he singled out as particularly to be avoided were artichokes, cabbage, carrots, French beans, and lettuce. Shellfish, or more specifically lobster, crayfish, and crab, and cold tea and coffee were recommended as actively slimming, and also white wine as a diuretic, but, as this suggests, slimmers were cautioned against drinking more of anything than was strictly necessary. This meant that, apart from lobster, the only item against which there was no objection was meat. Mercifully, Harvey included eggs and 'dry, firm'[34] (i.e. not cream) cheese in his diet, and also fish, probably because he accepted that it was not only unrealistic but would have been considered uncivilized to suggest that people should entirely omit the first course at dinner (presumably he considered soup, since it was both liquid and almost certain to contain fat, starch, and/or vegetables, even worse). Similarly, he permitted a token amount of fruit at dessert; he also acknowledged, perhaps because some of his patients, like Banting, had suffered from boils, that the complete exclusion of vegetables might produce 'bad effects',[35] in which case it was necessary to eat a very few. He did not, however, include any in the diet he gave, which consisted of: breakfast: beef, mutton, fish, bacon, or eggs, dry toast, and cold tea or coffee without milk or sugar or chocolate made with water rather than milk; lunch: cold game or 'dry, firm' cheese, one biscuit, and a glass of sherry; dinner: turbot, sole, salmon, perch or carp; meat; poultry or game; a very little fruit (no pudding), a little cheese, and three or four glasses of sherry, Madeira, claret, or other light wine.

Smith, consistently with his work on the diet of the poor, wrote not on how to get thinner, but fatter: thus, on the same basis, he was able to advise a thoroughly healthy, well balanced, albeit unfashionable plan of eating, with plenty of fish, fruit, vegetables, and starch, and less red meat than was customary among the higher classes (he was one of the very few doctors at that time prepared to acknowledge the viability of vegetarianism). Among the items he especially recommended were turbot, flounder, brill, and mackerel, cabbage, carrots, lettuce, and potatoes, oranges, nectarines, melons, and – interestingly (this was 1865) – mangoes, plus bread, soup, porridge, milk, and warm rather than hot tea and coffee.

Perhaps partly as a result of his subject – then as now, skinniness (as opposed to malnutrition) not being known to produce any physical ill effects – he was the only one of the three to express understanding of the misery of being either too fat or too thin (amusingly, in view of current ideas, the undesirable features of the latter which he singled out were hollow cheeks and 'apparent'[36] collar-bones). Also, since he published his pamphlet not under his name but merely as 'A London Physician', he felt able, as he did not in his report on the workhouses, to show very deep emotion on the subject of poverty and unemployment: 'It is curious to note, that two evils of exactly opposite natures affect mankind; the one consists in the melancholy fact, that at least one half of all the men, women, and children are unable to get enough to eat, while the other is just the reverse. . . . It is long, long ago since man tried to cure the first evil, but his efforts remain fruitless – starvation is still the great enemy of our race. . . . No doubt much of this misery is self-entailed, or the natural result of want of prudence, and indulgence in vice or idleness; but laying aside a large proportion for this culpable section, there remaineth a terrible mass of unmanageable misery, among which may often be seen that saddest sight which the sun beholds on our planet, men willing and able to work that they may earn food for themselves and those dear to them by natural ties, who are yet unable to procure it. Perhaps so ugly a feature in our social system was necessary to overcome man's reluctance to that labour which was imposed on him by the Creator, and no doubt its horror has a wholesome effect on the sluggard, but it is also stupefying.'[37]

10. *Children: Mutton or Cook-It-Yourself*

The monotony of higher-class children's diet was criticized even at the time. Until the age of about seventeen, when they left the nursery or school – where boys, but, needless to say, not girls, showed remarkable resource in breaking it – they were fed almost exclusively on milk, oatmeal, bread (ideally, eight days old), potatoes (again, old rather than new), mutton, and suet or rice pudding. The Dr Spock of the era, a paediatrician called Pye Henry Chavasse, whose books remained in print for almost a century, forbade any meat other than mutton or beef, all vegetables but old potatoes except for very occasionally, very small helpings of the four considered most digestible, i.e. asparagus, broccoli, cauliflower, and French beans, and all cakes and sweets – restrictions which were also supposed to apply to lactating women.

Pregnant women were told to eat fruit but little meat because 'the habit of body, at that time, is usually feverish and inflammatory';[1] once the baby was born, however, a bland and easily digested diet was considered essential to preserve the flavour and quality of the milk. Today it may be claimed that food has a negligible effect on the taste of mothers' milk: on the analogy of animals, however, the Victorians believed that flavours were readily absorbed by it. Chavasse said: '. . . if a cow feeds on swedes, the milk and butter have a turnipy flavour. This decides, beyond a doubt, that the milk does partake of the qualities of the food that she [the nurse] feeds on.'[2] Thus, as well as the limitations specified for children, he banned sauces and all salted, spiced, or pickled foods; in addition, for reasons of digestibility, soups were prohibited, and also, presumably as stimulants, green tea and wine (though he conceded that ladies who were used to wine should perhaps continue to drink a little). Since beer, despite being condemned as unladylike, was thought to be uniquely effective as a stimulant to the secretion of milk, he recommended a couple of glasses of mild ale a day; otherwise, the drinks he favoured were weak black tea, barley water, milk and water, and toast and water.

Besides the inconvenience and boredom of the diet, new babies were customarily fed every hour and a half (rather than four), and because there were no manufactured baby milks, breast-milk given for about a year (until they could eat a proportion of solid food). This meant that breast-feeding was an almost total commitment: when one remembers that families were unplanned, so that pregnancy and lactation threatened to be continuous, it becomes more understandable that higher-class ladies frequently opted out of it. There were also of course those who could not do it, and the considerable number of babies whose mothers died in childbirth. The traditional, and most obviously satisfactory substitute for the mother was the wet-nurse – who, however, brought a variety of problems; the next most favoured (and certainly less potentially trouble-some) was a donkey, whose milk had been shown by analysis to be nearer in composition to humans' than that of any other animal. Queen Victoria's daughter wrote to her mother thanking her for promising to send her one: 'I was quite ashamed to telegraph to you about a donkey for the children but really it will not do any longer without one, and Wegner [her children's doctor] has been advertising without end in the newspapers without any success. In the south of Germany one can only get them in April and May they say, so we were obliged to have recourse to your kindness.

'The nurse is no use whatever to poor Baby and the milk does not seem to agree with him so that we shall wean him as soon as the donkey comes. The cow milk here is shockingly bad.'[3]

As one might suppose, diet was one source of tension between the nurse and her employer. This would no doubt have applied in any case, but was aggravated by the fact that most lower-class women were either too ignorant or too poor to have heard of or been able to observe any prohibition when feeding their own children (salt or pickled pork in particular being a very likely component of their menu) and regarded the constraints imposed on them as merely ridiculous. Another cause of trouble was the use of laxatives and sedatives, against which Isabella gave an emphatic warning: 'There are two points all mothers should remember, and be on their guard against. The first is, never to allow a nurse to give medicine to the infant on her own authority: many have such an infatuated idea of the *healing excellence* of castor-oil, that they would administer a dose of this disgusting grease twice a week, and think they had done a meritorious service to the child. The next point is, to watch carefully, lest, to insure a night's sleep for herself, she does not dose the infant with Godfrey's cordial, syrup of poppies, or some narcotic potion . . . The fact that scores of nurses keep secret bottles of these deadly syrups, for the purpose of stilling their charges, is notorious . . .'[4] But even nurses who performed their duties impeccably must frequently have been looked on with ambivalence by mothers made to feel guilty or jealous, according to circumstances, by their presence; there was also their effect on fathers, who in some cases were suffering from the first shock of the loss of their wives. It was not so much grief at his bereavement, however, but pride which gave rise to Mr Dombey's distress at having to employ a nurse for his only son: '. . . he viewed with so much bitterness the thought of being dependent . . . on a hired serving-woman who would be to his child, for the time, all that even *his* alliance could have made his own wife that in every new rejection of a candidate he felt a secret pleasure.'[5] When Polly Toodle, the wife of a stoker, was finally engaged, 'For all his starched, impenetrable dignity, he wiped blinding tears from his eyes . . . and often said, with an emotion of which he would not, for the world, have had a witness, "Poor little fellow!" '[6]

If cows' milk had to be used, it was advised that it should be diluted with one third of water (which would have made it less rich than breast-milk), and, because it was thought that some of its properties were destroyed by heating, that it should be warmed by means of the water rather than the milk: it seems appallingly sad, in view of the risk of TB, that for this reason it was stressed that milk for children should never be boiled – unless, according to Chavasse, they had diarrhoea. The point he particularly emphasized, however, was that, to ensure consistent quality, it should always come from the same cow: obviously, this left the possibility that an infected animal might be chosen, but in overall terms would considerably have reduced the risk of disease.

Prepared milk was dependent on the production of dried milk powder, which did not become available on a large scale until the 1870s: the earliest equivalent was a recipe published by Liebig in 1867 which he claimed gave a mixture with almost exactly the same properties as human milk. This was (per feed) five ounces of cows' milk, one ounce of water, half an ounce each of wheat and malt flour, and thirty drops of solution of potash: the latter was added to balance the acidity of the starch in the flour. It was first produced from fresh milk by a firm called Liebig's Registered Concentrated Milk Co., which (of necessity) delivered daily and operated only in the London area but a few years later was marketed nationally in powder form by Lily & Co.

The traditional starch foods for babies were gruel made from arrowroot, semolina, crushed biscuits, bread, or flour: Chavasse recommended baked flour or bread or flour boiled for several hours like a pudding. Manufac-tured cereal foods, however, were already on the market and, according to Lily, the cause of an alarming rise in infant deaths from stomach disorders: the reason given, or rather implied, was that they were used as substitutes rather than supplements to milk and thus fostered nutritional deficiency, but insofar as that they encouraged bottle- as opposed to breast-feeding, another factor, of which by this time a few chemists were probably aware, was that bottles and teats were not sterilized. Bottles were cleaned simply

A child's fantasy (the cups contain, or rather contained,
either a cream or ice cream)

by rinsing in warm water, and teats, rather than being removed and
washed separately, often left on until they wore out, which might not be
for several weeks: this was because of the difficulty of attaching them,
which, since the calves' teats traditionally used could not be stretched over
the necks of the bottles, had to be done by tying them on with string.
Rubber ones had been introduced by 1860, but, despite their obvious
convenience, were unpopular because they were black, which the mothers
alleged put off the babies.

Once the child was on solid food, the routine of old bread, old potatoes
and mutton began. Soyer reported Mrs B—— as giving her children
carefully varied dinners: although main courses were usually roast and
boiled mutton and roast beef in rotation, less approved dishes such as
pickled pork or salt beef and dumplings were also occasionally served;

puddings might be milk (rice, tapioca, or pasta),* apple or rhubarb tart, or bread or 'very plain' currant pudding. It was felt necessary, however, to defend this: 'Many people may, perhaps, imagine that there is too much variety for children; but it is quite the contrary; change of food is to the stomach what change of air is to the general health . . .'[7] At the other extreme, Augustus Hare had roast mutton and rice pudding every single day without intermission; until reform, the scholars at Eton not only had boiled mutton and mashed potatoes every single day for dinner but the left-overs, and nothing else, for supper: if there were none, they went without. The bones from supper were kept to be used as bait for their evening sport of rat-catching, which was one of their ways of passing the time in the enormous dormitory, the 'Long Chamber', in which (to save the cost of supervision) they were locked from 5 p.m. in winter and 8 p.m. in summer until 7.30 the following morning – when, as the school did not provide them with breakfast, they had to find their own, the custom being for them to pay a woman in the town for breakfast, extra supper, and other necessities not supplied by the school. After reform (in the early '40s) they were given bread, butter, and milk for breakfast, tea of the same – tea as a meal being common in schools because dinner was at midday – with beef instead of mutton twice a week. At both Eton and Winchester, it was also traditional to celebrate Sunday by serving pudding, plum or otherwise (in terms of traditions, however, the Eton one was relatively recent dating only from 1785, when a fund for the puddings was donated by a sympathetic ex-pupil, Lord Godolphin). The scholars at Winchester had beef on Sundays and mutton every other day; fee-paying boys (who ate in a separate dining-hall) were given mutton four days a week and roast and boiled beef and roast veal on the other three (fee-paying Etonians had their meals in different boarding-houses, where the food varied). Very occasionally, carrots or greens were served at Winchester, otherwise, again, vegetables were always potatoes 'dressed after a curious fashion, something between boiled and mashed, and served in tin pannikins'.[8] Besides plum pudding for all on Sundays, fee-paying Wykehamists – known as 'commoners' – had apple or gooseberry pie, according to season, on Thursdays, and the scholars, or 'collegers', two puddings per week – the extra pudding, to judge from the latter's popularity, more than compensating for the greater frequency of mutton. Breakfasts and suppers for both groups were tea, rolls, and butter – which, however, were regarded as merely the foundation of the meal. No doubt partly for this reason, but also because of generous quantities and cooking which, by all reports, was unusually good, Wykehamists – in contrast to Etonians –

---

* Not only macaroni but vermicelli was used for milk puddings in a similar way to rice.

seem universally to have considered their 'Commissariat' excellent (though whether they were allowed to appreciate it was another matter).

To the extent that other factors impinged, neither Hare's unremitting diet nor the Eton and Winchester mutton were typical: the latter was partly a matter of economy and/or convenience, since both schools were endowed with estates on which sheep were reared, and the former part of a horrifyingly cruel upbringing by a pair of sado-masochistic aunts (one of their most unforgivable acts was to kill his pet cat because they felt that he had become too fond of her; also – more ludicrously – he was served with exotic puddings which he was then not allowed to eat). In general, however, children were given mutton (as the most wholesome sort of meat) and only the simplest and supposedly most digestible foods because their systems were thought to be, not merely less robust than adults', though this was also emphasized, but, on the basis that babies could only drink milk, immature in the sense of being incomplete. Esther Hewlett said: 'As to food, it is essential for parents to know that the stomachs of their children are in general not capable of digesting the same food that they themselves enjoy';[9] a doctor, in a wonderfully euphemistic passage, explained further: 'Compared with the adult, it [the child] stores up, in a more or less permanent form, a far larger proportion of the constituents of its *ingesta* among the tissues of its body. In other words, for equal amounts of food . . . a smaller quantity of effete matter is necessarily dismissed . . . by those various functions of which the *egesta* are the ultimate products. Now most of these functions are so strictly depurative; indeed, are so strictly the means of eliminating poisons casually mixed with the *ingesta*; that this contrast sufficiently explains why purity from such admixture is in the case of the infant a far more imperious require-ment than in the adult . . . Furthermore, a careful consideration of the processes which we sum up by the term "Digestion," would show that not only are the various metamorphoses thus comprehended conducted more feebly and imperfectly in the infant, but that there are grounds for supposing these conversions themselves to be chemically somewhat more limited.'[10]

The hardships caused by the excesses of the fagging system and general bullying and victimization of younger boys which characterized the public schools at this time are well known; perhaps less widely appreciated, however, is the extent to which they were connected with food – or drink. It is true that at Harrow, where Hare was sent for a short time, sport was responsible for some of the worst suffering: boys unable to run fast enough in football, for instance, were beaten until blood ran with thorn sticks, and Hare himself was clearly exhausted by hours spent cricket fagging (i.e.

fielding). The younger Harrovians' most formidable challenge, however, was being sent to the pub to buy porter – pubs being out of bounds at all the schools except (in practice) Eton: the penalties were either a flogging from the headmaster or, for not going, a 'wapping' from the sixth-form boys, which – necessarily – was the more dreaded (one has to remember that although pupils were forbidden to go into pubs, there was no law banning the sale of drink to children and drinking condoned – to the extent that table, i.e. weak, beer was served and sometimes brewed by the schools). Another, less risky but boring and time-consuming fagging duty was waiting on the seniors at meals – all the boys having or sharing their own rooms, to which the elder ones' breakfasts and teas were taken. As at Eton, pupils lived in different boarding-houses where conditions varied slightly: in some, the waiting was done by servants, but in others it fell to the fags, who, besides delivering and clearing away the dishes, had to sit on the floor outside the relevant doors for the duration of the meal to be ready to fetch further supplies or run any other errands which might be required. They were not, however, expected to prepare items – cooking being possible, as at virtually all schools, because of the use of open fires for heating, but, at any rate in Hare's house, forbidden: Hare and his friends nevertheless invested in a frying-pan and pipkin and regularly ran up snacks on their own account, their usual choice of dish (no doubt governed by pocket-money) being fried potatoes; on one occasion, how-ever, they tried (ironically) to roast a hare, but, after dealing with the innards 'with much the same difficulty and secrecy, and in much the same manner, as the Richmond murderess disposed of her victims', were caught long before it was cooked enough to be edible, not having realized how long it would take over the 'wretched embers'[11] of a small fire.

At Eton, although the boys were not allowed into pubs at large, they were tacitly permitted to use two – because, as was noted in the Clarendon Report, 'the beer given in the boarding-houses is not uniformly good'.[12] Here too, the fags had to act as waiters but not cooks: boys may sometimes have had private fry-ups, but the custom was for those from landed families to give dinners of game or poultry from their fathers' estates, the impracticality of preparing which on the premises was obvious: instead, such items were sent – via the fags – to the nearest inn (presumably one of the permitted establishments): 'At this moment there entered the room a little boy, the scion of a noble house, bearing a roasted goose, which he had carried from the kitchen of the opposite inn, the Christopher. The lower boy or fag, depositing his burthen, asked his master if he had further need of him; and Buckhurst, after looking round the table and ascertaining that he had not, gave him permission to retire; but he had scarcely disappeared, when his master singing out, "Lower boy, St John!" he immediately re-entered, and demanded his master's pleasure, which was that he should pour some water into the teapot. This being accomplished, St John really made his escape, and retired to a pupil-room, where the bullying of a tutor, because he had no derivations, exceeded in all probability the bullying of his master, had he contrived in his passage from the Christopher to have upset the goose or dropped the sausages.'[13]

The latter suggests that Etonian fags, at least if they were aristocratic, were treated a little more mercifully by the older boys than was the practice at Harrow – or Winchester, where before mid century quite as much cruelty was shown in the collegers' dining-hall as on the Harrow football pitch, and even at a later date it was impossible for any junior to sit down to a civilized breakfast or supper; correlatively, the prefects, as one Old Wykehamist put it, 'feasted in royal state, surrounded by a multitude of servants, which might have matched the train of an Indian prince, or a Jamaican nabob . . .'[14]

All Wykehamists customarily supplemented the rolls, butter, and tea provided at breakfast and supper with their own additions – only the crust of the rolls being eaten, the crumb, in age-old fashion, being squeezed into pellets and used as ammunition (which at least shows that the bread was fresh). The juniors, however, had to content themselves with instant items such as cold beef or meat pies which could be consumed in snatched intervals between or before they began their work as restaurateurs. Absurd as it sounds, the entire lower school was involved in preparing breakfasts for a total of twenty-four prefects (twelve collegers and twelve common-ers), who, since none of the boys had their own rooms, did not take them in private but in the dining-halls, where they occupied special tables placed on either side of the enormous fires needed for heating. Whereas in the commoners' hall the meal began with roll-call, which was taken by a master who remained present long enough for the younger boys to swallow their cold meat before applying themselves to their duties, no member of staff attended in college, where activity started at once; apart from this, and the fact that there were fewer scholars to share the work, the proceedings in both halls were virtually the same. The boys operated in a professional manner in teams, one of cooks proper, organized under a master chef, one of toasters, another of butterers, one of waiters, and one of errand-boys. The master chef supervised the cooking of major items such as chicken, sausages, and eggs; the toasters, who used hazel branches split at the ends as toasting-forks, worked in relays, each one having to complete a certain number of slices; as soon as the slices were done, they were buttered and delivered with the utmost haste to ensure, on pain of indignant rejection, that they reached their customers 'hot-and-hot';[15] meanwhile, the errand-boys, who in commons (where there were more of them) sat in a row on a cross-bench waiting for orders, were despatched in all directions for accompaniments such as egg-cups, spoons, pepper, mustard, and marmalade.

Dinner was more sedentary, but for the junior collegers had formerly been such an ordeal that only the awful consequences of being discovered skiving can have induced them to attend at all. As the meal was already hot, no cooking had been demanded of them; fetching accompaniments, however, had not only caused them to be deprived of their mutton but subjected to indiscriminate chastisement. The arrival of the prefects in hall had acted as the signal for serving to begin but at the same time heralded the exodus of half the diners, the items required in this instance including sauces, pickles, bread, beer, and extra knives, many of which had to be brought from distant parts of the school; meanwhile, the meat was distributed according to a tradition which dictated that it should be served only to boys who were actually seated at table – very few of the errand-boys being able to complete their missions until long after it had been withdrawn and even those who did being liable to be sent on another. (It should be said that the surplus mutton, rather than being eaten by the seniors or appropriated by the college servants, had, theoretically at least, been given to the poor). In addition, nominally to speed the boys on their way, two prefects had been stationed at strategic points, e.g. by the door and in the middle of the hall, and slashed everyone who went past with ash switches. Occasionally, terrified juniors had in fact absented themselves, and, to avoid discovery, hidden in empty beer-barrels in the cellar; once, one had been found imprisoned in a salting-tub, the lid of which he had succeeded in replacing but could not afterwards lift off over his head.

Until these practices were forbidden, the college dinner had been at 6 p.m.; thereafter, it was served at 1 p.m. in both halls, followed by supper at 6 – at which cooking took place in much the same way as at breakfast. Nor did this complete the prefects' gastronomic pleasures for the day, since they also had 'mess' at 8 or 9 p.m., which consisted either of tea or coffee plus 'fixings', or 'made beer', an ingenious concoction of school-brewed beer doctored with sugar and spice, bottled, and kept to strengthen. The 'fixings' may have been merely toast, perhaps with anchovy spread or potted meat, or something more luxurious from the confectioner's – probably from a shop called 'La Croix' (which was also a caterer's) situated just down the street from the college buildings in the house where Jane Austen spent the last few weeks of her life. In winter, this refreshment (the only meal not taken in hall) was savoured by the fires in their dormitories, but in summer was carried outside to 'a species of ex-tempore tea-gardens'[16] formed by the buttresses of the chapel.

As well as confectioners', schoolboys had the option of street-sellers, who offered anything from toffee to a beverage in ginger-beer bottles which was sold on the football pitch at Rugby at half-time and alleged to have an unfavourable effect on the standard of play. In addition to off-was on-the-premises consumption, and not only in permitted inns by Etonians – Rugbaeans displaying a somewhat ungentlemanly taste for the gin punch at their local 'Cock Robin' (at Rugby, cooking was as established a part of school life as at Winchester, but carried out in the boys' private studies). There were also the traditional school hampers – known among Wykehamists as 'cargoes' which, besides the fag's breakfast pies and cold meat might contain fruit pies, fruit, and fruit cake. Dickens described a hamper containing steak pie, mince pies, apple turnover, and cake; Isabella Beeton's sons (who went to a preparatory school at Exmouth and then to Marlborough) were sent fruit from their father's garden, chocolates (this was in the 1870s) and no doubt cake – the recipe given by their mother for children at school, however, not being for the sort of confectioners' creation probably bought for 'mess', but a suitably healthy kind of tea-cake with relatively little sugar and very little fat.[17] The situation was totally different in girls' schools, where, needless to say, cooking among themselves or waiting on other pupils would have been even more unthinkable than cookery lessons; nor could girls whose hunger overcame their sense of propriety resort to confectioners', since they were virtually never allowed outside the school grounds unsupervised; generally, their only excursions were accompanied walks in crocodiles, which served for exercise instead of games. Hence their much greater dependence on the school supply of bread and butter – rather than, as alleged, greater intrinsic needs than boys': 'I don't believe that any of the stories told about the ravenous fondness of schoolgirls for *Butterbrods* are exaggerated ... I hope I shall not be contradicted by physiologists when I assert, that in the majority of instances girls have a far more voracious appetite than boys. From nine to thirteen a girl would much sooner have a slice of bread-and-butter than a hoop, a doll, or a skipping-rope. This is why discreet governesses are able entirely to dispense with corporal punishment in girls' schools.* A boy doesn't care much about being deprived of a meal; a girl does ... Starvation is a quiet, genteel, unobtrusive punishment. It causes no frenzied struggles, no violent howling. It is very cheap; and the establishment saves money by the culprits who are put *au pain sec*.'[18]

Starvation, or dry bread and water, was also a very popular punishment in the home – and probably helped to promote a puritanical attitude towards food (although, if the meal in question was only bread and butter

---

* Corporal punishment was in fact very common in girls' schools.

A children's party at the Mansion House (*Illustrated London News*)

and milk or milk and water to begin with, it was a lesser deprivation than it sounds).

The only times when the strictness of children's diet was modified were at Christmas, perhaps Michaelmas (Michaelmas dinner was one of the two occasions in the year on which the regular menu at Winchester was changed – geese being served in the ratio of one per five boys) and parties. Even at the latter, however, as much attention was paid to health, and also, at least at the top end of society, decorum, as possible. In a pair of biting articles in *Punch*, Thackeray pointed out that a more intelligent regard for health would have indicated summer as the most popular season for giving them rather than the post-Christmas weeks of 'sleet, thaw, frost, wind, mud, and sore-throats'[19] – but, as usual, saved most of his fire for the sort of behaviour they engendered: '. . . attired in those absurd best clothes, what can you expect from [the children] but affectation and airs of fashion? . . . And look at them when they arrive at their places of destination; what processes of coquetry they are made to go through! They are first carried into a room where there are pins, combs, looking-glasses, and lady's maids, who shake [their] ringlets out, spread abroad their great immense sashes and ribbons, and finally send them full sail into the dancing-room. With what precocity they ogle their own faces in the looking-glasses! . . .

'As to the airs which wretches give themselves about dancing, I need not enlarge upon them here . . .'[20]

In fact, the food was the only major respect in which allowance was made for age at such parties, which were planned to be as nearly as possible identical to adult balls; they were held in the evening, albeit an hour or so earlier than was customary for the latter, the chief entertainment was dancing, and the children were dressed almost as elaborately as their parents. Except for the 'great immense' sashes, which might have been pink or blue, and, as the only colour in their costume, must have been very eye-catching, girls wore virginal white, from white flowers in their hair to unwashable, uncleanable white kid gloves and white shoes; boys as young as seven or eight were expected to wear similar evening dress to their fathers', which also included white kid gloves. Lady Frederick Cavendish excitedly described her preparations for a ball given by Queen Victoria for her third son, Prince Arthur's fifth birthday (Lady Frederick was fourteen at the time, but, just as little distinction was made between the way in which adults and children were entertained, so none was drawn between children of different ages, who were all asked to the same parties together): 'May 1st., 1855. A memorable day indeed! My head was washed by Strathearne, a hairdresser . . . He did Agnes [Gladstone] and my hair in the evening, at about 7. At 8½ we were to be at the Palace for the Queen's ball. We were rigged, figged, and launched into two carriages in tolerable time, and our dresses were something magnificent. A beautiful muslin frock trimmed with ruches and daisies, white silk stockins, white satin shoes with white bows, white kid gloves trimmed with white daisies, and a wreath of two rows of daisies on polls . . .'[21]

Her only comments about the supper were that the table was horse-shoe-shaped, that 'everybody stood' (it was evidently a buffet) and 'Nobody eat much' – which was presumably because they were too excited and overawed by the royalties present; the food, however, would have consisted of cold meats, beautifully garnished but without salads, patties – as opposed to vols-au-vent because of the richness of puff pastry – and perhaps meat, rather than egg or cheese, sandwiches; this would have been followed by decorative but basically plain biscuits, tarts, cakes, jellies, blancmanges, and custards, plus a dessert which included fruit and platters of sweets or bon-bons but not ices. The accepted drink at children's parties, and indeed peculiar to them, since it was not considered potent enough for adults, was negus (based on port or sherry); in addition would be freshly made cool, but not cold, lemonade, and after the meal weak tea and coffee (stronger tea and coffee often being offered to accompanying parents on arrival, on the assumption that they had just had dinner). Iced drinks and ice-cream were forbidden: 'The aged, the delicate, and children should abstain from ices or iced beverages; even the strong and healthy should partake of them in moderation. They should be taken immediately after the repast, or some hours after, because the taking these substances *during* the process of digestion is apt to provoke indisposition . . . It is also necessary to abstain when persons are very warm, or immediately after taking violent exercise, as in some cases they have produced illnesses which have ended fatally.'[22] Also prohibited were muffins and bread and butter, as opposed to sandwiches, because of the risk of butter on the white kid gloves, which could be taken off for a sit-down meal but were left on at a buffet. At a Christmas party, the dishes of sweets at dessert would have been replaced by crackers, which contained sweets, and, as one might guess from the idea of the latter with mottoes, were invented by confectioners, who originally conceived them merely as a style of wrapping; as yet, their contents included only sweets, mottoes, and presumably 'cracks' rather than hats or any other sort of present. When they were first introduced is uncertain: an early cracker-maker was a confectioner called Tom Smith, founder of the company of that name, who is said to have started making them in 1846,[23] but he can hardly have been the first, since Thackeray, in the course of his observations on parties, took them for granted only three years later: 'Among the very little children I confess I get a consolation as I watch them, in seeing the artless little girls walking after the boys to whom they incline . . . inciting them to dances, seeking them out to pull crackers with them and begging them to read the mottoes . . .'[24] A contributor to *The Ladies' Treasury* also mentioned them, referring to them, however (with accuracy), as 'cracker-bon-bons'.

In fashionable circles, the only permissible entertainments besides dancing were conjurors' and magic lantern shows; further down the social scale, however, perhaps partly because smaller numbers were involved, games such as charades or 'Historical Questions' (the equivalent to 'Trivial Pursuits' might be played, although the emphasis was still on dancing, with the assumption which it implied of attraction between the sexes among children of any age (sexual interest seems to have been presumed to be active virtually from birth). At this level, too, a rather more individualistic attitude was sometimes taken towards the refreshments: the writer in *The Ladies' Treasury* (who was not Aunt Deborah) recommended a centrepiece of 'a nice *rich* cake',[25] and expressed disapproval of alcohol for children, suggesting orgeat (a soft drink made from almonds) as an alternative to negus; there was also a mother – living of course in North London – who had no objection to alcohol but refused to serve either negus or confectioners' goods because of her concern about additives: her guests therefore made merry on ginger and blackcurrant wine, presumably home-made, accompanied by a feast of 'pies and puddings and custards'[26] which were not merely made at home but by, or at least partly by, the lady herself.

Although the poor themselves obviously could not give parties, it was traditional for landowners to entertain the local children at Christmas or on other occasions, and in the towns – though less often – charities might organize Christmas dinners for adults and/or children (e.g. a mammoth dinner at which Soyer roasted an ox). At these events, the reverse of the higher-class pattern applied inasmuch as that non-adult amusements were often provided for children in the form of sports and games (the assump-tion presumably being that they did not know how to dance) but – if the meal was dinner – the food for both invariably included roast beef and plum pudding. Nor, according to the details given in a squire's account book, did the quantities eaten by the two age-groups differ (admittedly, the book referred to the 1880s, but one has no reason to suppose that the children's appetites were significantly larger than they would have been twenty or thirty years earlier – indeed, rather the reverse, since they were probably better fed at home than before). At a Christmas schoolchildren's dinner, ninety of the latter plus ten adult helpers ate a total of 80 lb. of roast beef, accompanied by vegetables, 1 lb. or more each of Christmas pudding,* and, in the case of the children, sweets, oranges, and nuts and apples for which, by way of a game, they had to 'scramble': this was succeeded not long afterwards (they arrived at 1.30 p.m. and left at 4.30) by tea and coffee, bread and butter, tea-cakes, fruit and seed buns, jumbles, shortbread, a selection of other biscuits, various cakes, and dessert – none of the children, if of school age, being more than fourteen. When the same generous host subsequently gave them a tea, it was their consumption of liquid rather than solid refreshment which calls for comment (though the latter was not inconsiderable). This time, eighty guests ate 56 lb. of bread and butter and rather less than 30 lb. of cake, accompanied by tea made with 1½ lb. of tea, 4 gallons of milk, and 14 lb. of sugar. A pencilled note in the margin of the book said, 'A good deal too much cake. Bread and butter preferred'[27] – which was almost certainly not because of any intrinsic preference for bread and butter (nor a reflection on the quality of

---

* The recipe was: 42 lb. flour, 16 lb. suet, 21 lb. mixed fruit, 6 lb. sugar, lemon peel, and skimmed milk. This was made into 24 puddings which were boiled for nine hours.

the cake) but because they killed their desire for sweet food by drinking vast amounts of tea into which they put an average of 6 oz. of sugar per head. One assumes that the explanation for this was that the lower classes, although better off than previously and despite lower duty and prices, still could not afford tea for their families: thus the children regarded it as a special treat but were unaccustomed to its bitterness.

11. Nutrition: A Case of Direct Observation

'The question of food lies at the foundation of all other questions. There is no mind, no work, no health, no life, without food; and just as we are fed defectively or improperly, are our frames developed in a way unfitted to secure the greatest of earthly blessings – a sound mind in a sound body.' Edwin Lankester, *On Food*

'The health of both mind and body are dependent ultimately on how we eat. We are undoubtedly, to a certain extent, composed of what we eat . . .' Anton Mosimann, *Cuisine Naturelle*

Justus von Liebig showed no sign of brilliance as a child: possibly his lack of promise was due to dyslexia which he was able to overcome when he grew older, or he may simply have been bored and frustrated because at this date no scientific subjects were taught in schools. He was reported to be hopeless at all the available subjects and described in class as 'the plague of his teachers and the sorrow of his parents';[1] nor were his schoolmasters likely to have been impressed by his declaration that he wanted to be a chemist, since chemistry was only just beginning to be studied at the universities and still too new and avant-garde to be taken seriously as a career possibility – besides seeming totally unrealistic for a dunce.

At home, however, his ambition was probably viewed with more sympathy, since his father was a colour dealer, which involved the use of chemicals, and apparently interested in their wider possibilities: thus it was presumably from him that his original inspiration, if not also some of his talent, sprang. One can hardly blame the father, as a provincial tradesman – his business was in Darmstadt, just south of Frankfurt – and in the light of Justus's depressing academic record, for interpreting the word 'chemist' in its humbler sense, and, when the latter left school, apprenticing him to a druggist in the small town of Heppenheim. That the arrangement did not work out almost goes without saying – not because he seemed lazy or incapable but, rather to the contrary, because he tried to teach himself by carrying out experiments with his master's materials. Before long, again as must be expected, this led to an explosion, which, however, did no serious damage and was useful in that it curtailed the time he wasted with the druggist, who promptly sent him home. It seems that his father gave up at this point and made no further plans for him; Liebig, however, who was by now sixteen, continued his efforts at self-education in the local Darmstadt Court Library, where he read everything on chemistry he could find – which, as this included most, if not all, the major works on the subject to date, must have given him a fairly thorough academic grounding. He then persuaded his father to send him to Bonn University, which had recently been re-founded after destruction by the French and had a chemistry department headed by a professor called Kastner.

He evidently liked and respected Kastner, who in turn recognized that he had unusual talent; in terms of method, however, the teaching deeply disappointed him because the need to allow pupils to conduct experiments for themselves had not yet been appreciated, nor were the corresponding laboratories provided: thus they could not verify existing theories or experiment or gain any practical knowledge at all – which he considered the most important element in learning. It may have been because he was outspoken on this or other subjects, or – albeit more prudently than before – repeated his crime of experimenting privately, that he apparently got into trouble once again; or it may have been connected with personal relationships. A poet called Platen who knew him at this time described him yearningly: '". . . clear, definite, and solid in everything, and, above all, on the side of the affections, open and confiding . . . beautiful. Of slender form, a friendly earnestness in his regular features, great brown eyes with dark, shady eyebrows which attracted one instantly . . . Oh that I might after so many deceptions, find happiness and peace in this friendship, which seems to open up new future possibilities."'[2] Though in love the poet was not blinded by it, or at least not alone in responding to him: students at the department Liebig founded only two years later confirm that the ridiculed schoolboy grew up to be mesmerically attractive apparently even to those without homosexual tendencies, and later photographs show that he was quite extraordinarily handsome.

The desire to stay with Kastner, though it certainly played a part, may thus not have been his only reason for leaving Bonn and following the latter to Erlangen University, near Nuremberg, before he had finished his course; at Erlangen, however, he received his PhD and published his first paper, still aged only nineteen. He was then given a grant which enabled him to go to Paris, at that time the scientific as well as artistic centre of Europe, where, after initial embarrassment, he was introduced to two of the foremost scientists of the day, Joseph Gay-Lussac and the naturalist and explorer Baron Alexander von Humboldt, who launched him on his career by recommending him for the job of starting a chemistry department at Giessen University, in a quiet country town not far, as it happened, from Darmstadt.

He arrived at Giessen in 1824, aged twenty-one, and stayed thirty years, during which time his department became internationally famous, drawing pupils from all over the civilized world, while his work as a chemist, first in pure organic chemistry and thereafter in applied chemistry, earned him the acknowledged title of founder of the former and the right to that of founder, or at any rate co-founder, of the modern study of nutrition.

As a teacher, his particular contribution was, predictably, to introduce laboratory work for students: this became standard practice in a surprisingly short time, and proved an advantage to teachers as well as pupils, since the latter were able to further the former's research – Liebig's senior students carrying out literally thousands of experiments for him. For the rest, his effectiveness was assured by his personality: one reason why his students worked exceptionally hard may have been, as was cynically observed, that there was little else to do in Giessen, but it was also because they fell under his spell.

One, an American called Horsfield who later became a professor at Harvard, ascribed his fascinating quality almost entirely to the visible manifestation of his intellect: 'There is an expression of thought in all his attitudes and movements which I could scarcely have believed upon the mere relation [i.e. telling], and which the crayon cannot commit to paper ... He is all mind – and it beams as distinctly through his corporeal tenement as his chemical compounds are seen through the vessels that contain them. His detail of chemical decompositions and recompositions is clear and expressed without any circumlocution in terms, comprehended by everyone. Occasionally, these details bring him to review some investigations and theories of his own, and then a new animation is superadded to his ordinary bearing, and the illustrations are dramatic. His large eyes expand, and his features seem to glow. The gesticulations are sometimes so happy and so numerous that I have sometimes fancied one might understand some of his themes if he [one] were unable to hear.'[3]

His most fundamental achievement in the field of pure chemistry was to establish a method of analysing compounds, the one he adopted being the now classic oxidization or burning, which had been tried before but until then had not been systematically tested and modified for use with different substances; he also contributed towards finding a method of measuring molecular weight. The discoveries with more general applications included a cheap (and safe) way of producing potassium cyanide, which was relevant in several fields, including photography, and, most significantly, chloroform (which he found in 1832 but was not used in this country until 1847). In the later 1830s he turned his attention to fermentation and digestion, which he studied together because he believed that they were similar processes, and at about the same time started research into plant and animal nutrition, which led to his recognition of both the efficacy of inorganic fertilizers and importance of protein. His ideas on plant nourishment were put forward in the book which first made him famous outside academic circles and for which, at least in Britain, he is probably still best known, *Organic Chemistry in its Applications to Agriculture and Physiology* – which was not originally conceived as a book but merely a paper in response to an invitation to address a meeting of the British Association for the Advancement of Science, and (to save time) was translated as he wrote it by one of his students, a Scot called Lyon Playfair. His next book, completed a couple of years later, *Animal Chemistry in its Applications to Physiology and Pathology* (1842) dealt with animal nutrition; then, in accordance with an avowed policy of popularizing chemistry and the knowledge it made available, he set out his theories in terms adapted to the lay public in two volumes of *Familiar Letters on Chemistry and its Relation to Commerce, Physiology, and Agriculture* (1843 and '44).

Organic Chemistry ran to seventeen editions in eight years, four of which were in English, *Animal Chemistry* to three English editions in four years, and *Familiar Letters* reached a total of over thirty in ten languages.[4]

The starting-point of his study of nutrition was his discovery of the food chain, i.e. the interdependence of plants and animals, his research into plant nutrients and behaviour leading to his identification of protein: 'From carbonic acid, water, and ammonia – that is, from the constituents of the atmosphere – with the addition of sulphur and of certain constituents of the crust of the earth, plants produce the blood of animals . . .'[5] Essentially, since he distinguished it from carbohydrate by its nitrogen content (for formula he gave was $C_{48} H_{36} N_6 O_{14}$) and realized that it was essential to life, his concept of protein was correct; in detail, however, it was erroneous, as was virtually inevitable given the newness and complexity of the subject. Although he never used the single word protein but referred to it only as one of three forms, albumin (soluble), fibrine (insoluble), and casein (which he defined as a variation of it adapted for feeding the young, i.e. as in milk and eggs) he maintained that its composition was always identical and the three forms freely interchangeable, the differences in their properties being accounted for by differing arrangements of their elements.* According to this view, the value of plant and animal protein was precisely the same, which was especially relevant to vegetarianism; there was also the belief arising from the idea of

---

* i.e. he claimed that they were isomeric. Isomerism had been one of his particular subjects of study during the first half of his career at Giessen. He later modified this theory by attributing a higher nitrogen content to fibrine than albumin and casein.

Justus von Liebig
(Mansell Collection)

the solubility of albumin in the high protein content of soup and meat extract, which not only brought complications to the kitchen but laid him open to criticism partly because he gave his name to a brand of beef extract made to his specifications, Liebig's Extract of Meat, which later became Oxo. In addition, as was implied by, or at least consistent with the notion of its uniformity, he held that instead of being broken down during digestion and re-formed, protein was left intact and utilized unchanged. Further, he partly confused its role with that of carbohydrate, assuming, on the basis that muscle and the brain consisted of it, that it was burnt up rather than the latter by voluntary muscular or mental action, which caused him to overestimate the needs of people engaged in any kind of hard work (in fact, he assessed a manual labourer's requirements at double the actual figure); correlatively, he also misjudged the role of carbohydrate, which he took to be merely that of supplying energy for the basic metabolic processes of breathing and maintaining body heat.

Despite these mistakes and the fact that he was not the first to discover protein, credit for which goes to the Dutch chemist Mulder, with whom

Arthur Hill Hassall
(*Arthur Hill Hassall,
Physician and
Sanitary Reformer*)

he had a regrettable and much publicized quarrel, his contribution in confirming its existence and laying the foundations for its future study is enormous (a chemist who played a leading part in subsequent research and demonstrated that its composition varies was one of his pupils, Heinrich Ritthausen).[6] Most valuable of all, however, at least in immediate terms, was that, as with plants, he extended his work to its practical applications. In the course of his research, he analysed a number of everyday items, including milk, eggs, meat, grain, and potatoes, and divided them into two groups, those which do and do not contain protein, or, to use his terms, those which were 'plastic', i.e. capable of being transformed into tissue, and those which were 'respiratory'. This division was the first attempt ever made to classify foods on a scientific basis and, although too absolute in that it did not allow for the composite nature of most kinds, was used as the foundation of a nutritional guide which came to include not only a comprehensive range of foodstuffs but several additional categories, one of which, as a result of a further subject of his research, was mineral foods. Although he did not claim to have been able to identify the part played by minerals in the body, which made his work in this area less compelling than on protein, his endeavour to do so generated surprisingly sound advice and meant that the guide gave a wider coverage of nutritional needs than one might have been thought possible (as it was eventually presented, it also served a wider public than might have been thought possible, since it was comprehensible even to the barely literate).

The immediate cause of his dispute with Mulder was the explanation for variations in the properties of protein, Liebig's being isomerism and Mulder's its sulphur and phosphorus content (which was as near the truth as perhaps was possible at this stage); underlying and igniting it, however, were defensiveness on the one side and resentment on the other. It was extremely sad that notwithstanding his success and personal power of attraction, Liebig remained neurotically sensitive to public (as opposed to private) criticism, almost certainly as a hangover from his difficulties in childhood: hence presumably, combined with impetuosity, his notoriously quick, violent temper. One of his students described him as 'fiery and rash, seizing a new idea with enthusiasm . . . easily offended, hot-tempered, hardly master of his emotions . . .'[7]; Mulder himself, in anger but with justification, declared that he was 'morbidly irritable, always seeking to quarrel . . .'[8] and ready to attack anyone who opposed his views 'with a fury, such as was never exhibited in science.'[9] Mulder's situation was that he had published a paper on protein (with Liebig's help)[10] in 1838, three years before an introductory article on it by Liebig appeared: Liebig then followed up his article with *Animal Chemistry*, which, in establishing him as the acknowledged authority on the subject, left Mulder feeling slighted and ignored; when, some time later, Liebig (rather than he) brought up the issue of sulphur, which involved challenging the validity of his research, he was thus as ready as his opponent to take offence. The result was that instead of a constructive discussion the dispute became an undignified slanging match which is worth mentioning only as a reminder of Mulder's claim and example of Liebig's temperamental weakness. His vulnerability also led him to cling to his views in the face of evidence which now at any rate one would have thought was convincing over not only beef extract but fermentation, and possibly similarly to ignore the American series of experiments illustrating digestion (of which, however, it is possible that he had not heard, although the book in question was published in Germany).

His research on the minerals needed by the body enabled him to identify all the major ones and at least one trace element – zinc. The account of this aspect of his work in the 1847 edition of *Animal Chemistry* did not highlight calcium (of which in overall terms the body contains far more

than any other inorganic material), presumably because his experiments
were carried out only with flesh and blood: thus he was especially struck
by the amount of phosphorus, in the form of phosphates, which he found,
and also by the apparent importance of potassium in flesh and sodium in
blood. As with the details of protein but perhaps even more forcibly, or at
least – since he did not attempt it – more obviously, it was impossible for
him to ascertain their roles, the only observation he felt qualified to make
being that their presence was sufficient indication of their vital importance.
His reasoning in describing his proceedings, however, strongly suggested
that their functions were in some way regulatory, which, because the gap
in knowledge left by minerals and vitamins combined was obvious, led to
the hypothesis that they played the approximate part of both; more
particularly, since fruit and vegetables were already well known as the
cure for scurvy* and he had made it clear that vegetables were a primary
source of phosphates, it was suggested that the latter were the equivalent
of vitamin C. The implications of this possibility, and the importance of
minerals in general, were discussed by Lankester, first in *The Ladies'
Companion* and subsequently in the course of a series of lectures at the
newly established South Kensington Museum; otherwise, however, presumably for lack of definite information, the subject seems to have
attracted very little notice (even the vegetarians did not refer to it directly,
although they emphasized the first-hand, and hence by implication purer,
nature of food from plants as opposed to animals).

Nor was much attention paid to Liebig's ideas on digestion, in this case
because they were overshadowed by the American experiments, which
were not only based on tangible physiological evidence but (again like his
work on protein) accompanied by practical applications. As conformed to
traditional views, his central theory was that instead of being dissolved by
straightforward chemical action, food was broken down by the more
complex type of reaction which he believed brought about fermentation,
i.e. of the same nature as decay; he defended this on the grounds that
whereas, as he said, he would have expected a simple breakdown to yield
constant, predictable results, the same nutrients could be turned into
different products. His theory of how nutrients were distributed throughout the body was equally incorrect, since he believed that they travelled by
means of osmosis; he accompanied this with the suggestion (but it was no
more, though he clearly favoured it as a subsidiary explanation for the
enigma of the dissimilar use of the same materials) that the membrane and
cell walls through which they passed might effect some kind of chemical
change on them. Against this, however, he made three major contributions,

---

* Lemon juice was discovered as a remedy for scurvy *circa* 1780.

two of which were concerned with the ultimate use of food and one directly with digestion. The latter was that he discovered three amino acids, leucine (essential), tyrosine, and glycine, which, as with minerals, he recognized must have some significance but the role of which could not be determined until further research had been carried out on proteins. In addition, as was empirically known but had not been scientifically proved, he showed that carbohydrate could be turned into fat; thirdly, which makes his error over the use of carbohydrate seem trivial, he was the first to establish that body temperature is maintained by the combustion of nutrients.

In the summer of 1822 William Beaumont, a surgeon in the US army, was stationed at a village called Mackinac on an island in Lake Huron, which, because of its accessibility, was the principal trading-post of a large fur-trapping company. One morning he was called to the company store, which in the busy season sometimes became very overcrowded and, one can imagine, disorderly, to attend a trapper who had been accidentally shot at point-blank range. He arrived moments later to find the patient lying as if already dead with a gaping cavity in his left side from which jutted part of his lung and a displaced section of stomach, the latter having been pierced with a hole out of which had flowed the breakfast he had recently eaten. Beaumont, who was more dismayed by the position of the exposed piece of stomach than the hole, at first dismissed the case as hopeless, believing it impossible for him to live longer than a matter of minutes; he was thus extremely surprised when a little later he not only regained consciousness but had the strength to endure the extraction from the wound of shot, severed bits of bone, and as much other debris as Beaumont could find with fortitude (it was still another decade before Liebig discovered chloroform: possibly, however, the apparent stoicism of the young man, whose name was Alexis St Martin, was due to initial numbness in the affected area).

As soon as was practicable, Beaumont moved him to the military hospital (which was little more than a primitive wooden shed), where he treated and nursed him, keeping a remarkably full, meticulous record of his progress, for nearly a year. It was very soon obvious that the chief barrier to St Martin's recovery was not unseen internal injury, as the surgeon had presumably been led to suspect by the location of the damaged piece of stomach, but the fact that everything he ate escaped through the puncture: until it was possible to bind the wound, Beaumont fed him by means of anal injections, after which he blocked the opening with tight bandaging. Apart from this St Martin's stomach worked normally after three weeks, and, with an unpleasant intermission while further pieces of shot and bone were expelled, his side steadily healed – except round the hole, which was the diameter of a finger and showed no sign of diminishing or closing.

While he was in the hospital, he was maintained as a pauper, as in fact, since he could not earn and had no other resources, he became (he was also illiterate, or at any rate unable to write). By the middle of the following spring, however, to Beaumont's great disgust, the purse (or patience) of the local authority had run out and it was decided that he should be sent home, which, as he came from near Montreal, would have meant travelling two thousand miles. Beaumont thereupon took him into his own household, afterwards declaring that at that stage of his convalescence such a journey would have been fatal – which, if only inasmuch as that he would have starved without bandaging over the hole, was certainly true. Probably largely because of his charity, or one might say simply sense of responsibility towards his patient, he was later alleged to have treated him virtually from the first and deliberately kept the hole open with a view to using him for experiments. That this was not the case seems clear from his records, which admittedly he could have falsified but give a convincing impression of spontaneity: in them, he noted fairly early on trying every means he could devise of inducing the hole to close; subsequently, he described a way of bandaging it which he hoped would encourage the edges to knit together, and finally claimed that he urged St Martin to have stitches, to which, however, the latter apparently refused to agree. Also, he did not mention the curious possibilities it offered until after he had taken him into his home, i.e. a full year following the accident, and then not in connection with research but merely as a convenience for the insertion of medicine, which he reported giving him 'it is presumed, as never medicine was before administered to man since the creation of the world – to wit, by pouring it in through the puncture into the stomach'.[11] Considerably more time elapsed before he wrote, with wonder and enthusiasm, 'I can look directly into the cavity of the Stomach and almost see the process of digestion. I can pour in water with a funnel, or put in food with a spoon, and draw them out again with a syphon. I have frequently suspended flesh, raw and wasted, and other substances into the perforation to ascertain the length of time required to digest each; and at one time used a tent of raw beef, instead of lint, to stop the orifice, and found that in less than five hours it was completely digested off, as smooth and even as if it had been cut with a knife.

'This case affords an excellent opportunity for experimenting upon the gastric fluids and process of digestion ... I may, therefore, be able hereafter, to give some interesting experiments on these subjects.'[12]

Nor, even after the idea had struck him, did he succeed in summoning

sufficient confidence to plan and start to execute a research programme on
his own until goaded by resignation or despair (an important element in
his situation was that he was only a surgeon, which at that time meant a
practitioner who had trained via an apprenticeship rather than an academ-
ically qualified doctor). In the autumn of 1824 he wrote to his surgeon-
general reporting St Martin's recovery and evidently putting forward the
notion of experimenting, accompanied by a request for advice on how to
proceed – St Martin by then being not only fit and active but no longer in

William Beaumont
(*Life and Letters of Dr William Beaumont*)

need of bandaging, since, although the hole had not closed, a flap had
formed over it which acted as a valve preventing the emergence but not,
since it opened inwards and could easily be pushed ajar, the entry of items.
The surgeon-general, who was a personal friend of Beaumont and consistently did his best to further his research, replied by suggesting topics for
investigation and saying that he would try to send him a book on earlier
studies of the gastric juice as a guide – lack of access to both books and
live sources information, i.e. doctors and scientists, being a condition of

life on Mackinac which now apparently became so frustrating to Beaumont that it seems that he applied for a transfer to a less isolated post further east: at any rate, after six months' hesitation, he received a notice announcing his appointment at Niagara. This, however, was swiftly countermanded: in the event, it was reinstated a few weeks later, but in the interim believing that he would not be permitted to go, he finally

Alexis St Martin
(*Life and Letters of Dr William Beaumont*)

forced himself into action and carried out two or three experiments. He then moved to Niagara and, clearly determined to waste no more time, promptly applied for a sufficient period of leave to enable him to show St Martin's stomach to and consult scientists on the East coast; meanwhile, his wife, anticipating his movements, travelled straight on for a holiday in Plattsburgh, on Lake Champlain – as it happened, one of the nearest towns in America to Montreal. In the short period before his authorization for leave arrived, he carried out one or two more experiments, bringing the total he had completed to four.

In the course of these four, which, no doubt the more because of his uncertainty, he conducted with infinite care and the extreme meticulousness which both his book and the detail of his records show, was characteristic of him, he not only inserted and extracted items in different stages of digestion through the hole (later, he introduced inedible as well as edible articles) but, with the aid of a rubber tube, drew off samples of gastric juice, which he stored in bottles and employed for a set of experiments parallel to those in which digestion took place internally. Once, to ensure that the juice was free from nutrient, he insisted on St Martin's fasting for seventeen hours, which, however, he did not repeat, instead collecting it first thing in the morning; also, in order to simulate natural conditions as closely as possible, he took St Martin's stomach temperature (a procedure which at that date, or at least with his thermometer, took a quarter of an hour) and shook up the bottles to imitate gastric contractions.

As the passage of items through the hole was apparently perfectly painless, St Martin, unless he minded the sight of half-assimilated food, might have had no objection to the latter had it not entailed hanging about for hours at a stretch; nor was his boredom alleviated by any interest in the research, the point of which he could not understand, or, one suspects, by conversation with Beaumont of a kind which he was likely to have found entertaining. The removal of juice, however, was another matter, since, although careful to stress that so far as the hole was concerned it likewise caused him absolutely no pain, Beaumont also blandly reported that it produced a 'sinking feeling'[13] in the pit of the stomach which sometimes obliged him to desist. This would have been less significant if he had attempted it only occasionally, but, because of the part played by food in secretion, very little pure juice could be obtained at a time, which meant that he must have performed it relatively often, if not daily. Possibly at this stage and certainly later, a further source of distress to St Martin, which was not a direct result of the experiments but probably would not have occurred without the curiosity they aroused, was that he was severely teased about his hole.

It is possible that his subsequent behaviour was explained by the research alone, which, except perhaps for the suggestion that he was attacked with homesickness as a result of being in Plattsburgh, seems to have been all that Beaumont recognized; someone more imaginative, however, might have perceived that there were several other factors in his circumstances which probably caused him to be restless and discontent.

One was the difficulty he might be expected to have in adapting to middle-class routine after the outdoor and (the only practicable form of transport being by water) in effect seafaring life of a trapper (although he was only about nineteen at the time of the accident and thus could not have been employed for more than a few years, trapping was probably a traditional family occupation, his brother, or one of his brothers, being similarly engaged). Another was that he was dependent on charity, which, apart from being a humiliation in itself, added financial to physical constraint. A third was the loneliness (as distinct from homesickness) which he was likely to feel in a not merely strange but – since he was a French Canadian – foreign household. None of this, except perhaps the oppression of routine, might have signified if Beaumont had not been as he was, but, although faithfully served by friends who no doubt admired him for his unbending principles and determination, one can easily imagine that to his subject he seemed unfeeling, puritanical, humourless, and mean. Almost certainly, he lectured him, as he did his children, on the paramount importance of duty – and, more specifically, once he had resolved to proceed, his duty both to him and the world in general to co-operate in his research (in one conspicuous instance, he treated a military patient on a moral as opposed to medical basis, which ultimately earned him a presidential rebuke). His private writings show that he was not in fact entirely without humour; such as he had, however, was so dry that to St Martin it must have seemed formidable rather than funny; similarly, his benevolence and subsequent expenditure on him absolve him from the charge of meanness, but, as his constant reference to the costs of his generosity shows, he was nevertheless as careful with money as everything else.

Of all his characteristics, however, perhaps the most outstanding, and certainly the most damaging to himself, since it was the main cause of the various setbacks and embarrassments which dotted his career, was his obtuseness about people, as a result of which it evidently never occurred to him that, apart from his dislike of the experiments, St Martin might not be perfectly happy. That he did not connect his periodic disappearance on drinking bouts (which were almost certainly partly due to his need for escape) with his state of mind was to be expected, since the association was not yet recognized, besides which, if he had wanted a reason for his intemperance, he did not need to look further than the usual habits of trappers; on the other hand, the fact that his comments about him were invariably deprecatory gives the impression that he was basically antipathetic to him, and one would have thought that if this were the case, it would at least have crossed his mind that the reaction might be mutual (though it is possible that the criticism he expressed was merely retrospective bitterness). Although, as he later admitted, he was aware of St Martin's feelings about being used for research, he ignored them presumably on the basis that, in accordance with his precepts, his subject would nevertheless give precedence to duty: thus, without the least consideration for the opportunity it offered, he planned to stay in Plattsburgh (which was only a night's walking distance from the border) before proceeding east, and was utterly amazed when, shortly after arriving, St Martin absconded.

At this point, it is impossible not to feel sorry for Beaumont, who was described, with perhaps more than the usual justification for the hyperbole, as 'broken-hearted'[14] – the possibility of recapturing his subject in contemporary Canada at first probably not seeming even worth considering. His residence on Mackinac, however, had brought him into contact with several executives of St Martin's former company, to whom, when he had recovered from the initial shock and had time to think, he appealed. Their response, reported by Beaumont's biographer in words which reverse all sympathy, was to make 'every possible effort to bring him back to his benefactor. They were unremitting in their zeal to see him again serving the man to whom he owed so much and to whom he had proven himself so ungrateful.'[15] Had St Martin happened – or been foolish enough – to apply to them for work, their task would have been easy: in the event, it took them four years to discover him in the employment of a rival Canadian firm, by which time, as was scarcely surprising, he had married and had children. The process of disengaging him from his firm and shipping him back to Beaumont, complete with family, was accomplished only with 'considerable difficulty and at great expense'[16] – and on condition that Beaumont should undertake to pay him wages and support his family, which the latter clearly considered extremely hard but to which, since it was no more than he would have been expected to offer a married male servant, he could not reasonably object (after a time, the surgeon-general helped him out by putting St Martin on the Army pay-roll).

With financial independence and, at least to begin with, the company of his wife and children, St Martin allowed the experiments to proceed for several years, though not without intermissions. Having convinced Beaumont of his trustworthiness, he paid two visits to Canada, the first with his family, and duly returned; it seems likely, however, that the latter did not accompany him back, which, plus the death of one of his children, would have explained why his patience snapped on a third and he failed to reappear. This time his withdrawal was permanent: although Beaumont again sought the assistance of friends and eventually managed to communicate with him, he never succeeded in reclaiming him, nor saw him again;

nor would much have been achieved if he had, since, though still dissatisfied, he had by then carried out over 250 experiments and found out almost everything which it was in his power to discover.

By middle-class standards, St Martin's life thereafter was not particularly satisfactory, since he was always poor and at one time reported to have succumbed to drink; he fulfilled his own undoubted ambition, however, of maintaining his independence and living as he would have done had the accident never occurred. If his drinking constituted a problem, it does not seem to have been serious enough to disrupt his marriage or impair his health, which was also apparently unaffected by his wound and his part in the experiments, since he lived to be eighty-three.

One area in which Beaumont might have wished to continue his research (though he said nothing to suggest that this was his intention) was in extending the range of foods it covered, which as he left it was limited to the everyday fare of his family and included very few fruits and vegetables; also, which he made persistent efforts to determine, he could not give a precise analysis of the gastric juice (though he was able to state that it contained hydrochloric acid). With the aid of the surgeon-general, he eventually succeeded in attracting the attention of Robley Dunglison, Professor of Physiology at the University of Virginia, and subsequently Benjamin Silliman of Yale, to both of whom he sent specimens and at whose instigation a sample was also despatched to the Swedish chemist Jacob Berzelius, but in no case with satisfactory results; indeed, in the practical sense he gained very little from the association for which his desire had so nearly cost him the whole project, although Dunglison (as opposed to Silliman, who remained aloof) was evidently genuinely interested and excellent value in terms of morale.

In fact, so far as the research itself was concerned, his lack of academic guidance or training was probably an advantage, since, besides the likelihood that it strengthened his determination to proceed with scientific exactitude, it meant that he had no preconceptions or theories to support and thus, as he himself stressed, made his observations completely objectively. Where it told heavily against him, however, was in his presentation of his work, which was disastrous, partly because of his failure to organize and evaluate the mass of material which the large number of experiments he had conducted had yielded – all he did in effect being to add an introduction and two sets of conclusions to his original notes, which were laid out in long, repetitive succession in chronological order as they had details, which made the book far from attractive reading.

One of his conclusions, which represented a full summary of his work, was a numbered list of a total of fifty-one generalizations, or, as he termed them, 'inferences'; the other was a table extending to well over 100 entries

showing the times different articles of food took to digest, which, although
in the long term less significant, was the more widely quoted at the time,
at any rate in Britain, no doubt partly because many of his generalizations
dealt with relatively specialized physiological details, but also because it
had the same sort of memorability as Liebig's classification of foods. Its
bias against fruit and vegetables, which accounted for only thirteen of the
items tested, meant that the very first 'Inference', that animal and farin-
aceous food is more digestible than vegetable, remained unjustified: a later
one, however, that fatty or oily articles are slow to digest, was clearly
demonstrated, two of the longest times given being for beef suet and roast
pork with fat, at five and a half and five and a quarter hours respectively
(inside the stomach: he quoted double figures throughout, one for interior
digestion and the other for his experiments in bottles, the exterior times
being much longer). Several of his results conflicted with established
beliefs, notably in the case of mutton, which was shown as both not
especially quick and no faster than beef; similarly, the soup and chicken
favoured for invalids were listed as not very quick and decidedly slow,
whereas cheese tied with bread at the bottom of the average calculated for
a moderate meal (three to three and a half hours). For those with the
patience to pick them out (the table not being arranged in any particular
order), the swiftest items included were boiled rice and – as seems
somewhat surprising – soused tripe, which were given an (interior) time of
an hour; a raw whipped egg and eating apple clocked in at an hour and a
half; grilled* venison steak at an hour and thirty-five minutes; raw
cabbage, roast potatoes, boiled beans, and sponge cake at two and a half
hours; uncooked oysters at two hours fifty-five minutes; rare roast beef,
grilled steak, boiled mutton, and bean soup, three hours; roast mutton,
roast oysters, and grilled pork, three and a quarter hours; bread, cheese,
well cooked roast beef, stewed oysters, and boiled turnips, three and a half
hours; boiled cabbage, boiled salmon, roast and boiled chicken, roast
duck, and fried heart, four; boiled mutton suet, four and a half; and boiled
beef tendons, five and a quarter.

Among the inferences were:

 8. That bulk as well as nutriment is necessary to the articles of diet . . .
11. That solid food of a certain texture is easier of digestion than fluid.
12. That stimulating condiments are injurious to the healthy stomach.
13. That the use of ardent spirits always produces disease of the
stomach if persevered in.

* Beaumont used the actual word 'grilled', although in England 'broiled' would have been
employed.

14. That hunger is the effect of distention of the vessels that secrete the gastric juice . . .

18. That the natural temperature of the stomach is 100 F.*

19. That the temperature is not elevated by the ingestion of food . . .

21. That the agent of chymification is the Gastric Juice.

22. That it acts as a solvent of food and alters its properties.

23. That its action is facilitated by the warmth and motion of the stomach.

24. That it contains free Muriatic [hydrochloric] Acid and some other active chemical principles.

25. That it is never found free in the gastric cavity, but is always excited to discharge itself by the introduction of food and other irritants.

26. That it is secreted from vessels distinct from the mucous follicles.

27. That it is seldom obtained pure, but is generally mixed with mucous, and sometimes saliva. When pure, it is capable of being kept for months, and perhaps for years . . .

32. That it is capable of combining with a certain and fixed quantity of food, and, when more aliment is presented for its action than it will dissolve, disturbance of the stomach, or 'indigestion' will ensue . . .

48. That chyle is formed in the duodenum and small intestines by the action of bile and pancreatic juice on the chyme.

49. That crude chyle is a semi-transparent, whey coloured fluid . . .

51. That no other fluid produces the same effect on food that gastric juice does, and that it is the only solvent aliment [sic].[17]

Beaumont had particularly hoped that his book would be published in England and was thus very disappointed when he received a letter informing him that none of a number of publishers to whom it had been sent would accept it: notes of rejection from two of them were not explicit as to the reason, but their reactions were almost certainly similar to that of an (unnamed) aristocrat who condemned it on the grounds ' "that the subject was coarse and indelicate and calculated to disgust" '.[18] Its scientific worth, however, was recognized by an eminent Scottish doctor called Andrew Combe, one of whose specialities was dietetics and who was not only exceptionally highly thought of as a practitioner but extraordinarily successful as a writer.† Three years after the appearance of the book in

* The thermometer was not very accurate: he established, however, that the temperature of the stomach is the same as that of the rest of the body.
† Another area in which he specialized was phrenology, which, partly as co-founder of the *Phrenological Journal*, he did much to make fashionable at that time. In 1838 he was appointed Physician Extraordinary to Queen Victoria in Scotland, an honour which might have significantly have changed history, since (if the diagnosis was correct) he was a long-term sufferer from TB, which must have put all his patients at risk.

America, where, although in an edition of only a few hundred, it was extensively and considering its literary shortcomings, surprisingly well reviewed (one factor in its favour being that Americans clearly did not share British inhibitions about the discussion of food), he incorporated substantial chunks of it, duly set into context and acknowledged, into a book of his own, the *Physiology of Digestion* (1836); then, since the passages he had lifted amounted to about fifty pages, he was seized with guilt at the realization that ethically, though not legally (this was long before the establishment of copyright laws between the two countries), Beaumont should receive royalties rather than mere acknowledgement, and commissioned a reprint of the original in Edinburgh. Furthermore, he claimed that to give the latter a clear market, he had tried to expunge the quotations from it from the *Physiology*, but abandoned the attempt, partly because 'I found many of the extracts so mixed up with the practical conclusions they were used to enforce that I could not leave them out without materially weakening the argument',[19] in addition, the earlier rejection of the book was justified by the fact that very few copies sold: 'Dr Beaumont's volume is in the hands almost exclusively of professional men, and is thus likely to remain almost as little known to the general reader as if it were still confined to circulation to the other side of the Atlantic.'[20]

In fact, remuneration apart, Beaumont could hardly have been better served, since, even more than Liebig's books, the *Physiology* became an indispensable adjunct to every aware higher-class household, running to nine editions in as many years; meanwhile, a second, larger American edition of the original was published from Plattsburgh in 1847.

Liebig's theories, however, were publicized in this country not only via books but visual exposition. This was the inspiration of his former pupil and the translator of *Organic Chemistry*, Lyon Playfair, who became a personal friend, acting as his host and interpreter on two occasions when he visited England (1842 and '44) and continuing to correspond with him and promote his ideas for many years. In examples of letters to him, Liebig, far from giving the impression of irascibility, comes across as surprisingly mild and gentle – though neurotic, one of his chief sources of concern outside his work being his health, for the sake of which he ate brown bread (presumably made according to the recipe given by Eliza Acton) and adhered to a mainly vegetarian diet: thus he especially appreciated being sent some English cheese (almost certainly Cheshire) which he declared was the only sort which did not disagree with him. A situation arose over which he also gave evidence of his sensitivity: some while after, Playfair had left Germany, when he was depressed and felt the need for change, he expressed a wish to start an agricultural college in England where he could put his ideas on farming into practice, apparently having been led to believe that the British government would be prepared to pay him a modest salary (the amount he claimed to need being the almost ridiculously small sum of £300 a year); when told that public funds were not obtainable but that plans were being made to finance the project by subscription, he at once assumed that the proposal was a form of charity and was so overcome with horror and embarrassment that he not only begged that all thoughts of it should be dismissed but almost forgot the civility of asking that those who had supported it should be thanked.

Presumably because its object was to promote art and manufacture, i.e. material achievement rather than abstract knowledge, his ideas on nutrition not illustrated at the Great Exhibition, despite the fact that Playfair, as part of a team which included Sir Henry Cole, was one of its organizers, and that a considerable number (about 100) specimens of raw and processed foods, described in the catalogue with the emphasis on production, was shown. After the Exhibition, however, it was decided to spend the very considerable profit which it had made on founding the museum, originally known as the South Kensington, which was the (or rather, a) forerunner of the complex which now includes the Victoria and Albert, Science, and Natural History Museums, the Royal Colleges of Art and Music, and the Imperial College of Science. Cole and Playfair were appointed joint directors, initially with shared responsibility overall but which it was soon decided to split, Cole taking charge of the art department and Playfair of the science. The idea of creating a Food Collection in the science department was attributed, not to Playfair, but the tea merchant Richard Twining, and was in any case an expedient to accommodate circumstances, since, as soon as it became known that the Museum was planned, the directors were showered with gifts of articles which had either been displayed at the Exhibition or fell into the same categories, including foodstuffs, which it was felt that it would be ungracious not to accept but at first seemed difficult to use. The credit for the form the Collection took, however, belongs entirely to Playfair, who, rather than simply repeating the pattern of 1851, aimed both to make it as comprehensive as was practicable and, as the accompanying *Guide* proclaimed, to instruct people of all classes not only as to the sources of foods but their nature, i.e. their chemical and hence nutritive properties. In fulfilment of this, and having observed that a large proportion of visitors to the Exhibition could not read, he sought to explain food values by means of sets of cases filled to appropriate levels to represent the amounts of protein, carbohydrate, etc., contained in different items (later, he showed a similar realism and imagination in introducing competitive

examinations into the Civil Service and graded degrees, as opposed to
merely prizes and passes, in the universities). The system of cases made
such an impact that the teaching of nutrition by this method was widely
adopted, food collections arranged on his principles becoming a common
feature in museums all over the country. As with other spectacles and
entertainments, the effects of this can only be appreciated when one bears
in mind the lack of competition from modern forms of visual communica-
tion – two particular consequences which he himself noted being a boost
for the temperance movement (because it drove home to people that in
practical terms alcohol was bad value for money) and a demand for
cookery instructions, which came at a timely moment, since it coincided
with (and to which it may also have been partly due) a general rise in
working-class incomes and the availability of a wider range of relatively
cheap ingredients, e.g. imported frozen meat and a substitute for butter in
the form of margarine (the sale of which he was instrumental in legalizing).

Before the Collection was finished, which, no doubt because of its scope,
took some time, Playfair left South Kensington to become Professor of
Chemistry at Edinburgh, leaving its completion to the doctor and journalist
Edwin Lankester, who, apart from his professional qualifications, was well
equipped as his successor in that he was noted for his appreciation of food
and wine; he was also genial and humorous, as was particularly evident
from a series of lectures he gave soon after his arrival at the Museum and
which were afterwards published as a book, *On Food*. One of his first
tasks after taking up his post, however, was to write a *Guide to the Food
Collection*, which, although it also contained general information and
facts about production, as at the Exhibition, was an efficient practical
summary of Liebigian principles. Foods were divided on the basis of the
latter's classification into nitrogenous, carbonaceous, and mineral, to
which Lankester added several further categories under the general heading
of 'Auxiliary', or inessential, where he placed tea, coffee, alcoholic drinks,
acids and 'volatile oils', and fibre (the labelling of the latter as inessential
was inconsistent with Beaumont's observations although he made remarks
elsewhere which show that he was familiar with his work). His explanation
of the difference between protein and carbohydrate was admirably clear
and its significance duly emphasized; in the section on minerals, disap-
pointingly but clearly because he was writing for a mass readership, he did
not feel free to discuss mere hypothesis, he simply gave a list of the
minerals identified in the body and, so far as he could, their site – much of
the section, very rightly, being devoted to water and the importance of its
purity. He was misleading on the subject of tea, since, the leaves having
been found to contain protein, he advised adding soda to draw it out; his
comments on acids, however, which were in effect complementary to his

remarks on minerals in his lectures, showed surprising insight: 'There is reason to believe that ... they ... assist by their decomposition in oxidizing the materials of the blood. In all cases, they act medicinally or as auxiliaries to the first class of foods.'[21]

It was in the greater freedom of his lectures that he really succeeded in bringing nutrition alive, and although in so doing lent added currency to errors, also offered advice which sounds almost as if he were speaking today.) In explaining the significance of protein, he said: 'We think by the aid of our brain – of the nervous matter of which it is composed – and in this way every time we think we exhaust or destroy a certain portion of nervous matter ... You know that animals throw off certain portions of their body at certain seasons of the year, and we call that moulting ... In the human being we find this process of moulting is going on constantly – our skins rub off, our mucous membrane wears away, and our internal organs, all of them, disappear by a similar process, so that I calculate a human being loses about a fortieth part of his weight every day, and in this way you will find that the vital organs of the human body are renewed every forty days ...

'Nervous matter consists of about 7 per cent of albumin, not a very large quantity, but still this matter must be regarded by us as an intensely interesting product, because it is the material by which we are put in relation to the external world. It is this which enables us to think, to feel, and to be conscious of our existence. All this depends upon the state of the albumin in our system. Although we may sit at our breakfast egg, thinking of other things, yet the laws by which the egg becomes the source of our thought may be worth a thought.'[22]

Having stressed that fat and oil yielded twice as much energy as sugar and starch – in fact, he put the proportion at two and a half – he observed, with an understanding reminiscent of Savarin: '... too much fat in the human body is unhealthy. The causes of too much fat are both natural and acquired. Some persons, like some breeds of animals, get fat on a diet which produces no such effect on others. But many circumstances, over which people have entire control, tend to produce obesity. Indulgence in alcoholic liqueurs [sic], the free use of saccharine and oily foods, sedentary habits, and living in warm rooms, all assist in producing it ... When people are not unhealthy, avoiding butter at breakfast and bread at dinner is a good rule, with only one glass of wine in the day, and no sugar in tea, coffee, or chocolate. Hard biscuits may also be substituted for hot rolls at breakfast with advantage. Regular exercise, not excessive, in the open air, should also be taken daily. But alas! the obese are generally infirm of will ...'[23]

His lecture on minerals began: 'In this lecture I wish to bring before you what I have called the mineral substances of food . . . to which people, generally speaking, attach very little importance. Persons who prepare our food – cooks in the kitchen, ladies who superintend cooks, and order dinners for large families, and people who consume food from day to day [i.e. but a nicer way of putting it, those who did not have servants], never think of asking whether it contains the right proportions of these ingredients to secure health. Yet without these, babies get rickets, young ladies acquire crooked spines, fathers get gouty, and mothers have palpitations . . . if you will persist in rejecting the salt, and avoiding the liquor that meat is boiled in, you may get albumin and fibrine, but none of these other substances; and then the first attack of fever or cold may prove fatal . . .[24]

'The first substance I shall talk about is chloride of sodium, common salt . . . it may be asked, of what good is the salt? You may be sure that it does good. There are some people who are foolish enough to believe that man has been wrong in all ages, and that salt has done harm.*

'It facilitates the absorption of water into the system. This will also account for the thirst produced by taking excessive quantities of salt, or salted food of any kind.

'Another action of salt to which some physiologists have attached importance is, that it supplies to the system a certain quantity of chlorine which is necessary to the perfection of some of the vital processes. Thus during digestion a fluid is thrown out from the stomach, called gastric juice. This fluid contains free hydrochloride acid, and the chlorine of this compound could only be furnished by the salt taken with the food.'[25]

After salt, he turned, first to phosphates, then to potash: 'There are some plants which are called potash plants . . . Potatoes, for instance, contain potash . . .

'The salts of potash are found in other vegetables, as asparagus, radishes, turnips, carrots, and parsnips. Those who exclude these things from their diet are running the hazard of injuring themselves. It is even best not to throw away the water in which these things are boiled. Soups should be made of the water, and people should be encouraged to take them. Watercresses, lettuce, chicory, endive, and such plants, contain potash, and may be eaten with advantage in salads . . .[26] *It is even possible for cooking so to change the constituents of our food, that they may not convey to the system the elements in those forms in which they are most fitted for the nutrition of our bodies.*'[27] He then exhorted his listeners to eat raw vegetables, and finally, 'since people are so little used to eating salads',[28] gave a list of ingredients which included those he had already

---

* For details of the non-salt faction, see page 252–5. Although it was erroneous to suppose that much salt is desirable, it should be stressed that his basic point was simply that some is necessary.

mentioned plus beetroot, celery, cress, radishes, and, more adventurously, sorrel, dandelion, and beet spinach. In a subsequent lecture, he completed his recommendations with sound instructions on preparation and dressing: 'A salad properly prepared should have the leaves of the plant dried to such an extent that they will readily absorb the dressing poured over them, which should consist of two-thirds or three-fourths olive oil. I need not also add that the oil should not be rancid; but such is the thorough carelessness with which these articles are put on our tables, that in nine cases out of ten, the oil is rancid and unfit for use. This, perhaps, accounts for the flood of vinegar to drown its flavour.'[29]

12. The Vegetarian Movement: Heavenly Voices and the Garden of Eden

As depicted by his followers, the leader of the vegetarian movement was so saintly that it is difficult to portray him convincingly – as, however, was by no means the case with the founder of the sect which was its forerunner and inspiration. The latter was an offshoot of Swedenborgianism, which early in the century, when the secession occurred, was itself only recently established (it became a separate worshipping body in 1787). One of its most popular and scholarly, but also individualistic and perhaps ambitious preachers, William Cowherd, of Salford, quarrelled with the hierarchy at its seventh general conference (1808) and instead of attending the next, which had been scheduled to take place the following year, convened an independent meeting and formed a rival group which took the name 'Bible Christian'* and adopted doctrines substantially at variance with mainstream Swedenborgianism. As no record of it was made at the meeting, it seems that he did not bring up the issue of diet at this stage, which may have been because he had not yet considered it, but was more likely to have been due to his unwillingness to introduce it until he felt that his leadership was assured: presently, however, he proclaimed that an absolute condition of Bible Christianity was teetotalism and abstinence from flesh. The justification he gave for the second was that eating food which had involved the taking of life prevented man from rising to an original spiritual or mystical potential which gave the mind control over physical factors such as disease and enabled them to receive heavenly communications in the form of voices and visions: 'Open vision and audible dictation would again become man's daily experience'[1] (which was in the same tradition as the use of total fasting, i.e. starvation, as a means of inducing illusions or revelations).

This perhaps gained credibility from the fact that Cowherd had a wide reputation as a healer (he was often referred to as 'Dr'); also, although the conformist Swedenborgians were not vegetarians and condemned his ideas as the 'ridiculous whims and ebullitions of an unsound mind',[2] it was

---

* Cowherd's following is not to be confused with another Methodist sect of the same name based in Cornwall.

rumoured that in later life Swedenborg himself had become a vegetarian. In addition was the authority of Cowherd's scholarship (he was reported to be the only person to have read all the former's voluminous works in the original Latin) and coherence of his arguments, which were sufficiently convincing to impress not only four ministers and the future MP for Salford, Joseph Brotherton, who were present at his inaugural meeting and members of the original Bible Christian congregation, but, at least so far as abstinence from flesh was concerned, the American temperance lecturer Sylvester Graham. Nevertheless, and despite his caution in introducing it, it says much for his sway that his dietary edict was accepted, since vegetarianism at that time, before Liebig and subsequent studies of the poor had provided contrary evidence, was almost universally regarded by the educated classes as not merely insane but suicidal – as continued to be the general view even after Liebig's work became known and the Vegetarian Society was established (both his own relatively early death and that of the Society's patron half a century later being attributed to it with equal readiness).

As he must surely have recognized, in terms of establishing the sect it was a brilliant notion, since it gave his followers a cohesion and sense of loyalty which theology alone, and indeed perhaps nothing else, could have achieved. Initially, however, it presented the practical problem that members had no experience of vegetarian cookery combined with the complete lack of vegetarian cookery books (in fact, at this date relatively few cookery books of any kind were available): thus their only possible source of guidance was an uncertain number of independent vegetarians (some years later, the author of almost certainly the first vegetarian cookery book ever published gave a figure of 100, but it is not clear whether she meant the latter, in which case it was probably a considerable underestimate, or the Bible Christians themselves). Nor initially did the whole congregation (to begin with, there was only one) grasp the full implication of the ban: the tale was told of one woman who, on being asked what she had eaten, innocently replied that she never touched animal food but occasionally had a little mutton or broth or a red herring – whereupon, perhaps annoyed as much by stupidity as on other grounds, Cowherd, with a notable lack of patience or sympathy, excommunicated her.

In 1814 or '16 he died, at the age of just over fifty and evidently unexpectedly, though not before he had written his own epitaph, which included the words: ' "All feared, none loved, few understood" '.[3] The Bible Christians (who by this time had expanded to two congregations) were completely unprepared for his death and seem to have lapsed into such confusion thereafter that they failed to appoint a successor until about 1818; meanwhile, two of the ministers and forty-one others, presumably despairing of the sect's future in England, embarked for America. Eventually, the young Joseph Brotherton was appointed preacher, and continued to hold office, despite the fact that his parliament- ary career necessitated frequent absences in London, for forty peaceful but dietetically influential years – his wife, Martha, however, being far more influential with regard to food (as opposed to drink) than he, since it was she (under the signature of 'A Lady') who compiled the cookery book, which was not only seminal but, even allowing for a relatively substantial independent vegetarian readership, must have sold widely among the general public.

Her husband's equivalent in terms of authorship was that he wrote a tract which is generally accepted as the first to appear in this country advocating teetotalism; no doubt partly because of his career, however, he seems to have felt that one singularity of this kind was enough and deliberately to have kept a low profile on vegetarianism. Nor, perhaps following his example, did the members of his congregation make any discernible effort to promote it in the years before the formation of the Vegetarian Society (the idea of which, when it was duly put forward, did not originate with them and appears to have been doubtfully received both by him and its future leader, who was his relative and colleague). The Bible Christians in America, on the other hand, who almost certainly included the more fanatical members of the group, settled in Philadelphia and within a decade had made the town conspicuous as a centre of vegetarian propaganda. One can assume that a periodical devoted to diet and health founded there in 1829 was one of their ventures; a little later, Graham visited the neighbourhood and after discussions with them formulated a theory which, in that its ideal was purely physiological, was much more down-to-earth than Cowherd's but which, rather than ordi- nary vegetarianism, entailed a remarkably gastronomically unappealing form of veganism. It posited that, since man had originally been created to live as in the Garden of Eden on fruit, nuts, and seeds in their natural state, he was best adapted to a 'natural' diet of, so far as edibility allowed, uncooked, unrefined, and otherwise unprocessed plant food. Alcohol, drugs, tobacco, caffeine, all forms of animal produce, and also condiments were condemned as stimulants and, on the ground that stimulation was succeeded by depression, deleterious to health; similarly, he pronounced any kind of processing or cooking except the minimum necessary for softening cereals and (presumably) vegetables such as potatoes 'pernicious' and 'insalutary' because it 'violate[d] the laws of relation'[4] between the masticatory and digestive organs. This was supported by reference to the frugivorous habits of the orang-utan, which Graham (correctly) identified as the animal with alimentary apparatus the most like man's; also – as were among the commonest arguments afterwards cited by the vegetarians – he pointed to the tendency of children to dislike meat and the apparently excellent health of vegetarians in history.*

The Philadelphian periodical, the *Journal of Health*, which was the first of a series of three publications founded in the next few years, attracted the attention of an educationalist called William Alcott, who was a supporter of Pestalozzi and, although not yet a committed vegetarian, sympathetic to Graham's views partly as a result of his Pestalozzian beliefs, which, since the latter derived from Rousseau, were similarly based on a return to nature. When, after four years (which compared to its successors was a very creditable length of time), the *Journal* folded, he replaced it by starting a publication of his own; then, in 1836, he and Graham joined forces in mounting a campaign in Boston for dietary reform which had impressive immediate results and, although the enthusiasm engendered appeared to die down, was largely responsible for the foundation of an American vegetarian society fourteen years later.

A further probable consequence of the Boston endeavour was that a year or so afterwards (1838) a social reformer and Pestalozzian teacher called James Greaves founded an experimental school in Surrey, to which a community fed on Grahamite principles and otherwise run in accordance with his own social ideals was subsequently added. The house he selected for his enterprise, which he named Alcott House, after Alcott, was in a 'picturesque'⁵ spot on the edge of Ham Common, near Richmond, and evidently large, since it stood in 100 acres of land and, besides the school, accommodated a community of about twenty†: whether the addition of the Concordium, as the latter came to be called, was his original intention or an expedient forced on him by shortage of pupils one does not know. Regrettably, apparently as unexpectedly as Cowherd, he died before arrangements for the community were complete: his plans, however, were carried out by others with no relaxation of Graham's rules, which one presumes had been imposed from the outset at the school.

The Concordium's daily schedule, with approximate menus, of which the main meal at least was the same as the children's, was given in the later of two extremely short-lived periodicals which, (naively) the community apparently hoped would help it to pay its way.

5 a.m. Bell. Everyone got up bathed (almost certainly in cold water).
6.15. Work.

---

* Until recently, one might have dismissed his views (except with regard to the value of raw fruit) as mere period eccentricity, but the benefits of eating a high proportion of uncooked food are now fully appreciated and a theory which draws on his ideas (see Harvey and Marilyn Diamond, *Fit For Life*, 1987) has attracted a remarkable amount of notice.
† The house was demolished soon after the Concordium was disbanded.

8. Breakfast: this usually consisted of a choice of plain brown bread, brown raisin bread, porridge, figs, and 'cold', [6] i.e. (presumably) raw, vegetables.*

9. Work.

12. Children's dinner.

1 p.m. Adults' dinner. The menu for both adults and children was a main course of potatoes, cabbage, beet, parsnips, or other vegetables according to season, followed by fruit according to season and rice, barley, 'meal' (i.e. maize or cornflour), or pease-pudding.

2–4.30. Work.

4.30–6. Leisure.

6. Supper of brown bread, biscuits, figs, raisins, and/or other seasonal fruits or vegetables.

7.30–9. Class or meeting.

9. Bed.

At every meal, a member of the community read aloud, from whatever work they might desire, 'which generally affords abundant matter for conversation'.[7] The early hours were presumably to dispense with the need for candles, since Greaves (unlike Graham) included humanitarianism in his justification for avoiding animal products, and thus extended the ban to all types of article. The clothes and shoes worn, certainly by the adults, were made on the premises, shoes presumably being wooden clogs and clothes (which for men consisted of white trousers, brown smocks, and checked shirts 'without neckcloths or any other clumsy wrapper round the neck'[8]) made of cotton or linen rather than wool: hence work options included tailoring and shoemaking. Since, in order, or partly in order, to produce the periodicals, Greaves or his successors had invested in a press, another was printing: neither of the journals, the *Healthian* and the *New Age*, lasted more than a few months, but outside business may also have been undertaken. Leisure activities were expected to be cultural, i.e. drawing, music, reading, and presumably, while they lasted, writing and editing the magazines (the *Healthian* is not available, but the *New Age* was distinctly amateur). The classes in the evenings were almost certainly social studies or self-improvement sessions based on Greaves' ideal, the operative principle of which, as was made clear in an otherwise virtually unintelligible description of the Concordium's purpose, was love: 'Its basis being high, the principles, of course, are in accordance with it; and emanating from Love, as exhibited in the triune law of goodness, wisdom,

---

* Dennis Hardy, in *Alternative Communities in Nineteenth-Century England*, tells of a visitor to the Concordium who caused some embarrassment by asking for salt to accompany raw cabbage at breakfast.

and power, it aims to present the most loveful, intelligent, and efficient conditions for divine progress in humanity. Its members unite, for the purpose of submitting to this universal law until they accord or concord with it, and are, therefore, denominated Concordists – Love is the infallible standard to which all are called to submit'[9] (whether this covered sexual or free love was of course not indicated, but the possibility that it might could have been decisive in deterring Brotherton and his colleague from attending a meeting at the house).

The experiment ended, presumably for lack of funds, in 1848, the school having survived ten years and the Concordium (established in 1841) seven – which it would be an understatement to say was far too long, since from the point of view of the health, certainly of the children at the school, it should never have been attempted at all. The greatest care was taken over such items as were permitted: water, which was the only beverage drunk, was spring, fruit and vegetables grown on the estate, flour home-ground, and bread (which was almost certainly unleavened) home-baked. These precautions, however, could in no way compensate for the basic deficiencies of the diet, the most obvious of which, the more as nuts were apparently not served and pulses (in the form of pease-pudding) only occasionally, was shortage of protein; another essential which was virtually entirely absent was fat (the only sort available being animal) or oil (which was processed). One consequence of the latter was calorific, the effects of which were intensified by the fact that sugar, as both a processed product and classifiable as a condiment, was presumably also proscribed:* hence residents had to rely solely on starch and natural sugar for their needs – which explains, or partly explains, the regular consumption of beetroot and figs.† A further consequence of fat- and sugarlessness was that, in combination with egglessness, starchy foods were less varied than the menus suggest, since there was relatively little to distinguish biscuits, puddings, and bread; the disuse of sugar (and also honey) further curtailed variety by cutting out sharp fruit such as rhubarb and some sorts of gooseberry (though these might not have been favoured anyway because of the need for cooking).

No doubt the residents soon became accustomed to the absence of sweetening, as also of salt: nevertheless, it is hard to believe that dry, (probably) unleavened bread and plain water, milkless porridge and rice pudding, butterless potatoes, and raw vegetables with neither dip nor

---

* Unlike salt, it was not on a published list of forbidden articles; the latter, however, was clearly not intended to be comprehensive.
† It so happens that dried figs (as they must usually have been) contain not only more sugar but protein than most other fruit. In addition to being eaten for their sweetness, they were almost certainly favoured as a prevention of constipation.

dressing (perhaps a squeeze of lemon juice was permitted) can have had much interest beyond masochistic appeal.

An interested observer not only of the dietary practice of the Concordists but also their journalistic ventures was an author and possibly one-time, or at any rate would-be publisher called William Horsell, who had been converted to vegetarianism as a result of writing a book on hydropathy and at this time was running a vegetarian hospital at Ramsgate, in Kent (his allegiance to hydropathy as well as vegetarianism was not unusual, since, then as now, the similar appeal in terms of health of the latter and alternative medicine meant that they had an overlapping public). He was among the first to recognize the fundamental importance of Liebig's work to vegetarianism, which, because of the ideas that plants are the primary source of protein and all protein was identical, raised it from the realms of idealism to a not merely rational but considerably better scientifically validated choice than can be claimed for it today. As is shown by the fact that he afterwards remarked of the periodicals that they were 'before their age',[10] he was also aware that the new ideas did not immediately penetrate to the wider public: in 1846 or '7, however (four or five years after the first appearance of *Animal Chemistry*) which perhaps was sooner than he might have acted had the opportunity not arisen, he bought a publication called the *Truth Tester* from a temperance reformer with progressive ideas called Frederick Lees, who professed to be selling it because he was planning to emigrate to America. Soon after taking it over, Horsell received a letter, presumably from a reader, suggesting the formation of a vegetarian society: as one might expect in view of the obvious benefit to his purchase, the future of which was probably already of serious concern to him, and, in fairness, almost certainly also out of simple loyalty to the cause, he promptly followed it up and convened a meeting to discuss the possibility at – perhaps ill-advisedly – Alcott House. The first gathering was inconclusive, clearly mainly because of the absence of Brotherton and his colleague, (one suspects not only *per se* but, because without their influence it was difficult to counter the extremism of the Concordists); another, however, was held a couple of months later (September 1847) at the more acceptable venue of Horsell's hospital, to which, possibly after persuasion, the absentees duly came, and where the Society which is still in existence today was founded, with Brotherton's associate, James Simpson, as President, and Horsell as Secretary – Brotherton himself declining (one assumes that he was asked) to take office.

Under the aegis of Simpson, who, like Brotherton, was a Bible Christian (and in fact acted as the latter's deacon), the Society as it was finally constituted was as open and moderate as its *raison d'être* allowed, except that, in accordance with both Bible Christian and Grahamite principles, teetotalism was insisted on as a condition of membership; otherwise, the qualification was a very modest single month's abstinence from flesh alone. Necessarily, and again following the example of the Concordium (Greaves claiming no religious basis for his views) it was declared non-denominational – subsequent details of the membership, which included ministers (certainly more than had been among the original Bible Christian following) but no Church of England clergy and was predominantly upper lower-class, suggesting that it was largely nonconformist. For its first few months, it functioned merely as a 'correspondence'[11] society; the following summer, however, Simpson celebrated the occasion of its first annual general meeting by financing a banquet which for the next twelve years became a regular event and was not only a unique attraction but a remarkably effective publicity device; from this date also, the *Truth Tester*, under the title of the *Vegetarian Advocate*, was adopted as the official Society organ.

140 were present at the Ramsgate conference; by the time of the banquet, membership had increased to 315, rather fewer than 230 of whom attended (in fact, attendance was 232, but this figure included a proportion of non-, or prospective, members who had been invited as friends). A list of some ninety of those present was published but reveals little except that they comprised nobody of note besides Brotherton; almost certainly, however, it represented the middle-class proportion of the guests, the rest being tradesmen, technicians, and manual workers of one sort or another – perhaps plus their wives – who a couple of years later accounted for two thirds of the total membership (women constituting one third). As was stressed in a detailed report of the proceedings given by Horsell in the opening issue of the *Advocate*, many had come from long distances (as, one might remember, had also applied to Brotherton and Simpson when they went to Ramsgate) – considerations of travel probably being one of the reasons for the fact that the feast began at the somewhat surprising hour of three in the afternoon (which the next year was modified to five p.m.).

It was held in the ballroom (called the Assembly Room) of Hayward's Hotel, Manchester, where the company was accommodated at ten long tables, plus a top table for especially honoured guests, i.e. those who had been vegetarians for the longest time (periods of abstinence frequently being quoted rather as newspapers today give people's ages). Each table was 'provided for'[12] by one of the ladies present, the meaning of which is not altogether clear but appears to be that, because of the lack of staff at the hotel capable of vegetarian cooking, the work of catering had been shared by the women in this way: whoever had carried out the preparations, however, had done so, presumably under Mrs Simpson's and Brotherton's directions (and using the latter's recipes) in true upper-class

style: '... we could not enter the Assembly room ... without being forcibly struck by the beautiful and orderly arrangement which was there presented. The tables were decorated with Nature's choicest productions of flowers, fruit, and vegetables, intermingled with dishes of artistic cookery; and these ornamented with garnishes of pastry, beetroot, turnip, carrot, parsley, and cauliflower, cut into such shapes, and formed into such combinations with regard to colour, as to surprise us that these simple vegetables could be formed into such a pleasing variety of decorations. . . .' This was followed by an equally appreciative description of the aspect of the guests, which, although cloying by today's standards, was typical of the period and may have seemed perfectly acceptable to Horsell's readers: '... when we turned from these evident signs of refined taste, to view the "human face divine," as displayed in a happy distribution of age and sex around the festive board, glowing with health, vigor, and vivacity, and illuminated with such smiles of pure friendship and regard for each other as could only flow from hearts as pure, we could plainly see that all experienced a delightful stream of thought and happy joyous feeling.'[13]

Punch's view of the vegetarian banquet, 1849

Either to simplify the service or save time which was needed for speeches (or both), the meal consisted of only two courses, the second of which combined the puddings and dessert; nor, probably for the same reasons (rather than on Grahamite principles) was it succeeded by tea or coffee. The menu, however, which, as was the custom, was given according to the arrangement of the dishes on the table, was quite as long as at a fashionable party (See p. 261).

One would guess that the mushroom pie served at the first course was for the benefit of vegans, since it could be made with oil rather than butter and was among a number of recipes specified for them in a subsequent edition of Mrs Brotherton's book (though, virtually inevitably when it came to selecting dishes acceptable to others, none of the named first-course items except beetroot was acceptable to strict Grahamites). If there had been more courses, cheese, probably with celery or other salad, which vegetarians tended to favour, (presumably because of its protein content) instead of sweet dessert, might have been added. As it was the end of July, raspberries and strawberries can be assumed to have been over: the grapes, however, which almost certainly came from Simpson's hothouses, would have been considered a far greater luxury, and, displayed in long-stemmed epergnes, perhaps arranged between layers of vine-leaves, must have been at least as picturesque. To complement the visual and gastronomic appeal of the feast – and possibly as an equivalent to the Concordium readings – the food was eaten to the accompaniment of 'many lively airs ... performed with admirable effect on the pianoforte'.[15] (The next year an orchestra was employed; on this occasion also, the menu included not only strawberries but tea and coffee.)

The impact of all this on a group of people of whom many had almost certainly never been in a hotel before, let alone entertained in fashionable splendour, was perhaps to some extent expressed by the enthusiasm of their response to the speeches which followed the meal. Notwithstanding that these (interspersed, since the festivities included the Annual General Meeting, with reports on Society affairs) were sufficiently lengthy to take up seventeen pages of tiny print in the magazine (and despite the fact that only water had been drunk), every point, anecdote, joke, and exhortation was greeted to the last with varyingly loud rounds of applause, laughter, or shouts of 'Hear! Hear!' Apart from sectarian justifications, the points made included almost every argument heard before or since supporting the cause – Biblical sanction frequently being quoted and the religious propriety of abstinence stressed but, consistently with Society policy, discussed only in general terms. Much was made of the economic advantage of not eating meat, which was the more relevant, at least in the personal sense, because of the circumstances of the majority of the membership; similarly, its health claims were duly emphasized.

A temperance lecturer called Passmore Edwards* (who was one of the more amusing speakers of the afternoon) said: '... if there is one thing more than another that can promote the independence of man, it is the establishment of this system of diet ... It is in the fewness of our wants that we must seek independence of conduct. Very small means will do for the vegetarian ...' and declared (to cheers rather than jeers) that since becoming a vegetarian he had felt so fit that: 'I sometimes run after the butterflies and chase the sunbeams, just as I could at eight or ten years of age'[16] – Horsell having given the cue to this remark by claiming that in the mornings (after his cold bath) he often had 'so much elasticity and vigour, that I hardly know what to do with myself, and I have actually been obliged to run at the rate of six or seven miles an hour in order to expend the physical energy of my system (laughter and cheers).'[17] The latter also

* Presumably a forebear of the philanthropist who founded the Passmore Edwards Museum (London) and other institutions.

FIRST COURSE
Large Savoury Omelet
Vegetables
Rice Fritters
Vegetables
Beetroot

Small Vase of Flowers

Onion and Sage Fritters
Vegetables
Savoury Pie

Large Vase of Flowers

Mushroom Pie
Vegetables
Bread and Parsley Fritters

Small Vase of Flowers

Beetroot
Vegetables
Forcemeat Fritters
Vegetables
Large Macaroni Omelet

Water the only beverage

SECOND COURSE

Plum Pudding
Moulded Rice
Almonds and Raisins
Cheesecakes
Figs

Small Vase of Flowers

Custards
Grapes
Flummery

Large Vase of Flowers

Flummery
Gooseberries
Creams

Small Vase of Flowers

Nuts
Cheesecakes
Red and White Currants
Moulded Sago
Fruit Tarts

Water the only beverage.[14]

Sponge cake

Sponge cake

maintained that changing his diet had cured him of chronic indigestion; another member, a Mr Neeson, who had formerly weighed seventeen stone, reported that he was now down to ten. Brotherton brought up the subject of diseased meat, citing a colourful example of the importation of sheep alleged to be infected with smallpox; Liebig's principles were enunciated by Simpson, who (as President) spoke last.

But even the subject of health, crucial as its role was to the foundation of the Society and despite its relatively high entertainment value, could not compete with humanitarianism and the vision of universal peace which, independently of narrower religious ideals, set the mood of the day. A minister (who had also said grace) observed, in the course of one of the more ponderous speeches: 'The eating of animal food must certainly have an injurious influence upon the mind and temper, as well as upon the body; and we may conclude that this is its tendency, from the effect which is produced upon the animals themselves ... Such animals as prey upon one another, and those that are fed upon flesh, are savage and ferocious, whilst those ... that are fed upon vegetables, are mild and inoffensive in their nature. The temper even of the carnivorous animal is found to be greatly modified and altered, by the kind of food with which it is fed ... the Tartars, who live principally upon animal food, possess a ferocity of mind and character, such as is manifested only in carnivorous animals; whilst the Brahmins and Hindoos, who live on a vegetable diet, are mild and gentle in disposition.'[18] Brotherton, with the brisker style born of long parliamentary experience, declared: 'I am quite convinced that nothing would be a greater blessing to this nation, than that these principles should be extensively adopted. It would lead to sobriety, it would lead to humanity; lead men to be opposed to wars, and every kind of cruelty ...'[19] Neeson pleaded: 'Let us get above these artificial wants; let us by our industry in the cultivation of better tastes, make this what it was designed to be, an earth of purity, virtue, intelligence; a Paradise (immense applause).'[20] Passmore Edwards concluded his discourse: 'You find that this question of abstinence from flesh is closely connected with all other reforms; with everything that is calculated to advance the highest interests of humanity; to hasten the time when right shall dance on the grave of might, and when humanity shall be universally enfranchised.'[21]

The world, however, was not ideal, and even in vegetarian circles might, in the form of money (admittedly aided by a bright idea) still prevailed. Aside from occasional lapses into sentimentality (another occurred when he came to report the second banquet, when he referred to angels smiling down from the roof) and lack of culinary qualifications, Horsell was a capable editor and concise, straightforward writer – perhaps more than he liked: hence his attempts at compensation. The *Advocate*, which, since the Concordium publications (assuming that the *Healthian* did not belie its title) had had a broader *raison d'être*, can almost certainly be said to have been the first British magazine devoted not merely to vegetarianism but food, was as committed and lively as the banquet might lead one to expect – partly, similarly, because of the enthusiasm of members, who sent in numerous letters and other contributions which he almost certainly used the more freely not only because they added to its variety but represented free material and he was forced to operate on an extremely narrow budget. To begin with, its contents consisted of the latter, news items, both Society and otherwise, articles, and book reviews, plus, in the opening issue, a surprising number of advertisements, which bears testimony to his diligence but which, despite his undoubtedly continuing efforts, fell off to a modest sprinkling thereafter; in its second year (when it already faced competition) he added a children's page, and subsequently (too late, even had it been more satisfactory) a recipe column. The readers' contributions ranged from verses on the banquet to accounts of vegetarian happenings and propagandist activities; among the advertisements were one for a health food shop offering haricot beans, a patent pease flour for (almost) instant soup, and a product called 'Breakfast Powder' based on grain (probably corn- or rice flour) as a substitute for tea or coffee; there were also two for coffee-houses serving vegetarian meals (dinner at the first, Talfourd's, in Farringdon Street, cost 10d.). The reviews, although informative, were little more than self-advertisement, since, having set himself up to produce the magazine, he understandably – and indeed of necessity – sought to underpin it by extending his business into general vegetarian publishing, and not only fairly obviously wrote the reviews but brought out most of the books himself. In general, he restricted both the works thus publicized and the articles to subjects immediately relevant to diet, avoiding the idealistic and political arena, but one or two of the latter were more wide-ranging, in particular – which was notable at that date and for which one cannot give him too much credit – a remarkably uninhibited, modern-sounding essay advocating equal rights for women. When he did finally introduce a recipe page, it was almost certainly compiled by him without the help of a contributor and, like a cookery book he wrote a few years later, so unreliable as to be exasperating rather than useful (e.g. a soup which can hardly have been more than tainted water and lemonade for which 4 oz. instead of about 1 lb. of sugar per six lemons was given).

His troubles began in September 1849, soon after the *Advocate*'s first anniversary, when a rival magazine was launched by a young man called Frederick Pitman, brother of Isaac of shorthand fame. Isaac, a former schoolmaster, had adopted Swedenborgianism plus vegetarianism and invented 'Stenographic Sound-hand', as his system was first called, almost simultaneously a dozen years before, and by then, although the latter was not yet nationally known, had built up a substantial business in shorthand publications which he printed but did not publish himself. He was not listed as being present at the first banquet but at the second, which was Pitman-dominated in that a (different) brother (he had five altogether) acted as steward and both he and yet another were among the speakers, he was billed, no doubt as a result of a fat donation, as one of a number of vice-presidents. It so happened that just at that point Frederick (who was the youngest of the fraternity and fifteen years his junior) came of age and established himself as a publisher, primarily, or at least with the security of handling the shorthand list. One does not know how Isaac reacted to his aspirations on the vegetarian front, although as a business man he can hardly have approved, but that Simpson and Horsell registered a protest is strongly suggested by his introduction to the new magazine, in which he declared that he was setting out, not to compete with but complement the *Advocate*, his proposals being to publish only occasionally (the *Advocate* appeared monthly), to concentrate more on 'completeness in the information'[22] than variety, and, rather than aiming at existing vegetarians, direct his attention to the wider, as yet unconverted public. In addition, an announcement was made stating that the older publication remained the accredited Society organ – which was more than merely a matter of a few hundred sales to the membership, since (which explains the fact that a journal was viable at all) Simpson had agreed to underwrite it by

paying for the balance of copies required to bring the print order to the economic minimum. The surplus (which a decade later cost £12 per month and, since the price was 2d, must have constituted a minimum of 1,400 copies)* was distributed free as publicity material to libraries, schools, temperance hotels, and other places where potential members (i.e. the same public as Pitman claimed to be wooing) might gather.

For just two issues, the latter bore out his word over frequency of publication, the first number of the *Vegetarian Messenger*, as his magazine was called, appearing in September and the second not until December. In this second number, however, perhaps inspired by the banquet, he gave a fashionably elaborate, five-course menu for a Christmas dinner, plus a simpler, three-course adaptation for the more faint-hearted or less well off, with recipes appended. The meal began with a choice of soups, as at conventional dinner-parties, and ended with both cheese and a fourteen-dish dessert which included not only grapes and the customary figs but American apples, pears, prunes, dates, and Christmas cake. Over half the recipes came from Mrs Brotherton's book, with or without slight amendments; none were as disastrous as the examples in the *Advocate*, but one of Mrs Brotherton's, for a turnip hash, looks as if it would turn out inappropriately sloppy as well as almost unpalatably dreary, and a carrot soup (which did not come from her), though certainly more than mere water, must have been depressingly thin. Nevertheless, the idea produced sufficient response for him to repeat it with supper parties in January – after which he continued to publish monthly; nor, aside from the recipes, plus the fact that he favoured extracts from other publications rather than readers' contributions, was there much difference in content between the two magazines, the *Messenger* merely giving the impression of being more substantial because short items, instead of appearing in the main section, were placed in a separate 'Supplement' at the back.

Horsell sustained the rivalry for over a year; when (despite Simpson's subsidy) he was finally forced to withdraw, he did so in true vegetarian spirit, sadly rather than bitterly and with commendable generosity: '. . . To the *Vegetarian Messenger* we wish that success which, from its literary merit and philanthropic character, it so well deserves; for ourselves . . . we have that veneration for the cause of vegetarianism, that we cannot cease its advocacy, but on the contrary, feel impelled . . . to urge on the work of dietetic reform . . .'[23] This was a reference to a plan, which perhaps even he did not look on as more than an almost hopeless last resort, to replace the *Advocate* with a weekly newspaper – one of his later tactics in his

---

* One is uncertain whether Simpson paid the full or cost price; other details of the arrangement are also unclear.

struggle with Pitman having been fortnightly publication of the former: the paper, *the Pioneer*, was duly launched and survived for three issues. Thereafter, one's knowledge of his career is shadowy, but it seems likely from the addresses given in two works which he subsequently wrote, a tract, *The Vegetarian Armed at All Points*, and the cookery book, *The Science of Cooking Vegetarian Food**, that by 1856 he was concerned in a publishing venture called the Vegetarian Depot, with offices in Oxford Street, and also worked in collaboration with a presumably younger man named Job Caudwell. *The Vegetarian*, a straight defence of the cause, was pithy, comprehensive, and altogether journalistically excellent; the introduction to *The Science of Cookery* (in which his sympathy for women was evident) was also admirable, but otherwise one can only wish that he had not written it. Even before the demise of the *Advocate* – in fact, just after he began publishing fortnightly – he had ceased to be secretary of the Society, presumably having resigned for lack of time: thus both elements of his Society role ended after a comparatively short time. That his association with Simpson continued on a personal level, however, is suggested by the warmth of his tribute to him at his death some nine years later – the latter almost certainly not merely offering him moral support over this period but, as he did to many others (probably including Brotherton)† financial assistance as well.

Simpson's wealth was second-generation, his father, who was described as 'one of England's princes of trade', having made a fortune in the cloth-printing industry; his Bible Christianity was his inheritance from his mother, who had probably been a member of Cowherd's original congregation. He had been trained as a barrister but not pursued his career because 'his attention was drawn to the strong temptation to which gentlemen of the law are exposed to plead their client's cause, whether just or not. Being of opinion that no man could do this without injury to his own mind, he declined to expose himself to a position so full of peril.'[24] Though cited as a laudable example of conscientiousness, it is difficult not to feel that this was merely feeble; it is also tempting to assume that he lacked resolution in his dealing with Frederick Pitman, but here one knows too little about the situation to be able to make a valid judgement (and it has to be remembered that Pitman was only offering fair competition). Nor were his speeches (or speech) more than competent and informative (a journalist, trying, without much success, to ridicule the vegetarians, accusing him of making the same one at every annual banquet). Nevertheless, he seems to have commanded an authority

---

* He also wrote a book on bread, which is unobtainable.
† As Brotherton was not sufficiently well off to finance himself as an MP, his expenses, according to the *DNB* were paid by his constituents – i.e., one suspects, largely or entirely by Simpson.

and inspired an admiration which cannot be accounted for by money and education alone, or even the fact that, having abandoned the Bar, he spent not only much of his fortune but apparently all his time on good works – though his selflessness was one of the qualities on which few people failed to comment; another, which has to be seen alongside one's own suggestion that he was not in all respects strong, was his consistency in practising his principles (and not only in relation to diet). In one of the many adulatory appreciations of him, it was said: 'MR SIMPSON was a *Teacher* as well as a *Leader*; he taught us not only by precept, but more by example . . . by his life of purity, and his spirit of charity . . . by his catholicity, by his generosity . . . and by his unblenching adherence to truth, to principle, to honour, and to duty; he taught us the great and needful lesson, that mortal life, with all its capacities and activities, is a sacred trust . . .'[25]

Apart from a brief tract in the form of a letter on charitable soup, his only published work was a revision of Mrs Brotherton's book, which, as the two families were very close (they were in fact related), one can be sure that he carried out with her co-operation – unless he undertook it after her death, which was not unlikely, since the Brothertons were by then relatively old (Joseph himself died in 1857, aged seventy-four). Her absence or age presumably account for the fact that, although a number of new recipes, which she had presumably evolved over time, was added, and their presentation updated (but probably by Simpson or the publisher rather than her), insufficient attention was given to the directions, which, although in some cases admirably clear and precise, also contained unfortunate omissions. Simpson's most conspicuous but not necessarily helpful contribution in terms of sales was to expand the introduction from a simple statement into a comprehensive, forty-page manifesto; he also gave guides to menu planning for different degrees of vegetarianism, added a system of recipe reference for vegans, and could have been responsible for setting out the recipes with lists of ingredients at the top – in which case he rather than Isabella Beeton was the first to do. (This layout, however, may not have been adopted until after his death and the apparance of *Household Management*.)

Clearly because, except for her contact with the Philadelphian Bible Christians, who presumably account for several American preparations in the book (e.g. corn cakes), Mrs Brotherton had no access to foreign ideas, her inspiration derived solely from the English tradition: thus her general pattern, as was illustrated at the banquet, was main dishes plus vegetables rather than main vegetable dishes (although she used vegetables as the fillings for pies); despite a few additional recipes in the revised edition, very little advantage was taken of cheese, nor did she

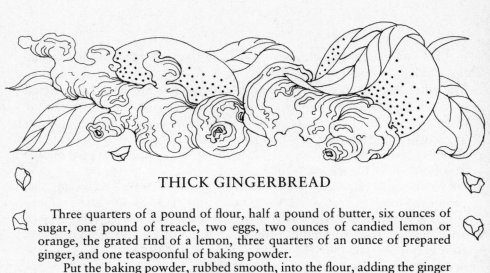

THICK GINGERBREAD

Three quarters of a pound of flour, half a pound of butter, six ounces of sugar, one pound of treacle, two eggs, two ounces of candied lemon or orange, the grated rind of a lemon, three quarters of an ounce of prepared ginger, and one teaspoonful of baking powder.

Put the baking powder, rubbed smooth, into the flour, adding the ginger and lemon-peel; beat the butter to cream; add the sugar, well rolled, and then the flour with the ginger and powder; mix all together with the treacle, warmed, and the eggs, well beaten, adding the candied fruit, cut in thin slices; spread the mixture about half an inch thick in a warm tin, well buttered with fresh butter, let it stand for a few minutes; then cut it into square pieces; lay it on a board till quite cold, and keep it in a tin box, with thin writing or tissue paper between each layer.

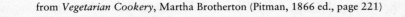

This is rich but refreshing because of the lemon peel.

Use black treacle and self-raising flour, omitting the baking powder; the candied peel can be omitted, or replaced with chopped walnuts.

It is simpler to melt the butter with the treacle rather than creaming it: mix together the dry ingredients, then add the butter and treacle, and stir in the eggs last.

Bake at 150°C, 300°F, gas mark 2, for 45 minutes.

from *Vegetarian Cookery*, Martha Brotherton (Pitman, 1866 ed., page 221)

include any savoury rice dishes such as risotto or curry, as she might have done had she, for instance, known anyone in the East India Company (though Simpson, who had studied Beaumont's work, would have disapproved of curry on health grounds). Principal items were restricted to pies, of which the mushroom was perhaps the most attractive, puddings based on eggs, which were essentially unwhipped soufflés, and other egg dishes such as fritters; since, like everyone else, she avoided the use of garlic, flavourings were chiefly leeks, onions (with which she was relatively free) and herbs. So far as savoury recipes are concerned modern vegetarians would therefore find her repertoire monotonous and the dishes extremely dull: that, as seems evident, contemporaries did not is easily understood when one recollects that the middle-class carnivorous equivalent was probably under- or overcooked mutton or sometimes beef, alternately roast and boiled.

If thus far the interest of the book is mainly historical, i.e. as a guide to how the early vegetarians ate, the balance changes when one comes to the parts on baking and sweets, where she was no longer bound by specific dietary considerations. In this, the recipe ranged from custards, moulds, and creams to oatcakes, tea-cakes, scones, crumpets, and muffins to numerous varieties of bread and no fewer than ten sorts of gingerbread. Not all were as good as they could have been – e.g. a dangerously hard 'Snap' gingerbread – but some, such as another kind of gingerbread (with lemon) or apple bread, remain among the best it would be possible to find even today.

With Simpson as leader, the Society had grown, not dramatically but steadily, from the original 140 in 1847 to nearly 1,000; in 1850 an American society under the presidency of Alcott had been formed, and in the same year, besides the coffee-houses, a remarkably ambitious dining establishment had been opened in Manchester; largely thanks to the banquets, considerable publicity had also been generated, most, but not quite all of which was as unsympathetic as might be expected. (surprisingly in view of his nutritional knowledge, a particularly sharp critic was Lankester, who published a vigorous condemnation of the movement in the *Ladies' Companion*). Although Simpson's death occurred when he was only forty-seven, it was not entirely unexpected, since it had been preceded by a long illness: thus forewarned, the Society was not incapacitated as apparently the Bible Christians had been many years earlier, and was swift in appointing a successor, their choice being an Alderman W. Harvey, who was his father-in-law. Whether or not sentiment played any part in his selection, Harvey (despite his age) proved brisk and businesslike – as he needed to be, since, as he revealed, Simpson had spent £5,000 in the last five years on the cause. There was no question of continuing the banquets; for a year the society also went without a journal, but in 1861 the *Messenger* was revived as a quarterly by Horsell's associate, or former associate, Job Caudwell. This continued without a break until 1958, when it merged with the *British Vegetarian*, now simply called *The Vegetarian*.

13. Eating Out: A Matter of Necessity rather than Pleasure

As near as comparisons are possible, the equivalent of tea-shops and cafés was coffee-houses, of motorway cafés, railway refreshment rooms, of fish-and-chip shops, oyster bars, of cheap restaurants, eating-houses, of spa-ghetti- and steak-houses, chop-houses, of wine-bars and pubs serving food, taverns, and of inns, hotels, and clubs, the same. As eating out was looked on as matter of necessity rather than pleasure, most establishments were utility rather than luxurious, and fashionable restaurants in the modern sense did not exist – fashionable dining being a matter of eating in (in the sense of in private houses) rather than out. For men, there were one or two exceptions, since they could dine at the clubs, which were the nearest equivalent to restaurants, or a handful of relatively high-class taverns, e.g. those specializing in fish at Greenwich and Blackwall or one in the City serving turtle soup; except for Greenwich, however, which was supposedly acceptable for women (though one has nevertheless found no record of a lady of standing going there), the only public places where the latter could dine respectably were inns and hotels – and even then they probably took their meals in private rooms (which, however, had formerly been the custom for both sexes and was still adopted when people wished to entertain in style away from home).

In general, like their French equivalent in name, the cheapest eating-places were the coffee-houses, which, according to a writer in *Household Words*, were so numerous that 'there is scarcely a street in London – certainly it would be difficult to find three together'[1] without one. In their early days, they had been rather like the clubs in that they had been places where literary, political, and other like-minded groups of the élite could gather to read the newspapers and pass the time of day, and still tended to attract distinctive types of customer and provided newspapers and maga-zines: because of the latter, however, combined with the fact that only non-alcoholic drinks were served, their image had changed with their status and they seem to have come to be looked on as worthy and conservative, a little like old-fashioned tea-shops today. As was character-istic of eating-places of the time, their interiors were dominated by a series of wooden stalls giving privacy to each table – the French lay-out of small

Simpson's-in-the-Strand c. 1880: wooden partitions
have been replaced by banquettes

tables in an open room having as yet been adopted in this country only at
the class of establishment likely to employ French chefs; for the rest, décor
was minimal: 'A plain room . . . fitted with plain Pembroke tables, papers,
periodicals, and magazines, not quite guiltless of coffee stains and bread-
and-butter spots, a neat waitress, economical of speech, and who is forever
ringing the changes between the two refrains of "coffee and slice," and
"tea and a hegg," – are common to all coffee-houses. There is more deal
in some, more mahogany in others; there are aristocratic coffee-houses;
where they serve you silver salt castors with your muffins, and silver
creamjugs with your coffee; there are low – very low – coffee-shops, where
there is sand on the floor, and an ill odour pervading the place "generally
all over" '[2] (the humbler sort were usually referred to as 'shops'; and sand
was used to absorb spilled items and other debris). Not only coffee and
snacks, but as is indicated by the two serving vegetarian dinners, full meals
were also available: at a shop frequented by cabmen, where it was claimed

that dinners accounted for 150lb. of meat a day, a portion of the latter, plus bread, vegetables, and service came to 6½d (as compared to 8½d at a neighbouring tavern, which, however, included a pint of beer).[3]

The journalist on *Household Words* cheerfully forgave sand and smell in the light of the virtues of temperance and reading matter; similarly, the writer of a companion article discounted grease on the walls in the face of the claims of gastronomy; in a later description of an eating-house in *All the Year Round*, however, nothing ameliorated the all-encompassing filth. This establishment, in Lambeth, was 'a low-roofed, dingy, dirty hole, littered with sawdust [instead of sand] and grease. The table-cloth was inconceivably dirty; the knives, forks, plates, etc., were of the rudest description, and clogged with black dirt.'[4] The usual charge at eating-houses seems to have been 1s, but at this one boiled beef, peas, new potatoes and bread, all too unattractive for the reporter to be able to eat, were 1s. 3d. without beer – well over twice as much as at the coffee-shop. One of the reasons for low standards and relatively high prices was that, like shops, the houses sold on credit: this was illustrated by Dick Swiveller in *The Old Curiosity Shop*, who was forced by 'a certain small account'[5] to send out for his plate of beef, not to his local, but a house several streets away where he was not known. The passage also shows that it was accepted practice to send out for meals rather than eat on the premises – which, although preferable to the alternative of dining in squalor, was a less enviable convenience than it might at first seem because of how cold the food would have become.

The most unmistakably identifiable eating-place discussed in a series of articles in Dickens's two magazines, if only because it was distinctively stated to be directly opposite the India House in Leadenhall Street, was the tavern specializing in turtle soup, which, as such, was certainly one of the most expensive in London – sufficiently expensive for prices not to be quoted and for the contributor, who assumed the character of a careful, provincial bachelor, to feel obliged to reassure middle-class readers with a preamble of excuses for going which took up half the article. After a rigmarole which included the claim that he had 'earned' his extravagance by saving 'six, eight, ten, fifteen shillings'[6] a day by staying in a lodging-house rather than a hotel, he went on to give a description of his visit to the tavern which, if it had been limited to the experience of dining only, would have been anticlimactic in its brevity – though the few comments he made were remarkably expressive. On the way in, he noticed a 'vast and solid chest' which he at first thought might contain a turtle: 'But, the correspondence between its bulk and that of the charge made for my dinner, afterwards satisfied me that it must be the till of the establishment.[7] The dining-room (then known at the better-class level of eating place as the coffee-room) was 'odiferous with Turtle, and the steams of thousands of gallons, consumed within its walls, hung, in savoury grease, upon their surface. I could have inscribed my name with a penknife, if I had been so disposed, in the essence of innumerable Turtles.'[8] This was all he said (or perhaps needed to say) about his surroundings: nor did he elaborate on his meal, which he had previously decided should consist simply of soup, with its traditional accompaniment of iced punch, and steak: 'My dinner came – and went. I will draw a veil . . . I will put a cover on the empty tureen, and merely say that it was wonderful – and that I paid for it.' But, as he sat 'meditating, when all was over, on the imperfect nature of our present existence, when we can eat only for a limited time'[9], the waiter approached him and asked if he would like to see the turtles, whereupon he was led into a spacious, gas-lit basement where : 'There were two or three hundred Turtle . . . all alive. Some in tanks and some taking the air in long dry walks littered down with straw. They were of all sizes; many of them enormous. Some of the enormous ones had entangled themselves into corners, with their fins over water-pipes, and their heads downwards, where they were apoplectically struggling and splashing, apparently in the last extremity. Others were calm at the bottom of the tanks; others languidly rising to the surface. The Turtle in the walks littered down with straw, were calm and motionless . . . Two athletic young men, without coats, and with the sleeves of their shirts tucked up to the shoulders, were in attendance on these noble animals.'[10]

As was probably relatively common among fish houses (Rules functioned similarly as both oyster-bar and fishmonger), the establishment clearly combined catering and supply: one imagines that it was from here that the turtles for the soup traditionally served at the Lord Mayor's banquets were obtained.

Another turtle dinner was eaten at one of the leading Greenwich/ Blackwall fish taverns, Lovegrove's, at Blackwall, the menu on this occasion also including whitebait from the river which, because they could be cooked within hours of being caught, were especially celebrated and the main gastronomic reason for the taverns' reputation. This dinner was given by the police magistrate with individualistic notions on health[11]* and unusually up-to-date ideas on dining, Thomas Walker, who conceived it as an experiment at which the latter could be put into practice. Besides his belief that instead of relying on servants, diners should be able to help themselves and each other to accompaniments, he held that dinner-party meals should be lighter, and in particular that it was a waste to serve game after the main-course dishes, when nobody had sufficient appetite to

* See also p. 191.

Turtle soup for the *bon viveur*

TURTLE SOUP

This soup, the delight of civic corporations, the friend of the doctors, and enemy of the alderman, has been, and perhaps ever will be, the leading article of English cookery. Its great complication has rendered it difficult in private establishments; I shall here, however, simplify it so as to render it practicable. Make the choice of a good turtle, weighing from one hundred and forty to one hundred and eighty pounds, hang it up by the hind fins securely, cut off the head and let it hang all night, then take it down, lay it upon its back, and with a sharp knife cut out the belly, leaving the fins, but keeping the knife nearly close to the upper shell; take out the interior, which throw away, first collecting the green fat which is upon it, then remove the fins and fleshy parts, leaving nothing but the two large shells, saw the top shell into four and the bottom one into halves; then put the whole of the turtle, including the head, into a large turbot kettle, and cover it with cold water, (or if not kettle large enough blanch it twice). Place it upon a sharp fire and let boil five minutes, to sufficiently scald it, then put the pieces into a tub of cold water, and with a pointed knife take off all the scales, which throw away, then take out carefully the whole of the green fat, which reserve, place the remainder back in the turbot kettle, where let it simmer until the meat comes easily from the shells and the fins are tender, then take them out and detach all the glutinous meat from the shells, which cut into square pieces and reserve until required. Fricandeau and a few other entrées are sometimes made from the fleshy parts, but the stringy substance of that mock meat is not worth eating. and few stomachs can digest it.

The Stock. – For a turtle of the above size (which is considered the best, for in comparison with them the smaller ones possess but little green fat,) cut up sixty pounds of knuckles of veal, and twenty pounds of beef, with six pounds of lean ham; well butter the bottom of three large stewpans, and put an equal proportion of meat in each, with four onions, one carrot, twenty peppercorns, ten cloves, two blades of mace, an ounce of salt, and a pint of

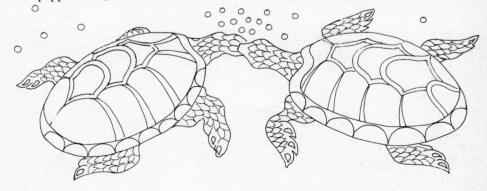

water; place them upon sharp fires, stirring them round occasionally until the bottom of each is covered with a brownish glaze, when fill them up with the water in which you blanched the turtle, taking more water if not sufficient; when boiling place them at the corners of the fires, let them simmer two hours, keeping them always well skimmed; then pass the stock through a fine cloth and into basins to cool. The stock after being drawn down in the three separate stewpans, may be turned into a large stock pot, but my reason for doing it in smaller quantities is, that it requires less ebullition, and consequently the aroma of the different ingredients is better preserved; after having passed the stock, fill them up again with water, let them simmer four hours, when pass it and convert it into glaze as directed.

The Soup. – Put three pounds of butter into a large stewpan with ten sprigs of winter savoury, ten of thyme, ten of basil, ten of marjoram, and ten bay-leaves; place it a few minutes over a moderate fire, but do not let it change colour, then mix in four pounds and a half of flour to form a roux, which keep stirring over the fire until it becomes lightly tinged, when take it off the fire and stir it occasionally until partly cold, then add the stock which should amount to ten gallons, place it again over the fire and stir it until boiling, then place it at the corner of the fire and let it simmer two hours, keeping it well skimmed, then pass it through a tammie into a clean stewpan, add the pieces of turtle, place it at the corner of the fire and let it simmer until the meat is nearly tender, when add the green fat, and let it remain upon the fire until the meat is quite tender, add a little more salt if required, and put it by in basins until ready for use; when ready to serve warm the quantity required, and to each tureenful add half a saltspoonful of cayenne, and a quarter of a pint of Madeira wine; serve a lemon separate. To make soup of a smaller sized turtle you must of course reduce the ingredients in proportion. The remains of the soup put in jars will keep a considerable time.

from *Gastronomic Regenerator*, Alexis Soyer (1846, p. 85)

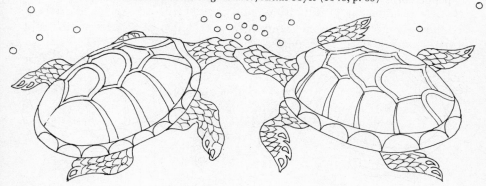

appreciate it. He therefore ordered all the accessories to the meal, e.g. lemons to go with the soup (which he specified should be halved rather than quartered to facilitate squeezing) to be placed at intervals round the table so as to be within easy reach of everyone, and planned a menu designed to ensure maximum enjoyment of each component. After the soup came the whitebait, then, with no intermediate dish, grouse, followed by a choice of apple fritters or jelly (the former being universally favoured, perhaps because the more filling), ices, a 'good'[12] dessert, and coffee; to drink were punch with the soup, as before, Champagne with the whitebait (usually, however, the latter were also served with punch), claret with the grouse, and, in the interests of moderation, one glass only per head of liqueur – port, Walker clearly felt, being superfluous, although he added that he might provide it if 'particularly wanted'.[13] The verdict on the dinner was not quite one hundred per cent favourable: nobody criticized the serve-yourself aspect of it, but the insufficiently grateful guests apparently later agreed that in fact there had perhaps not been quite enough to eat and that an additional fish course would have been an improvement.

Less seriously gastronomic was a dinner at the Trafalgar, in Greenwich, given for Dickens in 1844 to mark his departure for Italy; guests including Monckton Milnes, Cruikshank, Charles and Edwin Landseer, and Thackeray. Dickens apparently liked the Trafalgar because of its views of the Thames, referring to it as the place where Bella took her father in *Our Mutual Friend*: it was also distinguished, however, as the venue for the ministerial whitebait dinners which were held every July to mark the end of the parliamentary session – a custom, according to Ross Wilson,[14] which was introduced by the younger Pitt at the end of the eighteenth century, and was certainly a major factor in establishing the river taverns' standing.

To some extent, other fish houses, and in particular oyster-bars, seem, as the nature of their wares might suggest, to have shared the exceptional position of the fashionable taverns in that people certainly went to them for pleasure – both Dickens and Thackeray also visiting Rules; lower down the market, the former's Kit Nubbles took his mother, brothers, future wife Barbara, and her mother for a celebration supper at a bar where the stalls had been turned into private boxes by means of red curtains. (It should be pointed out, however, that such a celebration could not have taken place everywhere, since, just as there were very few fish shops in inland areas, it is extremely unlikely that in places such as, for instance, Oxford, there were oyster-bars.)

The gastronomic attraction of another fashionable tavern, the Albion, which was chiefly popular for after theatre suppers, did not rest on any particular speciality but merely relatively good cooking and perhaps a slightly larger choice of dishes than usual – Soyer, who went there regularly, observing to a waiter: 'I do not intend to criticize your bill of fare, which is as much varied, if not more so, [as] that offered at other large taverns, and . . . quite as well executed'[15]: he said this, however, as a prelude to suggesting that it might nevertheless be desirable to extend the menu, and, according to his account in *Culinary Campaign*, went on to compile a list of a total of some eighty dishes suitable for tavern suppers, which included items such as kidneys *à la Roberto Diavolo*, while he waited for his supper to be prepared. Meanwhile, the existing bill of fare (which, as was usual, was not written down but simply reeled off to each customer) apparently comprised raw and scalloped oysters, stewed tripe, broiled kidneys, broiled beef bones, chicken, chops, steaks, and Welsh rarebit – Soyer ordering scalloped oysters and Welsh rarebit 'made in my style'[16] (i.e. if he meant by the recipe given among the other tavern supper dishes, with sherry or Champagne and half a pound of cheese: possibly, this quantity was intended for more than one, but one notes that he also recommended that steaks should be one and a half to two pounds in weight).*

But, as with the Café Royal a little later, and as could not apply in quite the same way to the river taverns because of their location, which discouraged casual visiting, people did not necessarily go to the Albion for the food (or, perhaps, necessarily because they had been to the theatre). Even with relatively exact knowledge, it is sometimes difficult to explain why one establishment rather than another succeeds, though in this instance position was obviously a major factor: for whatever reason, however, it was frequented by 'crowds of celebrities' who 'meet nightly – some to restore themselves internally, others to sharpen their wits'.[17] At its busiest time, which, since performances ended much later than today, was at about midnight, the noise and confusion as described by Soyer, with the waiters reciting the menu and (as was also usual) shouting orders to the kitchen through speaking-trumpets, must have been far worse than at any modern theatre-bar during the interval – but was not unavoidable, since there were private rooms, in one of which Soyer sat undisturbed compiling his supper-dish list.

Nothing was said about prices at the Albion; its menu, however, was wide indeed in comparison to those at inns and hotels, where guests were lucky if they had any choice at all, a single set meal evidently being the

* Mrs Beeton, however, recommended only half a pound; nor so far as one can judge, were the quantities given in *Modern Housewife* especially large. One probable reason for the size of the portions given in these recipes was that suppers generally only consisted of one course; another was perhaps that consumers could be assumed to be male (the amounts look less excessive when seen alongside a series of recipes for the Army, where allowance was 1lb. meat per head per day, which in practice meant for dinner).

norm at all except the largest and most popular. Complaints – at least at English and Scottish hotels (the appellation 'hotel' had been introduced during the Napoleonic wars, and by now had largely superseded the older English term of 'inn') – centred on expense and the predictable preponderance of mutton. Nathaniel Hawthorne wrote '. . . the living at the best of English hotels, so far as my travels have brought me acquaintance with them, deserves but moderate praise, and is especially lacking in variety. Nothing but joints, joints, joints: sometimes a meat-pie . . . At the lake hotels, the fare is lamb and mutton and trout – the latter not always fresh, and soon tired of. We pay like nabobs, and are expected to be content with plain mutton.'[18]

Dickens in the Highlands wrote more cheerfully: 'The food (for those who can pay for it), "not bad," as M. [probably Thomas Mitton] would say: oatcake, mutton, hotchpotch, trout from the lake, small beer bottled, marmalade, and whiskey.'[19] The Princess Royal, on holiday in Scotland, reported similarly on the endless round of mutton, but, as she was by then married and living in Germany, was delighted by it – though she observed that it would not have suited her mother.

Thackeray in Ireland, however, told a very different tale. In Dublin, staying at the Shelbourne, which he said could be used 'either as an hotel or a boarding-house', he was 'comfortably accommodated' at the latter level 'at the very moderate daily charge of six-and-eightpence. For this charge a copious breakfast is provided for [guests] in the coffee-room, a perpetual luncheon is likewise there spread, a plentiful dinner is ready at six o'clock; after which there is a drawing-room and a rubber of whist, with *tay* and coffee and cakes in plenty to satisfy the largest appetite.'[20] (The hotel/boarding-house distinction was probably that the more expensive rate brought a private sitting-room in which meals could be served.) Subsequently – had he known beforehand, he would no doubt have stayed there instead – he discovered that another Dublin hotel, the Imperial, employed a chef whom he declared to be the equal of Soyer. At Kilroy's Hotel, in Galway, although a set dinner without choices was served, alternatives were clearly possible, since a Frenchman who had travelled from Sligo was able to order a turbot, for which he was charged 2s and which according to Thackeray would have been worth more than £1 at Billingsgate; this was followed by a most un-hotel-like main course of mutton chop and fried potatoes – Thackeray meanwhile accepting the standard meal, which cost 2s altogether and featured turkey (two birds between four people). On the other hand, reputedly the best inn in Waterford was so dirty that he could not find a surface without a thick coating of dust on which to put down his hat; dinner was 'plentiful and nasty – raw ducks, raw peas, on a crumpled table-cloth'.[21] In another dirty hotel in Skibbereen – the only one where he noted being given mutton, which, however, he pronounced extremely good – was Dan's pantry, where Dan the waiter kept the ingredients for breakfast: '. . . of all the wonderful things in Skibbereen, Dan's pantry is the most wonderful – every article within is makeshift, and has been ingeniously perverted from its original destination. Here lie bread, blacking, fresh [unsalted] butter, tallow-candles, dirty knives, all in the same cigar-box, with snuff, milk, cold bacon, brown sugar, broken tea-cups, and bits of soap. No pen can describe that establishment, as no English imagination could have conceived it.'[22] Most Irish of all, however, was a waiter at a dinner given to mark the first meeting of the Irish Agricultural Society at Cork, where haunch of venison was served: having been sent to fetch redcurrant jelly, he returned with the words ' "Sir . . . there's no jelly, but I've brought you *some very fine lobster sauce.*" '[23]

In conjunction with economic factors, the main agent in bringing about change was the railways, both indirectly and *per se*. One of their earlier and most conspicuous indirect effects was that, in encouraging, indeed, virtually creating, the tourist trade, they gave rise to the establishment of more, larger, smarter (but not necessarily pleasanter) hotels. In 1860, fifteen years after Thackeray's visit, Isabella Beeton went to Ireland and noted, not bargain turbot and dust, but (as a general comment) fashionable dinners ' "conducted quite in the French style" '.[24] In London, in yet another of Dickens's articles, an astonishingly modern-sounding, impersonal, company-owned hotel complete with glossy receptionist and lift (it was by contemporary standards a skyscraper, with eighteen floors) was described: here, the necessity to book in advance and a queue at the reception desk were illustrative of the increasing volume of trade; the new mood was exemplified by the 'great, rambling'[25] lounge, where, instead of after-dinner whist, lonely guests had no resort but the newspapers and plentifully provided pens and ink for writing letters.

Similarly, in making it practicable to commute, which meant a later dinner – not perhaps as late as in fashionable circles, but at seven p.m. instead of half-past five or six – the railways created a demand for a new, more upmarket, lunch-oriented type of eating-place. This was met by chop-houses, e.g. Stone's, which had been founded nearly a century earlier as a wine-shop and was turned into a coffee-house before graduating to chops, taverns specializing in lunches, such as Simpson's, which was transformed from a chess club to an eating-place in 1848 and was soon sufficiently well known to be commended by Soyer: an early menu consisted of a choice of two soups, two fish dishes, four roasts from the trolley with (as now) unlimited portions, plus one pudding, and cheese (Stilton, Cheshire, Wensleydale, or Welsh rarebit).

The direct effect of the railways was to introduce the now all-too-familiar cold convenient snack. As dining-cars were not introduced until late in the century (according to Alan Forrest, the first en-route meal – lunch, needless to say comprising mutton – was served in 1879),[26] refreshments could be obtained only at stations: this produced the need for items such as sandwiches, pork pies, and cakes which could be portioned and ready before the train stopped and if necessary taken back to the compartment to eat – sandwiches otherwise featuring, not during the day, but at cold suppers, and, at least before 1851, when they were probably one of the most popular items among the refreshments at the Great Exhibition, not yet very common.

The food provided at the Exhibition, which consisted of ham and other meats and/or ham and possibly other meat sandwiches, sausage rolls, pies and patties, buns, biscuits, cakes, pastries, jellies, and ice-cream supplied by the ice-cream-machine inventor, Thomas Masters, was (except for the ice-cream because of its impracticality as yet) a typical example of the then new-style collation (and in fact also a replica of the average supper-party menu). The number of sandwiches sold can only be estimated, since, although figures were given for all the other articles except ice-cream, presumably because they were purchased from outside, only ingredients were specified for both these and the latter (Masters being one of the subcontractors for the catering): if, however, leaving aside the rest of the meat, they accounted for all the ham consumed, around a million must have been served.* Of the other items, pies and patties, buns, and, because the sale of alcohol was prohibited, Schweppes soda water, lemonade, and ginger beer (Schweppes being the senior catering contractor) were the most popular, with sales of respectively nearly 60,000lb., two million, and one million bottles. On this occasion, according to a calculation based on a consumption of cream, ices also did well (on the streets, one may remember, they were a failure, but, with a more sophisticated public and perhaps the greenhouse effect of the sun on the glass of Crystal Palace, one might expect them to have been more successful).

Punch commented on how miraculously thinly the slices of ham in the sandwiches were cut; for the rest, however, criticism seems to have been concentrated on the lack of alcohol – and one would imagine that, whatever its quality otherwise, the fare was in truth fresh, if only because of the large turnover. On stations, as the railways were run by a number

---

* Thirty-three tons of ham were consumed: one has assumed that 1 oz. was used per sandwich.

of different companies, not only the quality but kind of refreshment varied, hot items as well as cold sometimes being provided (or supposedly provided): overall, however, early railway catering produced a volley of criticism perhaps unequalled since – and if sawdust sandwiches has become a cliché, it was certainly the station cafeteria example which originated it: 'The pork and veal pies, with their bumps of delusive promise, and their little cubes of gristle and bad fat, the scalding infusion satirically called tea, the stale bad buns, with their veneering of furniture polish, the sawdusty sandwiches, so frequently and so energetically condemned, and, more than all, the icy stare from the counter, the insolent ignoring of every customer's existence, which drives the hungry frantic . . .'[27] At Cambridge, a full dinner starting with soup was offered: 'We have seen some infatuated [sic] individuals sitting down to partake of the *table d'hôte* spread before them . . . but we never saw anyone get beyond the spontaneous combustion of his mouth with the burning soup, and we really believe that the rest of the dinner is a mere matter of fiction, which the rapid starting of the train after the first mouthfuls renders completely superfluous.

'Nothing can be easier than to start a *table d'hôte* on a railway line; for it requires only a tureen of boiling hot liquid and a few dramatic chickens, with a piece of roast beef done by a good stage carpenter . . . We verily believe that we have recognized the same "property" in plum-pudding on the table at one of the Stations for the last three months . . .'[28]

An obvious solution was to take a picnic, as Dickens did when he travelled over the country giving readings – the growing popularity of picnics (as entertainment as well as the answer to refreshment rooms) leading to the introduction of railway excursion picnics, celebrated in the following send-up in *Punch*: 'A few days ago the Station of the Eastern Counties, at Shoreditch, was alive with all the resources that beauty can derive from millinery; for a party of gay and lighthearted houris, in stiff muslins . . . thronged the platform . . . We were at first puzzled to make out the meaning of this group, assembled among porters and packages, luggage and luggage-vans . . . until, upon inquiry we ascertained that a Picnic party was going off by the railway, with sandwiches stowed away in the stuffing-box of the engine, hot water for tea in the boiler, hard eggs deposited in the cylinder, and some champagne . . . in the safety-valve.

'The Picnic came off, we believe, at one of the largest Goods Stations of the Eastern Counties Railway, and the eatables were set out upon one of those revolving pieces of machinery upon which the carriages are turned round, and which, acting as a sort of dumb-waiter, caused the wine to circulate with the utmost facility.'[29]

Into this situation stepped a remarkable partnership, which was later to found the Criterion theatre and restaurant but is also known in the cricket world as the initiator of the Test matches, the Australians Felix Spiers and Christopher Pond, of whom Spiers was the business brain and Pond the source of inspiration. Before 1860 they had operated in Melbourne, where their largest undertaking had been the catering for the Melbourne and Ballarat railway; in that year, however, Pond visited England, his specific purpose being to promote the tour which material-ized into the first Test series, but when he also noted the ripe opportunity offered by the British railways. A year or so later (1863) he returned, this time with Spiers, and proceeded to introduce, first on the new Metropol-itan Line underground and eventually on half a dozen above-ground lines, a system of catering of which the efficiency and emphasis on quality remind one, although the parallel is not direct, of Marks & Spencer. Once again, the tale was taken up in Dickens's columns, where the partners were described, with some surprise, as 'courteous men of business, with nothing to distinguish them from other mercantile or professional folk. Anything less like the conventional type of refreshment contractor than quiet well-mannered people before us it would be hard to find'.[30] At this stage, four years after their arrival, they were running eighteen railway refreshment rooms (ultimately it was 200), to which bread, buns, and confectionery were sent direct from their own bakery and factory each morning and unsold items returned the same evening, thus ensuring that nothing reached the customer which was not perfectly fresh; meat was bought wholesale in Scotland, and they imported their own wines. Their showpiece to date was a set of refreshment rooms on the Metropolitan Line at Ludgate Hill, known as the 'Silver Grill', which became a model for later extremely ambitious station establishments: this comprised not only platform cafeterias but first- and second-class dining-rooms and separate premises for ladies. A special feature of the first-class room, from which the name 'Silver Grill' was derived, was a custom-made silver modern-style grill on which steaks and other items were cooked; the menu, however, was sufficiently varied and sophisticated for it to be pronounced 'superior in some respects and equal in all'[31] to that of one of the leading clubs.

Hawthorne described having a dinner at the Reform Club in 1856: 'On Thursday, at eight o'clock, I went to the Reform club, to dine with Dr. –. The waiter admitted me into a great basement, with a tesselated or mosaic or somewhat figured floor of stone, and lighted from a dome of lofty height. In a few minutes, Dr. – appeared, and showed me about the edifice, which is very noble and of a substantial magnificence that was most satisfactory to behold – no woodwork imitating better materials, but pillars and balustrades of marble, and everything what it purports to be. The reading-room is very large, and luxuriously comfortable, and contains an admirable library: there are rooms and conveniences for every possible purpose; and whatever material for enjoyment a bachelor may need, or ought to have, he can surely find it here . . .

'The coffee-room occupies one whole side of the edifice, and is provided with a great many tables, calculated for three or four persons to dine at; and we sat down at one of these, and Dr. – ordered some mulligatawny soup and a bottle of white French wine. The waiters in the coffee-room are very numerous, and most of them dressed in the livery of the Club, comprising plush breeches and white silk stockings . . .

'After the soup we had turbot, and by-and-by a bottle of Château Margaux, very delectable; and then some lambs' feet, delicately done, and some cutlets of I know not what peculiar type and finally a ptarmigan . . . Then some cheese, and a bottle of Chambertin. It was a very pleasant dinner . . .'[32]

This was some half-dozen years after Soyer had left, the cooking at the Reform by this date being considered less good than it was at other clubs, notably the Travellers', Carlton, Coventry, and perhaps Brooks's (which, having been founded in 1764, was the oldest). A menu for a dinner at the latter is given on the following page, complete with spelling mistakes.

Whereas at the beginning of the century there had only been two or three, the number of London clubs was by now between two dozen and thirty; in Paris, where fashionable eating out dated from the revolution of 1789, when the great households had been broken up and the chefs thrown out of work, there were about 1,000 restaurants. The establishment of restaurants in this country would of course have come in any case; in the event, however, they were brought by social changes a generation before economics and war put them on the same footing as in France. These changes dated from the marriage of the Prince of Wales in 1863, after which, based at Marlborough House, he injected Society with a younger, 'faster', more blatantly hedonistic style, in which pleasure trips to Paris and its restaurants (facilitated by the railways) played a frequent part. Before this date, there were already a few French restaurants in London calling themselves such but which were not fashionable, e.g. one, Au Gourmet, in the Strand, which advertised itself in 1845 as a combined restaurant, wine- and provision-merchant, and pâtisserie, and which, since it claimed to offer 'exquisite and rare dishes',[34] may have been relatively high-class; a second, however, advertising in 1851, the Café Restaurant Français et Italien, in Ludgate Hill, was simply an eating-house, where roast meat and vegetables or alternatively 'meat-' (by which was presumably meant 'mock-') turtle soup plus bread were competitively priced at

FOX CLUB DINNER
4 Juin, 1859

Potages

La Tortue Claire   La Tortue Lié
Green Fat and Fins   Le Printanier

Poissons

Le Turbot, Sauce Hômard
La Saumon, Sauce Persil et Hollandaise
Les Rougets à l'Italienne
Les Filets de Merlans à la Cardinale
Les Crimped Soles (Côte)

Les Bouchées aux Salpicon

Entrées Doubles

Les Blanquettes de Volaille aux Comcombres
Les Cotelettes d'Agneau aux Pointes d'Asperges
Les Filets de Canetons aux Pois
Les Boudins de Lapereaux à la Financière

Relevées

Les Dindonneaux à la Toulouse
Le Jambin d'Espagne au Naturel
Le Noix de Veau en Bedeau Jardinière
Le Quartier d'Agneau Roti

Rots

La Poularde   Les Cailles Bardées
L'Oison   Les Poulets Printainier

Entremets Doubles

Les Gelées aux Fraises
Les Napolitains à le Chantilly
Les Pois à l'Anglaise
Les Asperges en Branches
Les Vol-au-Vents de Fruit
Les Chartreuse d'Abricôts

Relevées

La Bombe, à la Vanille
Les Fondûs au Parmesan

Table de Côté

Les Poulets   La Langue   L'Agneau
Le Jambon de York   Le Boeuf Roti   Le Selle de Mouton Roti
La Hanche de Venaison   Les Légumes
&c   &c   &c

1s; there was also the similarly Franco-Italian Bertolini's in Leicester Square, recalled with especial affection by George Augustus Sala. Another such, the Café Restaurant Nicols, was founded in 1864 in Glasshouse Street, off Regent Street, in somewhat inauspicious circumstances in that its owner, Daniel Nicolas Thévenon, was a bankrupt Burgundian wine-shopkeeper who, unable to pay for his premises, had to do so retrospectively out of his profits (supporting the seller *in situ* in the meanwhile) and that as it happened there was already a French Hotel Restaurant in the same street. The Café Nicols, however, was an immediate and spectacular success – again, for not altogether explicable reasons, though Thevenon's wife, who ran the business alone after her husband's death for twenty years, was clearly a brilliant manager and he himself had experience of wines (as no mention was made of the food in its first years, one has no reason beyond the Café's popularity to suppose that it was unusually good, or unusually good value – the cooking presumably being done, as certainly the marketing was, by Mme Thevenon herself, who in fact was by trade a seamstress). Within a few months, having paid for Glasshouse Street, they were able to move to a better site in Regent Street – their customers at this stage being said to be fellow French immigrants. Two years later, they changed the name of their restaurant to the Café Royal, which not only became fashionable but the most celebrated place in which to dine out in late nineteenth-century London, its customers including, in the words of Thevenon's grandson, 'kings, princes, prima donnas, artists, sculptors, judges, financiers, writers – in short, the Famous of the Land'.[35]

As by the late '70s Rules was certainly fashionable, one can assume that by this date the immigrants had been replaced by members of the smart set – or rather, its men, plus women whom them might wish to entertain in privacy. The story goes that Edward dined so often at Rules with Lillie Langtry (in a private room) that the management put in a special door so that he could enter and leave unobserved: this was in about 1880, by which time Spiers and Pond's Criterion (which had an American bar) had also been founded. By the turn of the century 'New' women were dining out (as is recorded by Guy Deghy and Keith Waterhouse, a sufficient number went to the Café Royal by this time for the management to change the lampshades from blue to a more flattering pink); for the average lady, however, it was still some years before dining out could be taken for granted.

References

1. Shops and Shopping Customs: Normal and Sharp Practices

1. *The Delectable History of Fortnum & Mason*
2. *Household Words*, 1851, pp. 241–6
3. *Englishwoman's Domestic Magazine*, Vol. II, New Series, 1866, 'The Depths of Poverty', pp. 87–9
4. *Household Words*, 1851, 'Poison Sold Here', p. 301
5. *Ibid.*, Vol. XI, 1852, 'The Miller and his Men', pp. 426–7
6. Parliamentary Papers 1852–3, Vol. XXXVII
7. *Ibid.* 1871, Vol. XXXVI, p. 112
8. *Ibid.*, pp. 111, 112 and 114
9. *Ibid.*, p. 42
10. *Ibid.*, p. 26
11. Earl of Beaconsfield, *Sybil*, 1919 ed., pp. 178–185
12. *Household Words*, 1852, 'The Miller and his Men', p. 427
13. *All the Year Round*, 28 Dec. 1867, 'The Butcher', p. 57

14. Henry Mayhew, *London Labour and the London Poor*, 1851 Vol. I, (1967 ed., p. 33)
15. *Ibid.*, p. 68
16. John Page (pseud. Felix Folio) *The Hawkers and Street Dealers of the North of England Manufacturing Districts* 1858, p. 125
17. *Ibid.*, p. 129
18. Mayhew, *op. cit.*, p. 61
19. *Ibid.*, p. 196
20. Charles Dickens, *Pickwick Papers*, 1836–7, 1972 ed., p. 335
21. Parliamentary Papers 1854–5, Vol. VIII, p. 296
22. Arthur Hill Hassall MD, *Food and its Adulteration*, 1855, p. 383

2. Markets, Fairs and Street-Sellers: Oysters Three a Penny

1. J. Stonehouse, *Pictorial Liverpool*, c. 1845, p. 234
2. Nathaniel Hawthorne, *Our Old Home*, p. 279
3. J. Stonehouse, *op. cit.*, p. 235
4. *The Porcupine*, 16 August 1873, 'Hour by Hour: A Series of Sketches by Day and Night. Six A.M. – At the Wholesale Vegetable Market', p. 315
5. *Ibid.*, 26 July 1873, 'Four a.m. . . .', p. 266
6. *Ibid., loc. cit.*
7. Charles Dickens, *Oliver Twist*, 1837–9, 1966 ed., p. 203
8. Parliamentary Papers 1849, Vol. XIX, p. 297
9. *Ibid.* 1850. Vol. XXXI, p. 393
10. Henry Morley, *Memoirs of St Bartholomew's Fair*, 1859, p. 493
11. *Ibid.*, p. 488
12. Hawthorne, *op. cit.*, pp. 234–5
13. *Ibid.*, pp. 237–8
14. 'English Amodeus', *Revelations of Life in Nottingham*, 1860, pp. 181–5
15. John Page, *The Hawkers and Street Dealers of the North of England . . .*, p. 10
16. Henry Mayhew, *London Labour and the London Poor*, 1851, Vol I, (1967 ed. p. 163)
17. Mayhew, *op cit.*, p. 90
18. *Ibid.*, p. 7
19. A. H. Slee, *Victorian Days in a Devon Village*, 1966, pp. 24–6
20. Mayhew, *op cit.*, p. 62
21. *Ibid.*, p. 76
22. *Ibid.*, p. 184
23. *Ibid.*, p. 192
24. *Ibid.*, pp. 205–6
25. Page, *op cit.*, p. 44
26. *Ibid.*, pp. 48–9

3. Produce: The Best in the World

1. *Household Words*, 1854, 'Beef', pp. 289–90
2. James Caird, *English Agriculture 1851*, 1852 (1968 ed. pp. 110–11)
3. *Life of Frances Power Cobbe* by herself, 1894, Vol. I, p. 142
4. Parliamentary Papers 1846, Vol. IX, Part I, p. 483
5. *Ibid.*, pp. 633 and 639

6. *Ibid.*, p. 632
7. William Cantelo, *A Practical Exposition of the Cantelonian System of Hatching Eggs*, 1849 (3rd edition)
8. Eliza Acton, *Modern Cookery*, 1859, p. 446
9. *The Servant's Magazine*, Vol. I, 1838, 'An Obstinate Cow', p. 105
10. Parliamentary Papers 1854–5, Vol. VIII, Select Committee on the Adulteration of Food, p. 295
11. *Household Words*, 1854, 'Cheshire Cheese', pp. 327–31
12. George Dodd, *The Food of London*, 1856, p. 312
13. Mrs Beeton, *Household Management*, 1861, p. 817
14. Mrs Gaskell, *Wives and Daughters*, 1969 ed., p. 162
15. *The Ladies' Treasury*, Vol. 1, 1854, 'Conduct and Carriage', p. 239
16. Richard Jefferies, *The Gamekeeper at Home*, 1978 ed., p. 25
17. Edwin Lankester, *Vegetable Substances Used for the Food of Man*, 1846, p. 150
18. *Ibid.*, p. 79
19. Mayhew, *op cit.*, Vol. 1, p. 84

4. *Products: The Worst in the World*

1. Thomas Hood, '*The Comic Annual*, 1842, p. 92
2. Parliamentary Papers 1847–8, Vol. LI, 'Copy of the Evidence given by Dr Guy before the Sanitary Commission in reference to the Persons Employed in the Baking Trade', p. 367
3. *Ibid*, p. 367
4. Parliamentary papers 1862, Vol. XLVII, 'Report on Grievances Complained if by the Journeyman Bakers', pp. 196–7
5. Isaac Mead, *The Story of an Essex Lad*, 1923, p. 24
6. Alice Catherine Day, *Glimpses of Rural Life in Sussex*, 1927, p. 13
7. Mrs Beeton, *op cit.*, 1861 ed., p. 833
8. Parliamentary Papers 1850, Vol. XXII, p. 27
9. *Punch*, Vol. 16, 1849, 'Victuals and Drink', p. 107
10. Edwy Godwin Clayton, *Arthur Hill Hassall, Physician and Sanitary Reformer*, 1908, p. 8
11. Arthur Hill Hassall, *Food and Its Adulterations*, 1855, p. 108
12. *The Times*, 1 January 1845
13. Charles Dickens, *Pickwick Papers*, 1836–7 (1978 ed., p. 546)
14. Hassall, *op cit.*, p. 296

15. Henry Mayhew, *London Labour and the London Poor* 1851, Vol. I, (1967 ed., p. 455)
16. Eliza Acton, *Modern Cookery*, 1859, p. 587
17. Hassall, *op cit.*, p. 18
18. *Ibid.*, p. 621
19. Alexis Soyer, *The Gastronomic Regenerator*, 1846, p. 558
20. *Ibid.*, p. 547
21. Mayhew, *op cit.*, p. 204

5. *Drink: The Grape v. The Gooseberry*

1. W. M. Thackeray, *Irish Sketch-book*, 1845, pp. 113–16
2. William Carpenter, *The Use and Abuse of Alcoholic Liquors*, 1851, pp. 54–5
3. William Beaumont, *The Physiology of Digestion*, 1847, p. 300
4. George B. Wilson, *Alcohol and the Nation*, 1940, p. 332; Parliamentary Papers, 1870, Vol. XX, pp. 386–7; P.P. 1859, Session 2, Vol. XXX, p. 272; the Brewers' Society; the Wine Development Board
5. Thackeray, *op cit.*, p. 55
6. *Ibid.*, pp. 54–5
7. See Lord Kinross,*The Kindred Spirit*, 1959
8. *The Oxford Illustrated Dickens*, 1981, 'Gin Shops', p. 183
9. Charles Elmé Francatelli, *The Cook's Guide and Housekeeper's Assistant*, 1861, p. 431
10. Jerry Thomas, *How to Mix Drinks, or, the Bon-Vivant's Companion*, 1862, p. 4
11. *Ibid.*, p. 4
12. *Ibid.*, p. 11
13. *Ibid.*, p. 49

6. *Cooking: Management of the Fire*

1. Esther Hewlett, later Copley, *The Housekeeper's Guide*, 1838, pp. viii – ix and 14
2. *Ibid.*, pp. 12–13
3. Mrs Beeton, *Household Management*, 1861 ed., p. 24
4. Eliza Acton, *Modern Cookery*, 1859, p. 304
5. Alexis Soyer, *The Gastronomic Regenerator*, pp. 627–8
6. *Illustrated London News*, 24 May 1851, p. 460
7. Beeton, *op cit.*, p. 261
8. Acton, *op cit.*, p. 105

9. Alexis Soyer, *Modern Housewife*, 1851, p. 70
10. See Dorothy Hartley, *Food in England*, 1979, pp. 46–7
11. *The Diaries of Hannah Cullwick*, ed. Liz Stanley, 1984, pp. 144
12. *New Monthly Belle Assemblée*, Vol. XXXIII, p. 244
13. Acton, *op cit.*, pp. 201, 205 and 243
14. Alexis Soyer, *Soyer's Culinary Campaign*, 1857, p. 557
15. Alice Catherine Day, *Glimpses of Rural Life in Sussex*, p. 45
16. *All the Year Round*, 'Leaves from the Mahogany Tree. Concerning Pies', 6 June 1868, p. 613
17. *The Letters of Charles Dickens*, Vol. II 1840–1, pp. 448–9
18. *All the Year Round, loc. cit.*
19. Acton, *op cit.*, p. 399
20. *Ibid.*, p. 410
21. *Ibid.*, p. 489
22. *Ibid.*, pp. 456–7
23. *Ibid.*, pp. 167–8
24. Alexis Soyer, *Gastronomic Regenerator*, pp. 208–10
25. Beeton, *op. cit.*, Preface
26. *Punch*, vol. 17, 1849, 'Mr Brown's Letters to a Young Man About Town: Great and Little Dinners', p. 1

7. The Cooks: Aspiring Heroines and Artistes

1. *Household Words*, 1850, 'A Good Plain Cook', pp. 272–3
2. James Caird, *English Agriculture 1850–51*, 1852, p. 84
3. Thomas Hughes, *Tom Brown's Schooldays*, 1857, (1953 ed. p. 32)
4. See Geoffrey Best, *Mid-Victorian Britain 1851–75*, 1979, p. 108
5. *The Ladies Companion*, 'The Housekeeper's Room: My Last Six Cooks', Vol. III, pp. 41–2. (The sixth cook of the title proved satisfactory and was still in the lady's employment when the article was written.)
6. *Household Words*, 'A Good Plain Cook'
7. Ann Barr and Paul Levy, *The Official Foodie Handbook*, p. 7
8. *The Ladies' Companion*, 1850, Vol. 2, p. 156
9. Abraham Hayward, *The Art of Dining*, 1883, p. 78
10. *Ibid.*, p. 75
11. Charles Elmé Francatelli, *Modern Cook*, 1846, p. vi
12. Hayward, *op cit.*, pp. 77–8
13. Richard Aldington, *Wellington*, 1946, p. 49
14. Hayward, *op cit.*, p. 17
15. *The Ladies' Companion*, 1856, Vol. 2, p. 156
16. Hayward, *op cit.*, pp. 37–8

8. The Cookery Writers: Frugality and Economy v. Extravagant Farragos

1. Esther Hewlett, *Cottage Cookery*, 1849, pp. 80–81
2. *Ibid.*, p. 18
3. Esther Hewlett, *The Housekeeper's Guide*, 1838, p. vi
4. Mrs Beeton, *Household Management*, 1861 ed., pp. 1–2
5. Esther Hewlett, *Cottage Comforts*, 1825, p. 66
6. *Ibid.*, p. 66
7. See Eric Quayle, *Old Cook Books*, 1978, p. 165
8. Eliza Acton, *Modern Cookery*, 1855, p. 540
9. *Ibid.*, p. x
10. *Ibid.*, p. 60
11. *Ibid.*, p. 220
12. Beeton, *op cit.*, pp. 10–12
13. *The Ladies' Treasury*, Vol 1 (1858), p. 62
14. Georgiana Hill, *The Breakfast Book*, 1865, p. 42
15. Abraham Hayward, *The Art of Dining*, 1883, p. 75
16. F. Volant and J. R. Warren, *Memoirs of Alexis Soyer*, 1859, p. 242
17. *Ibid.*, p. 71
18. Hayward, *op cit.*, p. 76
19. Soyer, *Culinary Campaign*, 1857, p. 118
20. William Kitchener, *The Cook's Oracle*, 1827, p. 7
21. *Ibid.*, p. 19
22. J. H. Walsh, *The English Cookery Book*, Preface

9. Meals and Entertaining: From Porridge to Poularde à la Nelson

1. Hon Geo. C. G. F. Berkeley, *Anecdotes of the Upper Ten Thousand*, 1867, Vol. II, p. 195
2. *Passages from the English Notebooks of Nathaniel Hawthorne*, 1870, Vol. II, pp. 122–3
3. M. E. Grant Duff, *Notes from a Diary 1851–72*, 1897, Vol. 2, p. 4
4. Georgiana Hill, *The Breakfast Book*, 1865, p. 130

5. George Augustus Sala, *Breakfast in Bed*, 1863, p. 225
6. Grant Duff, *op cit.*, p. 126
7. *The Diary of Lady Frederick Cavendish*, ed. John Bailey, 1927, Vol. I, p. 298
8. Grant Duff, *op cit.*, p. 137
9. Mrs Beeton, *Household Management*, 1861 ed., p. 949
10. Alexis Soyer, *Modern Housewife*, 1851, p. 418
11. Alexis Soyer, *Gastronomic Regenerator*, 1849 ed., pp.xiv and xv. The anecdote was quoted from Launcelot Sturgeon, *Essays, Moral, Philosophical and Stomachic*
12. Beeton, *op cit.*, p. 955
13. Brydges Williams Letters, quoted by kind permission of the Hon. Jacob Rothschild
14. See Abraham Hayward, *The Art of Dining*, 1883, pp. 80–84
15. *Ibid.*, p. 87
16. 'Nooks and Corners of Character: The Greengrocer who Waits at Parties', *Punch*, Vol. 18, 1850, p. 72
17. James Greenwood, 'The Depths of Poverty III; Poverty's Larder', *Englishwoman's Domestic Magazine*, Vol. II New Series, 1866, p. 61
18. *Ibid.*
19. Dr Edward Smith, 'Dietaries for the Inmates of Workhouses' Parliamentary Papers 1866. Vol. XXXV, p. 338
20. *Ibid.*
21. William Brinton, *On Food and its Digestion*, 1861, p. 470
22. Ian Anstruther, *The Scandal of Andover Workhouse*, 1973
23. *The London Standard*, 12 March 1985
24. J. A. Brillat-Savarin, *The Philosopher in the Kitchen*, trs. Anne Drayton, 1970, p. 205
25. *Ibid.*, pp. 219–20
26. *Ibid.*, pp. 221–2
27. *Dearest Child: Letters between Queen Victoria and the Princess Royal 1858–61*, ed. Roger Fulford, 1964, p. 90
28. *Punch*, Vol. 17, 1849, 'Mr Brown's Letters to a Young Man About Town', p. 1
29. William Banting, *Letter on Corpulence Addressed to the Public*, 2nd ed. 1863, reprinted in *Tracts on Hygiene 1862–72*, p. 10 and p. 13
30. Watson Bradshaw, *On Corpulence*, 1864, reprinted in *Tracts on Hygiene 1862–72*, pp. 8–9
31. *The Observer* 2 February 1986, p. 55
32. Watson Bradshaw, *op cit.*, p. 21
33. *Living Magazine*, May 1986, p. 52, 'The Diet Revolution'
34. John Harvey, *Corpulence, its Diminution and cure, without injury to health*, 3rd ed. 1864, reprinted in *Tracts on Hygiene 1862–72*, p. 36
35. *Ibid.*, p. 36
36. 'A London Physician', *How to Get Fat*, 1865 reprinted in *Tracts on Hygiene 1862–1872*, p. 12
37. *Ibid.*, pp. 10–11

10. Children: Mutton or Cook-It-Yourself

1. Pye Henry Chavasse, *Advice to a Wife*, 3rd ed. 1854, p. 53
2. *Ibid.*, p. 131
3. *Dearest Mama: Letters between Queen Victoria and the Crown Princess of Prussia 1861–64*, ed. Roger Fulford, 1968, p. 183
4. Mrs Beeton, *Household Management*, 1861 ed., p. 1024
5. Charles Dickens, *Dombey and Son*, 1846–8, (1964 ed., p. 26)
6. *Ibid.*, p. 29
7. Alexis Soyer, *Modern Housewife*, 1850, p. 33
8. H. C. Adams, *Wykehamica*, 1878, p. 275
9. *Family Economist*, Vol. II, 1849, p. 165
10. William Brinton, *On Food and its Digestion*, 1861, pp. 426–7
11. Augustus J. C. Hare, *The Story of My Life*, 1896, Vol. I, p. 244
12. Parliamentary Papers 1864, Vol. XX, Part I, p. 105
13. Benjamin Disraeli, *Coningsby*, 1948 ed. (first published 1844), pp. 54–5. The details given of life at Eton were researched and are generally accepted as authentic
14. Adams, *op cit.*, pp. 269–70
15. *Ibid.*, p. 269
16. *Ibid.*, p. 281
17. Beeton, *op cit.*, p. 855
18. George Augustus Sala, *Breakfast in Bed*, 1863, pp. 242–3
19. *Punch*, 'Child's Parties', Vol. 16 1849, p. 13
20. *Ibid.*, p. 35
21. *The Diary of Lady Frederick Cavendish*, 1927, Vol. I, pp. 25–26
22. Beeton, *op. cit.*, p. 761
23. See David Churchill, *Financial Times*, 22 December 1979, 'Tom Smith's Idea Grows into a £20m Snap'
24. 'Child's Parties', *loc. cit.*, p.35
25. *The Ladies Treasury*, Vol. IV, 'Christmas Guests', p. 11, The italic was added by the present author.
26. *All the Year Round*, Vol. XIX, 1868, 'Child's Parties', p. 187

27. Mss in the possession of Mrs Monica
    Burroughes

11. Nutrition: A Case of Direct Observation

1. W. A. Shenstone, *Justus von Liebig: His
   Life and Work*, 1895, p. 11
2. *Ibid.*, p. 16
3. Charles A. Brown, 'Justus von Liebig –
   Man and Teacher', *Liebig and After
   Liebig: A Century of Progress in
   Agricultural Chemistry*, 1942, p. 6
4. See *ibid.*, pp. 1 and 8
5. Justus von Liebig, *Familiar Letters on
   Chemistry*, 1851 ed., p. 350
6. See Hubert Bradford Vickery, 'Liebig and
   the Chemistry of Proteins' in *Liebig and
   After Liebig*, pp. 23–24
7. Shenstone, *op cit.*, p. 37
8. *Mulder's Reply to Liebig*, introduction by
   James F. W. Johnston, 1846, p. 2
9. *Ibid.*, p. 8
10. See Vickery, *op cit.*, p. 20
11. Jesse S. Myer, *Life and Letters of Dr
    William Beaumont*, 1912, p. 114
12. *Ibid.*, p. 117
13. William Beaumont, *The Physiology of
    Digestion*, 1847, p. 24
14. Myer, *op cit.*, p. 122
15. *Ibid.*, p. 134
16. *Ibid.*
17. *Ibid.*, pp. 201–2
18. *Ibid.*, p. 280
19. Andrew Combe, *Physiology of Digestion*,
    1845 ed., p.x
20. *Ibid.*, p. xi
21. Edwin Lankester, *A Guide to the Food
    Collection in the South Kensington
    Museum*, 1860, p. 66
22. Edwin Lankester, *On Food*, 1861,
    pp. 121–6
23. *Ibid.*, pp. 105–7
24. *Ibid.*, p. 33 and 35
25. *Ibid.*, pp. 36, 40–41, 42
26. *Ibid.*, pp. 51–2
27. *Ibid.*, p. 58 The italic is the author's
28. *Ibid.*, p. 59
29. *Ibid.*, p. 116

12. The Vegetarian Movement: Heavenly Voices and the Garden of Eden

1. Commentator on Cowherd: Swedenborgian Institute, London WC1
2. Robert Hindmarsh, *Rise and Progress of
   the New Jerusalem Church*, 1861, p. 194

3. *Dictionary of National Biography*, 1887
   ed., Vol. 12, p. 379
4. Sylvester Graham, *The Physiology of
   Feeding*, 1897, p. 76
5. *New Age*, Vol. 1, No. 1, 1843, p. 8
6. *Ibid.*, pp. 15–16
7. *Ibid.*, p. 16
8. *Ibid.*, p. 16
9. Quoted from Dennis Hardy, *Alternative
   Communities in Nineteenth-Century
   England*, 1979, p. 61
10. William Horsell, *The Vegetarian Armed
    at all Points*, 1856, p. 43
11. *Vegetarian Advocate*, Vol. I, No. 1, 1848,
    p. 6
12. *Ibid.*, 'Report of the First Annual Meeting
    of the Vegetarian Society', p. 1
13. *Ibid.*
14. *Ibid.*, pp. 2–3
15. *Ibid.*, p. 2
16. *Ibid.*, p. 15 (both quotations)
17. *Ibid.*, p. 14
18. *Ibid.*, p. 8
19. *Ibid.*, p. 5
20. *Ibid.*, p. 17
21. *Ibid.*, p. 16
22. *Vegetarian Messenger*, Vol. I, No. 1,
    1849, p. 1
23. *Vegetarian Advocate*, Vol. III, 1851,
    pp. iii–iv
24. *Vegetarian Messenger*, Vol. X, 1859,
    p. 120
25. *Ibid.*, p. 30 (Supplement)

13. Eating Out: A Matter of Necessity Rather Than Pleasure

1. *Household Words*, 1852, 'A Cup of
   Coffee', p. 159
2. *Ibid.*
3. See Henry Mayhew. *London Labour and
   the London Poor*, 1851
4. *All the Year Round*, Vol. XV, 1866,
   p. 589
5. Dickens, *The Old Curiosity Shop*, 1841
   (1974 ed., p. 108)
6. *Household Words*, 1851, 'Lively Turtle',
   pp. 193
7. *Ibid.*, p. 194
8. *Ibid.*
9. *Ibid.*, p. 194
10. *Ibid.*, pp. 194–5
11. John Harvey, *Corpulence, its Diminution
    and cure . . .*
12. Abraham Hayward, *The Art of Dining*
    1884, p. xx; see also Ross Wilson,
    Financial Times, 1983, p. 13, 'No other
    Fish but Whitebait . . .'
13. *Ibid.*, both Hayward, p. xx, and Wilson

14. See Wilson, *loc. cit.*
15. Alexis Soyer, *Culinary Campaign*, 1857, p. 7
16. *Ibid.*, p. 6
17. *Ibid.*, p. 3
18. *Passages from the Notebook of Nathaniel Hawthorne* 1870. Vol. 1, pp. 276–7
19. *The Letters of Charles Dickens, Vol. I, 1840–41*, eds. Madeline House and Graham Storey, 1969, p. 323
20. W. M. Thackeray, *Irish Sketchbook*, Vol. I. 1845, p. 10
21. *Ibid.*, p. 50
22. *Ibid.*, p. 172
23. *Ibid.*, p. 108
24. Sarah Freeman, *Isabella and Sam*, 1977, p. 177
25. *All the Year Round*, Vol. XV, 1866. 'Inns Old and New', p. 562
26. *Financial Times*, 16 November 1979, p. 7
27. *All the Year Round*, Vol. XIX, 28 December 1867, 'Genii of the Cave,' p. 60
28. *Punch* Vol. 15, 1848, p. 54, 'A Dinner on the Eastern Counties'
29. *Ibid.*, p. 39, 'Railway Picnics'
30. 'Genii of the Cave', *loc. cit.* p. 62
31. *Ibid.*, p. 64
32. *Passages from the English Notebooks of Nathaniel Hawthorne* Vol. II, 1870, pp. 6 and 8
33. Menu supplied by Brooks's
34. *The Times*, 3 January 1845, p. 1
35. Captain Daniel N. Pigache, *Café Royal Days*, 1933, p. 18

Select Bibliography

BOOKS

Acton, Eliza, *Modern Cookery*, Longman 1845 (1st) and 1859 eds.
—— *The English Bread Book*, Longman 1857
Adams, H. C., *Wykehamica*, Winchester 1878
Adshead, Joseph, *Distress in Manchester*, Hooper 1842
Agogos, *Hints on Etiquette and the Usages of Society*, Longman 1839 (1st published 1834; reprinted Turnstile Press 1946)
Agriculture, Fisheries, and Food (Ministry), *Manual of Nutrition*, HMSO 1985 (9th ed.)
Aldington, Richard, *Wellington*, Heinemann 1946
Allen, H. Warner, *Sherry and Port*, Constable 1952
Anon. (presumed Joseph Brotherton), *First Teetotal Tract on Abstinence from Intoxicating Liquor*, 1821, reprinted in *Tracts on the Drink Question 1855–94*, Onward Publishing, Manchester 1894
Anon., *Truths about Whiskey*, written for John Jameson & Son, William Jameson & Son, John Power & Son, The George Roe & Co., London 1878
Anstruther, Ian, *The Scandal of Andover Workhouse*, Geoffrey Bles 1973
Augustine, *Footprints of Father Theobald Mathew*, M. H. Gill & Son, Dublin 1947
Banting, William, *Letter on Corpulence Addressed to the Public*, published by the author, 2nd ed. 1863
Barker, Alfred, *The Life of Sir Isaac Pitman*, Pitman 1980 (1st published 1908)
Barr, Ann, and Paul Levy, *The Official Foodie Handbook*, Ebury Press 1984
Beaconsfield, Earl of, *Coningsby*, John Lehmann 1948 (1st published 1844)
Beaumont, William, *The Physiology of Digestion, with Experiments on the Gastric Juice*, Chauncey Goodrich, Burlington, 1847
Beeton, Isabella, *Household Management*, facsimile of original ed., Cape 1971 (1st published 1861)
Berkeley, Hon. George, C. G. F., *Anecdotes of the Upper Ten Thousand*, Bentley 1867
—— *A Pamphlet in Defence of the Game Laws*, Longman 1845
Best, Geoffrey, *Mid-Victorian Britain 1851–75*, Panther 1973
Booth, David, *The Art of Wine-making in All its Branches*, F. J. Mason 1834
Bowden, Gregory Houston, *British Gastronomy: The Rise of Great Restaurants*, Chatto & Windus 1975
Bradshaw, Watson, *On Corpulence*, published by the author 1864, reprinted in *Tracts on Hygiene 1862–72*
Brillat-Savarin, Anselme, trs. Anne Drayton, *The Philosopher in the Kitchen*, Penguin 1970
Brinton, William, *On Food and Its Digestion*, Longman 1861
Broadley, A. M., *Piccadilly 1686–1906: For a Century and a Half the Home of the House of Fortnum & Mason*, 1906, reprinted in *Topographical Tracts 1904–9*
Brook's Club, *Memorials of Brook's*, 1907
Bucknell, William, *The Eccaleobion*, published by the author 1839
Burnett, John, *Plenty and Want*, Nelson 1966

Byron, George G. B. (Lord), *Don Juan* (cantos I and II 1st published 1819)

Caird, James, *English Agriculture 1850–51*, Frank Cass 1968 (1st published Longman 1852)

Cantelo, William James, *A Practical Exposition of the Cantelonian System of Hatching Eggs and Rearing Poultry*, William Strange 1849 (3rd ed.)

Carlyle, Thomas, *Past and Present*, Chapman & Hall 1897 (1st published 1843)

Carpenter, William, *The Use and Abuse of Alcoholic Liquors*, Charles Gilpin & John Churchill 1851

Cavendish, Lady Frederick, *The Diary of Lady Frederick Cavendish*, Murray 1927 (2 vols.)

Chavasse, Pye Henry, *Advice to a Wife*, Longman 1864 (3rd ed.)

Clayton, Edwy, G., *Arthur Hill Hassall, Physician and Sanitary Reformer*, Baillière, Tyndall & Cox 1908

Cluny, Hilaire, *Louis Pasteur*, Souvenir Press 1965

'Clutterbuck, Lady Maria' (Catherine Dickens), *What Shall We Have for Dinner?* Bradbury & Evans 1852

Cobbe, Frances Power, *Life of Frances Power Cobbe*, Bentley 1894

Cobbett, William, *Cottage Economy*, Oxford University Press 1979 (1st published 1822)

Combe, Andrew, *Physiology of Digestion*, Maclachlan & Stewart, Edinburgh 1845

Cullwick, Hannah, *The Diaries of Hannah Cullwick*, Virago 1984

David, Elizabeth, *English Bread and Yeast Cookery*, Allen Lane 1977

Day, Alice Catherine, *Glimpses of Rural Life in Sussex*, The Countryman, Oxford 1927

Deghy, Guy, *Paradise in the Strand: The Story of Romano's*, Richards Press, 1958

Deghy, Guy, and Keith Waterhouse, *Café Royal: Ninety Years of Bohemia*, Hutchinson 1956

Denman, J. L., *Wine and its Adulterations*, Spottiswoode 1867

Diamond, Harvey and Marilyn, *Fit for Life*, Bantam 1987

Dickens, Charles, *Pickwick Papers*, Penguin English Library 1978 (1st published 1836–7)

—— *Oliver Twist*, Penguin English Library 1966 (1st published 1837–8)

—— *The Old Curiosity Shop*, Penguin English Library 1974 (1st published 1841)

—— *Dombey and Son*, Signet Classics 1964 (1st published 1846–8)

—— *Little Dorrit*, Penguin English Library 1967 (1st published 1857)

—— *Our Mutual Friend*, Penguin 1987 (1st published 1864–5)

—— *Letters of Charles Dickens*, Vols. II and III, eds. Madeline House and Graham Storey, Vol IV, ed. Kathleen Tillotson, Clarendon Press, Oxford, 1969, '74, and '77

—— *Oxford Illustrated Dickens*, 1981

—— *Sybil*, Longman 1919 (1st published 1845)

Dodd, George, *The Food of London*, Longman 1856

Duff, Mountstuart Elphinstone Grant, *Notes from a Diary 1851–72*, Murray 1897 (2 vols.); *1873–81*, Murray 1898 (2 vols.)

'English Asmodeus', *Revelations of Life in Nottingham*, 1860

Fortnum and Mason, *The Delectable History of Fortnum and Mason*, produced by Colman, Prentice, & Varley (undated)

Francatelli, Charles Elmé, *Modern Cook*, Bentley 1886 (1st published 1846)

—— *Cook's Guide and Butler's and Housekeeper's Assistant*, Bentley 1868 (1st published 1861)

—— *Plain Cookery for the Working Classes*, Bentley 1861

—— *Royal English and Foreign Confectioner*, Bentley 1862

Freeman, Sarah, *Isabella and Sam*, Gollancz 1977

Gaskell, Elizabeth, *Wives and Daughters*, Penguin Books 1983 (1st published 1866)

Gilbert, A., *Recollections of Old Nottingham*, H. B. Saxton, Nottingham 1901

Glasse, Hannah, *The Art of Cookery Made Plain and Easy*, facsimile of original ed., Prospect Books 1983 (1st ed. 1747)

Goddard, Ebenezer, *Illustrated Prospectus of the Patent Portable Asbestos Gas Stove*, 1851

Graham, Sylvester, *The Physiology of Feeding*, Ideal Publishing Union 1897

Grant, M. P., *Louis Pasteur*, Ernest Benn 1960

Great Exhibition Descriptive Catalogue, HMSO 1851

Griffiths, Sir Percival, *The History of the Indian Tea Industry,*, Weidenfeld & Nicolson 1967

Haining, John, and Tyler, Colin, *Ploughing by Steam*, Model and Allied Publications, Hemel Hempstead, Herts, 1970

Hardy, Dennis, *Alternative Communities in Nineteenth-Century England*, Longman 1979

Hare, Augustus J. C., *The Story of My Life*, George Allen 1896

Harrison, Brian, *Drink and the Victorians*, Faber 1971

Hartley, Dorothy, *Food in England*, Macdonald & Jane's 1979

Harvey, John, *Corpulence, its Diminution and cure, without injury to health*, 3rd edition 1864

Hassall, Arthur Hill, *Food and its Adulterations*, Longman 1855

Hawker, James, *A Victorian Poacher: James Hawker's Journal*, Oxford University Press 1961

Hawthorne, Nathaniel, *Passages from the English Notebooks*, Strahan 1870
—— *Our Old Home*, Ohio State University Press 1970

Hayward, Abraham, *The Art of Dining*, Murray 1883 ed. (1st published 1852)

Hewlett, Esther (later Copley), *The Little Cowslip-Gatherers*, William Darton 1824
—— *The Old Man's Head*, London 1825?
—— *Cottage Comforts*, Simpkin & Marshall 1830 (1st published 1825)
—— *The Housekeeper's Guide*, Longman and others 1839
—— *The Poplar Grove*, Thomas Tegg 1841
—— *Cottage Cookery*, Groombridge 1849
—— (ed.) *Hints of Happy Homes; or, Family Experiences*, Dean & Son 1859

'High Elms' (Sir Edward Levett Darwin), *The Game Preserver's Manual*, The Field, London, and Bemrose, Derby, 1859

Hill, Georgiana, *Everybody's Pudding Book*, Bentley 1862
—— *The Breakfast Book*, Bentley 1865
—— *How to Cook Apples shown in One Hundred Different Ways*, Routledge 1864.
—— *How to Cook Vegetables in One Hundred Different Ways*, Routledge 1868
—— *Women in English Life*, Bentley 1896

Hindmarsh, Robert, *Rise and Progress of the New Jerusalem Church*, Hodson 1861

Hood, Thomas, *Whims and Oddities*, G. P. Putnam 1886

Horsell, William, *The Science of Cooking Vegetarian Food*, Vegetarian Depot 1856
—— *The Vegetarian Armed at All Points*, Horsell & Caudwell 1856

Hughes, Thomas, *Tom Brown's Schooldays*, Collins 1953 (1st published 1857)

Jefferies, Richard, *The Gamekeeper at Home* and *The Amateur Poacher*, Oxford University Press 1978 (1st published 1878)

Jeffs, Julian, *Sherry*, Faber 1970

Johnston, James F. W., *The Chemistry of Common Life*, Blackwood 1853–5 (2 vols.)

Kilvert, Francis, *Kilvert's Diary 1870–79*, Penguin 1978

Kinross, Lord, *The Kindred Spirit*, Newman Neame, 1959

Kitchener, William, *The Cook's Oracle*, Cadell, Edinburgh 1840 (8th ed; 1st published 1817)

—— *The Art of Prolonging Life*, Hurst Robinson 1826

—— *The Housekeeper's Oracle*, Whittaker, Treacher & Co. 1829

'A Lady' (Martha Brotherton), *Vegetable Cookery*, William Clowes 1833 (4th ed.; 1st published circa 1820); as *Vegetarian Cookery*, with an introduction by James Simpson, Pitman 1866

Lankester, Edwin, *Vegetable Substances Used for the Food of Man*, Charles Knight 1846

—— *A Guide to the Food Collection in the South Kensington Museum*, HMSO 1860

—— *On Food*, Hardwicke, 1861

Liebig, Justus von, *Researches on the Chemistry of Food*, Taylor & Walton 1847

—— *Familiar Letters on Chemistry and its Relation to Commerce, Physiology, and Agriculture*, Taylor & Walton 1851 (3rd, enlarged ed.; 1st published 1843)

—— *Food for Infants. A Complete Substitute for that Provided by Nature*, James Walton 1867

—— *Baron Liebig and the Children*, Lily & Co. 1873; reprinted in *Medical Tracts 1857–73*

Liebig and After Liebig: A Century of Progress in Agricultural Chemistry (various authors), American Association for the Advancement of Science 1942

Livingstone, Josiah, *Some Edinburgh Shops*, James Thin, Edinburgh 1894

'London Physician' (Edward Smith), *How to Get Fat*, John Smith 1865

MacClure, Victor, *Scotland's Inner Man: History of Scots Food and Cookery*, Routledge 1935

MacCulloch, *Remarks on the Art of Wine-making*, Longman 1816

MacGuire, John Thomas, *Father Mathew, A Biography*, Longman 1863

Mackenzie, Jeanne and Norman, *Dickens: A Life*, Oxford University Press 1979

MacMullen, T., *Handbook of Wines*, D. Appleton & Co., New York, 1852

Manchester Corporation, *Water for the Millions: Manchester Corporation Waterworks 1847–1974*, 1974

Masters, Thomas, *The Ice Book*, Marshall 1844

—— *A Short Treatise Concerning some Patent Inventions*, Patent Journal Printing Office 1850

Maxwell, Sir Herbert, *Half a Century of Successful Trade: Being a Sketch of the Rise and Development of the firm of W. and A. Gilbey*, privately published 1907

'Maxwell-Lyte' (Sir Henry Churchill), *History of Eton College 1440–1875*, Macmillan 1889

Mayhew, Henry, *London Labour and the London Poor*, facsimile of original ed. Frank Cass 1967; 3 vols. (1st published 1851)

Mead, Isaac, *The Life Story of an Essex Lad*, A. Driver & Sons, Chelmsford 1923

Metropolitan Water Board, *Water Supply of London*, 1961

Miall, Edward, *The British Churches in Relation to the British People*, Virtue 1849

Mitford, Mary Russell, *Our Village*, Sampson Low 1879 (1st published 1824)

Morgan, Brian, *Express Journey*, Newman Meame 1964

Morley, Henry, *Memoirs of St Bartholomew's Fair*, Chapman & Hall 1859

Morning Chronicle Survey of Labour and the Poor, Caliban Books 1980

Morris, Helen, *Portrait of a Chef: Alexis Soyer*, Cambridge 1938

Morton, J. C. (ed.), *Cyclopedia of Agriculture*, Blackie & Son 1855

Mulder's Reply to Liebig, Edinburgh 1846

Myer, Jesse, S., *Life and Letters of Dr William Beaumont*, Mosby, St Louis, 1912

Newbigging, Thomas, and W. T. Fewtrell (eds.), *King's Treatise on the Science and Practice of the Manufacture and Distribution of Coal Gas*, William King 1882

Newmarch, C. H., *Recollections of Rugby, by an Old Rugbaean*, Hamilton & Adams 1848

Osbaldeston, George, *Squire Osbaldeston: His Autobiography*, John Lane Bodley Head 1927

Page, John, *The Hawkers and Street Dealers of the North of England Manufacturing Districts*, Abel Heywood, Manchester, 1858

—— 'The Story of the Manchester Fairs', *Papers of the Manchester Literary Club*, Vol III 1877

Periera, Jonathan, *The Elements of Materia Medica and Therapeutics*, Longman 1842 (2nd ed.)

Pigache, Captain Daniel N., *Café Royal Days*, Hutchinson 1933

'Piscator' (William Hughes), *Fish, How to Choose and How to Dress*, Longman 1843

Poultry Book for the Many, by contributors to the *Cottage Gardener and Poultry Chronicle*, Cottage Gardener 1857

Prothero, Rowland Edmund (Baron Ernle), *English Farming Past and Present*, Heinemann/Frank Cass 1961 (1st published 1912)

Quennell, Peter (ed.), *Mayhew's London*, Kimber 1951

Rance, Charles, E. De, *Water Supply of England and Wales*, Stanforth 1882

Read, Jan, and Maite Manjon, *The Great British Breakfast*, Michael Joseph 1981

Redding, Cyrus, *Every Man his own Butler*, Whittaker & Co. 1839

—— *Modern Wines*, Henry Bohn 1851

—— *Abstract of the Evidence given before a Select Committee of the House of Commons upon the Import Duties of Wines*, Charles Skipper & East 1852

Reid, Sir T. Wemyss, *Memoirs and Correspondence of Lyon Playfair*, Cassell 1899

Roby, Kinley, *The King, the Press, and the People*, Barrie & Jenkins 1975

Saintsbury, J., *Notes on a Cellar-Book*, Macmillan 1920

Sala, George Augustus, *Breakfast in Bed*, Maxwell 1863

—— *Living London: or, Echoes Re-echoed*, Remington 1883

Sanger, George, *Seventy Years a Showman*, C. A. Pearson 1910

Scarborough, Christopher, . . . *About Oxo in its Golden Jubilee Year 1965*, Spectator Publications 1965

Shenstone, W. A., *Justus von Liebig: His Life and Work 1803–73* Cassell 1895

Sigmond, George Gabriel, *Tea: its Effects, Medicinal and Moral*, Longman 1839

Simon, André, *Port*, Constable Wine Library 1934

Simpson, James, *A Letter to the Right Honourable H. Labouchère, on . . . Soup Kitchens*, Manchester 1847

Slee, A. H., *Victorian Days in a Devon Village*, published by the author 1966

Soyer, Alexis, *Gastronomic Regenerator*, Simpkin, Marshall 1846

—— *Charitable Cookery, or, the Poor Man's Regenerator*, Simpkin, Marshall 1848

—— *Modern Housewife*, Simpkin, Marshall 1851

—— *The Pantropheon*, Simpkin, Marshall 1853

—— *Shilling Cookery for the People*, Routledge 1855

—— *Culinary Campaign*, Routledge 1857

Stonehouse, James, *Liverpool, its Highways, Byeways, and Thoroughfares by Land and Water*, James Cornish 1852

—— *Pictorial Liverpool*, Lacy, c. 1845 (undated)

Strong, L. A. G., *The Story of Sugar*, Weidenfeld & Nicolson 1954

Sugg, Walter, T., *The Domestic Uses of Coal Gas*, Walter King 1884

Taine, Hippolyte, *Notes on England*, Strahan 1870

Tennent, Sir James Emerson, *Wine, its Use and Taxation*, James Madden 1855
Thackeray, William Makepeace, *Irish Sketch-book*, Chapman & Hall 1845 (2 vols.)
—— *Book of Snobs and Sketches and Travels in London*, Smith & Elder 1869
Thomas, Jerry, *How to Mix Drinks, or, the Bon-vivant's Companion*, Dick & Fitzgerald, New York, 1862
Thompson, Flora, *Lark Rise to Candleford*, Penguin 1983 (1st published 1939)
Timbs, J., *Hints for the Table*, Kent & Co. 1859
Twining, Stephen H., *Twinings, Two Hundred and Fifty Years of Tea and Coffee 1706–1956*, R. Twining 1956
Ude, Louis Eustace, *The French Cook*, Ainsworth 1827
Victoria, Queen, *Dearest Child: Letters between Victoria and the Princess Royal 1858–61*, ed. Roger Fulford, Evans 1968
—— *Dearest Mama: Letters between Victoria and the Crown Princess of Prussia 1861–64*, ed. Roger Fulford, Evans 1968
Volant, F., and J. R. Warren, *Memoirs of Alexis Soyer*, Kent 1859
Walker, Violet, *Goose Fair*, paper read at Nottingham Northern Branch Library 1948
Walsh, John Henry, *A Manual of Domestic Economy*, Routledge 1857
—— (ed.) *The English Cookery Book*, Routledge 1858
—— (ed.) *The British Cookery Book*, Routledge 1883
Warren, C. Henry, *Essex*, Robert Hale 1950
Weinreb, Ben, and Christopher Hibbert (eds.), *The London Encyclopedia*, Macmillan 1983
Wheaton, Barbara Ketcham, *Savouring the Past*, Chatto & Windus 1983
Whitworth, George, *Shudehill Markets Mismanagement*, Manchester Corporation
Williams, Trevor I., *A History of the British Gas Industry*, Oxford University Press 1981
Wilson, C. Anne, 'Eight Centuries of the British Restaurant', *Good Food Guide 1986*, Consumers' Association/Hodder & Stoughton
Wilson, George B. *Alcohol and the Nation*, Nicholson and Watson 1940
Wilson, Ross, *Scotch Made Easy*, Hutchinson 1959
Wright, T., *Some Habits and Customs of the Working Classes*, Tinsley Brothers 1867
—— *The Great Unwashed*, Tinsley Brothers 1868

PARLIAMENTARY PAPERS

Agricultural Wages

1900, Vol. LXXXII, p. 557. Report by Mr Wilson Fox on the Wages and Earnings of Agricultural Labourers in the United Kingdom

Bakeries

1847–8, Vol. LI, p. 367. Copy of the Evidence given by Dr Guy before the Sanitary Commission, in reference to Persons Employed in the Baking Trade
1862, Vol. XLVII, p. 1. Grievances Complained of by the Journeymen Bakers.
1863, Vol. I, p. 133. Bakehouse Regulation Bill
1865, Vol. XLVII, p. 261. Report on the 1863 Bakehouse Regulation Act

Drink

1852, Vol. XVII, p. 1 (whole volume). Select Committee on Import Duties on Wines
1852–3, Vol. XXXVII, p. 1, and 1854, Vol. XIV, p. 231. Reports from the Select Committee on Public Houses
1854, Vol. LXV, p. 737. Wine and Spirit Consumption
1859, Session 2, Vol. XXX, p. 197. Reports on the Effect of the Vine Disease

Hansard, Vol. CLVI, column 832. Commercial Treaty with France (1860)
1870, Vol. XX. Reports from Commissioners: see p. 189

Food and Drugs
1854–5, Vol. VIII, p. 221. First Report from the Select Committee on the Adulteration of Food
1857, Session 2, Vol. I, p. 9. Bill for Preventing the Adulteration of Articles of Food
1859, Session 1, Vol. I, p. 5, and 1860, Vol. I, p. 49. Amendments to above
Hansard, Vol. CLVI, column 2025. Adulteration of Food or Drink Bill.

Game
1830, Vol. II, p. 373. To Consolidate and Amend the Game Laws and Authorize the Sale of Game
1830–31, pp. 491 and 517, and 1831, Vol. II, pp. 9 and 29. Amendments to above
1831–32, Vol. II, p. 105. For the More Effectual Prevention of Trespasses in Pursuit of Game . . . in Scotland
1837, Vol. III, p. 241. Reparation of Injury done by Game in Scotland
1846, Vol. IX, Parts I and II, p. 1 (whole volume) of both. Report from the Select Committee on the Game Laws

Poison (sale of)
1851, Vol. VI, pp. 1 and 7. Sale of Arsenic Regulation Bill
1857–58, Vol. IV, p. 335. Act to Restrict and Regulate the Sale of Poison

Public Schools
1864, Vol. XX, Part I, p. 1 (whole volume). Public Schools Commission (Clarendon) Report

Shop Hours
1886. Vol. XII, p. 1. Report from the Select Committee on Shop Hours Regulation Bill

Smithfield
1849, Vol. XIX, p. 243. Report from the Select Committee on Smithfield Market
1850, Vol. XXXI, p. 355. Report of the Commission on Smithfield Market
1851, Vol. VI, pp. 77 and 93. Smithfield Market Removal Bill
1857–58, Vol. XLVIII, p. 417. Smithfield Market Site
1859, Vol. XXIII, p. 339

Sugar
1852–3, Vol. XCIX, p. 567. Return on the Quantities of Sugar Imported 1800–52
1860, Vol. LXIII, p. 561. Quantities of Sugar imported 1800–59

Tea
1840, Vol. VIII, p. 578. Opinions on Assam Tea
1843, Vol. LII, p. 26. Quantities of Tea Imported 1830–42

Truck
1870, Vol. IV, p. 701. Appointment of a Commission to inquire into the Truck System
1871, Vol. XXXVI, p. 1 (whole volume). Report of Commission on the Truck System
1887, Vol. VI, p. 527. Bill to Amend and Extend the Law Relating to Truck
1887, Vol. LXVI, p. 631. Report of Alexander Redgrave on the Truck System in Scotland

Water
1850, Vol. XXII, p. 1 (whole volume). Report by the Board of Health on the Supply of Water to the Metropolis
1850, Vol. XXXIII, p. 435. Commission on Metropolitan Sewers

1857, Vol. XIII, p. 149. Report on the Microscopical Examination of the Metropolitan Water Supply by Arthur Hill Hassall

1867, Vol. IX, p. 1. Report from the Select Committee on East London Water Bills

Workhouse Diets

1866, Vol. XXXV, p. 321. Dietaries for the Inmates of Workhouses, by Dr Edward Smith

Workhouse Education

1851, Vol. XLIX, p. 31. Reports on the Education and Training of Pauper Children in 1850

1875, Vol. LXIII, p. 343. Letter by Mrs Nassau Senior upon her Report on Pauper Schools

1877, Vol. LXVII, p. 559. Instruction in Cookery

PERIODICALS

All the Year Round
Athenaeum
The Comic Annual
Englishwoman's Domestic Magazine
Family Economist
Family Friend
Financial Times
Gentlemen's Magazine, 3rd series
The Grocer
Group News (Crosse & Blackwell)
Household Words
Illustrated London News
Ladies' Companion at Home and Abroad (1849–50); continued as *Ladies' Companion and Monthly Magazine*
Ladies' Treasury
Living Magazine
London Standard, now *Evening Standard*
National Co-operative Leader
New Age
New Monthly Belle Assemblée
Nottingham Weekly Guardian
Observer
Penny Magazine for the Society for the Diffusion of Useful Knowledge
The Porcupine (Liverpool)
Punch
Quarterly Review
Servants' Magazine
The Times
Vegetarian Advocate
Vegetarian Messenger

Index

DATE DUE